INTRODUCI
COMPUTER ASSISTED
LEARNING

INTRODUCING COMPUTER ASSISTED LEARNING

Philip Barker and Harry Yeates
Interactive Systems Research Group,
Dept of Computer Science, Teesside Polytechnic

Prentice/Hall International

Englewood Cliffs, NJ London Mexico New Delhi Rio de Janeiro
Singapore Sydney Tokyo Toronto Wellington

British Library Cataloguing in Publication Data

Barker, Philip
   Introducing computer assisted learning.
   1.   Computer-assisted instruction
   I.   Title   II.   Yeates, Harry
371.3'9445   LB1028.5

ISBN 0-13-477308-X

ISBN 0-13-477308 X

Prentice-Hall, Inc., Englewood Cliffs, New Jersey
Prentice-Hall International, UK Ltd, London
Prentice-Hall of Australia Pty, Ltd, Sydney
Prentice-Hall Canada, Inc., Toronto
Prentice-Hall Hispanoamericana, S.A., Mexico
Prentice-Hall of India Private Ltd, New Delhi
Prentice-Hall of Japan, Inc., Tokyo
Prentice-Hall of Southeast Asia Pte, Ltd, Singapore
Editora Prentice-Hall do Brasil Ltda, Rio de Janeiro
Whitehall Books Ltd, Wellington, New Zealand

10   9   8   7   6   5   4   3   2   1

Printed by A. Wheaton & Co. Ltd, England

To our Friends

Through education a better world.

CONTENTS

vii

5. APPROACHES TO MULTIMEDIA CAL

6. THE FUTURE OF CAL

PREFACE

The use of computers as teaching aids is growing at a significant rate
within virtually all subject areas and at all levels of instruction –
primary, secondary and tertiary. Furthermore, as an instructional tool
the computer is finding a multitude of applications in areas other
than schools, colleges and universities. Its use in industrial and
commercial training, for example, is growing at an increasing pace.

This book is intended to bring together a selection of material
relevant to the needs of those involved in or who are intending to
introduce techniques for computer assisted instruction. Consequently,
this text will be useful to teachers and instructors in all areas of
education and training. It could also be used to support courses in
instructional/educational technology as no assumption is made of any
previous knowledge of programming languages or computing. The text is
concerned with the development, application and evaluation of systems,
techniques, and aids to improve the process of learning.

Educationalists, at all levels, experience pressures which prevent
them from keeping abreast of the latest innovations in educational
technology. The authors believe this book will bridge a gap in the
current literature.

ACKNOWLEDGEMENTS

The authors are indebted to Durham University, Teesside Polytechnic and Sunderland Polytechnic for the assistance and help that they have given us during the preparation of this book. We would also like to acknowledge the following individuals/organisations for their help (and where appropriate) permission to reproduce material from their publications:

Dr D.M. Towne, Behavioural Science Laboratory,
    (University of Southern California).
Colin Robinson, SCICON Limited.
Alan Cook, Barclaycard.
Geoff Hutt, BL Systems.
Colin Mansell, Control Data Limited.
R.J. Elder, Dundee College of Education.
Dr C. Bryce and A. Stewart, Dundee College of Technology.
John McCann, Department of Trade and Industry.
John Tickle, Ferranti Computer Systems Limited.
Jim Slater, Independent Broadcasting Authority.
Dr J.H. Cable, IBM (UK) Limited.
Neil Ker and Steven Donald, Kodak limited.
Andrew Colchester, Marconi Radar Systems Limited.
Stuart Chilvers, Mills and Allen Communications Limited.
Dr M. Marples, Dr Ann Jones, Dr Diana Laurillard, and
    Dr Tom Vincent (The Open University).
Mr L.A. Yeazel, Pioneer Video Inc.
Mr G.W.G. Winkfield and Simon Turner, Philips Industries.
Mark Lindsay, Realmheath Video Limited.
Bryan Edwards, Speedwriting/Speedtyping Limited.
Star Microterminals.
Stewart Anderson, Texaco Limited.
Allan Kennedy, Training Technology LImited.
Professor John King, Department of Maritime Studies,
    (University of Wales Institute of Science and Technology).
Captain K.H. Waters, Cardiff Ship Simulator.
Stephen Bond, Videotel Marine International Limited.
John Richardson, Viscat Limited.

PGB would particularly like to thank John Lindley, John Darby, John Steele, John Wilford, Ravinder Singh, Dennis Moss, Giles Wright and Ruth Freestone for the help that each has given him during the preparation of this book.

ABOUT THE AUTHORS

PHILIP BARKER
As a State Scholar, Philip Barker studied Chemistry at the University
of Wales. He graduated with a first class honours degree in 1965 and
was awarded the Ayling Prize for the best honours degree performance
in Chemistry. After successfully completing studies for a Ph.D., he
held research fellowship and computer consultancy posts. In 1971 he
became a Lecturer in Computer Science at Teesside Polytechnic and in
1973 took up a post as Lecturer in Computing at the University of
Durham. Dr. Barker returned to Teesside Polytechnic in 1979 as
Principal Lecturer in Computer Science. He currently leads research
into human–machine interaction one aspect of which relates to studies
of computer assisted learning. He has published a number of articles
in various research journals and has recently completed a textbook
entitled: 'Computers in Analytical Chemistry.' He is currently writing
a book on human–machine interaction.

HARRY YEATES
Harry Yeates is a member of the Chartered Institute of Cost and
Management Accountants. He spent several years as a Systems Accountant
specialising in the analysis and design of business systems in both
the chemical and construction industries. He entered the field of
computing in 1964 and for four years was Computer Manager of an IBM
installation which served the United Kingdom subsidiaries of a multinational machine tool organisation. In 1968 he was appointed Group
Management Services Manager for this organisation with
responsibilities for industrial training. At this time he developed an
interest in educational/training technology. Since 1972 he has been a
Senior Lecturer in the Department of Business Management, Sunderland
Polytechnic. His association with Philip Barker began in 1978 with a
research project which combined their common interests in using the
computer as an audio–visual teaching resource. Experiments in using
microcomputers to interface with conventional audio–visual materials
followed and in 1981 he was awarded an M.Sc. from the University of
Durham for his thesis 'Man–Machine Interaction in Computer Assisted
Learning'.

OVERVIEW

Chapter 1 provides an introduction and examines education and training as an interactive process. The scope of computer assisted learning is discussed and the types of system used for the integration of teaching resources are outlined.

Chapter 2 reviews the subject of courseware which is the generic term used to describe the many different types of computer based instructional resource used in educational and training environments.

Chapter 3 outlines the development of author languages. The philosophy behind this type of facility is that the computer should handle the programming and let the teacher concentrate on the preparation of instructional material. Author languages are designed specifically for teachers who are not computer specialists.

Chapter 4 introduces the ideas behind multimedia CAL and discusses the principles of interfacing instructional devices to computers. A detailed example is then given of a simple multimedia CAL unit that has been used for instruction both in academic and industrial training environments.

Chapter 5 follows up the theme of workstations for multimedia CAL. This is done through a series of case studies that together cover a wide range of CAL applications. The problems of courseware authoring for multimedia CAL are also discussed. Some examples of languages that are specifically orientated towards this mode of teaching are then briefly outlined.

Chapter 6 reviews the current trends in information technology and the future prospects for instructional uses of the computer.

LIST OF ILLUSTRATIONS

INTRODUCING COMPUTER ASSISTED LEARNING

Chapter I

USING COMPUTERS FOR EDUCATION AND TRAINING

1.1 ON THE NATURE OF COMPUTERS

The world around us consists of a multitude of different objects. These objects vary quite significantly in both their form and complexity. Their sophistication ranges from simple elementary structures, such as a pot or a knife, through to complex machines such as a motor car or an aeroplane. The various entities from which the world is composed are often categorised into two broad classes: animate and inanimate. Those in the first class are distinguished from those in the second by the fact that they experience some form of life cycle.

Life is an extremely complex process. It commences at birth and terminates at death. During their life cycle, in order to survive, animate entities are critically dependent upon their ability to acquire and process signals and data that are derived from various stimuli. This data may originate from two basic sources. Firstly, there is data that originates from within the species itself; secondly, there is that which arises from the external environment within which the species has to exist. During their lifetime all living entities must learn how to interpret the plethora of data derived from each of these sources.

Learning is the general term used to describe those processes which animal species use in order to acquire the skills necessary to live and exist within their containing environment. In general, learning

1

may be loosely thought of as involving the acquisition of:

(1) data, information and knowledge from both the internal and external worlds mentioned above,
(2) techniques for processing this data and information, and
(3) skills that are needed to secure the species' future needs (such as decision making, control of motor effectors and so on.

Information and data may take a variety of different forms. Some of the most common examples are those based upon sound or light stimuli. For this reason, many animals possess very advanced physiological systems for processing signals produced by the stimulation of sight and hearing organs (Lindsay and Norman, 1972). This is particularly so in the case of the human species. Humans use a variety of different forms of text, pictures and speech for the purpose of communicating knowledge and data.

Of all the different forms of animal life, the human species is unique in that it has developed a number of important tools to aid the fundamental tasks involved in handling information. Some of the simpler examples of these include devices such as the slide rule (Saffold and Smalley, 1964) and the pocket calculator (Wyld and Bell, 1977). These information processing tools have both been designed to help people to overcome some of the difficulties they encounter when performing mathematical computations. Word processing systems (Simons, 1981) have likewise developed in order to assist with the handling of textual information. Similarly, image processing systems (Hwang, 1983) enable a variety of different operations to be performed on pictorial information. Fundamental to the human's more advanced information processing tools is some form of computer system.

A computer is essentially a device for performing automated information (or data) processing tasks. It may be thought of as a machine that takes raw data or information as its input and produces, as output, new or transformed data/information. The relationship between the input to and output from a computer is shown in figure 1.1. Here, the computer is conceptualised as a 'black box'. Data flow, into and from the computer is represented by large arrows. Typical examples of input and output data are illustrated in table 1.1.

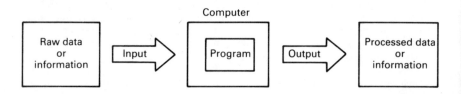

Figure 1.1   The basic function of a computer system.

Table 1.1   Examples of input and output data.

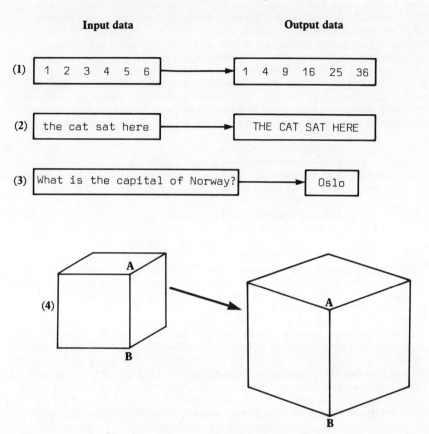

In the first example the input data consists of a sequence of integer numbers. The output produced from this sequence is a second list of numbers. Each of the values in the output list represents the square of its corresponding input value – on a positional basis. The second example provides an illustration of simple text (or word) processing. Here the input data is a simple sentence written in lower case letters. The output data produced from this is a second sentence in which all the letters have been capitalised. Like example two, example three involves the input and output of text. However, in this instance the input to the computer takes the form of a question while the output corresponds to the answer to that question. The final example in table 1.1 illustrates the input and output of graphical data. The output image has been produced from the input by enlargement and slight rotation about a vertical axis passing through the central edge labelled AB.

In each of the three examples described above a set of input data has
been transformed into a new form by the computer. Transformations of
this type are accomplished by means of special groups of instructions
stored within a computer system. A collection of instructions resident
within a computer system and which is responsible for controlling the
activity of the computer is generally referred to as a program.
Programs are usually formulated in terms of a special type of
artificial language that the computer is capable of understanding.
Such languages are referred to as programming languages. Common
examples include: BASIC, FORTRAN, COBOL and COMAL. An example
of a simple computer program written in BASIC is shown below:

PROGRAM

```
10   INPUT N
20   ANS=N*N
30   PRINT ANS
40   GOTO 10
```

This example program contains four fundamental instructions (or
statements) that tell the computer what information handling tasks
have to be performed. The first of these (INPUT N) is an input
instruction which causes the movement of data from the outside world
into the computer system (see figure 1.1). The second statement
(ANS=N*N) specifies how the input data is to be processed. This
involves calculating the value of the quantity ANS by squaring the
previously acquired value of N. The third instruction (PRINT ANS)
causes the value of the newly created data (ANS) to be output from
within the computer system to the outside world. The final statement
(GOTO 10) is used to make the computer repeat the previous three steps
again. It thus automates the basic procedure embodied in the first
three statements. Indeed, this simple program would continue to input,
process and print out data values indefinitely – provided a
sufficiently long list of input numbers was available.

Computer programs are available for a wide variety of purposes,
particularly for teaching and learning. Some of these will be
described in more detail later. The term software is often used to
refer to collections of computer programs used to operate a computer
system. Software is discussed in more detail in section 1.1.3.

In order to enter data into a computer system and receive results back
from it, appropriate input and output channels are required. The
nature of these channels will depend upon the type of computer
facility being used – for example, whether it is a mainframe, a
minicomputer or a microcomputer system – and the nature of the
processing tasks for which it is employed: batch or interactive. Each
of these modes of computer usage will be described in subsequent
sections of this book. Predominantly, however, this text will be
concerned with interactive systems in which the user (for example, a

teacher or a student) interacts directly with the computer. Special types of communication channel are needed to facilitate this type of computer usage. The most popular mode of data input will be via a typewriter-like keyboard. This is used to effect data transfer from the user to the computer. Data flow in the reverse direction is facilitated by means of a TV-like cathode ray tube (CRT) screen. Each of these peripherals will be discussed in more detail in the part of this chapter devoted to the user interface (see section 1.1.4).

Interactive facilities may be provided via a microcomputer, a minicomputer or a time-shared mainframe computer system. For the majority of users in schools or in the home, the microcomputer will probably be the most readily available means of gaining access to computing resources. In view of this, the micro will be taken as a reference point for the discussion of computer systems. Subsequent parts of this section are therefore used to introduce the relevant terminology necessary for an understanding of microcomputer based systems.

1.1.1 The Structure of a Microcomputer
There are many different microcomputer systems currently on the market. Typical examples include: Sinclair ZX81, Commodore VIC-20, Sinclair Spectrum, Dragon 32, Texas Instruments TI-99/4, Atari 400, Colour Genie, Video Genie and the BBC Microcomputer. The external appearance and structure of a representative example of such a system is depicted in the photograph presented in figure 1.2. The keyboard and CRT screen are its most prominent visible components. The unit that contains the screen is also used to house many of the other important parts of the computer - for example, its processing unit, its memory elements, its power supply unit and so on. These latter items of hardware only become visible when the protective casing containing the screen is removed. The term hardware is one which is generally used to describe the various electronic and mechanical components from which a computer is constructed. Thus, the CRT screen, the keyboard, the memory boards, the floppy disc units (see later) are each examples of computer hardware.

A complete computer system consists of an appropriate combination of both hardware and software. Previously, the word software was introduced as a generic term to describe a collection of computer programs. These are needed to control the hardware. Without suitably designed software the hardware from which a computer is built would not be able to function. This would mean that the computer could not be used to achieve any of the data processing transformations that were described earlier. Because of their importance, the hardware and software structures of a typical microcomputer system are described in the following two sections.

1.1.2 The Hardware System
Although there may be some differences in the fine detail of their individual architectures, the majority of microcomputers are

constructed from fairly similar arrangements of common types of hardware component. These are selected in such a way that they enable:

    (1) the input and output of data,
    (2) the temporary or permanent storage of this data, and
    (3) the processing of the stored data.

Figure 1.2   Basic appearance of a microcomputer system.

The hardware elements contained within a microcomputer system are usually inter−connected by means of a special type of communication channel called a bus (Witten, 1980; Camp et al., 1979). The purpose of this is to enable control signals and data to flow between any of the constituent parts of the computer. The structure of a typical bus orientated computer system is illustrated in figure 1.3.

The input and output of data is achieved by means of the I/O peripherals. The keyboard and CRT screen (see figure 1.2) are the commonest examples of such I/O devices. Most microcomputers are also equipped with a printer. This permits data values arising from internal computations to be written out onto paper. Such a facility provides a means of keeping a permanent record of the results of data processing operations. While a printer is an extremely useful accessory, a device of this type is not essential for simple computing applications.

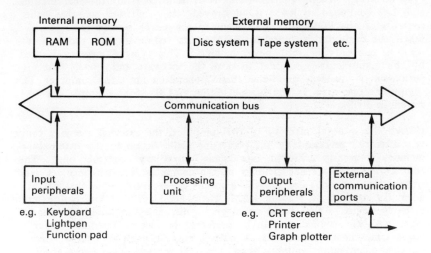

Figure 1.3   Hardware structure of a typical microcomputer.

The processing unit is that part of the computer that is responsible for all control activity and also for performing all the data processing tasks that have to be undertaken. Thus, when the computer is asked to compute the value of the expression 2+3 it is the processing unit that performs the basic computations involved. Amongst other items, the processing unit will contain one or more microprocessor chips – the word chip is a synonym for integrated circuit or IC. Some examples of integrated circuit chips of this type include: Zilog's Z80, MOS Technology's MOS6502, Intel's 8086, Motorola's M68000, etc. Further details of microprocessor chips are given elsewhere (Hordeski, 1979).

The storage of data is achieved by means of the computer's memory units. These fall into two broad types: internal and external. Internal memory is that which is permanently built into the computer and which the processor can access directly. There are two common types of internal memory:

>   RAM   random access memory
>   ROM   read only memory

The RAM section of the memory space is used to hold the data and information that is entered by the user through the keyboard or which is generated by programs running within the computer. Notice that a program must be resident within the computer's internal memory before it can become active or operational. When in such a state, the program controls the hardware components and the overall effect that the computer has. Random access memory is often referred to as being volatile memory because its contents can easily be changed. Consequently, when the computer is switched off, all the information and data contained in RAM is destroyed. In contrast to this, the contents of the ROM section of memory can never be changed – even when the computer is switched off. As its name implies, the data it contains can only be read, never modified. This type of memory is used by the manufacturer in order to store the software and data that is permanently needed for the basic operation of the computer. The computer's operating system (see section 1.1.3), for example, is stored in ROM.

Unlike the internal memory of the computer, the external memory cannot be directly processed by the processing unit. Access to the external memory is usually achieved via some auxilliary control unit. The function of the external memory of the computer is to enhance its data storage capacity and also provide a means of archiving data that might normally need to be held in RAM. There are two basic kinds of external memory device – that based on magnetic disc and that based on magnetic tape. Of the two, disc is to be preferred because of its much faster access time. That is, data can be written to and retrieved from disc systems much more quickly than it can from tape. Two types of disc system are currently available: flexible and hard. Flexible (or 'floppy') discs are probably the most well known. Both flexible discs and magnetic tape provide a convenient means of transporting data between different microcomputer systems.

Another useful method of transferring data and programs between micros is via their external communication ports (Barker, 1982a). A computer that is fitted with ports of this type allows other peripherals and computers to be plugged into it. Communication ports (or interfaces) may be of two basic types: standard and non-standard. The latter are usually designed by particular computer manufacturers and are available only on specific ranges of computers; a typical example is the user port on Commodore PET microcomputers (Commodore, 1979). Standard interfaces are independent of particular manufacturer's conventions. Their structure and mode of operation will usually have been agreed upon internationally. This type of communication port is to be preferred wherever possible. Two of the most popular interfaces in this category are the IEEE–488 (Fisher and Jensen, 1980) and the RS–232–C (Zaks and Lesea, 1979) standards. Most of the better quality micros are fitted with each of these – and may contain some non-standard interfaces as well. The external communication ports enable the micro to be attached to (1) a variety of more sophisticated peripherals (Barker, 1982b; 1982c), and, (2) different types of local area network (Tropper, 1981). These types of application will be discussed in more detail later.

1.1.3 The Software System
The computer programs that are used to control a micro system fall into two broad classes:

(1) system software, and
(2) applications software.

Usually, those programs that fall into the first of these two categories are provided by the computer manufacturer or supplied by a software vendor. The two most important classes of system software are operating systems and language translators.

An operating system (OS) provides a series of software interfaces that enable both the user (see section 1.1.4) and other programs to control the computer hardware. The operating system is usually built into the computer's ROM space. However, in some computers the OS is partly committed to ROM and partly disc resident. Some micros have operating systems that are unique to their manufacturer (compare the communication ports discussed in the previous section). The more sophisticated micros usually provide a 'standard OS'. Two examples of widely used microcomputer operating systems of this type are CP/M (Fernandez and Ashley, 1980) and UNIX (Thomas and Yates, 1982).

As will be discussed in the next section, for the majority of users the initial interface to a microcomputer system will be by way of a set of primitive commands that cause the computer to perform certain well-defined functions. Typical examples of such commands might be:

LOAD	to load a program from external memory,
SAVE	to save a program on tape or disc,
ERASE	to remove a program from memory,
RUN	to activate (or execute) a memory resident program.

In order to carry out the various operations needed to implement each of these commands the operating system will contain appropriately designed sections of program code. When the user issues one of the above commands the relevant section of the operating system takes over control of the hardware for the time needed to execute the basic operations associated with the command. As well as servicing commands issued via the keyboard, most operating systems also contain a series of special entry points that enable users' application programs to call upon the services offered by the OS.

Language translators provide the means whereby the computer user can prepare and execute application programs for specific needs – for example, payroll, computer assisted instruction, computer based learning and so on. The most widely used language translator on microcomputer systems is probably BASIC (Spencer, 1975). In some micros, for example the Commodore PET (see Osborne and Donahue, 1980) a BASIC interpreter is often built into ROM and so is immediately available for use as soon as the system is powered up. Other micros provide this facility in the form of a disc based program (Microsoft, 1982) which has to be loaded into the computer's memory before it can be used. Some of the other popular programming language translators available on micros include PASCAL (Grogono, 1978) and PL/I (Barker,

1983a). In addition to using these high level programming languages to prepare software it is also possible to use special machine orientated (or low level) languages. These are often referred to as assembler systems. Program development using these is usually much more difficult than when high level languages are used, mainly because they require a more detailed understanding of the computer's hardware architecture (Barker, 1981; Fernandez et al., 1982). The major advantages of programs written in low level languages are the enhanced speed of execution and the compactness of the code produced. A major drawback to their use arises from the poor portability of the resultant software. That is, programs cannot easily be moved between computers having different hardware architectures.

As well as writing programs, another important source of software is through program packages. A software package is simply a set of computer programs that have been designed and implemented to meet some specific application. There is a wide variety of software packages available for educational use, both for teaching and for administration purposes (Johnson, 1971; Smith, 1982). Packages are often distributed (both nationally and internationally) via software vendors or through special organisations that act as program exchange centres. Usually, software distributed by this method will be written in a high level language – unless it has been purposely designed for running on a particular type of computer. A further factor influencing the portability of software packages is the availability of a standard computer operating system, for example many application packages are designed to function under the CP/M system. Micros that do not have this OS cannot therefore use such packages.

Application packages and computer programs that have been designed for teaching applications are referred to by a special term: courseware. As will be described later, this term can be used to include more than just computer programs. Thus, audio recordings, slides, video tapes and many other teaching resources are often classified as courseware. A much more detailed description of courseware will be given in the chapters that are to follow.

1.1.4 The User Interface
Human interaction with computer systems may be achieved via a multitude of different kinds of communication channel (Witten, 1980; Meadow, 1970; Guedj et al., 1980). In the introductory section of this chapter these were broadly categorised into two types:

(1) those in which there was no direct (or real–time) communication between the computer and the user, and
(2) those that involved some form of real–time interaction with the computer.

Techniques that fall into category (1) formed the physical basis of many early approaches to using computers with batch processing techniques (Bohl, 1976). Of more importance to the subsequent material in this book are communication channels that fall into category (2). The wide scope of these techniques is summarised in the simple sketch presented in figure 1.4 (Barker, 1983b). This depicts some of the basic ways in which data/information can be made to flow between a human and a computer system.

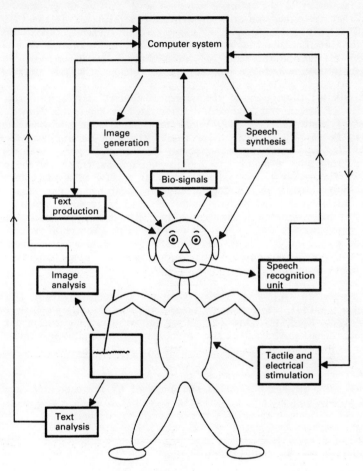

Arrows denote information flow

Figure 1.4 Basic mechanisms for human–computer interaction.

Undoubtedly, the most common method of setting up interactive human–computer communication systems is through the use of a typewriter (QWERTY) keyboard and a CRT display screen (see figure 1.2). Data flow to the computer is then achieved through the tactile manipulation of the key set from which the keyboard is constructed. This mode of

keyboard operation generates sequences of characters constituting
messages that are passed to the computer (as input) for processing.
Responses from the computer to the user (that is, output messages) are
displayed on the screen of the CRT. Most often these will take the
form of character strings that the user is able to read. Sometimes,
visual stimulation of the retina is achieved with the use of graphical
images that are either statically or dynamically displayed on the CRT
screen. The usefulness of graphical images often depends upon the
degree of detail that can be achieved (that is, the resolution that
the screen offers) and the range of colours that it will support –
this depends upon whether a monochrome or coloured CRT is employed.

A more detailed illustration of the human–computer interaction process
(via a CRT screen and keyboard) is illustrated in figure 1.5. Notice
that the keyboard and CRT may belong to a stand–alone microcomputer or
they may be part of a visual display unit (VDU). In its simplest form
a VDU is an unintelligent peripheral (or terminal) device used for
communicating with a mainframe or minicomputer system. From the point
of view of appearance, there is little difference between a VDU and a
microcomputer, particularly if the latter is an inexpensive one that
has no built-in disc units. Often, micros are used as terminal devices
to larger mainframe/minicomputer systems (Barker, 1982d). Similarly,
the more expensive VDUs are nowadays being equipped with
microprocessors and some form of local storage; used as an attachment
to a more powerful computer, VDUs of this type are often referred to
as intelligent terminals.

When a human interacts with a computer (either a micro or a larger
system via a VDU), the interaction takes the form of a simple dialogue
(Barker, 1983b; Kidd, 1982; Martin, 1973) in which information is
exchanged. The procedural steps involved in this dialogue are as
follows:

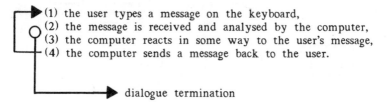

(1) the user types a message on the keyboard,
(2) the message is received and analysed by the computer,
(3) the computer reacts in some way to the user's message,
(4) the computer sends a message back to the user.

dialogue termination

The basic four–step procedure presented above may be repeated
indefinitely, with the computer and user each taking it in turn to
send a message. The cyclic nature of the dialogue is reflected by the
solid arrow; this is used to indicate that as soon as step 4 is
completed, the whole sequence is repeated again (and again and again
...) from step 1. Sooner or later all dialogues must come to an end –
for example, the user may finish his/her computational tasks; require
a coffee break or exceed his/her allowed resource allocation.
Alternatively, of course, the computer could break down or there might

be a sudden cut in the power supply. The dotted line leaving the dialogue cycle is used to indicate that the loop must, at some stage, terminate.

An example of a simple human–computer dialogue is shown in table 1.2. This shows how a computer user initiates a dialogue (by typing START), performs some numerical calculations in BASIC and then activates a simple quizzing program. The latter is intended to test the user's knowledge of capital cities. More sophisticated examples of human–computer dialogues and teaching programs will be described later in this book.

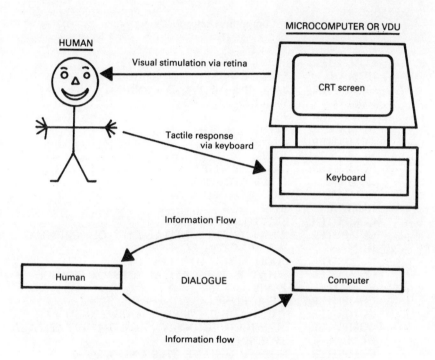

Figure 1.5   A human–computer dialogue system.

Inspection of the basic format of the dialogue contained in table 1.2 will reveal that all information flow takes place by means of character strings. These are either typed by the user or generated by a program resident within the computer. Other techniques could, of course, be used. These might involve the analysis and/or generation of hand–printed/written text or speech processing methods. Thus, speech generation equipment attached to the microcomputer could be used to produce audible text strings. Such sonic information would be a useful asset to those who are without sight and who, therefore, cannot respond to visible text images on the screen. Similarly, the availability of high quality, rapid response speech analysis and voice recognition units could prove equally useful for those unable to manipulate a keyboard device. In addition to these more sophisticated sound processing machines there are many applications for less powerful equipment. Thus, simple sound generation circuits capable of driving a loudspeaker (at various frequencies and for different durations) can often be used to successfully augment the conventional CRT/keyboard combination in a number of ways. Some of the more advanced applications of this involve the use of such equipment for generating simulated sound effects (for example a squeaky door, a police siren, a steam engine, etc) and for the production of computer generated music.

Table 1.2   A Human–Computer Dialogue Trace

HUMAN:	START
COMPUTER:	ENTER COMMAND
HUMAN:	LOAD BASIC
COMPUTER:	BASIC LOADED AND RUNNING
HUMAN:	PRINT 3+6
COMPUTER:	9
HUMAN:	PRINT (3+6)*2-14
COMPUTER:	4
HUMAN:	EXIT
COMPUTER:	OK – GOING BACK TO COMMAND LEVEL
HUMAN:	LOAD GEOGPROG
COMPUTER:	OK – LOADED
HUMAN:	RUN
COMPUTER:	EXECUTION BEGINS
COMPUTER:	WHAT IS THE CAPITAL CITY OF AMERICA?
HUMAN:	WASHINGTON DC
COMPUTER:	GOOD – YOU ARE CORRECT
COMPUTER:	WHAT IS THE CAPITAL CITY OF FRANCE?
HUMAN:	PARIS
COMPUTER:	WELL DONE.
COMPUTER:	YOU HAVE 2 CORRECT ANSWERS SO FAR.
COMPUTER:	OF WHICH COUNTRY IS OSLO THE CAPITAL?
HUMAN:	SWEDEN
COMPUTER:	NO – YOU HAVE THIS ONE WRONG
COMPUTER:	YOU SHOULD HAVE TYPED NORWAY
COMPUTER:	OF WHICH COUNTRY IS ROME THE CAPITAL?
HUMAN:	ITALY
COMPUTER:	etc

o

o

o

Image processing and its application to high quality human–computer interaction is still a subject in which many rapid developments are taking place. Programming techniques that are orientated towards the generation of images are often referred to as computer graphics. It is a well documented and understood topic within many areas of science, engineering and technology (Newman and Sproull, 1973). However, much work yet remains to be done before humans will be able to communicate effectively with computers using free format pictorial forms.

From what has been said above it is easy to see that many of the current advances in user interface technology are likely to be of substantial benefit to computer users who are in some way handicapped or disabled. Studies in this area are extremely important since a significant number of potential users of computers have some form of impairment that prevents them from using the conventional methods (see figures 1.2 and 1.5) of communicating with a computer. Fortunately, as can be seen from figure 1.4, this mode of communication represents just one of the many possibilities that exist for bridging the gap between the computer and its human user. As we shall see later, the human's ingenuity can be used in a multitude of ways in order to utilise the other possibilities that exist.

1.2 THE NATURE OF EDUCATION, LEARNING AND TRAINING

Of the many different types of living entity, the human species is undoubtedly one of the most complicated. This point was emphasised earlier in section 1.1. The complexity of the human species is reflected in a number of ways such as (1) its very advanced brain function, (2) its ability to effect changes in its surroundings, and (3) the ease with which it can react to and accommodate changes in its environment. One of the major functions of the human brain is to store information, process data derived from internal and external sources, make decisions and initiate appropriate control action to secure its owner's survival. The nature of the information that the human brain has to handle is both complicated and varied (Lindsay and Norman, 1972; Kent, 1981).

In general, members of the human race are extremely versatile and very active. This is evidenced by the wide range of activities in which people participate. Consider, for example, the multitude of work functions and professions that exist; the numerous leisure pursuits available; the diverse techniques used for preparing food; and the variety of criminal behaviour in modern societies – and the legislation needed to cope with it. As a direct consequence of activities of this sort, the human species generates, and needs to have access to, significant volumes of knowledge and information. Typical examples of such information include bus and railway timetables, house prices, share/stock values, telephone numbers, commodity prices, medical treatments, cookery recipes, and social protocols. This information is needed in order to provide rules and guidelines that enable members of the human species to survive when placed in different (possibly unfamiliar and hostile) situations.

Everyday, people have to make a multitude of decisions. The outcome of
these decisions can critically influence the way in which individuals
live, their prosperity and their happiness. Successful living is
intimately related to a person's ability to make correct decisions and
therby plan (and execute) courses of action that are most beneficial
to his/her well—being. Information is important because it is the
vital commodity that is needed in order to make rational decisions.
The human species uses information become more knowledgeable. The
processes of acquiring knowledge and information are intimately
related to education and learning, as we shall see later in this
section.

1.2.1 The Growth of Knowledge and Information
An important consequence of the active nature of the human species is
the continual generation of significant volumes of new information.
This manifests itself in a variety of different ways, the production
of new books, the availability of a wide range of daily newspapers and
magazines and, of course, the continually expanding and diverse
spectrum of research journals and specialised text books that are
published. In quantitative terms, it has been estimated (Jackson,
1974) that the volume of recorded knowledge doubles roughly every
twenty years. This substantial growth rate in the volume of
information available for human consumption is reflected in the
exponential distributions depicted in figure 1.6. The shape of each of
these curves is often said to be characteristic of an 'information
explosion'. That is, a situation in which information is generated at
an ever increasing rate.

The data points from which figure 1.6 is constructed are taken from
two different sources. The open circles represent the growth in
documented chemical information during the period 1907 through 1976.
The measurement metric used to obtain these points was simply the
cumulative size of the American Chemical Society's publication
entitled 'Chemical Abstracts'. The fact that the information explosion
is not restricted to just one subject is supported by the curve that
passes through the solid circles. These depict the increase that has
taken place in the number of different computer journals published
during the thirty year period commencing in 1940.

Combined with the large volume of knowledge that currently exists, the
rapid growth rates suggested by figure 1.6 create a number of problems
for those who use information (decision makers) and those who are
concerned with its storage and dissemination. It is important to
realise that the dissemination (or transfer) of information is of
fundamental relevance to education. A useful model that is often used
to depict the generation, transformation and transfer of knowledge is
that proposed by King (1978). This is depicted in figure 1.7.

The overall information transfer mechanism involved in this model
depends upon eleven basic steps. These are numbered 1 through 11 in
the diagram. Most of the steps are self—explanatory; further details

may be obtained from the original paper. From the point of view of education and teaching the most important phase is that involved in step 10 – assimilation by the user. In the following section steps 1, · 10 and 11 will be examined in more detail.

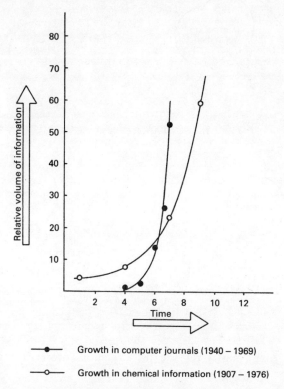

Figure 1.6   The exponential growth in documented knowledge.

Many problems have accompanied the information explosion that has taken place over the last decade or so. It is important to realise that the computer is a vital tool to aid the solution of some of these problems. Other important technologies are those associated with new storage methods (for example, optical/video discs) and data communication methods (for instance, satellite transmission systems). Together, advances in these three new technologies are likely to have a significant impact on the storage, manipulation and dissemination of information (see King's model shown in figure 1.7). They will therefore have a direct influence on the assimilation of information and, of course, upon educational practice.

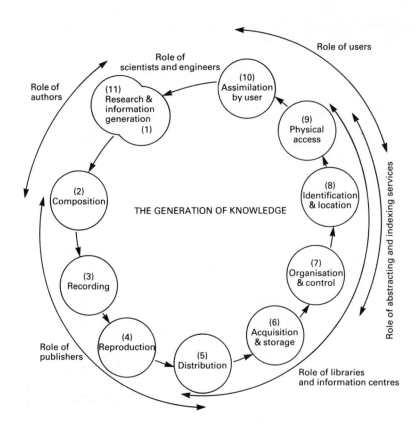

Figure 1.7 King's model for scientific/technical information transfer.

1.2.2 Information Transfer within Education

Knowledge and information are often sub-divided and classified into a finite number of subject areas, for example mathematics, physics, chemistry, biology, engineering, etc. The collection of knowledge and information that relates to and is relevant to a particular area of study is often referred to as a universe of discourse. It was established in the previous section that the volume of material in any particular subject domain (for example chemistry or computer science) is continually changing – usually expanding. These expansive changes in volume occur as a direct result of research activity conducted by scholars and researchers.

As new information is generated it is archived in a variety of different storage media, such as books, learned journals, microfilm, computer stores and so on. These are usually housed within a special type of organisation known as a library. A library is basically an institution that acts as: (1) a depository for recorded knowledge, (2) a means of sharing and disseminating information, and (3) a learning centre, that is, a medium to facilitate people's knowledge acquisition. The importance of learning centres will be discussed later.

Although all forms of stored information have considerable latent (or potential) value, the real worth of information is only realised when it is used for decision making to aid problem solving and goal seeking behaviour. For this to happen, appropriate subsets of the information contained in one or more universes of discourse have to be assimilated by those who need to use it. One of the fundamental roles of an educational system (in the broadest sense) is to provide the various mechanisms that enable these objectives to be realised.

Undoubtedly, the most widespread method of implementing a basic educational system is through the use of a graded collection of institutes of learning (such as schools, colleges and universities) and those experts (teachers, lecturers, researchers, scholars and so on) needed to run them. The function of an institute of learning (and of teachers) is thus to facilitate the assimilation of knowledge and its use for the realisation of both personal and collective objectives. Personal objectives are those that are relevant to a particular individual. Collective objectives are those deemed to be of importance to the society in which individuals have to exist.

The information/knowledge transfer processes that are characteristic of most primitive educational systems are summarised schematically in the diagram presented in figure 1.8.

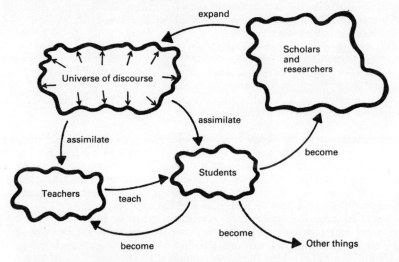

Figure 1.8   Knowledge transfer processes relevant to a conventional educational system.

This diagram is used to bring together some of the ideas presented so far in this and the previous sections. It is a pictorial way of indicating that scholars and researchers produce knowledge. Teachers assimilate this knowledge and pass it on to learners (or students). Clever students may be capable of assimilating this knowledge for themselves, once they have achieved a particular threshold age. Students use their acquired knowledge to realise their personal objectives, particularly with respect to acquiring a profession. Some students become teachers, scholars or researchers, thereby propagating the cycle inherent in figure 1.8. However, many others use their acquired knowledge to achieve a multitude of other personal objectives.

As can be seen from figure 1.8 two types of entity are of vital importance to the process of educational information transfer: teachers and students. Within some universe of discourse, a teacher is an entity that is regarded as being information rich. In contrast, a student is one who is thought of as being information deficient within this domain. The function of the teaching process is to achieve the transfer of information from the teacher to the student. To secure this transfer some channel (or medium) of communication must link the entities involved. These ideas will be discussed further in section 1.2.4.

Because of their importance, it is worth examining some of the basic prerequisite attributes of a teacher. A teacher is:

(1) an agent for the dissemination of information and knowledge,
(2) a motivator for the development of learning skills,
(3) a means of measuring the effectiveness of (1) and (2),
(4) adaptable and patient,
(5) able to modify teaching strategies to the needs of individual students, and
(6) always available when needed.

A fundamental thesis which this book attempts to promote is that computers can make good teachers.

The dissemination of knowledge through the conventional institutions of learning is just one way of achieving information transfer. Many other ancillary transfer channels also exist. Some examples of these are depicted in figure 1.9. It is important to realise that humans never stop learning. Education thus takes place throughout a person's lifetime. While channels A and B are important in very early life, channels B through E become of increasing value in later life. Indeed, the home and work environments are two of the most effective ways of disseminating educational information. In all of these contexts − education in the home, industrial/commercial training, education for leisure, and so on − the computer has a significant contribution to make, as we shall see later.

1.2.3 The Role of Education, Learning and Training

An educational process is one in which a person's knowledge of a universe of discourse is increased. This may arise either (1) via · introspection or (2) as a direct consequence of interaction with external knowledge sources. Frequently, these two techniques are complementary and need to be used together in order to optimise potential increases in knowledge.

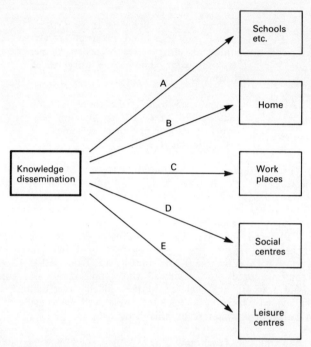

Figure 1.9   Basic information transfer channels.

As was discussed in the previous section, one of the prime functions that an educational system must fulfil is the provision of mechanisms that enable the transfer of information between living species, thereby influencing a person's knowledge acquisition through method (2) above. Of course, there are many other functions that an educational system must support. To summarise it must:

(1) aid the dissemination of knowledge,
(2) foster the development of new knowledge,
(3) shape the minds of people,
(4) produce a workforce capable of handling the problems of society,
(5) encourage cooperation and collaboration where this is beneficial to society, and
(6) provide guidelines for human existence.

The broadest possible definition of education, that encompasses all of these requirements, is simply that it should be a preparation for the world of today and tomorrow. This definition is probably one of the most widely accepted.

There are two important facets of education which need to be defined: learning and training. Definitions for each of these are presented below:

> LEARNING   a term used to describe those internal mental processes (and external activities) which an entity uses in order to increase its knowledge about some universe of discourse;

> TRAINING   a term used to describe those processes that enable an entity to develop and improve its performance in some task orientated skill.

Learning and training have considerable degrees of similarity in that their objective is to improve an individual's ability to solve problems and realise the goals that they set for themselves. Another fundamental thesis that this book supports is that computers can be used to augment each of the above processes. Indeed, computer based learning (CBL) and computer based training (CBT) are nowadays instructional techniques that are widely used in a large number of institutions – both educational and industrial. Two other frequently used acronyms used to describe the application of computers to learning and training are CAI (computer aided instruction) and CAL (computer aided learning). Each of these will be considered in more detail in subsequent chapters of this book.

1.2.4 Mechanisms for Teaching

It was established earlier (in section 1.2.2) that teaching was primarily concerned with the communication of knowledge and skills from one who is rich in these commodities (a teacher) to one who has a deficiency of them (a student) (see figure 1.8). The term communication refers to those techniques that may be used to facilitate the movement of signals, data, information and knowledge from one location to another. For this to happen an appropriate communication channel must exist between the two (or more) entities (or locations) involved in the communicative process. Increasingly, computer systems are being used to facilitate the movement of information from one place (a source) to another (a recipient). This is depicted schematically in figure 1.10.

The term instructional medium is used to describe the channels of communication used for teaching. Within education, media selection (Berman, 1974; Romiszowski, 1977) is an important factor to be considered when preparing instructional material. Figure 1.11 shows

just a few of the different possibilities that exist. In the first of
these (case A), the teacher (as an author) writes a text book. The
information that this contains is then assimilated by the student (as .
a reader). This mechanism of instruction lacks very many of the
requirements of a good teaching system. For example, information flow
is essentially unidirectional; there is thus no feedback to the
author. Furthermore, learning by this approach requires only a passive
involvement by the learner. Usually, unless a programmed instruction
text is used, there is no mechanism by which the instructional
strategy can be modified to meet the requirements of individual
learners.

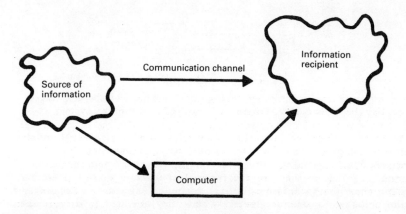

Figure 1.10   Communication – the movement of information.

Example B shows the conventional classroom situation. The teacher
prepares (or authors) a lesson. The contents of this are then
presented to a group of students in a class. The instructor is able to
evaluate each student's performance by setting regular homework and
periodic examinations. There is therefore some form of feedback from
the students to the teacher. This enables modifications to be made to
the course material (and its mechanism of presentation) should this be
necessary. Unfortunately, the teacher is unable to easily modify the
contents of a lesson in order to meet the individual requirements of
each particular student. For this reason it is customary to aim the
level of the lesson at the 'average' student. However, unlike the
book, a well planned lesson can involve the student in active learning
– through the use of practical sessions and activities designed to
stimulate direct student participation.

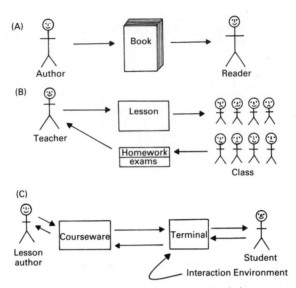

Figure 1.11   Examples of instructional media: (A) the text book,
(B) the classroom environment, and, (C) a computer system.

The third medium of instruction (case C) shown in figure 1.11 involves
using a computer system as the channel of communication for
instructional material. In this situation the teacher and/or lesson
author creates lessons in the form of courseware units (see section
1.2.5). These are then loaded into a computer system (a mainframe,
minicomputer or microcomputer) where they are used to drive a special
type of terminal device. This is used to create and control an
interaction environment for the student. The environment is designed
and built in such a way that it is able to present instructional
material to the student and also gather a variety of different types
of response data. In principle, the courseware provides: a highly
active learning experience; individualised instruction (that is,
strategies that are automatically tailored to the needs of each
individual student); and feedback to the teacher and lesson author.

A visual display unit or microcomputer system (see figures 1.2 and
1.5) often provides the basis for most interaction environments.
However, as we shall see later, it is possible to augment these with a
variety of other peripheral devices thereby producing sophisticated
interactive multimedia teaching machines. It is important to realise
that the type of interaction environment that was depicted
schematically in figure 1.4 will also form the basis for the design
and implementation of terminal systems for the support of computer
assisted learning and computer based training.

We believe that computer based systems can help to improve the quality
and efficiency of instruction. Indeed, there is experimental evidence
to support this claim (Kenny and Schmulian, 1979). However, it is

imperative to realise that computer based systems are not a panacea for all instructional problems. The computer is just one of many types of instructional medium. The lesson author/teacher must therefore carefully choose the one that is most appropriate for the fulfilment of particular pedagogical objectives.

1.2.5 The Computer as a Teaching Resource

As a teaching resource the computer can offer a number of interesting possibilities (Barker, 1979; 1984). For example, it is able to provide:

(1) sound effects and analysis,
(2) static and dynamic imagery through computer graphics,
(3) text handling facilities,
(4) control of external devices and of learning progress,
(5) a variety of data capture techniques,
(6) facilities for data archival, retrieval and dissemination,
(7) a means of achieving highly individualised instruction,
(8) a highly interactive learning environment, and
(9) facilities for pattern matching, computation
    and decision making.

Together, these basic facilities provide a wealth of resources from which to construct instructional material. When using the computer as a teaching resource two basic modes of usage are involved: author mode and learner mode. These are depicted in figure 1.12.

In author mode the computer is used as an aid to prepare the courseware that is to contain the instructional material and . which embodies the author's required teaching strategies. Two basic approaches can be used for the acquisition of courseware. Either, a special package is 'bought in' or the teacher/author produces it. In the former case, ready-made packages often have to be modified to meet local needs. Where it is applicable, this can provide a cost effective approach. However, in situations where the teacher has to generate the courseware from scratch, some form of programming has to be undertaken – this could mean higher costs. The production of courseware with this latter technique is achieved either by using a programming language (such as BASIC or PASCAL) or by means of a special author language (such as PILOT or MICROTEXT – see later). An author language is a special high level tool that is specifically designed to facilitate the preparation of instructional software. Each of these techniques for courseware development will be discussed in more detail in chapter 2.

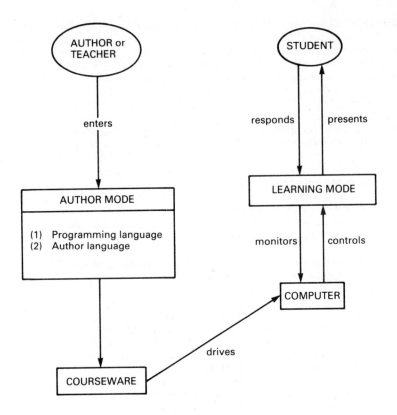

Figure 1.12   Modes of using an instructional computer.

Once the courseware has been developed, it is loaded into the computer
where it then controls the student's interactive learning environment.
This is now called learner mode. In this mode, the computer presents
instructional material (sound, graphics, text, etc) to the student and
monitors the responses produced. These are then used to determine the
subsequent direction that the course of instruction will take. During
learner mode, all student responses can be archived and subsequently
analysed by the computer. The results of the analysis can be passed
back to the author/teacher thereby providing valuable feedback on
student progress and courseware performance.

As a teaching resource the computer has a valuable role to play in
education and training. Some of the many instructional applications of
the computer will be outlined in the subsequent chapters of this book.
In order to form an introduction to these, the next section of this
chapter is used to outline the scope of computer assisted learning.

1.3 THE SCOPE OF COMPUTER ASSISTED LEARNING (CAL)

Computer assisted learning and computer assisted instruction may be thought of as domains that encompass any activity in which a computer is used to augment (or initiate) a learning or training process. In this context there are two fundamental approaches to the use of computer systems. There are those applications in which:

(1)   the computer itself is not only the medium of instruction but is also the subject of instruction — computer studies is now an extremely popular part of the curriculum in many centres of learning, and

(2)   the computer just acts as one of the many media that are used in the teaching of some other discipline — such as mathematics, English, reading, foreign languages, science, history, geography, music, dance, cookery, medicine and a host of other subjects.

No matter what the subject that is taught, the objectives of CAL remain the same. It is intended to be used as a means of:

(1) augmenting conventional teaching/training methods,
(2) accelerating the learning process,
(3) experimenting in course development,
(4) providing remedial instruction,
(5) providing individualised instruction,
(6) providing enrichment material,
(7) achieving consistently higher teaching standards,
(8) providing cost effective instruction,
(9) providing 'on-demand' instruction.

The last of these is particularly relevant to the implementation of Open Learning Systems (Coffey, 1978) in which students can gain access to instructional material as and when they need it, no matter where they are geographically located. As we shall see later, the use of computer communications networks will be of significant importance in promoting this type of learning environment.

The scope of CAL includes a wide variety of instructional functions. These have to be realised in terms of a limited number of CAL modes. The CAL functions to be performed and a selection of the CAL modes available for their implementation are listed in table 1.3. Each of these functions and modes is applicable to all levels of education and training. Because of their importance they will therefore need to be dealt with in considerable depth. In view of this, a more detailed exposition must be delayed. These topics will become the subject of subsequent chapters.

The scope of CAL application areas is probably as diverse as the number of subject areas in which it has been employed. For this reason it will be beneficial to attempt to classify applications of CAL into four broad categories, namely schools, colleges, industry and the home. Each of these is briefly outlined below.

Table 1.3   The Scope of CAL: Functions and Modes

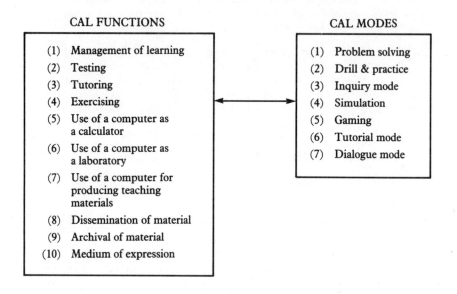

CAL FUNCTIONS

(1)   Management of learning
(2)   Testing
(3)   Tutoring
(4)   Exercising
(5)   Use of a computer as
        a calculator
(6)   Use of a computer as
        a laboratory
(7)   Use of a computer for
        producing teaching
        materials
(8)   Dissemination of material
(9)   Archival of material
(10) Medium of expression

CAL MODES

(1)   Problem solving
(2)   Drill & practice
(3)   Inquiry mode
(4)   Simulation
(5)   Gaming
(6)   Tutorial mode
(7)   Dialogue mode

1.3.1 CAL in Schools

Until the beginning of the 1980's CAL in schools was very slow in getting underway. One of the prime reasons for this slowness (at least within the UK) has been the distinct shortage of resources (both hardware and software) available to support this type of activity in an adequate way. Indeed, even at the time of writing this book, there is still a major gap in the provision of software for CAL. Furthermore, to make things worse, despite the growing availability of hardware for schools use, its suitability for CAL is often questioned. Prior to 1980, the hardware available in schools was most often employed for the teaching of mathematics and computer studies.

Before the availability of microcomputers, many schools were serviced by a time-sharing terminal that was linked through a telephone line to some form of mainframe or minicomputer system. The computing resources were then provided by a computer owned by the local education authority or by an industrial/commercial organisation. Many local authorities allocated a fixed amount of computer time to the provision of this type of application thereby allowing a reasonably regular schools service to be scheduled. Undoubtedly, the benevolence of industrial organisations was often less dependable since they could only allocate spare resources for schools use. This meant that any form of service was often on an unscheduled or ad hoc basis. The use of microcomputers in schools now means that a regular computing service can be organised.

School involvement with CAL can occur at three distinct levels: primary, secondary and tertiary. Although some form of computer usage has been taking place in the latter areas for some time, it is only very recently that interest at the primary level has actively developed. At the higher levels of school education the use of CAL will mainly be orientated towards the teaching of specific subjects. However, in the primary sector it is likely to be employed as an aid to the acquisition of basic skills (reading, writing, spelling, game playing, etc) and the more rapid development of basic concepts – such as colour, sound, touch, movement and so on. There is a very wide spectrum of avenues of investigation to be explored in this area, particularly the application of computers as an aid to overcoming the learning problems of physically and/or mentally retarded school children.

Because of the importance of education about computers and the significant potential that they offer as teaching tools, many awareness projects have been initiated. Within the UK, for example, the BBC is one of the many large organisations that are helping to promote computer literacy and the use of computers in schools (British Broadcasting Corporation, 1982). The government itself, through its Microelectronics Education Programmes (MEP and SMDP), is also actively involved in attempting to increase the extent of computer involvement in schools (Microelectronics in Education Programme, 1982).

1.3.2 CAL in Further and Higher Education
In principle, the use of CAL in higher and further education is controlled by similar objectives to those that govern its use in schools. It can be used in exactly the same way as in schools however, the complexity of the domain orientated material that is used is likely to be much greater. Because of this, the type of hardware employed, and the nature of the courseware that drives it, is likely to be much more sophisticated than its counterpart at school level. This is particularly so with respect to the teaching of scientific and engineering skills using CAL. There is a basic requirement in this area for very high quality software that is able to generate realistic and effective instructional dialogues. Undoubtedly, this objective will only be achieved by building a high degree of 'intelligence' into the software used for teaching at this level.

When planning for the CAL requirements of higher education there are at least three important factors that need to be taken into consideration. First of all, it is important to bear in mind the educational maturity of students in colleges and universities, and, incidentally, those who are attending part-time evening or day-release courses. Students in these categories are able to study on their own

and require far less personal attention from teachers than do learners
in a school environment. The second important factor relates to how
courses meet student requirements. Students in higher education prefer
to select combinations of courses which are able to meet the
requirements posed by their intended career pathways. Quite often, in
conventional class–room orientated teaching environments timetabling
clashes can preclude certain important combinations of options, unless
they are taught on an untimetabled self–study basis. The third factor
to be considered is the teaching of minority interest subjects.
Because of the availability of staff many useful courses in this
category fail to run. This situation often arises either because (1)
it is not cost effective to employ a subject specialist to teach the
course, or, (2) a staff member who is capable of teaching it has to be
timetabled for other duties.

Each of the types of problem outlined above can be solved in an
effective way through the use of appropriately designed open learning
systems. We have indicated previously that CAL can play an important
role in this type of approach to education, as indeed it can in
helping to solve directly some of the problems outlined above.

1.3.3 CAL in Commercial and Industrial Training
The objectives of industrial training are, of necessity, often very
different from those of an academic institution. The most significant
differences probably stem from:

(1) the breadth of instruction available; usually, in
     conventional educational establishments, a much wider
     range of subjects will be involved than is the case in
     a commercial or industrial environment;

(2) in general, in industrial/commercial training there
     is more emphasis on basic skill acquisition rather
     than on the teaching of fundamental principles or the
     learning of broad concepts;

(3) the type of instruction available in non–academic
     institutions is most often very 'organisation
     orientated'. That is, instruction and training are
     about and relate very closely to the organisation
     itself (for example, banking, insurance, steel making)
     and the specific tasks and processes (manufacturing,
     administration, financial, and so on) that take place
     within it.

To describe the educational applications of computers in
industry/commerce the term computer based training (cbt) is often
used. This term is usually interpreted as referring to a much narrower
range of objectives than the more general ones associated with the
term CAL.

CBT techniques are important where (1) there is rapid change in
technology such that employees continually have to be retrained in

order to work with the latest type of material and equipment, (2) there is a high turn-over and movement of staff within an organisation, and (3) the range of products and/or services tendered by a company is wide and continually changing. In each of these situations CAL and CBT can offer very effective induction and re-training courses.

Very many large organisations are committed in a significant way to the use of computer based training. For example, the wellknown computer manufacturing company IBM (International Business Machines) uses CBT techniques both for its own internal training programme (for engineers, sales people and technical support staff) and for the presentation of courses for the education of its customer base. IBM, along with another American company called Control Data Corporation (CDC) were amongst the first commercial organisations to become deeply involved with the use of CBT. Control Data's current interest in this area centres around the world famous PLATO system (Bitzer, 1976) which will be described in more detail later.

Many other commercial and industrial concerns are now using computer systems in order to effect in-house training and education programmes. Some of the more wellknown of these include Barclay's Bank, Imperial Chemical Industries (ICI), British Airways and International Computers Limited (ICL). In order to provide help and advice to those wishing to use CBT, the UK's National Computing Centre (NCC) has set up an advisory section to which potential users can turn (National Computing Centre, 1982). There are also many commercial companies who specialise in the design and provision of CBT packages to meet the requirements of industrial clients (Sturridge, 1981). Undoubtedly, there is currently a rapidly growing market for good quality CBT material.

1.3.4 CAL in the Home and for the Disabled.
Most modern societies are based upon the principle that a family unit, a pseudofamily or an individual will be domiciled within some form of 'home environment'. Typically, this might be a house, a flat or a bedsitter. In all probability, the home environment is likely to provide access to a television and a telephone. Each of these can provide a source of CAL material – provided that some form of home computer facility is also available. A wide range of microcomputers have recently been introduced for use in the home, either as stand-alone units or for attachment to an existing television set. Some of the most well-known examples of home computers include the BBC micro, the Sinclair ZX81 and Spectrum, Commodore's VIC-20, and Texas Instrument's TI-99/4.

Television can provide a significant range of CAL software using direct broadcasting techniques. Naturally, a suitable electronic adaptor must be available which will allow the connection of the home computer to the TV set and its reception system. Programs for CAL use that are transmitted and acquired in this way are referred to as telesoftware (Hedger, 1978). Another source of CAL software may be derived from the telephone. It is possible to buy a special adaptor that enables a home computer to be connected to the public telephone network (Barker, 1982d; 1982e). This enables the computer to be indirectly connected to a remote mainframe or minicomputer system. The CAL software resident in these can be used on the remote host system or transferred over the telephone network to the home computer. In addition to the use of the television and telephone as a source of CAL materials for home consumption, it is also possible to purchase special packages in the form of cassette tapes and/or flexible discs (these storage media were described in section 1.1.2).

When they are not at work or school, people spend a considerable amount of their time in their home environment. It is therefore quite natural to assume that within this environment a considerable amount of education takes place. This might be for leisure or pleasure, a form of pre-school instruction or for the fulfilment of unrealised career objectives. Of course, there is also a significant number of people who actually work from their home environment or are restricted to it. Examples of the latter include those who are geographically isolated, old people and those who are disabled or physically handicapped. From these examples it is easy to see that education in the home can cover a wide range of possibilities. CAL in this environment must, if possible, be capable of subsuming all of these possibilities.

Undoubtedly the market for CAL packages for home use is one which is likely to show considerable growth potential. However, because the educational attributes (such as knowledge level, learning ability, preferred instructional modes) are relatively unknown (compared with school children or students), the design of applicable courseware could provide significant problems, unless very sophisticated software design and programming techniques are employed. Courseware aimed at the home user will thus need to be exceptionally 'clever' if it is to react in the correct way to a spectrum of users that between them exhibit an extremely diverse range of abilities and levels of interest. The courseware must therefore incorporate some form of programmed intelligence. This topic, and intelligent software, will be discussed briefly in the following section and in subsequent parts of this book.

1.4 APPROACHES TO CAL

There are many different approaches to the provision of CAL facilities. In the final section of this chapter a brief indication will be given of some of the ways in which a CAL facility (1) has been provided in the past, (2) is currently implemented, and (3) is likely to be provided in the future. The material in this section is, of necessity, introductory in nature and will be expanded upon in subsequent chapters.

1.4.1 General Approaches
In terms of providing a CAL facility three basic types of
computational resource can be employed: a mainframe system, a
minicomputer system and/or a microcomputer (see section 1.4.2). These
may be used to support courseware packages that are bought-in as such
(and then modified to meet local requirements) or produced in-house
using either a programming language or an authoring system (see figure
1.12). No matter how the courseware is produced it will involve the
dissemination of information to a student population and analysis of
subsequent response patterns. The software, and its accompanying
hardware, must motivate the student in a positive way. That is, it
should encourage the student to learn about and explore the universe
of discourse (see figure 1.8) with which it deals.

Undoubtedly, most modern approaches to CAL involve some form of
interactive dialogue with the computer (see figure 1.5). The different
functions of CAL, and the modes of CAL usage needed to exploit these,
have been listed previously in table 1.3. Each of the basic modes
presented in this table has its advantages (and limitations),
depending upon the type of learning situation involved. The courseware
author must therefore be familiar with each mode and must then attempt
to formulate an approach to CAL that best exploits the advantages of
each. Sometimes the effects of each mode cannot be determined
beforehand and so there is considerable merit in adopting an
experimental and adaptable approach to their use. Indeed, perhaps one
of the most useful rules to remember when using CAL is: monitor and
modify. In other words, always attempt to monitor the performance of
courseware. Then, if need be, modify it in the light of experience in
order to optimise its performance. Performance can be measured in
terms of student satisfaction and attainment. High ratings in these
metrics are the hallmark of quality software.

1.4.2 Types of System
The early types of CAL system were almost all based on the use of a
large time-shared computer system (a minicomputer or mainframe). To
this was attached a number of student terminals or workstations. There
was thus a one-to-many relationship between the computer and the
student base that it supported. Typical examples of this approach to
the provision of CAL facilities include:

(1) the PLATO system (an acronym for Programmed Logic for
     Automatic Teaching Operation) at the University of
     Illinois (Bitzer, 1976) the development of which was
     sponsored by the Control Data Corporation,
(2) the TICCIT system (Time-shared Interactive Computer
     Controlled Information Television) that was produced
     by the Mitre Corporation (Merrill, 1980), and
(3) the various projects sponsored by the National
     Development Programme in Computer Assisted Learning
     NDPCAL – (Hooper and Toye, 1975).

Both (1) and (2) each represent typical American approaches to CAL on large machines while the third example gives an indication of the nature of the UK effort in this area. Within the NDPCAL programme two important examples of successful projects that were based upon the use of time–shared computers are worth noting. These are (1) the Computational Physics Laboratory at the University of Surrey (Jackson, 1975), and (2) the Clinical Decision Making Project at the University of Glasgow (Taylor, 1975a; 1975b).

Although this mode of CAL implementation has led to many very successful projects, in general, this approach can often be thwarted by a number of significant limitations:

(1)   the relatively high cost of this type of computer system,
(2)   the questionable reliability of the hardware,
(3)   the low overall availability of the CAL system,
(4)   the easily degraded performance, and
(5)   the limited interaction environment that
       is normally available.

An alternative approach to the use of large machines is the use of small computers, in particular the utilisation of micro systems and personal computers. Indeed, the arrival of this type of computational resource has brought about an explosive revival of interest in CAL, after the somewhat disappointing experiences with it on large machines.

The distinguishing feature about a micro or personal computer is the fact that there is a one–to–one relationship between the computer and the student (contrast the large machine situation). That is, each student has his/her own computer. Frequently, this will provide facilities for sound generation and a screen that is able to provide high resolution graphics along with a multiplicity of different colours. Of the many advantages of using personal computers for CAL, the following are probably amongst the foremost:

(1)   the relatively low cost of microcomputer systems,
(2)   their high reliability,
(3)   their potentially continuous availability,
(4)   their constant performance level, and
(5)   the fact that they can provide the basis for a
       much more complex interaction environment.

For many applications of CAL and CBT, microcomputers can thus offer an extremely useful implementation medium.

Future approaches to CAL (as we shall discuss later) are likely to involve the integration of each of the two basic methods outlined previously. This integration is likely to be achieved through the use of highly distributed computer communications networks similar to that depicted schematically in figure 1.13.

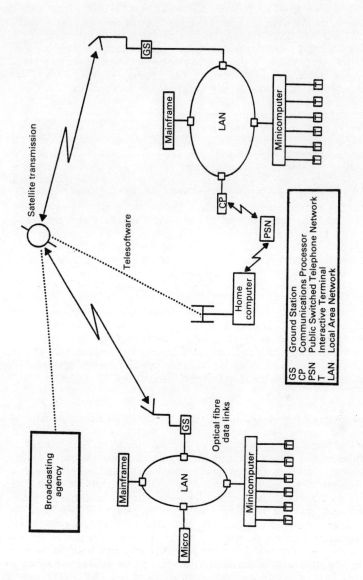

Figure 1.13 A computer based open learning system for CAL.

This diagram shows how Local Area Networks (LANs) and global nets can be combined to produce an integrated highly distributed CAL system. In principle, the use of direct broadcasting using satellite transmission systems (Fox, 1982) will permit (via telesoftware methods) the implementation of quite sophisticated computer based open learning systems. These should then permit the facile dissemination of educational material to virtually any geographical location.

1.4.3 The Integration of Teaching Resources

We have previously indicated that the process of teaching is, in part, one of information transfer from a teacher to a student. The communication channels by which this takes place can be varied and numerous. For example, a teacher most often uses a spoken narrative that may be supported by lecture notes, a blackboard, textbook references, slide/cine projection, TV video/sound recordings and a host of other communication methods. These teaching resources are often used both in sequence and in parallel. They may be combined in many ways to produce a particular pedagogical outcome in the most effective way. An analogous situation arises when a student interacts with a computer system. There are thus many potential channels of communication that the CAL author can employ in order to effect information/knowledge transfer.

In a CAL system, the student's interaction environment plays the role of the teacher. This environment can contain a multiplicity of channels to facilitate the flow of information both from the computer to the student and in the reverse direction (see figure 1.4). The available channels of communication may be broadly sub-divided into four types: textual, sonic, graphical and activity based diversions.

A textual channel is one that involves computer based generation/analysis of textual information. Similarly, sonic channels relate to the production and analysis of sound by computer: speech generation/analysis, the production of music and so on. Graphic channels involve the use of pictures for communication. Activity based diversions are processes that involve the student in a learning task requiring his/her direct participation in an 'on the job' context. During this participation the computer always closely monitors student performance and provides guidance when this is necessary. This type of teaching channel forms an important part of industrial computer based training applications of the computer.

In order to integrate and optimise the use of the available teaching channels in a CAL system a special type of multimedia workstation is required. It is this that provides the student's interaction environment mentioned above and which was illustrated in figure 1.11. As a means of controlling such an integrated environment, powerful programming facilities are required. These requirements will be discussed in more detail later, as will our approach to fulfilling them, namely the MUMEDALA system (MUltiMEDia Authoring LAnguage).

1.4.4 Intelligent Teaching Systems

In the last section we suggested that a significant part of the teaching process involved information transfer from a teacher to a student. Of course, it involves much more than just this. A teacher must observe and record the behaviour of his/her class and then respond to this in an appropriate way. For example, a teacher must attempt to assess the ability of individual students and then try to adopt an overall instructional strategy that is appropriate to the needs of that student. Each individual student will, in principle, require the use of a slightly different instructional strategy in order to effect an optimal knowledge transfer. Naturally, the ability to cater for this requirement will be difficult to realise in the case of a human teacher who has to deal with very many students. However, this should not be the case in a CAL environment. Another important task that a teacher has to perform is that of assessing the rate and degree of knowledge uptake for each student (this is different from an assessment of ability), since the pedagogical strategy should be markedly influenced by these factors. Modifications to the teaching mechanism should then be made in such a way that the rate and degree of knowledge uptake is optimised without forcing the student to go too fast or, on the other hand, impeding his/her progress. Human teachers are good at assessing situations and then taking appropriate action so as to maintain control of a learning situation.

Human instructors are intelligent teachers. It seems reasonable, therefore, that CAL software should be designed and fabricated in such a way that it attempts to implement at least some of the intelligent behaviour that human teachers exhibit – as was outlined above. Of course, this will require that the software has the ability to handle ad hoc and unanticipated situations in a way in which a human teacher might, that is, it would use similar types of decision rule in order to determine what to do in any particular situation. A requirement for intelligence in CAL software has already been hinted at in section 1.3.4. This requirement can best be met through the use of programming techniques developed as a result of studies in the area of artificial intelligence (Gable and Page, 1980).

There is now a whole area of CAL/CAI devoted to a study of the applications of artificial intelligence to the construction of intelligent tutoring and teaching systems (Sleeman and Brown, 1982). Some of the important topics that are of current interest include: modelling the student, studies of rule making, game playing and hypothesis formation. Of these, one of the most extensively studied is the area of student modelling (Self, 1974; Self and Hudson, 1982). Many designers of CAL courseware believe that it is important that the software is able to build up a mathematical model of the student in terms of his/her ability, preferred learning modes and knowledge states. By comparing the values of characteristic parameters of the model (for given student instances) with the desired values, appropriate teaching strategies can then be automatically and dynamically created. These can then be used to automatically control the path that the learning process takes for each individual student. Software that fulfils these objectives exists on the larger types of computer system. However, whether the complexity of this software will permit its implementation on small computers remains to be seen. It is certainly a worthwhile goal to aim for in view of what has been said previously in section 1.3.

1.5 CONCLUSION

Modern life is an extremely complex process. Much of this complexity is caused by the increasing need for members of the human species to develop methods for handling large volumes of data and information. This data arises from a wide variety of different sources. Nowadays, computers play a significant role in helping to process and store data that is derived from all forms of human activity. It is questionable whether the unaided human brain could cope with the increasingly complex demands that are placed upon it. For this reason, personal computers are likely to be of significant importance in future years.

Education, teaching and training cannot escape the onward strides of technology. It is therefore time that the role of computers in education was critically assessed. To some extent this has been attempted in the initial chapter of our book. We believe that computers can:

  (1)   enrich a learning environment,
  (2)   enhance the learning process,
  (3)   make education more widely available, and
  (4)   produce cost effective solutions to the
        dissemination of knowledge.

Furthermore, we envisage an increasingly important educational role for computers in the future. Computer aided learning and computer based training are sophisticated tools that can offer significant opportunities for the teacher and the student. Never before has an educational medium as powerful as the computer presented itself. Let us hope that all those who read this book will go forward with technology and enjoy, utilise and benefit from the educational potential of the computer. If they do not, one thing is certain: others will.

1.6 BIBLIOGRAPHY

Barker, P.G., The computer as an audio–visual resource, Computers and Education, 3, 23–34, 1979.

Barker, P.G., How a bubble sort can test code efficiency, Practical Computing, 4(7), 125–131, 1981.

Barker, P.G., Data transfer between micros, Electronics and Computing Monthly, 2(5), 21–25; 46–49, 1982a.

Barker, P.G., Programming a hand print terminal, Electronics and Computing Monthly, 2(7), 17–20; 67, 1982b.

Barker, P.G., Data base interaction using a hand print terminal, International Journal of Man–Machine Studies, 17, 435–458, 1982c.

Barker, P.G., PET as a terminal device, Practical Computing, 5(1), 106–109, 1982d.

Barker, P.G., Networking small computers, Wireless World, 88(1556), 35–40, 1982e.

Barker, P.G., Programming with PL/I–80, Electronics and Computing Monthly, 3(1), 26–31; 3(2), 78–81, 1983a.

Barker, P.G., Dialogue programming with PILOT, Electronics and Computing Monthly, 3(3), 78–80; 3(5), 70–72, 1983b.

Barker, P.G., Computers as an educational resource, Analytical Proceedings of the Chemical Society, 21(4), 140–142, 1984.

Berman, I., Learning media: theory, selection and utilisation in science education, in New Trends in the Utilisation of Educational Technology for Science Education, 101–142, UNESCO, Paris, 1974.

Bitzer, D.L., The wide world of computer based education, Advances in Computers, 15, 239–283, 1976.

Bohl, M., Information Processing, Second Edition, Science Research Associates, Chicago, IL, 1976.

British Broadcasting Corporation, Insight Into Computing – A Teacher's Guide to the BBC Provision on Computer Literacy, Broadcasting Support Services, London, 1982.

Camp, R.C., Smay, T.A. and Triska, C.J., Microprocessor Systems Engineering, Matrix, Portland, OR, 1979.

Coffey, J., Development of an Open Learning System in Further Education, Working Paper 15, Council for Educational Technology, London, 1978.

Commodore Business Machines, CBM Professional Computer User Manual, Commodore Business Machines, Santa Clara, CA, 1979.

Fernandez, J.N. and Ashley, R., Using CP/M: A Self–Teaching Guide, John Wiley, New York, NY, 1980.

Fernandez, J.N., Tabler, D.N. and Ashley, R., 6502 Assembly Language Programming, John Wiley, New York, NY, 1982.

Fisher, E. and Jensen, C.W., PET and the IEEE–488 Bus (GPIB), Osborne/McGraw–Hill, Berkeley, CA, 1980.

Fox, B., Satellite TV starts the ultimate craze, New Scientist, 95(1322), 680–683, 1982.

Gable, A. and Page, C.V., The use of artificial intelligence techniques in computer assisted instruction: an overview, International Journal of Man–Machine Studies, 12, 259–282, 1980.

Grogono, P., Programming in PASCAL, Addison–Wesley, Reading, MA, 1978.

Guedj, R.A., ten Hagen, P.J.W., Hopgood, F.R.A., Tucker, H.A. and Duce, D.A., Methodology of Interaction, Proceedings of the IFIP Workshop, Seillac, France, May 1979, North Holland, Amsterdam, 1980.

Hedger, J., Telesoftware: home computing via teletext, Wireless World, 84(1515), 61–64, 1978.

Hooper, R. and Toye, I., Computer Assisted Learning in the United Kingdom: Some Case Studies, Council for Educational Technology, London, 1975.

Hordeski, M.F., Microprocessor Cookbook, Tab Books, Blue Ridge Summit, PA, 1979.

Hwang, K., Computer Architectures for Image Processing, IEEE Computer, 16(1), 10–12, 1983.

Jackson, D., DF–1/03 Computational physics teaching laboratory, in Two Years On – The National Development Programme in Computer Assisted Learning, edited by R. Hooper, 92, Council for Educational Technology, London, 1975.

Jackson, P.C., Introduction to Artificial Intelligence, 65, Petrocelli, New York, NY, 1974.

Johnson, M.C., Educational Uses of the Computer: An Introduction, Rand McNally, Chicago, IL, 1971.

Kenny, G.N.C. and Schmulian, C., Computer assisted learning in the teaching of anaesthesia, Anaesthesia, 34, 159–162, 1979.

Kent, E.W., The Brains of Men and Machines, Byte/McGraw–Hill, New York, NY, 1981.

Kidd, A.L., Man–Machine Dialogue Design, British Telecom Research Laboratories, Volume 1, Study 1, issued by Martlesham Consultancy Services, Ipswich, 1982.

King,   D.W.,   Statistical   indicators   of   scientific   and   technical
communication (1960–1980), in Key Papers in the Design and   Evaluation
of Information Systems, edited by D.W. King, 299–304, American Society
for Information Science, Knowledge Industry, 1978.

Lindsay, P.H. and Norman, D.A., Human Information Processing: An
Introduction to Psychology, Academic Press, London, 1972.

Martin, J., Design of Man–Computer Dialogues, Prentice–Hall, Englewood
Cliffs, NJ, 1973.

Meadow, C.T., Man–Machine Communication, John Wiley, New York, NY,
1970.

Merrill, M.D., Learner control in computer based learning, Computers
and Education, 4, 77–95, 1980.

Microelectronics in Education Programme, Project Director: Richard
Fothergill, Newcastle Polytechnic, Newcastle–Upon–Tyne, 1982.

Microsoft, MBASIC User's Manual for Intertec's Video Computer Systems,
Microsoft, Bellevue, WA, 1982.

National Computing Centre, Manchester, 1982.

Newman, W.M. and Sproull, R.F., Principles of Interactive Computer
Graphics, McGraw–Hill, New York, NY, 1973.

Osborne, A. and Donahue, C.S., PET/CBM Personal Computer Guide, Second
Edition, Osborne/McGraw–Hill, Berkeley, CA, 1980.

Romiszowski, A.J., The Selection and Use of Instructional Media: A
Systems Approach, Kogan Page, London, 1977.

Saffold, R. and Smalley, A., The Slide Rule, The English Universities
Press, London, 1964.

Self, J.A.,   Student   models   in   computer   aided   instruction,
International Journal of Man–Machine Studies, 6(2), 261–276, 1974.

Self, J.A. and Hudson, R.W.A., A dialogue system to teach database
concepts, Computer Journal, 25(1) 135–139, 1982.

Simons, G.L., Introducing Word Processing, National Computing Centre,
Manchester, 1981.

Sleeman, D. and Brown, J.S., Intelligent Tutoring Systems, Academic
Press, London, 1982.

Smith, C., Microcomputers in Education, Ellis Horwood, Chichester, 1982.

Spencer, D.D., A Guide to BASIC Programming, Second Edition, Addison-Wesley, Reading, MA, 1975.

Sturridge, H., A lesson in computer lessons, Computer Management, 28–31, 1981.

Taylor, T.R., Computer assisted learning in clinical decision making, in Computer Assisted Learning in the United Kingdom: Some Case Studies, edited by R. Hooper and I. Toye, 199–214, Council for Educational Technology, London, 1975a.

Taylor, T.R., DP-1/04 Clinical decision making, in Two Years On – The National Development Programme in Computer Assisted Learning, edited by R. Hooper, 92, Council for Educational Technology, London, 1975b.

Thomas, R. and Yates, J., A User Guide to the UNIX System, Osborne/McGraw-Hill, Berkeley, CA, 1982.

Tropper, C., Local Computer Network Technologies, Academic Press, London, 1981.

Witten, I.H., Communicating with Microcomputers – An Introduction to the Technology of Man-Computer Communication, Academic Press, London, 1980.

Wyld, B.A. and Bell, D.A., The Calculator Revolution: How to make the Most of Your Calculator, White Lion, London, 1977.

Zaks, R. and Lesea, A., Microprocessor Interfacing Techniques, SYBEX, Berkeley, CA, 1979.

Further Reading

Burke, R.L., CAI Sourcebook – Background and Procedures for Computer Assisted Instruction in Education and Industrial Training, Prentice-Hall, Englewood Cliffs, NJ, 1982.

Crawford, F.R., Introduction to Data Processing, Prentice-Hall, Englewood Cliffs, NJ, 1968.

Evans, C., The Mighty Micro: The Impact of the Computer Revolution, Gollancz, London, 1979.

Gaines, B.R. and Shaw, M.L.G., The Art of Computer Conversation – A New Medium for Communication, Prentice–Hall, Englewood Cliffs, NJ, 1984.

Godfrey, D. and Sterling, S., The Elements of CAL – The How–to Book on Computer Aided Learning, Press Porcepic, Victoria, British Columbia, 1982.

Hartley, R., Computer assisted learning, in Human Interaction with Computers, edited by H.T. Smith and T.R.G. Green, 129–159, Academic Press, London, 1980.

Hawkridge, D., New Information Technology in Education, Croom Helm, London, 1983.

Leiblum, M.D., Screening for CAL, Computers and Education, 3(4), 313–324, 1979.

O'Neil, H.F. (editor), Computer–Based Instruction: A State–of–the–Art Report, Educational Technology Series, Academic Press, New York, NY, 1981.

Rushby, N.J., An Introduction to Educational Computing, Croom Helm, London, 1979.

Smith, P.R. (editor), Computer Assisted Learning, selected papers from the CAL '81 Symposium, April 1981, University of Leeds, Pergamon, Oxford, 1981.

Stonier, T., The Wealth of Information – A Profile of the Post–Industrial Economy, Methuen, London, 1983.

Chapter 2

PREPARING, OBTAINING AND EVALUATING COURSEWARE MATERIAL

2.1 WHAT IS COURSEWARE?

The term courseware is often used in a generic sense to describe materials that are specifically designed and produced for use within some form of teaching machine. Courseware can best be regarded as a combination of three essential commodities. Its essential constituents are (1) a set of instructional strategies, (2) their associated domain dependent subject matter, and (3) the storage media to which each of (1) and (2) are committed.

In this book we are concerned with courseware for teaching machines that are in some way based upon the use of a computer. Consequently, much of the instructional strategy and domain dependent subject matter will be embedded within some form of computer program. Most of the courseware that is of interest to us will therefore have characteristics similar to those of computer software. However, because some of the teaching material for a lesson may reside on other media (such as slides, films or videotape) the direct analogy to software will not be over-emphasised.

Courseware for computer based systems will consist predominantly of software (or programs) which is augmented by material resident on other types of storage media. This chapter will therefore be concerned with techniques for developing educational software (such as programming and the use of author languages), the selection of ancillary media, techniques for evaluating courseware and methods by which it may be distributed. However, before embarking on a more

44

detailed discussion of these topics, we present a brief historical narrative that describes some of the early work upon which the foundations of modern courseware development are based.

2.1.1 Historical Background

The United States of America, in the 1950s, was probably the first country to study the instructional uses of the computer. Developments in CAI arose out of the work of Skinner at Harvard University (Skinner, 1961) who originated a technique called programmed instruction (PI). This proposed that the best way of tackling a learning task was to break it down into a series of small subtasks and then tackle each one of these in turn. As a means of reinforcing learning, student mastery of a subtask would be rewarded in an appropriate way. As soon as a subtask had been successfully completed the student would be encouraged to tackle the next one. In situations where difficulty was encountered the learner's progress would be impeded until the necessary level of attainment had been achieved. This was effected by means of extra help and tuition – that is, remediation. Remedial strategies often involved presenting concepts in slightly different ways, or, subdividing subtasks into even smaller units which would be much easier to assimilate.

Programmed instruction involves the creation of self–instructional learning materials. Their design and production will usually have involved consideration of a number of important factors. The most important of these are listed in table 2.1.

The early teaching machines used to implement PI were usually restricted to the use of multiple–choice questions. In contrast, the development of CAI offered greater flexibility. The computer could be programmed to 'understand' a wider range of responses from the student terminal.

The earliest computer assisted instruction program is thought to have been developed at one of IBMs research centres in the late 1950s (Rath, 1959). It was part of a project concerned with basic psychological research into memory and learning. In these experiments a student was presented with a problem and then asked to type in the answer through a typewriter–like console. The answer was checked as each character was entered. If an error resulted, the computer assumed control and typed out the word 'wrong'. An incorrect answer then caused the generation of another problem of similar difficulty. After a number of successive incorrect answers a problem of lesser difficulty would be generated. This type of use of the computer, as an automated teaching machine, dominated educational applications of computing in the early 1960s. The courseware to support such applications was based upon the use of the same techniques as were used in the preparation of programmed instruction texts.

Table 2.1   Important Factors in the Development of PI Material

(1)   analysis of the expected performance of the
       learner on completion of the study assignment

(2)   definition of behavioural objectives that will
       reflect whether or not the student has learnt
       the material

(3)   design of a specific criterion–referenced
       test for the material

(4)   specification of a minimum acceptable test
       performance on completion of the learning

(5)   provision of information (feedback) to students
       on their performance at various times during
       the learning sequence

(6)   pilot trials using the material on an
       equivalent group of learners

One noteworthy example of an early computer system developed for instructional applications was the IBM 1500 Instructional System (Bunderson and Dunham, 1968). This was developed out of a joint project between IBM and the Institute of Mathematical Studies at Stanford University. The IBM 1500 was probably the first CAL system to integrate multimedia learning techniques. It consisted of a CPU (with bulk storage maintained on magnetic tape and exchangeable discs), a station controller and a range of peripheral devices that included a card reader and a line printer. The student terminal consisted of a CRT, a keyboard and a lightpen (Shepherd, 1982). The light pen was the means by which touch responses could be made on the surface of the CRT, that is, it enabled the student to perform simple pointing operations. There was also an image projector having a capacity of 1000 slides which could be randomly accessed under computer control. A set of earphones and a microphone completed the multimedia resources available. Audio messages could be played to the student from a bank of audio–tape devices. Like the slides, the audio messages could also be randomly accessed under computer control. Of course, the slide, audio and computer–based material could be augmented by coloured filmstrips and reference to textbooks and other conventional learning media.

Using this system, one of the most well–known series of projects at Stanford University began under the direction of Patrick Suppes in 1965. These projects were aimed at elementary level teaching and were applied in several states in the USA. Stanford's major contribution in CAI for higher education was probably their two–year introductory

Russian course that was taught exclusively by computer and language laboratory sessions.

Another important historical development took place in 1960. A committee was formed at the University of Illinois. Its brief was to consider the possibility of using computers in the teaching of psychology, education and engineering. This committee was unable to reach any agreement and concluded that nothing should be done. The report of the committee was subsequently evaluated by Donald Bitzer (Bitzer, 1976) who recommended that the computer should be used initially for sorting and tracking students' pedagogical behaviour. Subsequently, an attempt to program a computer to teach computer programming was initiated. This work formed the basis of the first PLATO CAI system (Bitzer et al., 1962).

Until recently, countries other than the USA have been less active in CAL development, and hence in the production of courseware. Within Europe, activity in this area began in earnest during the 1970s. In most cases interest was promoted as a result of government incentive in the form of financial investment in various national projects. For example, the French National Experiment in Educational Computing began in 1970. It was aimed, in the main, at secondary education. An important facet of this project was the provision of intensive in-service training courses in computing and CAL for a nucleus of teachers. Once they had been trained it was intended that these teachers should then produce courseware and disseminate it to their colleagues in other parts of the country. Similarly, within the UK, the widespread development of CAL was first proposed by the NDPCAL (see section 1.4.2). Some 35 projects were set up - the majority in higher education and a smaller number in schools and military/industrial training establishments. These two examples serve adequately to illustrate the direction which national efforts in courseware development have taken in previous years.

One of the major drawbacks to the application of CAL has been the lack of suitable hardware for the cost effective utilisation of computer based teaching resources. However, as we have already outlined in chapter 1, the availability of low cost microcomputers is likely to remove this restriction. Unfortunately, the rapid developments in hardware technology have not been paralleled by similar developments in courseware production. In the future there is thus likely to be much greater emphasis given to this aspect of CAL.

2.1.2 The Origins of Courseware
As we have implied in the previous section, nationally sponsored CAL development projects represent a substantial source of significant amounts of CAI courseware. In order to disseminate CAL material nationally and to facilitate its exchange across international boundaries, special types of organisation known as Courseware Exchange

Centres have been set up. Because of their importance   as   sources   of
courseware,   a   more   detailed   description of these will be presented
later in this chapter.

In addition to courseware developed by teachers/lecturers   in   schools
and   colleges   (perhaps   on   a   commissioned basis), there are several
other   important   places   from   which   CAL   materials   may   originate.
Probably,   the most familiar of these will be (1) educational software
suppliers, (2) industrial/commercial training establishments, and   (3)
the rapidly developing 'cottage' industries.

Educational software suppliers come from a variety of backgrounds; two
of   the   most   common   are those with significant experience in either
computing or publishing. Indeed,   many   computing   professionals   have
turned their skills towards the development of software packages aimed
specifically at the educational market–place. Similarly, many textbook
publishers   are   now   starting   to   realise   the extensive market that
exists   for   the   sale   of   courseware.   Authors   are   therefore   given
considerable   encouragement   to   submit their work for publication and
distribution through publishers' textbook networks.   Two   examples   of
this approach to courseware distribution are: 'LOGO Challenge' (Govier
and   Neave,   1983)   and   'Computer   Applications   Packages' (Hennessey,
1983). The first of these is a   software/book   package   developed   for
primary and lower school pupils. The programs are written in BASIC and
simulate   the   turtle graphics [1] aspect of the LOGO language (Roper,
1983). The package consists of a student's book, teaching notes and   a
computer   program, the latter being supplied either on a flexible disc
or a cassette tape. Similarly, the   'Computer   Applications   Packages'
courseware   package   provides high quality material for use in schools
and   institutes   of   further   and   higher   education.   The   materials
(programs,   teacher's   notes   and   student's   book) are suitable for a
variety of examination and non–examination courses.

Industrial   and   commercial   courseware   can   be   obtained   from   many
different kinds of organisation. Those that employ CAL will very often
develop courseware to meet both general and specific in–house training
requirements,   for example development of typing skills (such as speed
writing,   speed   typing   and   word   processing),   machine   operation,
computer   programming,   familiarity   with office procedures, and so on.
Once it has been   developed,   courseware   that   is   capable   of   being

----

[1]   The   LOGO   language was developed at the Massachusetts Institute
of Technology (MIT) by Seymour Papert. An important part of this
language   is   a   mechanical   device   called a 'turtle'. This is a
hemispherical transparent drawing machine about 10 cm in diameter
which is controlled by LOGO commands entered through a computer
keyboard.   The   student   can   thus   write   programs   to   generate
pictures and hence explore the effect of programs   in   a   graphic
way. This is discussed in more detail in section 5.2.8.

transferred to other organisations can be either offered for sale or made available on a rental basis. Computer and microelectronic technology are two areas where developments are so rapid that there exists a continual need for employees to be retrained in order to keep abreast of progress. Courseware for this type of knowledge/skill update is thus often made available (for an appropriate fee) by computer manufacturers and other specialist organisations involved in the development of new types of microelectronic equipment. The PLATO system, for example, is used quite extensively for retraining applications in this area.

The widespread availability of inexpensive microcomputers within the home environment could lead to two important developments:

(1)   an increase in demand for courseware that is suitable for use in this type of environment, and

(2)   an increase in the number of people involved in the development of some form of courseware.

It is therefore likely that the cottage industry (item (2)), as a source of courseware, is one which will show a substantial growth rate in the next few years. Indeed, provided it is used wisely and with caution, this industry could well offer a solution to many of the problems we are currently facing as a result of either inadequate or unavailable courseware.

2.1.3 Future Directions
We believe that the directions in which CAL courseware development will proceed in the future will be significantly influenced by the widespread availability of the personal computer. A recent market research prediction by Isaacson and Juliussen (1983) does indeed predict a significant increase in the requirement for software for use in both schools and in the home. The anticipated growth trend for the next few years is depicted graphically in figure 2.1. It is worth speculating upon the areas from which this demand will arise.

Since learning to use a computer is becoming a crucial issue in today's society, there is likely to be a continuing and growing demand for computer literacy software. There will undoubtedly be a similar requirement for courseware to teach people how to use the popular application packages – such as VisiCalc, Mail–Merge and Wordstar [1]. Educational software for pre–school use, to teach maths, reading and other skills, is also likely to become very popular. Adult education is another area that could provide a further outlet for courseware packages. The educational software market is full of opportunities for existing companies, new start–up companies and firms engaged in other

---

[1]   These are tradenames of particular software packages that are available commercially for use on microcomputer systems.

activities. At present, educational games seem to offer the greatest opportunity. However, in the future there are likely to be many other educational software opportunities for innovative courseware publishers. Some examples include social studies, music, foreign languages, simulation of geographical topics, library literacy – teaching students to find and retrieve information, economic literacy, electronic money transactions and hosts more.

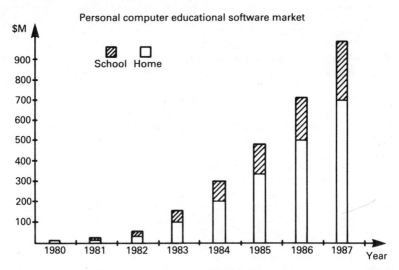

© November 1982 Future Computing, Inc., Canyon Creek Center, Richardson, Texas 75080

Figure 2.1   Predicted personal computer educational software market.
(Courtesy of Future Computing, 1982).

2.2 TECHNIQUES FOR COURSEWARE DEVELOPMENT

In this section we attempt to provide an overview of the various techniques and methodologies which need to be taken into consideration during the development of courseware materials. The general steps involved in preparing instructional material (audio–visual, lectures, PI and CAI) are illustrated diagrammatically in figure 2.2 (IBM Corporation, 1975).

Obviously, the discussion presented in this section will relate most closely to courseware that is intended for use within computer based systems. Indeed, as far as our own interests are concerned, the computer is the primary medium of instruction, with other media playing a less important ancillary role. This approach will naturally constrain our interest. We do not apologise for this since we believe

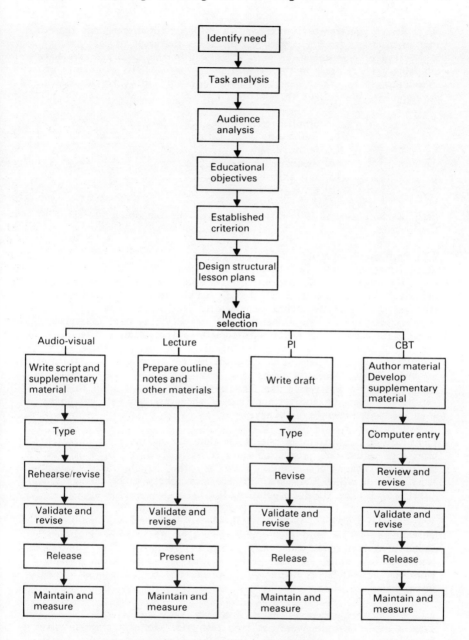

Figure 2.2   Courseware development stages.
(Courtesy of IBM.)

that some constraint is necessary in view of the tremendous breadth
that instructional technology covers. It is far too great to be given
any form of comprehensive treatment within the space that we have
available. Therefore, in what follows, we have given major
consideration to those factors most relevant to CAL courseware
development. We believe these to be:

(1) problem recognition,
(2) courseware specification,
(3) lesson design,
(4) media selection,
(5) implementation, and
(6) testing and revision.

Each of these aspects is briefly discussed in the remaining parts of
this section.

2.2.1 Problem Recognition

Recognition of the fact that a training problem exists is the first
step involved in the preparation of any form of instructional
material. In this context, two broad possibilities may be envisaged:
firstly, the need to produce courseware to meet new
training/educational requirements; and secondly, the need to replace
existing instructional material with something that is more effective,
less costly and/or easier to use. Within most organisations there will
usually be a requirement to continually review training and teaching
methods. This is necessary in order to ensure that they are performing
their stated objectives in the most appropriate way. Should this not
be the case then a critical reappraisal of the instructional methods
involved will often be necessary.

Identification of training needs is thus one of the most important
aspects of courseware production since it is this which sparks off the
subsequent chain of events. Some of the problematic training
situations in which CAL and CAI are most likely to be called upon are
listed in table 2.2 (IBM Corporation, 1975).

While these situations relate most closely to instructional problems
within industry, most of the situations that are listed will also be
found in conventional school and college environments. The guidelines
inherent in table 2.2 can thus be used as a good initial starting
point in the search for potential applications for computer based
instruction.

2.2.2 Courseware Specifications – Objectives

Once a need for courseware has been identified the next stage involves
formulating the requirements that this courseware is to fulfil.
Primarily, this involves specifying the instructional objectives that
must be realised. In addition, a statement must be made of the
constraints within which the courseware developer must work, for

Table 2.2   Identification of CAL Training Situations

(1)   many total students
(2)   many simultaneous students
(3)   many student locations
(4)   varied student backgrounds
(5)   high employee/student turnover
(6)   new employees lack qualifications
(7)   an uneven training load
(8)   lack of qualified instructors
(9)   standardisation of instruction is needed
(10)   student completion of course must be guarenteed
(11)   student records must be kept
(12)   employee/student testing is necessary
(13)   training in terminal operation is needed
(14)   course is not needed immediately
(15)   long course life expected
(16)   there is a change in job procedure planned
(17)   many classes with 10 or fewer students

example resource availability, cost, time constraints, and so on. A very simple example of a courseware specification is illustrated in figure 2.3 (Barker and Singh, 1983). In this example the training requirement was for an automated method of teaching trainee technicians in electronics how to read and evaluate resistor colour codes. Obviously, this is a very simple task which, in consequence, is easy to specify. In contrast, most training/learning situations will involve a much more detailed task analysis and statement of objectives which will therefore result in substantially more than two pages of documentation (see figure 2.3). Task analysis is a precursor to courseware specification. It involves a structured study of a job or activity in order to identify each of the basic tasks that the student/trainee must do in order to perform it. The amount of detail contained in the task analysis will obviously be dependent upon the job in question. However, it is important to realise that even simple jobs (for example, telephone answering) can involve a significant number of tasks. Once the tasks have been analysed and specified – and any necessary objectives/constraints enumerated – the work involved in course/lesson design can commence.

2.2.3 Lesson Design – Strategy and Content
Course design can be subdivided into the following three major steps:

(1)   formulation of the course plans,
(2)   preparation and organisation of the
       course material, and
(3)   formulation of suitable evaluation metrics.

The first of these involves specifying (i) the detailed way in which the course objectives (in terms of student attainment) will be realised, (ii) the teaching media that are to be employed (see section 2.2.4), and (iii) the various instructional strategies that are to be used within the lesson. In addition to defining how (and under what conditions) the main–line instructional material is to be presented, the course plan will also specify the types of remediation and reinforcement strategies that are to be used. Step (1) is most often subject matter independent.

CASE STUDY — RESISTOR COLOUR CODES

Before you attempt this case study make sure you have completed Parts 1 and 2 of the questionnaire that has been issued to you.

Practical Exercise

You are required to construct a software package that will:

1. enable trainee technicians in electronics to acquire a knowledge of how to generate and evaluate resistor colour codes,

2. exercise the technician in the application of these skills, and,

3. evaluate how well the required skills have been acquired by the trainee.

The program that you develop is to run on the PRIME minicomputer system and it should perform its teaching function via a VDU terminal.

Use the PILOT author language in order to implement the software. All the necessary domain dependent instructional material that is needed for this case study is contained on sheet 2 of this courseware specification.

* * *

Pilot Evaluation

When you have completed the exercise – or at the end of the practical session – (whichever is the sooner), please make sure that you complete Part 3 of the questionnaire and return it to Dr P.G. Barker.

Sheet 1

Figure 2.3 Learning tasks and courseware specification.

In contrast to step (1), step (2) is highly subject matter orientated since it involves the direct specification of the domain dependent material that is to be used in the lesson. If the course developer is not a subject matter expert in the area being considered then this step could involve a considerable amount of background research in order to collect together the required material. Where suitable material does not exist, or cannot be found, it may have to be generated in some way.

How to Read and Evaluate a Resistor Colour Code

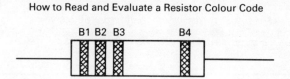

A resistor is marked with four coloured bands (labelled B1, B2, B3 and B4 in the above sketch) that together specify its value. One of the bands, which is usually silver or gold, stands on its own at one end of the resistor while the others form a group of three located at the opposite end. In order to calculate the resistance value, proceed as follows:

1. View the resistor in such a way that the orientation of the bands is similar to that shown in the sketch above. That is, the group of three bands lies on the left hand side as you view it.

2. Only the three left most bands are used in computing the resistance value.

3. The significance of the bands is as follows:
    (a) the colour of the leftmost band gives the first digit of the resistance value,
    (b) the next band then gives the second digit of the resistance value,
    (c) the third band specifies the number of zeros that follow the first two digits.

4. The numerical value associated with the various colours is as follows.

Colour	Value
Black	0
Brown	1
Red	2
Orange	3
Yellow	4
Green	5
Blue	6
Violet	7
Grey	8
White	9

Sheet 2

Figure 2.3   (Continued.)

Step (3), the formulation of evaluation metrics, serves two basic purposes, the assessment of student performance and the evaluation of the utility of the courseware. The first of these is necessary in order to (i) select an appropriate learning pathway for each individual student, and (ii) estimate how well student performance measures up to the requirements specified in the courseware objectives. The need to evaluate the utility of the courseware is of paramount importance since if it does not 'teach', then it will be of little real value. Once a suitable means of assessing the worth of the courseware has been formulated it must be applied (in conjunction with the courseware itself) to suitably chosen student test groups. If the courseware fails to realise its required objectives it must be modified and re-evaluated. These topics are discussed in more detail in sections 2.2.6 and 2.7.

---

(1) Explain the meaning of resistance

(2) State Ohm's Law and give the formula that relates current (*I*), voltage (V) and resistance (*R*)

(3) Randomly select one of *I*, *V* or *R* for computation

(4) Ask student to state the formula for calculating the required quantity

(5) Analyse the student's reply

(6) If correct then go to step 8

(7) Give student some remedial information and return to step 1, 2 or 3 depending upon the extent of help needed

(8) Test student's numeric ability by generating random values for use in the formula for computing the unknown selected in step 3

(9) Ask student to calculate the unknown value

(10) If the student's answer is correct then increment right answer counter

(11) If ten exercises have not been performed then return to step 3

(12) Give student percentage test score

Figure 2.4   Lesson design for a simple teaching task.

A simple example of a lesson design is depicted schematically in figure 2.4. This shows the strategies that are likely to be encountered in a scheme designed to teach students about Ohm's law. It does this by presenting the subject matter material (details of the mathematical relationship between voltage, current and resistance) and then gets the student involved in a 'drill and practice' session. This is used in order to exercise the student in the required skills and also to determine how well the student understands the material. At the end of the session the student is given his/her score for the exercises that were undertaken.

2.2.4 Media Considerations

The various media employed for CAL courseware production must, together, perform the basic functions of (1) storing the lesson material, (2) communicating the subject matter to the student, (3) allowing student feedback, and (4) storing students' responses. Feedback is important since it enables (i) student responses to be monitored, and (ii) the sequencing of lesson material to be controlled by these responses. As we have suggested previously (see chapter 1) media may be thought of as communication channels which may offer either unidirectional or bidirectional information flow. The channels for use in a CAL system will vary quite considerably with respect to the facilities they offer in the context of items (1) through (4) above and in their directionality.

When humans communicate with each other they use only a relatively small number of primitive modes (Wells, 1978). These involve the use of text (including numbers), pictures and actions. The last of these, of course, will encompass all forms of non–verbal communication (Argyle, 1975). Some of the many ways that have been used to support the requirements of these basic modes are listed in table 2.3 (Barker, 1979).

Table 2.3   Techniques for Communicating Instructional Material

(1) printed tables
(2) printed narrative
(3) recorded spoken narrative
(4) live spoken narrative
(5) still pictures and graphs
(6) silent motion pictures
(7) recorded spoken narrative with pictures (tape/slide)
(8) live spoken narrative with pictures (an illustrated lecture)
(9) sound motion pictures or video recordings
(10) man–computer communication through a computer terminal
(11) one to many live tutorial (with 'props')
(12) one to one live tutorial (with 'props')
(13) integrated multimedia communication techniques.

A comparison of the directionality of some of the support channels listed in this table is presented in figure 2.5 (Barker and Yeates, 1981). In this diagram, typical sources of information might be a teacher or a courseware author; students and trainees would then be destinations (or recipients) of information. Each of the channels listed in table 2.3 and figure 2.5 differs with respect to their capacity to communicate information and their 'interactivity'. This term is used to describe the balance and frequency of information flow between an information donor and recipient. High interactivity is achieved when the roles of donor and recipient interchange with substantial rapidity, as might be the case in a human–computer dialogue similar to that depicted in table 1.2 (see section 1.1.4).

Interactivity will be discussed in more detail in subsequent chapters since it is a very important consideration in CAL systems that are to sustain active learning.

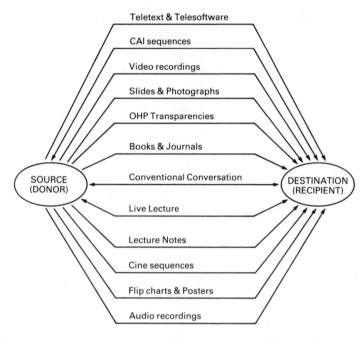

Figure 2.5   Directionality of some common communication media.

As we have emphasised earlier, we are particularly interested in systems where the computer (supported by other media) is the primary teaching (and control) medium. We refer to such arrangements as integrated multimedia CAL systems. Within arrangements of this type two broad possibilities exist, depending on the extent of the involvement of the computer in the teaching process. Firstly, there are those systems in which the major part of the instructional process is undertaken by the computer; we shall discuss systems of this type in more detail in chapters 4 and 5. Secondly, there are systems in which a significant proportion of the teaching is performed through media other than the computer itself. In these systems the computer is used more for the management of learning rather than for the primary medium of instruction. Systems of this type which employ several media, but in which greater emphasis is placed on the use of the computer for the control (or management) of learning are often referred to as computer managed instructional (CMI) systems. Within arrangements of this type, student/trainee activity is distributed between the computer and other media in a fashion similar to that depicted in figure 2.6.

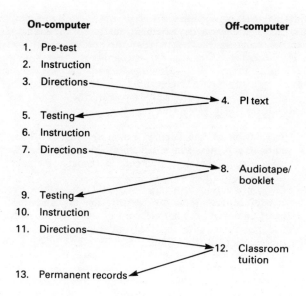

On-computer	Off-computer
1. Pre-test	
2. Instruction	
3. Directions	
	4. PI text
5. Testing	
6. Instruction	
7. Directions	
	8. Audiotape/ booklet
9. Testing	
10. Instruction	
11. Directions	
	12. Classroom tuition
13. Permanent records	

Figure 2.6   CMI – a particular form of multimedia CAL.

In this schema (or instructional strategy) the student is given a pre-test (see section 2.7) and some initial instruction using the computer. Based upon the outcome of this, the computer directs the student to an appropriate entry point within a programmed instruction textbook (see, for example, the reference to Saffold and Smalley's book at the end of chapter 1). Upon completion of this assignment the student returns to the computer, is tested again, completes another CAL module and is then directed to appropriate material contained within an audio-tape library; this is used in conjunction with its accompanying workbook. The final stage of the overall instructional process is accomplished through conventional classroom tuition. All records of the students' instructional progress are held within the computer and are always available for future reference should the need arise.

Despite the sparse treatment we have given this topic, the importance of instructional media cannot be emphasised too greatly. Their significance arises because they are the means by which, as instructors, we convey our knowledge to others. They are the fundamental building blocks by which we fabricate our instructional systems. For further details relating to media considerations, the reader is urged to refer to some of the many excellent textbooks that are devoted to this topic (Berman, 1974; Romiszowski, 1977).

2.2.5 The Implementation Phase

This phase of courseware development refers to the actual activities involved in constructing the lesson that the students will use. It is thus chiefly concerned with the techniques that are necessary to 'move' the lesson from the 'drawing board' across to the media selected for its support. Multimedia CAL and CAI activities cover a wide range of topics (see figure 2.2). However, they can be broadly classified into three basic categories:

(1) preparation of the support material such as slides, audio recordings, video sequences, guidebooks, PI texts, experimental equipment, textbooks, reference lists, and so on;

(2) the construction of computer software for the overall control of resources, the presentation of computer based material, the monitoring of student progress and the preparation of feedback reports for teachers; and

(3) construction of the final lesson by consolidating the results of the effort expended in categories (1) and (2). This phase will also involve checking that the complete lesson runs according to its design specifications with respect to time constraints and its pedagogical effects upon students.

Software construction – item (2) – will involve the production of a number of different kinds of computer program. These can be created by the courseware designer if he/she possesses the required skills. Alternatively, other people can be commissioned to write them. Two basic programming methodologies are most frequently used for this purpose. These involve the use of conventional computer programming languages (such as BASIC, FORTRAN or APL) or some form of author language (for example PILOT or MICROTEXT). These approaches are discussed in more detail in section 2.3 and section 2.4 respectively. Testing and revision are briefly discussed in the following section and an in-depth discussion of courseware evaluation (which can significantly influence the revision of courseware) is presented in section 2.7.

2.2.6 Testing and Revision

Testing and evaluation of courseware are often regarded as similar and synonomous activities. However, as far as we are concerned there is a distinct difference. We regard the testing of courseware as an activity which a development team uses in order to confirm the correctness of the software. On the other hand, evaluation is a process that is used by potential consumer's of the courseware in order to determine how well it is likely to fulfil their requirements. Of course, the results obtained from each of these sources can provide valuable guidelines for the revision of courseware units. Courseware revision is a fairly straightforward process. It involves modifying the software and other learning materials in order to accommodate those   changes   deemed to be   necessary   as a   result   of testing/evaluation.

Courseware testing can be used for three essential purposes:

(1)   to ensure that there are no errors (or 'bugs') either in the teaching material or in the mechanisms that are to be used for its presentation,

(2)   to confirm that the lesson actually imparts information/knowledge to, or develops particular skills within, the members of the student group for which it is intended, and

(3)   to guarantee that any feedback information that the courseware provides is an accurate reflection of the student population with which it is used.

The   degree   of   difficulty   associated   with each of these aspects of testing increases in the same order as that in which   they   have   been listed.   Testing   operations   within   category   (1)   are   fairly straightforward. A simple example is presented in figure   2.7   (Barker and Yeates, 1981).

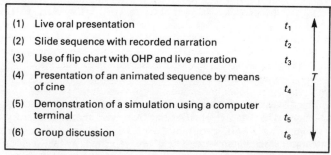

(1)	Live oral presentation	t_1
(2)	Slide sequence with recorded narration	t_2
(3)	Use of flip chart with OHP and live narration	t_3
(4)	Presentation of an animated sequence by means of cine	T / t_4
(5)	Demonstration of a simulation using a computer terminal	t_5
(6)	Group discussion	t_6

Figure 2.7   Testing the timing of a CAI lesson.

Here   a   variety   of   techniques   are   used   in   order to realise some particular instructional goal within a time constraint represented   by the   value   of T. It is   assumed   that   each   of   the   individual instructional units (1 through 6) of the lesson has   been   tested   for content   correctness   and flow control. The next set of tests must now be   performed in order to measure the time required for   the   execution of   each unit. The individual times must then be summed and the result compared with the time constraint inherent in the value of   T.   Should the total exceed this value, selected courseware units will need to be revised in such a way that their time requirement is reduced – thereby bringing the overall lesson time within specification.

Testing   with   respects   to   categories   (2)   and (3) is slightly more difficult.   Each   of   these   involves   testing   the   courseware   with preselected   groups   of   students (control groups) whose abilities and characteristic learning profiles are known. The effects that the courseware has on the learning rates and knowledge states of members of the control groups can then be used to assess the validity of the teaching material with respect to the categories (2) and (3). This approach to testing (and evaluation) relies heavily on pre–testing and post–testing – a topic which is discussed in section 2.7.3.

2.3 USING PROGRAMMING LANGUAGES

As we have explained in chapter 1, a programming language is simply a special kind of linguistic notation used to prepare computer programs. These programs specify the detailed instructions that (when executed) control the information processing activity of the computer. In educational establishments BASIC will undoubtedly be the most familiar and commonly available programming language, particularly on microcomputers. For those who are seriously thinking of developing their own CAL software, BASIC should be considered as a potential candidate for use. Although there are other more powerful languages available for dialogue programming, the simplicity of BASIC offers considerable attraction. It is not the intention of this book to teach programming or to discuss the relative merits of different programming languages as tools to aid courseware development. Instead, the function of this section is simply to (1) alert readers to their existence, and (2) present a few descriptive comments on specific examples of these languages (namely BASIC, FORTRAN and APL). Of necessity, our treatment here will be kept to the basic minimum necessary to support material presented elsewhere in the text.

2.3.1 BASIC
Some outline discussion of this language was presented in sections 1.1 and 1.1.3. From the simple illustration that was given, it is easy to see the format of a BASIC program. Essentially, a program consists of a series of numbered statements. These are executed by the computer in the order in which they are listed, unless some form of branch statement is encountered. The format of a BASIC program statement is thus:

| LINE NUMBER | STATEMENT BODY |

Line numbers will always be whole numbers, that is integer values. The computer uses these numbers as a means of keeping the program statements in ascending order of line number – irrespective of the order in which they may have been entered into its memory. The statements used to construct a program fall into about twelve different categories. Some of these are listed in table 2.4 (Microsoft, 1982).

Table 2.4   BASIC Statement Summary

Function	Statement keyword
Storage reservation	DIM
Output of Information	PRINT
Input of Information	LINE INPUT INPUT
Program annotation	REM
Unconditional branch	GOTO
Conditional branch	IF
Subroutine Invocation	GOSUB RETURN
Repetitive looping	FOR NEXT
Repetitive looping	WHILE WEND
Assignation	=
File handling	OPEN CLOSE

The dimension statement (DIM) is used to reserve storage for variables that are used to represent arrays of values. For example, the statement DIM X(10), Y(200) would reserve storage space within the computer's memory for two variables called X and Y. The first of these would be capable of storing 10 numeric values while the second could store up to 200 such values. Arrays are often used for storing lists of values, such as student names, exam marks or sets of drill and practice questions. Individual items from within the list contained in an array are identified and referenced by means of a numeric index. This index simply specifies the ordinal position of the item within the list that contains it.

Variables are used within a program in order to represent quantities to be calculated or to be used in calculations; they are also used to represent items which are to be remembered for future use. Before a variable can be used in a calculation it must be given a value, either a number or a string of characters. This is achieved by means of a process called value assignment. The assignation process is denoted by the = symbol. When a statement containing this symbol is executed, the expression on the right-hand side of the = symbol is evaluated. The result of the evaluation is then assigned to the variable that is named on the left-hand side of the = symbol.

Information output to the user is effected by means of the PRINT
statement. The value of the variable(s), constant(s) or expression(s)
that follow the PRINT keyword are displayed on the student's CRT
screen when the statement is executed. Sometimes this statement is
used to send cursor control information to the CRT thereby influencing
the way in which the information on the screen is displayed to the
user. Notice that in the context of dialogue programming, the PRINT
statement is very long–winded compared with the corresponding PILOT
statements (T: and :), (see section 2.4.3). As we shall see below, a
variant of the PRINT statement is also used as a means of archiving
data values from the computer's internal memory onto external files
held on flexible disc.

Input from the user is achieved by means of the INPUT and LINE INPUT
statements. The data values that are typed by the user on his/her
keyboard are assigned to the variable(s) that follow the INPUT
keyword. In addition to their use for dialogue programming, the INPUT
and LINE INPUT statements are also used in order to transfer data
contained in a disc file into the computer's main memory.

When writing courseware it is important to remember to include
explanatory notes within the body of the program so that other people
can easily deduce what the various sections of code are designed to
do. Program annotation is facilitated by the REM statement – REM is a
contraction of REMARK. Statements commencing with the REM keyword
are not executed by the computer; any characters that follow it are
intended for the use of human readers only. There is no limit on the
number of REM statements a program may contain. However, because they
do occupy space within the computer's memory, it is advisable not to
be too liberal with their use.

The GOTO statement is used to implement a program branch or jump.
Branching is a technique that is used to move from one point in a
program to another – thereby skipping over sections of a program that
are not to be executed. Sometimes the GOTO is used to make the
computer go back to an earlier part of the program so that its
execution can be repeated. The GOTO facility provides a mechanism to
enable unconditional branching, that is, the branch defined by this
statement is always taken. Situations in which a condition has to be
met before the branch is executed are catered for by the IF statement.

One of the most useful aspects of a computer is its ability to perform
a task repetitively, that is, over and over again until it is told to
stop. This repetitive execution is achieved in the following way. The
set of statements that define the process to be executed are listed;
these constitute what is called the loop body. The statements
contained in the loop are then executed in turn; when the last
statement has been executed, the computer goes back to the first
statement in the loop body and then executes the whole sequence again.
This process continues until some pre–defined condition (called the

loop termination condition) is met. Repetitive looping then stops and the   computer executes the statement that follows the loop termination statement (NEXT or WEND – see below).

The requirement for this type of operation is catered for by two types of BASIC statement: the FOR/NEXT and WHILE/WEND facilities. Looping is an extremely important programming facility, hence the availability of special types of command to enable its implementation. However, these are   not   strictly   necessary   since equivalent effects can be accomplished through the use of GOTO and IF statements.

In many applications of programming, situations arise in which a particular group of statements has to be executed from many different points within a program. This facility is normally provided   by   means of   subroutine and/or function subprograms. In BASIC, the code contained within a subroutine is activated by means of a GOSUB statement. The last executable statement in a subroutine must be a RETURN command that instructs the computer to return to the statement following   the GOSUB that was used to invoke it. Subroutine facilities are probably one of the most important requirements of a programming language since they facilitate the facile 'top–down' method of software development (Bleazard, 1976).

Another very important facility that a programming language has to provide is that of file handling, the ability by which user's programs can   store   data on flexible discs and later retrieve it (see sections 1.1.2 and 1.1.3). BASIC has quite good file   handling   facilities   for both   sequential and direct file access. In sequential processing, the records (or lines of information) that the file contains are processed one after the other starting at the first and progressing sequentially through the file. This type of access   is   useful   for   storing   large amounts   of   information that is only to be retrieved and displayed on the screen of a VDU, as is often typical of an instructional dialogue. Direct access to a file implies that any of the individual records   it contains can be accessed quite independently of any of the other records present. This mode of file access is   useful   for   maintaining class lists and marks, particularly when an   instructor wants to examine/update the marks for individual students.

In this section we have presented a very brief overview of BASIC. Our intention   has   been to be informative rather than instructional. That is, we have tried to indicate some of the facilities that exist within BASIC rather than to teach how to use them. We have purposely skipped over   this   latter   requirement   since   we   feel that it is adequately fulfilled by other books, typically   those   by   Spencer   (1975);   and, Osborne and Donahue (1980) which are listed at the end of chapter 1.

2.3.2 FORTRAN
FORTRAN developed as a mathematically orientated language for use by scientists and engineers. In these areas it is probably still the most

widely used programming language. Like BASIC, because of its
simplicity it is easy to learn. The details of the language are
described in many of the standard reference texts devoted to it
(McCracken, 1974; Wagener, 1980; Davis, 1981).

One of the strongest motivations for the use of FORTRAN as a high
level programming language has always been the program portability
that it is claimed to offer. That is, computer programs can easily be
moved from one computer to another (of a different type) without the
need for extensive redevelopment/code conversion projects. This is the
main reason why many CAL packages (see section 2.5) have been
developed using standard versions of this language, such as FORTRAN-IV or
FORTRAN-77. An example of this approach is the STAF author language
(which is briefly described in chapter 3). This CAL authoring facility
was developed entirely in FORTRAN and is available for use on a wide
range of mainframe, minicomputer and microcomputer systems (Ayscough,
1983). Indeed, in principle, there is no reason why this package could
not be made available on any computer system that supports the
FORTRAN language.

Now that BASIC is so widely available, it has largely superseded
FORTRAN as the preferred language for CAL authoring. Provided only the
'common subset' of commands and functions are used for courseware
development, it is possible to make BASIC programs virtually as
portable as those written in FORTRAN.

2.3.3 APL
APL is an acronym for A Programming Language (Grey, 1976; Gilman and
Rose, 1974; Pakin, 1972). It is a dialogue programming language which
operates in a fashion akin to BASIC. Unlike the latter, APL is quite
difficult to learn and is a much more complicated language. However,
the facilities that it offers (in terms of data manipulation and
program compactness) far exceed those of BASIC. The APL system uses
its own special alphabet that contains many unusual symbols each of
which represents a particular type of information processing
operation. These symbols are not found on a normal QWERTY keyboard.
Consequently, APL requires the use of a special keyboard and display
system. The problems associated with the provision of these facilities
probably explain why this language has not been as extensively used as
BASIC (at least in the UK) for the development of CAL software. The
language is far more popular in the USA where it has been used by a
number of CAL authors for the production of quite sophisticated
teaching packages (Macero and Davis, 1976). The program unit with
which the APL system deals is called a workspace. Workspaces exist for
a variety of purposes including the administration of a drill and
practice lesson on APL itself. Although program exchange centres exist
for APL courseware, programs written in this language are not as
portable as those written in BASIC. Furthermore, APL is not as widely
available as either FORTRAN or BASIC. Courseware authors who require
portability of their products should therefore avoid the use of APL.

2.4 USING AN AUTHOR LANGUAGE

Earlier, in figure 1.12, we indicated that there was an alternative way of preparing courseware material, namely the use of an author language. Such languages often offer an easier route to courseware. than that described in the previous section (that is, via conventional programming languages). In this section we provide a brief introduction to the function that an author language fulfils and indicate the format of courseware written in one of these languages; the PILOT system has been choosen for this purpose. Only a superficial treatment of this topic is presented in the following sections (2.4.1 through 2.4.3) since the remaining chapters of the book are devoted to this subject.

2.4.1 The Function of an Author Language

Undoubtedly, the major function of a CAL author language is to ease the burdens associated with courseware development and thereby greatly improve its user's productivity. An authoring facility attempts to fulfil these goals by providing a more facile interface to the computer than that provided by conventional programming languages. This can be achieved by providing:

(1) sets of built-in functions and subroutines that are specially designed to cater for the types of operation that are most often performed in instructional dialogue programming,

(2) facilities to enable the control of external instructional support media such as slide projectors, tape recorders, TV and video discs,

(3) an easy to use (and comprehensive) set of commands that are orientated towards the requirements of the CAL author, and

(4) facile file handling facilities to enable the storage of instructional material for presentation to students and the archival/retrieval of response data collected during an instructional dialogue.

The degree to which different author languages measure up to these requirements varies quite considerably. Several different examples of languages of this type are briefly described in chapter 3.

2.4.2 Mode of Operation

Most author languages operate in the same way as the conventional language translators (compilers and interpreters) which are provided with a computer system. That is, they take a previously prepared file containing source statements and translate these into an executable machine code program. When this is subsequently activated it controls the computer's activity for the duration of a student's instructional session. Using an author language is thus a three step process:

> (1)   preparation of the source file,
> (2)   translation of the source file, and
> (3)   activation of the courseware module.

Steps (1) and (2) are the responsibility of the CAL author while step (3) is for the student to perform. In order to prepare the source file containing the CAL program statements an editor system is usually used. This is a special program that enables the author to:

> (a)   create a named file on a disc,
> (b)   enter records into that file, and
> (c)   modify the stored records in various ways.

Phases (a) and (b) of editor usage are depicted in the dialogue trace presented in figure 2.8. This shows each of the three steps involved in using a CAL authoring facility.

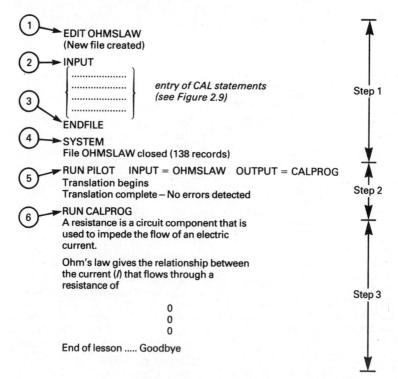

Figure 2.8   Steps involved in using an author language.

At the point labelled 1 the author invokes the computer's editing program by typing the EDIT command; the parameter that follows this keyword specifies the name of the file that is to be used to store the

CAL program. At point 2 the user issues an INSERT command.in order to
enter CAL statements into the previously created file, the actual
statements entered are listed in figure 2.9. When all of these have
been entered into the file the user types ENDFILE (point 3) in order
to inform the editor that there are no more lines to be entered into
the file. The editing session is then terminated by the command SYSTEM
which is typed at point 4. This returns computer control from the
editing program back to the computer's operating system (see section
1.1.3). The CAL author language translator is next invoked by the RUN
command issued at point 5; this specifies the names of the translator
to be used (PILOT), the file containing the source statements and the
file that is to hold the translated executable CAL module. Finally, at
step 6, the CAL courseware module is activated and the instructional
session commences.

Further details of the PILOT courseware module referenced in the above
example are given in figure 2.9. It was developed on a PRIME 750
minicomputer using a version of PILOT supplied by the University of
Surrey (Gilbert, 1981). The CAL module is discussed in more detail in
the following section.

2.4.3 An Example

The PILOT program illustrated in figure 2.9 represents an
implementation of the Ohm's law case study that was briefly discussed
earlier in section 2.2.3 (Barker and Singh, 1983). The reason for
including this listing is simply to indicate the general appearance of
courseware written in the PILOT language. Readers who are familiar
with BASIC will probably notice many similarities between the two –
however, there are many subtle differences.

Each PILOT statement in figure 2.9 commences with a command letter –
for example: d (dimension); c (compute); a (accept); t (type); j
(jump); and so on. To the right of the letter that represents the
command operator (and separated from it by a : character) lies the
command operand. The only exception to this basic command structure is
found in the type statement; because screen output operations are used
so often its key–letter (T) may be omitted. Thus, statements that
commence with a : character are (by default) type statements, that is,
all information to the right of the : is displayed on the user's
terminal. Notice how labels (which commence with a * symbol) are
interspersed through the listing. These denote branch points or the
commencement of subroutine definitions. We return to a discusion of
PILOT later in chapter 3. However, for those who are interested,
further information about this language is given by Conlon (1984).
Similarly, a more detailed description of the PILOT program presented
in figure 2.9 is given by Barker and Singh (1983).

```
 1) R: PILOT PROGRAM FOR TEACHING OHM'S LAW
 2) d: $find(3)
 3) d: $form(3)
 4) c: $find(1)="voltage"
 5) c: $find(2)="current"
 6) c: $find(3)="resistance"
 7) c: $form(1)="V=I*R"
 8) c: $form(2)="I=V/R"
 9) c: $form(3)="R=V/I"
10) c: p=prompt(">")
11) c: #fok=0
12) c: #nok=0
13) c: #count=0
14) c: #rem=0
15) c: $y=chr(26)+chr(7)+chr(10)+chr(10)
16) c: $y2=chr(10)+chr(10)+chr(10)
17) c: $b="                        "
18) *start
19) t: $y
20) t: A resistance is a circuit component that is used to impede
21)    the flow of an electric current.
22) t: $y2
23)  · Ohm's Law gives the relationship between the current (I)
24)  : that flows through a resistance of value R when a potential
25)  : of V volts is applied across it.
26) t: $y2
27)  : This may be expressed in several different ways:
28)  :
29)  :     V=I*R          (to calculate voltage)
30)  :
31)  :     I=V/R          (to calculate current)
32)  :
33)  :     R=V/I          (to calculate resistance)
34)  :
35)  : Press any key to proceed.
36) ah:
37) *loop
38) t: $y
39) t: $y2
40) c: #count=#count+1
41) c: #y=int(3*rnd(0))+1
42) t: $y2
43) c: $s1="What formula would you use to calculate a "
44) c: $s2=" value?"
45) c: $q= $s1+$find(#y)+$s2
46) t: $q
47)  ·
48) th: $b
49) a: $ans
50) c: $x=ucase($ans)
51) j($x=$form(#y)): *correct
52) t. No. You're wrong.
53)  : You will need to revise this.
54)  :
55)  :
56)  : Press a key in order to continue.
```

Figure 2.9 CAL courseware written in PILOT.

```
57) ah:
58) c:  #rem=#rem+1
59) j:  *start
60) *correct
61) t:  You are correct.
62) t:
63) :
64) :  Press a key in order to continue.
65) ah:
66) c:  #fok=#fok+1
67) r:  student got formula OK
68) r:  now test numeric ability
69) c:  $f=$form(#y)
70) c:  $v1=mid($f,3,1)
71) c:  $v2=right($f,1)
72) c:  $v3=left($f,1)  '
73) c:  $op=mid($f,4,1)
74)
75) c:  #v1=int(100*rnd(0))+1
76) c:  #v2=int(100*rnd(0))+1
77) j($op="*"): *mul
78) c:  #v3=int((#v1/#v2+0.005)*100)
79) j:  *ntest
80) *mul c:  #v3=#v1*#v2*100
81) *ntest
82) c:  $q2a="Suppose the value of "+$v1+" was "+str(#v1)
83) c:  $q2b="and the value of "+$v2+" was "+str(#v2)+". "
84) c:  $q2c="What would the value of "+$v3+" be?"
85) t:
86) :  $q2a
87) :  $q2b
88) :
89) :  $q2c
90) :
91) th: $b
92) a:  #ans
93) c:  #x=int((#ans+.005)*100)
94) j(#x=#v3): *corr2
95) t:  No.
96) :  You haven't got it right.
97) c:  $ca=str(#v3)
98) c:  #k=len($ca)
99) c:  $c1=left($ca,#k-2)
100) c:  $c2=right($ca,2)
101) j($c2="00"): *blank
102) c:  $ca=$c1+"."+$c2
103) j:  *print
104) *blank c:  $ca=$c1
105) *print
106) c:  $f="You should have typed "+$ca
107) t:
108) t:  $f
109) u:  *wait
110) j:  *linc
111) *corr2
112) t:  Well Done.
```

Figure 2.9   (Continued.)

```
113) t: You have it correct!
114) c: #nok=#nok+1
115) u: *wait
116) *linc
117) j(#count<10): *loop
118) r: Now give student results
119) c: '$f1="Your score on formulas was "+str(#fok)
120) c: $f2="Your score on numeracy was "+str(#nok)
121) c: $f3="Your remediation count was "+str(#rem)
122) t: $y
123) t: $y2
124) t: Here are your results.
125) :
126) : $f1
127) : $f2
128) : $f3
129) :
130) : End of lesson..... Goodbye
131) j: *finish
132) *wait
133) t:
134) t: Press any key in order to have another go.
135) ah:
136) e:
137) *finish
138) e:
```

Figure 2.9   (Continued.)

2.5 USING PRE-PACKAGED COURSEWARE

As we indicated earlier in chapter 1, a courseware package is a pre-programmed set of CAL modules which a teacher or instructor buys and uses (hopefully) without the need for any subsequent modification. Generally, packages may be supplied in either of two forms: (1) as source programs, or, (2) as machine code 'dumps'. In both cases, the courseware will probably be provided on a magnetic tape, disc or (less often nowadays) paper-tape. Usually, these packages are accompanied by documentation that describes how to use them, and what to do if anything goes wrong. The way in which such packages are used is described below.

2.5.1 Mode of Using a Package
As an example, we consider the use of a package supplied in the form of a flexible disc for use on a microcomputer. This is a reasonable case to consider since disc based microsystems are now becoming quite commonplace. Obviously, the description that follows also applies (in principle) to packages that are available for use on time-shared mainframe and minicomputer systems.

Usually, a package will exist as a series of named files on the disc upon which it is supplied. In order to determine the disc's contents its directory must be read. The directory is just a list of files stored on the disc. Most microcomputer operating systems provide a simple command to perform this function, for example DIR ·in the ÇP/M system (see section 1.1.3). A typical directory listing is presented in table 2.5.

Table 2.5   Directory Listing for a Disc Based CAL Package

Disc name: GEOGPROGS, PGB, 01	
Files:	
CONFIGURE	LESSON31
EXPLAIN	LESSON32
EXPLAIN01	LESSON33
EXPLAIN02	MAKEFILES
EXPLAIN03	SEEMARK
LESSON11	REPORTER
LESSON12	STUDTEST1
LESSON13	STUDTEST2
LESSON21	STUDTEST3
LESSON22	FINALTEST
Total: 20 files	
Free space: 56 Kbytes	

On this disc there are five basic categories of file. These perform the following functions:

    (a)   documentation (eg EXPLAIN),
    (b)   system initialisation (eg CONFIGURE),
    (c)   teaching (eg LESSON11),
    (d)   student testing (eg STUDTEST1),
    (e)   progress reporting (eg SEEMARK and REPORTER).

The documentation files are used to support and augment the conventional written material (reference manual and teacher's notes) that normally accompany a package. By loading and executing the EXPLAIN program, the teacher/student can get explanatory notes (via the CRT screen) about the package and what it is intended to do. Any explanation files that the student is not to have access to can be 'locked' by the instructor prior to releasing the disc for student use, alternatively, copies of such files can be omitted from discs distributed to students.

Before the package is released for use, the disc on which it resides will normally have to have some additional files created on it. In

addition the teaching software will need to be tailored to the
requirements of the computing configuration on which it is to run.
These operations are done by the CONFIGURE and MAKEFILES programs.
The configuration program enables the instructor to specify whether the
particular disc is intended for group or individual use; it also
enables details of the host computer to be specified, such as memory
size, number of discs that are available for use, printer availability
and so on. The MAKEFILES program creates all the additional files that
are necessary to run the package, for example student name files,
marks files, monitoring files and any others that are needed. Both
configuration and file creation programs are of an interactive nature,
that is they prompt the instructor for information and then use this
to perform system initialisation.

The teaching function of the package illustrated in table 2.5 is
performed by the program modules whose names commence with the stem
LESSON. There are three basic lessons contained in the package.
Because the individual lessons are too big to fit completely into the
computer's memory space, they are subdivided into sections. The first
and third lesson each contain three segments while the second lesson
contains two. Once a lesson has commenced, the loading of individual
sections is totally transparent to the learner. After each lesson the
student is given a test (using the programs STUDTEST1, STUDTEST2 and
STUDTEST3) and the results of these tests are stored in the files
created during system initialisation. At any time the instructor can
examine individual student's marks and progress by means of the
SEEMARK program. If the disc is one which is common to a group of
students then a class listing of the progress and marks for all the
members of the group can be obtained via the REPORTER program.

The basic way in which the lesson dialogue proceeds is similar to that
which was depicted earlier in table 1.2. However, the exact nature of
the dialogue that takes place between the courseware package and the
learner will obviously depend upon the objectives to be achieved and
the teaching strategies that individual lessons embody, for example
simulation, drill and practice, game playing and so on. Most packages
will not use a single instructional mode but will contain the most
appropriate combination of each of the available techniques. A brief
overview of some of these will be presented in the following section.

2.5.2 Types of Package Available
Any attempt to provide a comprehensive taxonomy of CAL packages would
be beyond the scope of this section. However, it is worthwhile
mentioning a few of the ways which have been most often used for
categorising CAL packages: by subject; by the nature of the skill
orientated task that they teach; and by the instructional strategy
that they implement.

By far the simplest classification scheme is by subject category. A
wide variety of subject disciplines have benefited from the

availability of CAL packages of one form or another. Some of the earliest application areas for which CAL materials were developed include the science based subjects (physics, chemistry, biology, mathematics, and so on); the engineering disciplines (electrical, mechanical, civil, control, etc); and medicine (for example medical diagnosis, nurse training and the teaching of the handicapped and· disabled). Today, the range covered by packaged CAL courseware has extended considerably to encompass such areas as English teaching, foreign language instruction, and the teaching of subjects as diverse as geography, economics, music, law, dance and art. As a result of interest in particular areas of the curriculum, many organisations have developed specifically to meet the need for CAL package production in that subject area. For example, the CALCHEM project (Ayscough, 1983) was set up primarily to meet the growing demand from university and college teachers for CAL packages to aid the teaching of physical chemistry. Similarly, on a slightly broader front, the Computers in the Curriculum Project at Chelsea College in London (Cox, 1982) has been involved in developing packs of CAL units since about 1969; the materials from this project were aimed at the sciences, economics, history and geography.

Another method of classifying the types of CAL package that currently exist is by means of the nature of the task that the package is designed to instill into its user. Thus, there are CAL packages designed to teach basic reading and writing skills; spelling, word usage, numeracy skills and a variety of more practically orientated subjects. Some typical examples of CAL packages that fall into the latter category include the development of keyboard skills, training in office skills, circuit board construction, soldering, computer programming, car maintenance, radio construction, circuit diagnosis, and so on. Many CAL/CBT packages intended for use in industrial and commercial training are often classified by skill rather than by subject area; this can create problems for those who have to catalogue CAL software, unless extensive cross indexing is used. Naturally, courseware cataloguing is important in the context of its distribution, a topic to which we turn in section 2.6.

The third classification scheme for CAL packages is based upon the mode of CAL that they implement. Unfortunately, this method is less useful than the other two because, as we mentioned in the last section, many large CAL systems will contain a mixture of different instructional modes. Some of the basic CAL modes were listed in table 1.3 of section 1.3. Based upon the entries in this table we can now list the following broad types of CAL package:

      (a)   tutorial packages,
      (b)   drill and practice packages,
      (c)   inquiry based systems,
      (d)   dialogue based packages,
      (e)   simulation packages,

(f) gaming packages,
(g) testing, monitoring and reporting packages,
(h) integrated packages.

In the remaining parts of this section we briefly outline the principle upon which each of these types of CAL package is based.

(a) Tutorial Packages
In their simplest form, tutorial programs comprise a linear series of factual statements interspersed with predetermined questions and responses. Regardless of ability, performance or prior knowledge, each student is required to proceed through the same material. In their more complex form, tutorial packages are composed of parallel sequences of different levels of difficulty. In some cases programs are structured into three levels; the student can move from the mainstream of instruction to branching paths for remedial or enrichment material. Other programs have a series of instructional loops to which the student can branch briefly for remedial or supplemental study and then return to the main sequence of the program. Tutorial packages designed to run on a computer permit a much more complex branching structure than either programmed texts or conventional teaching machines. The focus of the instruction is on the subject material and on the student's mastery of it.

(b) Drill and Practice Packages
Where course requirements and student performance call for reinforcement and remediation techniques, the drill and practice mode of computer instruction has become an effective aid. The computer presents the student with some information and then exercises the student in the use of that information. Computer based drill can offer significant assistance to students who are expected to master a specialised vocabulary. Other uses are to demonstrate rapid recall of mathematical or scientific data. Similarly, practice sessions administered via computer terminals can offer an effective and motivating learning experience in mastering new skills, such as speedwriting and speedtyping.

(c) Inquiry Based Systems
Packages that utilise the inquiry mode usually require the student to solve a problem or answer a question by posing inquiries to a base of information embedded within a specialised program. The computer then provides answers to the inquiries based on information that is pre-stored in it or available to it through its own computational capabilities. The program makes no attempt to guide the student to the correct answer or conclusion. Usually, a situation is presented to the student who, through the use of a specialised vocabulary, asks for more information. Eventually, the student accumulates sufficient information to suggest a solution or draw a conclusion.

(d) Dialogue Based Packages

Packages based upon the dialogue (or Socratic) mode of CAL resemble those that utilise the inquiry mode: the student controls the progress of the lesson by finding his/her own path through the material made available by the computer. The Socratic technique extends the interaction of the student with the program by establishing a two-way conversation between the student and the computer, usually, via a typewriter keyboard (see table 1.2 and figure 1.5). The students question, assertion or request for data can result in any one of a wide variety of responses from the machine. The computer may pose a question, attempt to coach the student into trying a different approach or guide the student in a review of earlier background material.

(e) Simulation Packages

Although direct experience is usually the best form of instruction, reality in education must often be sacrificed to factors of time, cost, safety and equipment availability. Simulation programs provide the student with artificial experience of a dynamic real-world environment. The student is usually called upon to take actions that affect the modelled situation. Computer based simulation can represent a complex chemical reaction, a problem in physics, a diagnosis of patient illness or the management of a large business firm. In simulation, there is often no 'correct' solution that produces a single optimum outcome. Simulated environments are dynamic, the goal being to achieve (over some period of time) the best possible set of policies. A simulator device is applicable where there is a risk factor (as in medicine), where the costs of using the actual equipment are great (as in pilot training) or where it is impossible to obtain real life experience (as in space travel).

(f) Gaming Packages

A game involves a competition between two or more players (one of which may be a computer program) in order to achieve a specific defined goal. In this way, gaming differs from simulation wherein there is usually no correct solution producing a single, optimum outcome. Computer controlled games developed from games which have been popular for many years in industry as a training mechanism for executives and managers. Games are based around a set of rules, the nature of which may change dynamically during the game. The student is required to learn the rules, through experience with the package, and then apply them to achieve particular pre-defined objectives. Games achieve intense student involvement (particularly when they involve group participation) and they are regarded as a valuable educational resource, particularly for the teaching of subjects such as economics and business. One of the most well-known elementry games ('How the West was Won') was written for use on the PLATO system; it is described in detail by Burton and Brown (1982). This package

illustrates   all   the   principles   involved   in   implementing   gaming
coarseware.

(g) Testing, Monitoring and Reporting Packages
Broadly, the functions of testing, monitoring and reporting of student
progress constitute important components of packages that are designed
to implement various types of computer managed instruction (CMI).
Packages of this kind are often employed when the instructor
responsible for a particular course requires assistance with the
routine management tasks associated with its implementation.
Sometimes, packages of this type can also include additional
facilities which enable the prescription of particular learning
pathways for each individual course member, based upon an analysis of
the data acquired during the testing and monitoring phases of its
operation.

Record keeping is important since their analysis provides a valuable
guide to both student and curriculum performance. When classes are
small in size the process of record keeping is easily accomplished
without computer assistance. However, for large classes the computer's
clerical and analytical aid can be invaluable. In addition to student
evaluations, the teacher can be given details of those course segments
(or examination questions) that have caused particular difficulty for
students. If need be, these can then be reviewed in order to
accommodate any changes that are thought to be necessary.

The importance of testing, monitoring and reporting of both student
and courseware materials cannot be over-emphasised. This is reflected
by the increasing number of packages that are becoming available to
aid the CAL designer implement these tasks.

(h) Integrated Packages
A comprehensive or integrated CAL package can best be described as one
which provides several different modes of instruction and management
for a single course. Thus, the course author will have appropriately
combined tutorial, drill and practice, simulation, gaming, inquiry and
Socratic modes of CAL in order to provide an optimum learning
environment for the student. Indeed, several alternative approaches
may be provided within the same lesson so that the one best suited for
a particular student can be selected and applied. In addition, as an
aid to both the student and the instructor, such systems will
invariably provide a variety of monitoring, recording, testing,
diagnostic and prescriptive aids.

Of course, to support these integrated courseware packages,
appropriate instructional media are required. Over the last decade the
technologies of television, telecommunications and computers have been
rapidly converging. The technology to support comprehensive integrated
CAL systems via multimedia instructional techniques now exists. We
therefore discuss this topic in considerably more detail later.

2.6 COURSEWARE DISTRIBUTION

The term coarseware distribution is used to describe the various techniques that authors and distributors employ in order to make CAL materials available to others. The means of distribution may vary considerably, ranging from the use of postal services (via flexible disc or tape cassette) through computer based communication networks to the most recent type of telesoftware facility. The type of mechanism that is employed will really depend upon the extent of involvement of the organisations concerned. The direct dispatch of courseware via telesoftware facilities will obviously be beyond the reach of the majority of organisations; usually, indirect distribution via some service similar to PRESTEL (Brown, 1980), CEEFAX or ORACLE (Brighton Polytechnic, 1982) would normally be used. The use of distributed computer based communication networks (Barker, 1982a) is probably a more realistic approach for the majority of distributors. Access to such systems is becoming increasingly easy and cost effective. In many situations an ordinary telephone can be used to interconnect a microcomputer system to some distant computer thereby enabling courseware to be transmitted between the two (Barker, 1982b). Currently, most CAL software is distributed via flexible discs; transfer takes place either on an ad hoc basis between individual authors or through a more formal arrangement based upon the use of program exchange centres (these are discussed in section 2.6.3). Because of the importance of courseware distribution, the following sections briefly outline the major motivations for distributing courseware and some of the problems involved.

2.6.1 Why Distribute?

Undoubtedly, one of the major motivating factors influencing the need to distribute coarseware is its extremely high cost of production. This arises because the generation of CAL material is often a labour intensive, complex process, particularly when authoring involves not only the production of software, but also the creation of sound recordings, artwork, video materials and so on. Because of the many facets that are involved, it is difficult to give any detailed costings or exact estimates of the effort needed to produce CAL courseware (Fielden, 1974). However, Boyd (1972) has suggested that an hour of instruction – whether it be PI, television, AV, language lab or CAI – seems to require between one hundred and four hundred hours of professional time to produce and validate.

With the high costs that this type of involvement implies, it is imperative, therefore, that they are shared by as wide a user base as is conceivably possible. Distribution of courseware, at a reasonable fee, therefore ensures that as many users as possible bear its cost of production. Of course, the concept of shared development cost is very important when considering the more advanced types of courseware that involve technologies such as video disc; here, the cost of preparing the courseware and putting it onto the disc will be far more than the average CAL user can afford. Consequently, shared funding is imperative if cost effective courseware is to be produced.

Another important reason for distributing courseware relates to the need (in many situations) to standardise on instructional content. That is, students must be educated/trained to meet particular objectively stated requirements, both with respect to educational task and level of attainment. For example, it is often necessary to train members of a geographically distributed organisation (such as a large bank) with skills that are applicable throughout that organisation. By distributing the same training software to each location, the type and level of training can, in principle, be made quite uniform. This factor, standardisation or uniformity of training, is undoubtedly more important in the context of industrial/commercial CAL distribution than it is in the academic sectors of education.

There are several other factors that influence the need to distribute courseware. Many of these are also closely associated with the motivations for wanting to use CAL in conjunction with open learning systems and 'on the spot' training. Typical reasons for employing these technologies include: (1) the fact that trainees cannot be released from their normal employment in order to attend courses that are held at distant locations, (2) the high cost of travel to and subsistence at host centres, and (3) the fact that courses at training centres may not be available when they are required. Each of these provides an additional, although indirect, reason for wanting to distribute courseware from host centres for local use. However, these factors are of secondary importance compared with those of cost effectiveness and standardisation which were outlined at the beginning of this section.

2.6.2 What are the Problems?
When software is distributed between different locations, only in ideal conditions does the transfer take place without encountering any problems. The difficulties encountered are often referred to as transferability problems. They arise for a variety of reasons. However, the major ones are:

(1) media incompatibility,
(2) hardware differences, and
(3) software differences.

These are fairly straightforward to understand. As an example of media incompatibility one could cite the problems associated with transferring CAL courseware resident on 8 inch discs to microcomputer systems fitted with only 5 inch discs. Similar types of media incompatibility can arise when transferring materials held on other media such as video tape (Betamax/VHS), cine film (8/16 mm) and video disc. Differences in hardware can also offer significant problems. For example, courseware that is designed to run on one range of computers will not necessarily run on another, or might produce different effects; the classic example of this is in random number generation. The problems of hardware incompatibility are undoubtedly most significant when programs for CAL are actually written in machine code. Because of this, most software for CAL is nowadays written in a high level language. However, software problems can also cause a variety of difficulties. For example, differences in dialects of programming/authoring languages, availability of suitable host software and differences in operating systems within different computers can cause significant barriers to courseware distribution. To overcome these problems a very high degree of standardisation has to be introduced. Some of the different types of standards currently in use (within the UK) and recommendations/guidelines for the selection of suitable CAL courseware equipment have been outlined in a series of USPECs (User SPECifications) prepared by the UK's Council for Educational Technology (Council for Educational Technology, 1982). Adoption of the guidelines contained in these specifications will undoubtedly help to minimise some of the transferability problems outlined above.

Two other problem areas likely to cause difficulties are:

(1)   modification of courseware to meet local needs, and
(2)   updating operational courseware.

Undoubtedly, once a software package has been purchased, it will often need to be modified to meet local needs if it is to be successfully integrated into an existing instructional framework. The ease with which this can be done varies considerably. Some CAL authors encourage recipients of their courseware to tailor it to meet their own particular requirements. However, many courseware producers are totally opposed to the user making any modifications to their instructional material. Of course, in order to make any changes, the user must be familiar with the programming/author language in which the software is written. This cannot be guaranteed, in which case a software consultant may have to be called in. Care must be taken when purchasing courseware packages supplied in the form of a binary dump since it is virtually impossible to make any modifications to these at the local centre.

Usually, courseware packages are designed to have a reasonable working lifetime. However, during the time it is in use it is inevitable that some errors (which escaped the author during testing) will appear. Naturally, these will need to be corrected. Of course, it is not unlikely that CAL material will need to be updated in order to accommodate slight changes in course structure and course content, particularly in rapidly changing high technology areas. These requirements introduce problems with respect to courseware updating. Normally, these can be overcome by distributing software updates and

new   releases   of courseware. Each release of a courseware package has
an associated version number; as changes and modifications are made to
a courseware package its version number is increased to indicate this.
When a package has a large user base, keeping its users informed about
new releases and distributing minor amendments to existing versions
can   present significant problems to courseware authors. However, they
must   be   overcome   if   teaching   materials   are   to   be   successfully
distributed.

Three   other   problem   areas   that effect the usefulness of courseware
distribution schemes are:

        (1)   inadequate documentation,
        (2)   ineffective technical support, and
        (3)   inefficient cataloguing.

If a software package is to be successfully employed it must   be   easy
to set up and operate; when something goes wrong, rectification of the
error   situation   must   also   be   a   facile   task.   To   achieve   these
requirements   courseware   packages   must   be   adequately   documented.
Unfortunately, few packages   meet   the   requirements   of good
documentation standards, either because the necessary material is   not
available   or   because   it   presents   an   additional   burden   for   the
courseware distributor. The latter factor is   particularly   true   when
the   documentation   is   paper   based; the problems associated with the
distribution of this medium can   be   removed   if   CAL   package
documentation is distributed in electronic form (see the EXPLAIN files
in table 2.5 of section 2.5.1).

When users of a courseware package encounter technical difficulties in
using it they will obviously need to talk to someone who can help them
with their problems. Failure to provide adequate technical support for
a CAL package is   one   sure   way   of   helping   to   minimise   its
effectiveness. If a user of a package gets into difficulty and   cannot
resolve   the   problems   that   present   themselves,   then,   in   all
probability, the package will not get   used.   Unfortunately,   few   CAL
authors (and distributors) provide the level of technical support that
is sufficient to ensure the widespread and satisfactory utilisation of
their packages.

As   we   shall see in the following section, courseware distribution is
increasingly taking place via the intermediacy of courseware   exchange
centres   (CECs).   Naturally,   these handle a significant number of CAL
packages. Unless   an   efficient   cataloguing   scheme   is   employed   it
becomes   impossible   to   trace   courseware   items.   This   means   that
potential users will not be aware of   their   existence,   and   so   will
either   revert   to   using non–computer based instructional methods, or
else they will   attempt   to   duplicate   development   effort   that   has
already been invested. Consequently, if courseware distribution from a
CEC is to proceed without these sorts of problem then it is imperative

that (1) an adequate indexing system is employed in order to facilitate the location and retrieval of CAL packages from the CEC's archive, and (2) suitable catalogues are available to ensure that potential user's are aware of what exists. The mode of operation of exchange centres is discussed in more detail in the following section.

2.6.3 Courseware Exchange Centres
As we indicated in the last section, the primary motivation for the development of courseware exchange centres was to facilitate mechanisms for courseware distribution. As a consequence of the importance of computer programs as a component of CAL courseware, organisations that archive and distribute these materials are also sometimes referred to as program exchange centres. Naturally, these centres can operate at different levels and can be funded by a variety of different sources. Typical of the levels at which courseware exchange centres exist are:

Local	through local authorities
Regional	through universities and polytechnics
National	through national projects/organisations
International	through international collaboration.

Many local education authorities have set up educational computing centres which have been delegated with the responsibility of acquiring courseware from various sources and distributing this to schools and colleges in their local area. Universities and polytechnics often play a similar role on a regional basis; these organisations often foster international links and also interface with local centres. Various national projects (see NDPCAL and MEP in chapter 1) and organisations (such as CET – Council for Educational Technology in the UK) also attempt to promote courseware distribution on a national scale. International collaboration can be fostered in a variety of different ways at each of the other levels of involvement. At each level in the above scheme, a network of CECs usually exist to facilitate easy courseware exchange. This may be achieved using conventional media (such as discs and tapes) or with newer techniques involving the use of telesoftware (Hedger, 1978).

While the type of structure outlined above may be suitable for the distribution of CAL materials between academic institutions, it may not necessarily apply to the dissemination of industrial/commercial courseware. Here, for obvious reasons, there will not be uncontrolled access to learning and training materials. However, while there may be little (if any) interorganisational exchange of courseware, it is not inconceivable that intra—organisational program dissemination could not proceed along similar lines to those outlined above. Thus, in multi—national companies, such as International Business Machines (IBM) or Digital Equipment Corporation (DEC), each of the four levels of distribution mentioned above are usually represented even though there might be little exchange of courseware between the two companies themselves. Some computer manufacturing organisations (such as DEC) distribute both their own training software and courseware that is contributed to their archives by their users. Usually, catalogues of courseware are periodically distributed and access to the available material is granted for an appropriate handling fee.

We have already mentioned the fact that many conventional textbook publishers are getting increasingly involved with courseware distribution both at a national and international level. In addition, many educational software companies are starting to emerge, for example Applied Systems Knowledge (1983); these will undoubtedly help to solve some of the problems of courseware distribution that were outlined in the last section. It is quite possible that as soon as companies of this type become more well established and hence networks of dealers emerge, the need for more formally based courseware exchange centres will decline. However, the educational software industry is still in its infancy and so it will be some time before this happens.

The volume of educational software, which is becoming available, is growing at an extremely rapid rate. In view of this, it is impossible for any courseware exchange centre to offer a comprehensive range of materials. Consequently, CECs have tended to specialise. Currently, there are three avenues along which specialisation has tended to proceed, according to educational level, subject area and implementation language.

Educational level really refers to the category of student for which the courseware is intended. For example primary, secondary, tertiary, and so on. A number of organisations now specialise only in the distribution of courseware aimed at particular age groups. Within the UK, two important associations actively involved in attempting to promote facilities distribution are:

MAPE   (Microcomputers And Primary Education, 1983)
MUSE   (Minicomputer Users in Secondary Education, 1983)

As their names suggest, the first of these is concerned with the use of computers at the primary level while the other is concerned with their use in the secondary sector. Many other specialised types of educational association are now springing into existence in order to meet the need for collaboration and co-operation with courseware development/distribution. Particularly important are those orientated towards the dissemination of CAL courseware to aid the teaching of the disabled and handicapped. The SEMERCs (special education microElectronics resource centres) within the UK represent one example of the extensive interest in this area (Adams, 1983).

The second avenue of CEC specialisation is in subject area. That is, particular institutions deal with courseware packages relating to particular subject areas. For example, the chemistry centre at Leeds University distributes software developed under the CALCHEM scheme (Ayscough, 1983). Similarly, GAPE (Geographical Association Program Exchange (Walker, 1982)), which is based at Loughborough University of Technology, is concerned with the evaluation and distribution of courseware that is relevant to the teaching of geography. Sometimes organisations deal with a wider range of courseware than is the case with a single subject area. Thus, the Central Program Exchange (CPE) (previously known as the Physical Sciences Program Exchange) covers a number of scientific disciplines. This CEC is based at Wolverhampton Polytechnic. A useful function that some of the CECs fulfil is that of forming international links thereby facilitating the exchange of software between different countries. The Educational Computer Centre at the London Borough of Havering (Broderick, 1983) is an example of an organisation that performs this type of function. This CEC has undertaken the task of distributing (within the UK) the contents of the software library of the Minnesota Educational Computing Consortium.

The final avenue of specialisation which we shall mention is that of the host language in which courseware is written, certain CECs deal only with material written in a given programming/author language. This is often a useful approach since centres that specialise in this way are often able to offer much useful advice about problems that arise when using the host systems in which they specialise. Many centres have adopted BASIC as their standard courseware language, particularly in Europe. However, there are many centres specialising in the distribution of courseware written in other languages. Typical examples of centres that have specialised in this way include:

(1)   the APL/PIE system at Suny Binghamton,
      New York (APL/PIE, 1974),
(2)   the PILOT exchange scheme based at Iowa
      (PILOT Exchange, 1981), and
(3)   the PLATO CBL laboratory at Illinois (PLATO, 1980).

Each of these organisations is based in the USA. The first specialises in the distribution of APL software (PIE is an acronym for Program Information and Exchange) while the second specialises in the distribution of courseware written in PILOT. The Computer Based Learning (CBL) laboratory at the University of Illinois was at one time involved in the distribution of PLATO material (written in the TUTOR authoring language) but this role has now been taken over by the commercial organisation that was originally responsible for funding the PLATO project (Control Data Corporation).

One of the major problems facing the organisers of courseware exchange centres is that of providing documentation and cataloguing the various items contributed to their archives. The magnitude of these problems have been hinted at earlier. In the past, CECs have usually advertised and announced the availability of various courseware items using conventional paper—based catalogues (Entwistle, 1975; CALCHEM, 1980; Pritchard, 1981). Unfortunately, the problem with this type of catalogue is that they become out of date so quickly and are also very difficult to update. Nowadays, there is increasing interest in the use of electronic cataloguing techniques based upon the use of information systems such as PRESTEL (Brown, 1980). Methods of this type are to be preferred since (1) they can be made more widely available than printed catalogues, and, (2) they are extremely easy to update.

Because of the many problems associated with cataloguing and indexing courseware (and computer software resources in general) a project to study possible solutions has recently been initiated (Templeton, 1983). The project is called SoCCS (Study of Cataloguing Computer Software). It is hoped that the results of the investigation will provide recommendations on cataloguing standards and a brief manual of practice. The importance of projects of this type cannot be over-emphasised since without effective cataloguing projects a significant amount of human development effort can be needlessly wasted.

2.7 EVALUATING COURSEWARE MATERIAL

One of the basic requirements of any evaluative study of courseware is obviously to assess its usefulness and quality. An item of courseware is useful if it performs a function which, for one reason or another, the teacher/instructor is unable to perform. Courseware quality is a more difficult thing to define and is something which is quite often just subjectively assessed, usually on a three point scale: good, average and bad. Obviously, such an evaluative classification is not very meaningful.

The basic function of courseware material is to teach, train or instruct those who use it. In view of this, it would seem that the evaluation of this type of teaching resource would be an easy matter. Unfortunately, this is not the case since many factors are likely to contribute to a good CAL package. Any objective evaluation of courseware thus involves an analysis of many different aspects. Some of these are outlined below.

2.7.1 The Problems of Assessment
One of the major problems often encountered during courseware evaluation is the subjective way in which many teachers/instructors approach the task. This situation is probably forced upon them because of the absence of any formal method of assessing the value of courseware units. Obviously, what is needed in order to overcome this difficulty is some form of objective evaluation metric that can be applied in a standard way to each of the courseware items to be evaluated. When designing such a metric a number of important contributing factors will need to be taken into account. Most of these are embodied in the list of questions enumerated below:

(1)   Is the courseware easy to use?
(2)   Does it teach?
(3)   Does it cater for individualised instruction?
(4)   Does it utilise ancillary media?
(5)   Does it use these to optimum effect?
(6)   Is there good technical support?
(7)   Is it easy to modify – if the need arises?
(8)   Is it free from technical/procedural errors?
(9)   Does it motivate the student?
(10) For what it does, is it cost effective?

When attempting to answer these questions it is important to bear in
mind two important points. Firstly, the answers to many of the
questions will not be simply 'yes' or 'no'; hence, a scale of values
will need to be introduced. Secondly, each of the factors that
contribute to the assessment metric will probably be allocated
different degrees of importance. Once these issues have been sorted
out, a simple method of compounding the factors is next needed. One
possibility is through the summation formula:

$$V = \text{SUM}[R(i).W(i)] \quad \text{for } i = 1 \text{ TO } N$$

where R(i) is the rating of the courseware unit with respect to
dimension i (see the list of questions above) and W(i) is the
corresponding weighting (or importance) associated with that
attribute. Because the rating scales may not all be the same they may
need to be normalised through the use of multiplicative normalisation
factors.

Support for the idea of an evaluation metric, similar to that outlined
above, has been provided by several other people. For example, one
researcher has recently presented a list of guidelines that relate to
software evaluation for microcomputer programs for teaching in schools
(Harris, 1983). It is suggested that the following factors should be
considered:

(1)   User Friendliness
(2)   Style of Presentation
(3)   Cost Considerations
(4)   Technical Considerations
(5)   Teacher's Reaction
(6)   Student's Reaction
(7)   Management Requirements

A detailed discussion of each of these is presented in the original
report, so nothing further will be said about them here. However, it
is important to conclude that this list does support our initial
premise that courseware evaluation is a multi–faceted task that
requires considerable thought and planning. This is particularly the
case in complex multimedia instructional systems (McIntosh, 1974; Hill

et al., 1977) in which a very large number of variables may be involved. When dealing with courseware for this type of system it is imperative that the person responsible for the design of the evaluation metric consults some of the standard textbooks devoted to the topic of curriculum material evaluation (Eraut, 1972).

There are two other important problems which have to be faced when attempting to perform courseware evaluation. Firstly, it is important to decide upon the methods to be used in order to acquire the information needed for the assessment metric. Secondly, some consideration must be given to the mechanisms by which these methods should be administered. These factors are discussed in more detail below.

2.7.2 The Use of Questionnaires

Undoubtedly, the most popular technique for acquiring evaluative information is via the use of some form of questionnaire. These are important because they enable people's reactions to an item of courseware to be documented for subsequent analysis – if need be, using statistical processing software such as SPSS (Nie et al., 1970) [1]. Successful design of a questionnaire is imperative if it is to solicit the required information from its respondent. Whenever it is feasible, the services of a professional survey researcher should be sought in order to discuss the best approach to adopt. If this is not possible then the standard textbooks on questionnaire design will need to be consulted (Moser, 1968; Oppenheim, 1973).

Naturally, the questionnaire should seek to solicit information relating to all aspects of the courseware, provided this does not make it unduly long. Copies of the questionnaire can then be distributed along with the courseware, either to all users or just to a preselected sample. It is not the purpose of this section to discuss the design details underlying the use of this type of evaluation tool. Rather, it is our intent only to mention how it is used and to point out a few of the problems involved. More detailed discussions of the use of this approach are given elsewhere (Yeates, 1981; Barker and Singh, 1983).

Undoubtedly, two of the most difficult problems to overcome when using a questionnaire are: (1) failure of the respondent to understand some of the questions – thereby resulting in incorrect feedback, and (2) ensuring that they are completed and indeed returned for analysis. The first of these problems can be overcome by preparing a guidebook or a

----

[1]   SPSS is an acronym for Statistical Package for Social Scientists. This is a collection of computer programs which may be used to perform a variety of different standard statistical tests and processing tasks. The programs are well documented and are used in many scientific research applications.

series of explanatory notes that the respondent can refer to if any doubt arises with respect to particular questions. Alternatively, a telephone number might be included on the form so that respondents can contact the evaluator directly. Unfortunately, it is much more difficult to provide any guarantee that completed questionnaires will be returned. One incentive, perhaps, is to offer free versions of software updates to those who co-operate in the courseware evaluation exercise.

2.7.3 Pre-testing and Post-testing

In order to evaluate certain aspects of courseware utility, such as items (2) and (6) in the lists presented in section 2.7.1 – it will be important to let students interact 'with it. This interaction must take place in such a way that the effect of the courseware on the student can be assessed. One of the most frequently used methods of performing this type of assessment is through the use of pre-testing and post-testing. These techniques are quite well documented in the literature and so we present only an overview of the steps involved. The basic strategy that is normally employed is as follows:

(1)   select a test group of students having a known
       ability range,
(2)   subject the test group to a pre-test in order to
       ascertain their knowledge/skill levels with respect
       to the courseware that is to be evaluated,
(3)   let the test group interact with the courseware,
(4)   perform a post-test on the student group, and
(5)   determine if there is any significant enhancement
       in the knowledge/skill levels of the test group.

Both the pre-testing (step 2) and the post-testing (step 4) can, of course, be conducted by the computer, as can the application of the statistical tests that need to be performed on the raw results obtained. However, there is no reason why each of these steps could not be performed using conventional manual techniques based on quizzes or other forms of specially compiled test material.

This approach to courseware evaluation can provide useful feedback for the CAL author who can then modify the material in order to accommodate any changes deemed to be necessary.

2.8 CONCLUSION

In this chapter the importance of courseware has been emphasised. We have examined its history, current status and likely future directions of development. In its simplest form, courseware is a special type of software resource. Techniques for its generation are therefore similar to those used for preparing conventional computer programs. Two broad approaches are used for the preparation of CAL packages: programming languages and author languages. Examples of each of these have been presented. Special attention will be given to author languages in the subsequent chapters of this book; we will be particularly interested in those systems that facilitate the development of courseware for use in multimedia instructional systems. When considering the use of CAL courseware packages several important factors need to be considered. Perhaps the most important of these are (1) its distribution, and (2) its evaluation. Each of these topics has been discussed in this chapter.

In the following chapter we turn our attention to the use of author languages as a means of developing courseware. The motivation for this stems from the fact that courseware authoring systems do provide a facile method for the preparation of CAL material.

2.9 BIBLIOGRAPHY

Adams, J., (editor), Learning to cope – computers in special education, an educational computing special, Educational Computing, 1983.

APL/PIE Computer Centre, Binghamton, NY, 1974.

Applied Systems Knowledge, President Professor Tom Stonier, London, 1983.

Argyle, M., Bodily Communication, Methuen, London, 1975.

Ayscough, P.B., CALCHEM reaches 50, CALNEWS, (21), Council for Educational Technology, London, 1983.

Barker, P.G., The computer as an audio-visual resource, Computers and Education, 3, 23–34, 1979.

Barker, P.G., Computer networks, Wireless World, 88(1563), 74–78, 1982a.

Barker, P.G., PET as a terminal device, Practical Computing, 5(1) 106–109, 1982b.

Barker, P.G. and Singh, R., A practical introduction to authoring for computer assisted learning. Part 2: PILOT, British Journal of Educational Technology, 14(3), 174–200, 1983.

Barker, P.G. and Yeates, H., Some problems associated with multimedia data bases, British Journal of Educational Technology, 12(2), 158–175, 1981.

Berman, I., Learning media: theory, selection and utilisation in science education, in New Trends in the Utilisation of Educational Technology for Science Education, 101–142, UNESCO, Paris, 1974.

Bitzer, D.L., The wide world of computer based education, Advances in Computers, 15, 239–283, 1976.

Bitzer, D.L., Braunfeld, P.G. and Lichtenberger, W.W., PLATO II: A multiple–student, computer controlled automatic teaching device, in Programmed Learning and Computer Based Instruction, Proceedings of the Conference on Applications of Digital Computers to Automated Instruction, October 10–12, 1961, 205–216, John Wiley, New York, NY, 1962.

Bleazard, G.B., Program Design Methods, National Computing Centre, Manchester, 1976.

Boyd, G.M., The derivation of programmed lessons from recorded protocols, in Aspects of Educational Technology, edited by K. Austwick and N.D.C. Harris, Pitman, London, 1972.

Brighton Polytechnic, Telesoftware and Education Project, Report on the Joint BBC/ITV and Brighton Polytechnic Research Project, Summer 1982, Brighton Polytechnic, Brighton, 1982.

Broderick, W.R., Havering – MECC software distribution, CALNEWS, (21), 12, Council for Educational Technology, London, 1983.

Brown, J., Central Program Exchange, CALNEWS, (20), 5–6, Council for Educational Technology, London, 1982.

Brown, M., PRESTEL and Education II: A viewdata telesoftware system for education, in Proceedings of the 4th International Online Information Meeting, 115–118, Learned Information, London, 1980.

Bunderson, C.V. and Dunham, J.L., The University of Texas Computer Assisted Instruction Laboratory, University of Texas, Austin, TX, 1968.

Burton, R.R. and Brown, J.S., An investigation of computer coaching for informal learning activities, in Intelligent Tutoring Systems, edited by D. Sleeman, and J.S. Brown, Academic Press, New York, NY, 1982.

CALCHEM – Computer Assisted Learning in Chemistry – Catalogue of Programs, Project Director: P.B. Ayscough, University of Leeds, Leeds, 1980.

Conlon, T., PILOT – The Language and How to Use it, Prentice–Hall, Englewood Cliffs, NJ, 1984.

Council for Educational Technology, User Specifications (USPECs), News Sheet, Council for Educational Technology, London, 1982.

Cox, M., The computers in the curriculum project – Chelsea College, CALNEWS, (20), 4–5, Council for Educational Technology, London, 1982.

Davis, W.S., FORTRAN: Getting Started, Addison–Wesley, Reading, MA, 1981.

Entwistle, R.P., Computers Across the Curriculum: Listing of Computer Packages for Schools, Northampton College of Education, Northampton, 1975.

Eraut, M., Strategies for the evaluation of curriculum materials, in Aspects of Educational Technology, edited by K. Austwick and N.D.C. Harris, 238–246, Pitman, London, 1972.

Fielden, J., The financial evaluation of computer assisted learning projects, International Journal of Mathematics Education Science and Technology, 5, 625–630, 1974.

Gilbert, G.N., PILOT – A Guide to the PRIME Implementation of the PILOT Programming Language, Version 3.2, University of Surrey, 1981.

Gilman, L. and Rose, A.J., APL: An Interactive Approach, John Wiley, New York, NY, 1974.

Govier, H. and Neave, M., LOGO Challenge, Addison–Wesley, Reading, MA, 1983.

Grey, L.D., A Course in APL With Applications, Addison–Wesley, Reading, MA, 1976.

Harris D., Software evaluation for microcomputer programs, CALNEWS, (21), 4–6, Council for Educational Technology, London, 1983. 1983.

Hedger, J., Telesoftware: home computing via teletext, Wireless World, 84(1515), 61–64, 1978.

Hennessey, K., Computer Applications Packages, Addison–Wesley, Reading, MA, 1983.

Hill, P.J., Lincoln, L. and Turner, L.P., Evaluation of Tape–Slide Guides for Library Instruction, British Library Research and Development Report No. 5378–HC, 1977.

IBM Corporation, Computer Based Training – User Guide, IBM Corporation, White Plains, NY, Form: GE20–0484–0, 1975.

Isaacson, P. and Juliussen, E., Personals spur educational software mart, ISO WORLD, 44, 1983.

Macero, D.J. and Davis, L.N., Computer–assisted instruction in chemistry at Syracuse University: an overview, Computers and Geosciences, (2), 107–112, 1976.

McCracken, D.D., A Simplified Guide to Fortran Programming, John Wiley, New York, NY, 1974.

McIntosh, N., Evaluation of multimedia educational systems – some problems, British Journal of Educational Technology, 5(3), 43–59, 1974.

Microcomputers and Primary Education, B. Holmes, MAPE Secretary, St. Helen's Primary School, Bluntisham, Cambridgeshire, 1983.

Microsoft, MBASIC User's Manual for Intertec's Video Computer Systems, Document No. P010, First Edition, Microsoft, Bellevue, WA, 1982.

Minicomputer Users in Secondary Education, MUSE, Bromsgrove, Worcestershire, 1983.

Moser, C.A., Survey Methods in Social Investigation, Heinemann, London, 1968.

Nie, N., Bent, D.H. and Hull, C.H., SPSS – Statistical Package for the Social Sciences, McGraw-Hill, New York, NY, 1970.

Oppenheim, A.N., Questionnaire Design and Attitude Measurement, Heinemann, London, 1973.

Pakin, S., APL/360 Reference Manual, Science Research Associates, Chicago, IL, Publication No. 13–5, 1972.

PILOT Exchange, Mason City, IA, 1981.

PLATO, Computer Based Education Research Laboratory, University of Illinois, Urbana–Champaign, IL, 1980

Pritchard, A., Small Computer Program Index, ALLM Books, Watford, 1981.

Rath, G.J., The IBM Research Centre Teaching Machine Project, in Automatic Teaching – State of the Art, edited by E. Galanta, John Wiley, New York, NY, 1959.

Romiszowski, A.J., The Selection and Use of Instructional Media: A Systems Approach, Kogan Page, London, 1977.

Roper, C., French flock to computer centre, New Scientist, 97(1344), 358–361, 1983.

Shepherd, M., A light pen for microcomputers, Wireless World, 88(1588), 30–32, 1982.

Skinner, B.F., Why we need teaching machines, Harvard Educational Review, No. 31, 1961.

Templeton, R., SoCCS: cataloguing computer software, CALNEWS, (21), 10, Council for Educational Technology, London, 1983.

Wagener, J.L., Principles of FORTRAN-77 Programming, John Wiley, New York, NY, 1980.

Walker, D., GAPE and teaching geography, CALNEWS, (20), 3, Council for Educational Technology, London, 1982.

Wells, G., How to Communicate, McGraw-Hill, London, 1978.

Yeates, H., Some Experiments in Man–Machine Interaction Relevant to Computer Assisted Learning, M.Sc. Thesis, University of Durham, 1981.

Further Reading

Bunderson, C.V., COURSEWARE: conceptions and definitions, in Computer-Based Instruction – A State-of-the-Art Assessment, Academic Press, 91–125, New York, NY, 1981.

Bunderson, C.V., Instructional strategies for videodisc courseware, Journal of Educational Technology Systems, 8(3), 207–210, 1979/80.

Chapter 3

AUTHOR LANGUAGES FOR CAL – AN OVERVIEW

3.1 INTRODUCTION

Author languages provide a means to facilitate the development of courseware material for use in computer–based instructional systems. In this chapter the nature and role of an author language is explained. Some examples of those currently available (or under development) on large, medium and small computers are then briefly described. Particular emphasis is given to exploring the author's interface with these systems. Future developments in author languages are likely to be significantly influenced by current trends in microelectronics, telecommunications, video and information storage technology. Some of the implications that each of these factors are likely to have on the development of author languages will be discussed in a subsequent chapter.

3.1.1 The Importance of Communication

In order to secure its long term survival the human species uses a number of complex biological processes. One of the most important of these is communication. The human's communicative skills are manifest in a variety of ways: through mathematics, natural language, the creation of music, literature and other forms of fine art. Through the process of education, knowledge and experience in each of these domains may be passed from one generation to another.

As a process of information transfer, education is closely related to communication. Although education is a far more complex process, for many purposes the two terms may be regarded as synonymous. Education is essentially an interactive process in which some form of information transfer takes place between two general classes of entity. One of these (the teacher) is information rich, while the other (the student) is deficient in this commodity, at least in the domain that binds members of the two classes together.

To permit the exchange of information between teachers and students, appropriate channels of communication are necessary. A variety of these currently exist (lessons, lectures, books, films, radio, TV, and so on). More detailed descriptions of some of the more important media have been presented elsewhere (Barker and Yeates, 1981). Increasingly, computer systems are being used as communication agents to bring about the transfer of instructional material between those who prepare resources and those who use them.

An educational process often involves the use of several different channels of communication (sound, pictures, text, and so on). These may be used simultaneously or in sequence. Parallelism with respect to media utilisation is likely to be a highly effective tool if used correctly. The importance of the computer as an educational resource depends upon the fact that it is able to support any of the conventional modes of communication using suitably constructed sonic, textual or pictorial interfaces. Furthermore, it can be made to operate in a highly parallel fashion and to exhibit significant interactivity, hitherto not available through any other type of teaching medium.

In conventional approaches to the use of computers as information transfer agents, some skills in the techniques of computer programming have often been a prerequisite. Many people believe that this provides an unnecessary hurdle to the fundamental process of educational communication through computers. In order to overcome this barrier, several different approaches have been explored. Typical of these are the many load–and–run teaching packages that currently exist (see section 2.5) and the growing number of teacher–orientated high–level application languages. These enable instructional material to be generated and administered automatically without the need for sophisticated computer programming skills. Historically, these latter systems have often been referred to as author languages. In more modern lesson development centres, the author language plays a vital role in linking together those who create educational material and the students who use them.

It is important to emphasise that in this chapter we intend to explore the end–user's interface with a number of different author languages. We are therefore less interested in the mechanisms of cognition, concept development, learning/teaching strategies and the detailed nature of learning processes. This is the domain of educational psychology and these topics are adequately covered in the literature of this subject. Instead, we concentrate on investigating the interface that exists between teachers, students and computer technology. We describe a number of different approaches to the provision of authoring facilities. Examples are taken from three categories of system. These are based on the use of mainframe computers, minis and micros. The problems of author language evaluation are then briefly outlined in section 3.5.

3.1.2 Tools for Courseware Development

Computer assisted instruction and computer aided learning are critically dependent upon the availability of suitable courseware units for their effective implementation. As we outlined in the last chapter, courseware is the generic term used to describe the many different types of computer-based instructional resource used in an educational environment. Typical examples of courseware items include drill and practice programs, simulations, animations, student quizzes and testing systems. A more detailed description of courseware has been presented by Bunderson (1981).

People who prepare computer-based materials for teaching are often referred to as courseware authors. The major tasks of the author involve (1) deciding upon the subject matter to be presented to the student, (2) structuring the material in a fashion suitable for presentation by computer, (3) deciding upon the instructional strategies to be employed, (4) selecting the media (or channels) necessary to convey the instructional material, and (5) if necessary, specifying appropriate evaluation metrics to enable the performance of both the courseware and the student(s) to be assessed.

Once the author has decided upon the instructional content of a lesson, its format and strategy of presentation, the only remaining task is that of communicating it to the computer. A variety of tools is available for this purpose. In the context of CAI, we have suggested in chapter 2 that these can be divided into two broad categories: general-purpose programming languages and author languages. The former are used for implementing a wide range of computer applications, while the latter are specifically designed for those who prepare computer-based instructional material. Whichever type of language is used, it should enable the smooth creation, testing and running of courseware modules. These, in turn, should reflect the author's aims in terms of the learning methods and expected goals to be achieved by the learner.

A substantial amount of courseware is coded in one or other of the general-purpose high-level programming languages referred to above. Indeed, a recent study (Kearsley, 1976) indicated that of the ten most commonly used CAI development languages, six were of the conventional programming variety. The most popular were APL, BASIC and FORTRAN (see section 2.3). Another recently announced language, called COMAL (Christensen, 1981; Atherton, 1981) is likely to become a further example of this category. Programming languages for instructional use are adequately described elsewhere Zinn (1969a; 1969b, 1972) and will not be further discussed here.

Unfortunately, the specific needs of CAI authors were never a design feature of any of the languages mentioned above. They were produced to satisfy the needs of mathematicians, engineers, business administrators and teachers of computer programming. Such languages contain specialised vocabularies and syntax which usually reflect the backgrounds of their user population. Thus, in order to produce good quality courseware, CAI authors have to familiarise themselves with the specific syntax and semantics of the programming language they elect to use. Having done this, there is still no guarantee that the resulting courseware will reflect their preferred teaching methods.

Another limitation of these conventional programming languages is the restrictions they impose on the input/output peripherals that can be used. Often only an alphanumeric VDU is supported. They do not facilitate the use of any of the wide range of audio-visual aids that are nowadays widely available in the classroom.

In addition to the general-purpose languages outlined above, there are several other more specialised ones such as LOGO (Papert, 1971; Kahn, 1977), SMALLTALK (Kay and Goldberg, 1977; Goldberg, 1979; Kay, 1980) and PROLOG (Clocksin and Mellish, 1981; Ferguson, 1981) which claim some support. However, there is no widespread evidence for their success or measure of the extent of their use as languages for the preparation of instructional material. Another area of growing interest is the use of videotex systems and their application for instructional purposes (Aston, 1980; Brahan et al., 1980; Barker and Yeates, 1981). As yet, there are few author languages available to enable this type of facility to be readily used although a considerable amount of work is currently being conducted in this area (Watson and Bevan, 1980; Hoskyns, 1982).

From what has been said above, several things become apparent. An author is expected to be skilful in the computer representation of knowledge, possess subject matter expertise and be a fairly good programmer. Such a combination of skills is rarely found in a single individual. Consequently, in order to overcome these limitations and to encompass some of the more modern aspects of computer usage within education, CAI author languages have been developed.

3.1.3 What is an Author Language?
It is important to understand the role of both a computer and an author language as instructional resources. In view of this it will be useful to compare conventional approaches to instruction with those which are based upon the use of a computer system. Such a comparison

(in   terms   of   entity/data–flow   graphs)   is   presented   in   figures   3.1 and   3.2.

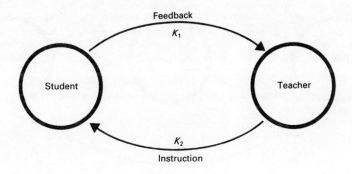

Interactivity, I (T : S) = K_1 / K_2

Figure 3.1   Conventional Instruction.

Figure 3.1 depicts conventional   instruction.   The   representation   is
very   approximate   since it does not indicate the fuzzy nature (Zadeh,
1965; 1976) of the entity classes involved, nor does   it   reflect   the
multiplicity   of   communication   channels   likely   to   be   invoked.
Furthermore, it fails to show the relationships of any of the entities
within the universe of discourse from which the instructional material
is derived. It is thus a   very   simplistic   view.   Despite   this,   the
diagram   does   depict   one   important   fact: there   is   (ideally)
bidirectional   data   flow   between   a   teacher   and   a   student.   The
interactivity   of the relationship between the two I(T:S), is given by
the ratio of the data–flow functions (k1) for the feedback   channel(s)
and   the corresponding function (k2) for the instructional channel(s).
These functions depend upon a number of parameters: the volume of
information despatched, its type, its value, its direction, the way in
which   it   is   partitioned   over   the   available channels and its time
dependence.

Figure 3.2 shows how the   introduction   of   a   computer   (as   a   third
entity)   may   influence   the data flow between a teacher and a student.
Essentially,   some   fraction   of   the   instructional   process   is   now
delegated   to   a   computer.   The nature of the tasks and the extent to
which they become computer based depends totally upon each   individual
teacher's   discretion.   In   order   to   prepare the materials needed to
produce computer based resources, some means of interacting   with   the
computer   is   (for   many)   a   prerequisite.   As   we   have   established
previously, two types of facility are usually   available: programming
languages and authoring systems.

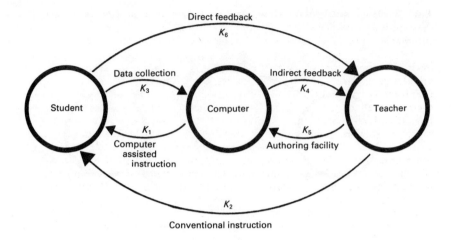

$$\text{Interactivity, } I(S) = I(C:S) + I(T:S)$$
$$= K_3 / K_1 + K_6 / K_2$$

Figure 3.2   Computer augmented instruction.

An authoring system is a programming facility that is specifically
orientated towards those who are involved in the development of
learning material that is to be administered by a computer. It allows
the author to organise CAI resources and permits the specification of
the conditions governing their display. In addition, it provides
systematic monitoring of the responses made by the student. Using such
a language, an author is likely to construct a data base [1]
containing the necessary course material. This data–base will usually
consist of a collection of frames which, in the main, are segments of
material to be displayed on a VDU screen. The frames expose the
learner to a concept (teaching frame) or pose a question (testing
frame).   Through the latter an attempt is made to assess the student's
understanding and retention of the subject matter that has been
presented.

––––––––––––––––––––––

[1]   The   term data base is a technical one used to describe a stored
       collection of electronic information held within a computer
       system (Barker and Yeates, 1981; Barker, 1982b; 1983a). Data
       bases differ from conventional file storage systems in that (1)
       there is an attempt to minimise the duplication of data, (2) data
       sharing is encouraged, and (3) a number of well–defined user
       operations are available – such as insert, update, retrieve and
       delete.

Author languages are, in general, easy to use. When used by a teacher they provide a comprehensive tool that enables a wide variety of automated teaching strategies to be implemented. Typically, these include tutorial mode, drill and practice, diagnostic testing, inquiry mode, counselling, simulation, gaming, problem solving and calculation. Each of these is adequately described in the CAI literature (Former, 1973; Aird, 1976; Kearsley, 1976). In addition to their information dissemination role, author languages also provide powerful facilities for data collection, data analysis and result reporting. Some of the most useful features, however, are the aids they provide for the utilisation of multimedia channels of communication - sound, images, text and the incorporation of a variety of ancillary teaching equipment. The importance of these multimedia interactions lies in their ability to provide the means to enable the construction of work models (Bunderson et al., 1981). This approach to instruction is based upon the belief that a teaching/learning environment should provide life-like working models to which a student can relate.

In 1973 Hoy and Wang (1973) produced a comprehensive index to computer based learning. This index lists 62 different languages. Of these, 16 were assembly level (see section 1.1.3) and 46 were general purpose. Included in the latter were authoring systems such as COURSEWRITER, TUTOR, CAILAN and ISL-II. Since this index was compiled, several new CAI languages have emerged. Some of these are experimental while others are intended to be used on a large scale. A few of the more popular of these are NATAL-74, PILOT, SMITH, ALERT and IPS. In addition to these, there are many less well-known ones in existence.

Most of the languages listed above provide authors with facilities to construct CAI lessons. Typically, these are likely to include (1) presentation of text via frames, (2) student-testing, (3) receiving and analysing student responses, (4) provision of remedial and reinforcement material, and (5) branching facilities, the direction of which depends on the nature of the student response.

Branching is a very important facility because it provides a mechanism to enable a high degree of individualisation of instruction to be accomplished. Since branching involves the address of positions to be branched to, most of the conventional CAI languages are often described as address-orientated (Osin, 1976). These languages do not possess the capability of handling frame contents, they merely obey the logic of branching. In contrast, other types of language allow the creation of a data base of structured information covering a certain subject area. These systems are able to explore the structure of a subject with a view to presenting information to the student based upon his/her previously determined ability. Languages of this type are called information structure orientated languages (Carbonell, 1970).

In the remaining sections of this chapter we present a brief
description of some of the more popular author languages. Our
intention is to (1) give the reader an indication of some of the
facilities that are available, and, (2) provide an indication of the
type of user interface that the various systems present to CAI
authors. We do not attempt to perform any critical comparison of these
systems since this task has been admirably undertaken by other authors
(Lower et al., 1979; Pashkin, 1979).

3.2 LANGUAGES AVAILABLE ON MAINFRAME COMPUTERS

In the past, most CAI material was developed for use on large
mainframe computers capable of servicing a number of student terminals
simultaneously. It is therefore quite natural to expect that there
would be several author languages available for use in this kind of
environment. We present below five examples of languages currently in
use on large computer systems.

3.2.1 COURSEWRITER
This is a group of languages developed by International Business
Machines (IBM) for use in conjunction with their 1050 student/author
station (International Business Machines, 1969). These stations were
linked to an IBM System/360 mainframe. They possessed multimedia
capabilities thereby making it possible to display static images using
slides, play audio messages and present typewritten information. It
was possible to use each of these resources individually or in various
combinations.

The author language is similar to English. Most users should therefore
find it relatively easy to learn. Its designers claim that it can be
used equally well by both novices and experts. However, there is no
evidence to support this claim. On the contrary, it is reported (Yobb,
1977) that teachers using COURSEWRITER find it both complex and
inflexible. The language consists of a small collection of commands, a
subset of which is presented in figure 3.3. Using these it is possible
to present information to students (ty and qu) and then record their
responses. These can then be matched against author defined
anticipated answers (ca and wa) and unanticipated ones (un). Depending
upon the nature of the response made the flow of control may branch
(br) to the next section of the lesson or to a remediation sequence.
The appearance of a section of a COURSEWRITER CAI program is
illustrated in the upper part of figure 3.3. Based upon this example
one might conclude that the user interface with this system is quite
friendly. However, this is not really true since the complexity of the
program text increases substantially as soon as the author attempts to
undertake more sophisticated teaching tasks (International Business
Machines, 1976).

```
Question 1
        qu   What is the product of 12 and 3?
        ca   36
        ty   correct
        br   question 4
        wa   15
        ty   No, the answer you gave is the sum.
             of 12 and 3.   Try again.
             Make sure that you have typed a numeric answer
             Try again.

                 o

                 o

                 o
```

Command	Action
qu	question to student - await a reply
ca	anticipated correct answer
ty	type out
br	branch
wa	anticipated wrong answer
un	unanticipated answer

Figure 3.3   Section of a COURSEWRITER lesson.
(Courtesy of IBM.)

Currently, there are three instructional system program products available from IBM to support computer based training. These systems are COURSEWRITER III (described above), the Interactive Training System (ITS) and the Interactive Instructional System (IIS) which combines features of the first two. Further details of IIS, courseware options and typical examples of commercial training applications are given elsewhere (International Business Machines, 1977; 1978).

3.2.2 ASET
This is an instructional system designed for use on large UNIVAC mainframe computers. A synonym for Author System for Education and Training, ASET is a sophisticated tool that enables the creation of a variety of instructional strategies (UNIVAC, 1975a; 1975b).

An ASET lesson consists of a lesson header and a series of units. The header contains various directives that are used to specify how the overall lesson is to be managed and presented. The options included in a header may be used to control such features as session time, response time, number of retries, whether phonetic analysis is required, and so on. A unit is the fundamental instructional segment of a lesson and consists of four parts: (1) the unit name, (2) the initial text, (3) a set of command strings, and (4) its supporting secondary text. The appearance of a typical unit is shown in figure 3.4.

The unit name (101 in line 1) is used for branching purposes and can be used as the target of a GOTO statement. The initial text (lines 2 and 3) is used to define the textual material to be presented to the student while the command string section (lines 5 through 12) controls lesson flow. In addition, it prints reinforcements (and other feedback messages) and makes decisions about student responses. In the example, lines 7 and 8 handle unanticipated incorrect answers; line 9 provides the required response to an anticipated correct answer based upon phonetic matching; and, lines 10, 11 and 12 specify the action to be taken for anticipated incorrect answers. The secondary text (from line 14 onwards) section is introduced by the keyword TEXT and contains material that is to be displayed to the student by means of the PRINT statements within the command section. ASET permits the use of both author variables and reserved data entry words. An author variable is essentially a counter that can be used to sum incorrect/correct responses and then advise the learner on the progress being made. They can also be used to determine where to reroute a student if his/her performance is above/below that deemed average for the unit concerned. In figure 3.4, N (lines 5 through 8) is an example of an author language variable. Examples of reserved data entry words are contained in lines 22 and 23. NAME is used to hold the value of the student's name so that it can be included, wherever necessary, in feedback messages. INPUT is used to store the value of the most recent item keyed in by the student through the VDU keyboard. It too can be used to construct appropriate feedback responses to the student.

```
**101///
        WHICH PLANET IS NEAREST THE EARTH?  TYPE IN YOUR ANSWER
        BELOW NEXT TO THE CURSOR.                                    101-1.1
COMMANDS
   N=0.
X  N=N+1.
   IF N.EQ.1, PRINT* E, GOTO X.
   IF N.EQ.2, PRINT* F, GOTO A102.
  +IF (VENUS) PHONETIC, PRINT* B, GOTO A102.
   PRINT* A, GOTO A090.
   PRINT* C, GOTO A090.
   PRINT* D, DO SR01, GOTO A101.
TEXT
A THE MOON IS NOT ONE OF THE PLANETS.  LET'S REVIEW.//
                                                                     101A
B YES, VENUS IS CLOSER TO THE EARTH THAN ANY OTHER PLANET, ONLY
     26 MILLION MILES AWAY./
                                                                     101B
C NO, MERCURY IS INCORRECT.  LET'S REVIEW PLANET DISTANCES.//
                                                                     101C
D NO, \NAME\, NEPTUNE IS NOT CORRECT.  LET ME HELP YOU MORE.//
                                                                     101D
E NO, \INPUT\ IS NOT RIGHT. TRY ONCE MORE.////
                                                                     101E
F \INPUT\ IS NOT RIGHT.  THE ANSWER IS: "VENUS" CONTINUE.////
                                                                     101F
```

Figure 3.4   Section of an ASET lesson.
(Courtesy of UNIVAC.)

Lessons may be constructed interactively through a terminal or on coding forms that are then transcribed to punched cards. The files containing the lessons are then processed by an assembler program (see section 1.1.3) which reorganises them into an executable format which can be used by the ASET interpreter when it executes the lesson for the student.

Although ASET is a powerful system, its ease of use is significantly impaired by the complexity of the computer software that surrounds it – the operating system and its job control language (see section 1.1.3). This means that computer non–specialists would have considerable difficulty in using it. Furthermore, in the environment in which we have used this system there have been no facilities for developing multimedia instructional strategies.

3.2.3 TUTOR

This is the author language used to construct PLATO lessons (Bitzer, 1976). PLATO is a large multi–terminal CAI system based at the University of Illinois. It uses a Control Data Corporation (CDC) Cyber computer. Access to the system is through special multimedia terminals that permit many different kinds of student (or author) interaction. Initially, most of the terminals were located at the central campus. However, many of them are now distributed at various sites throughout North America. These are linked to the central computer at the Illinois campus by means of a special type of communication network. Some centres, however, have set up their own in–house PLATO systems. The University of Delaware (Hofstetter, 1980) is one such example. Although developed by academic researchers, the system is currently being actively marketed in the USA and Europe by Control Data Corporation for industrial training applications.

One of the outstanding features of the TUTOR language is the capability it offers for handling interactive graphical images. These are produced on high resolution touch–sensitive screens attached to special terminal devices (Stifle, 1974; Francis, 1976). In addition, there is a powerful set of judging commands provided which facilitate the smooth flow of human–machine communication. Using these commands, student responses can be evaluated against author–specified synonymous words or concept phrases. The apparent simplicity of authoring in TUTOR is illustrated by the program shown in figure 3.5. This depicts the sequence of commands necessary to draw a rectangle on the student's screen and then test to see if he/she can recognise it as such.

Inspection of figure 3.5 would suggest that TUTOR is a highly teacher-orientated author language. Instructional units are constructed from a series of commands (the leftmost column in the diagram), their associated operands (the centre column) and supporting documentary material (on the right). Comments, introduced by the double dollar

mark, are used by an author in order to explain to others what he/she
is attempting to do within a particular section of an instructional
program. Thus, apart from the details of the draw command (line 5),
the comments embedded within figure 3.5 make it easy for the reader to
deduce what is happening. The draw command, however, needs some
further explanation. It can operate using both course grid–coordinates
(line number and character position within line) or a fine grid system
based upon the 512 x 512 matrix of pixel dots that comprise the
screen. In the example, the course grid system is used. Starting at
line 5, character position 10 a vertical line is drawn to line 15,
character position 10. A horizontal line 30 character positions long
is then drawn. The rectangle is completed by moving vertically to line
5 and horizontally back to the starting position at 510. The text,
'What is this figure?' is then written on line 18 (commencing at
character position 12) and a prompt arrow is generated on line 20. The
system then waits for a student reply which is subsequently analysed
and acted upon.

Unit	geometry	$$Name of course unit
next	moregeom	$$Name of next mainstream course unit
help	help1	$$Name of sequence to be entered if student presses HELP key
draw	510; 1510; 1540; 540; 510	$$Draw rectangle with specified corners (using course grid system)
at	1812	$$Positions text (line/position)
write	What is this figure?	
arrow	2015	$$Enters judging mode, positions response
specs	okcap	$$Accepts responses in lower or upper case
answer	rectangle	
write	Very good	$$Progress to next part of 'geometry' or 'moregeom' if this is the last part
wrong	square	
write	The sides are not equal	$$Comments for specific wrong answers
if	ntries=2	
nextnow	review1	$$Route to unit 'review1' after two wrong answers
endarrow		$$Revert to 'presentation' mode

Figure 3.5   Section of a TUTOR lesson.

The development of the TUTOR language has continuously accommodated
the changing requirements of the user. It has, therefore, evolved with
the various trends that have taken place in CAI. Since the language
was designed to support PLATO, its use outside this system might be

expected to be somewhat limited. However, TUTOR has recently been used as the basis of a new computer based education system called SIMPLER (Modular Computer Systems, 1981). This is less sophisticated than PLATO but is less expensive and runs on a minicomputer rather than on a mainframe system.

TUTOR is a more powerful system than either COURSEWRITER or ASET. Particularly important is the fact that it is much more end-user orientated than either of these other languages. Furthermore, it provides a true multimedia capability. Both TUTOR and PLATO have been described by a variety of authors (Sherwood, 1974; Ghesquiere et al., 1975; Barker, 1979). It is probably one of the oldest and most well known of all the computer based educational systems.

3.2.4 NATAL-74
The multiplicity of author languages has always made the exchange of courseware a difficult, if not impossible, task. In order to resolve this problem, the National Research Council of Canada commissioned the development of a NATional Author Language (Brahan et al., 1980). Four basic goals were considered to be important: (1) ease of use, (2) language portability, (3) terminal independence, and (4) computational, logical and file handling functions.

NATAL differs from older CAL approaches in that it emphasises the open-system approach. This means that in this system teaching material can be described independently of the student terminal upon which it will ultimately be used. It is then modified at run time to meet the requirements of the specific terminal actually used for course delivery. In contrast to this, the closed system approach used by PLATO requires every student to have the same terminal. Course material is then prepared in a way is orientated towards the use of this terminal (Brahan and Godfrey, 1982).

The language is constructed using three fundamental types of module: unit, procedure and function. Unit is the only mode of interaction between the student and the system. It allows the display of information and permits editing and categorising of student responses. In addition, it provides information to reinforce a correct response and to guide the student towards a desired one. Units can also be used for gathering student response data such as time taken to respond, category of response, number of attempts, and so on.

NATAL-74 has been available on a DEC System-10 at the Canadian National Research Council, Ottawa, since 1977. Initially, it was used to construct drill and practice programs for simple arithmetic concepts involving the addition, subtraction, multiplication and division of whole numbers. The results of initial experience with the system suggest that the language could easily be learned and applied to the large-scale production of CAI courseware. Since its implementation on a DEC computer, it has become available on an IBM-

MVS based mainframe and a Honeywell Level-6 minicomputer (Brahan and Godfrey, 1982). Currently, there is considerable interest in attempting to interconnect the NATAL author language with the Canadian videotex system TELIDON.

3.2.5 IPS

This Instructional Programming System has been developed by the Simon Fraser University in Canada (Lower, 1980; 1981). It attempts to combine the best features of CAI authoring languages (such as COURSEWRITER and TUTOR) with those other facilities only found in high level programming languages such as APL, PASCAL and SNOBOL. An illustrative section of an IPS lesson is presented in figure 3.6.

```
[1]    BEGIN

[2]    WRITE      'What is the most abundant metallic element'

[3]               'in the earth''s crust?'

[4]    ACCEPT

[5]    SCAN(F)    'al'

[6]    WRITE      'Very good!'

[7]    CALC       COUNT <-  COUNT + 1

[8]    SCAN(B)    'o';'ox'

[9]    WRITE      'Oxygen is the most abundant element,'
[10]              'but it is not a metal.  Please try again.'

[11]   UNREC

[12]   WRITE      'Sorry, I don''t recognise that answer.'

[13]   BEGIN
```

Figure 3.6   Section of an IPS lesson.

In appearance the CAI code in this figure looks very similar to that of the TUTOR system. This similarity is more than just superficial since it extends to the basic statement structure. Each statement consists of a command (either explicit or implicit) followed by its associated operand string. A command may be preceded by a label (for use in branching) and qualified by a modifier (enclosed in parentheses). If required, comments can be appended to the statement following the operand section - compare TUTOR. Commands are of two types: major and minor. Major commands are always executed when they are encountered in the flow of the program. Minor commands always follow a comparison command; they are executed only if the matching operation specified in the associated comparison command is successful.

The BEGIN command (see figure 3.6, line 1) always introduces a group of questions. Following this (line 2) the WRITE statement is used to present text to the student – line 3 contains an implicit WRITE command. At line 4 the student's response is accepted. It is then analysed using the SCAN commands. If the argument of the command in line 5 matches the student's reply, the statements in lines 6 and 7 would be executed. A forward branch (because of the F modifier on ' the SCAN command) would then be made to the next BEGIN statement (line 13). Should the match fail, the statement contained in line 8 would be performed. This time, a successful match (notice there are two options) would cause a remediation message to be printed out (lines 9 and 10) and then a backward branch (because of the B modifier) to the previous ACCEPT command would be taken. If the UNREC command in line 11 is reached, because this always matches, the indicated remedial message would be printed out and program control would then pass on to the next BEGIN group.

IPS is not very different from other authoring languages but does provide facilities to enable randomised selection of problems/text, complex answer analysis (through pattern matching) and the separation of instructional strategy from instructional content. The language is extensible and contains extensive graphic facilities that permit the author to define, store and dynamically relocate screen displays or portions of them. The system is implemented as an interpreter and runs on IBM System/370 type computers (an IBM 4341 is used at Simon Fraser University) under the Michigan Terminal System (MTS). The interpreter for IPS is written in SPITBOL, a fast version of the SNOBOL-4 programming language. It is the facilities available in this language that provides IPS with its powerful capability for answer analysis.

3.3 LANGUAGES AVAILABLE ON MINICOMPUTERS

A steady decrease in the cost of minicomputers has made CAI in college and university environments more popular. This has created the need for authoring systems which do not rely on the large store capacity and the sophisticated software support provided by mainframe computers. Some authoring systems have been developed in order to satisfy this need. In this section we briefly outline a selection of these.

3.3.1 TICCIT
This is an acronym for Time-shared Interactive Computer Controlled Information Television. It is a CAI system that was originally developed by the MITRE Corporation and which is now marketed by Hazeltine in the United States of America (Rappaport and Olenbush, 1975; MITRE Corporation, 1976). The system combines minicomputer and television technology in order to produce highly individualised learner controlled instruction for as many as 128 students. It achieves this through the use of computer-generated colour displays, videotapes, audio facilities and a specially designed interactive keyboard.

The author's interface with the TICCIT system is by way of a series of special authoring forms. These may be computer generated (for on-line courseware production at a VDU) or they may be of the conventional paper variety (for off-line use). These forms act as templates that permit the entry of learning rules (of varying degrees of difficulty), instances and examples. Using these it is possible for the author to construct multi-colour learning frames for display to the student. Other forms are then used to specify how frames are to be displayed and the way in which answers are to be processed. In essence, authoring thus reduces to a sophisticated form-filling exercise. Through these the author is able to control all the learning resources. No knowledge of computer programming is required.

3.3.2 DECAL
This authoring language has been produced by Digital Equipment Corporation (1980) for use on their PDP-11 range of minicomputers. The system is written in BASIC and can be used for all levels of instruction within any subject area. During lesson creation, DECAL prompts the instructor by asking for information and by giving explanations of the options available. In all, there are 15 built-in language elements that enable the teacher to structure the lesson according to its intended application. The lesson can present textual material to a student, provide additional help when requested, anticipate and respond to correct and incorrect answers and dynamically determine the course of the lesson on the basis of the student's responses. In addition, built-in limits can be imposed on the student, thereby restricting the amount of time spent on a given question and the number of attempted answers permitted. Lessons can contain up to 50 segments, can be linked with other lessons to form courses and can be shared among classes or schools.

3.3.3 SAL
Simple Authoring Language is essentially a multimedia authoring facility developed for use on a Hewlett Packard HP-2100 minicomputer having 24K words of store (Henry and Howard, 1977). The original CAI system contained audio-visual learning resources consisting of an audio-cassette player and a slide projector having a rear illuminated screen. In addition, it contained a variety of computer controlled stimulus, measurement and switching instruments.

In order to generate lessons the author prepares a series of slides and a set of ancillary parameters describing how the images are to be used during a teaching session. This control information is then entered into the computer system by means of an on-line dialogue. Two segments of an authoring session dialogue are illustrated in figure 3.7. The left-hand sections of these diagrams show the contents of question slides. Example A illustrates how a simple numeric answer is processed while example B depicts the parameters needed for a multiple-choice question.

The author language acts as a simple program generator. In response to the values entered by the author the generator produces a BASIC program in which the parameters are used as arguments in subroutine calls to general purpose CAI software.

EXAMPLE (A)

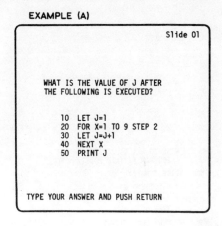

```
                                    Slide 01




    WHAT IS THE VALUE OF J AFTER
    THE FOLLOWING IS EXECUTED?

        10   LET J=1
        20   FOR X=1 TO 9 STEP 2
        30   LET J=J+1
        40   NEXT X
        50   PRINT J



TYPE YOUR ANSWER AND PUSH RETURN
```

```
>LOAD SAL
>RUN
DO YOU NEED INSTRUCTIONS (YES OR NO)?    NO
INPUT APPROXIMATE NUMBER OF QUESTIONS
            IN YOUR LESSON?   2
WHAT IS YOUR FIRST NAME?   RAVINDER
WHAT IS YOUR LAST NAME?   SINGH
WHAT IS THE TITLE OF THE LESSON?   BASIC-8
WHAT IS THE FILE NUMBER?   MTS-23
WHAT IS THE DATE?   25 JAN 1982
DO YOU WISH TO LET STUDENT WRITE A
            PROGRAM AT THIS POINT?   NO
INPUT SLIDE NUMBER?   01
HOW MANY QUESTIONS ON THIS SLIDE?   1
MULTIPLE CHOICE (1) OR NUMERIC (2)
            TYPE ANSWERS?    2
HOW MANY TRIES ALLOWED TO ANSWER QUESTION?   2
WHAT IS THE CORRECT ANSWER (NUMERIC)?   6
RETURN TO AUDIO TUTORING AT THIS POINT
            IN THE LESSON?   NO
IS THERE ANY MORE TO THIS LESSON?   YES
```

Figure 3.7   Authoring with SAL.

EXAMPLE (B)

```
                                              Slide 02

WHAT IS WRONG WITH THE FOLLOWING PROGRAM?


        10   DIM A(5), C(2,3)
        20   LET B(9) =5
        30   FOR T= 1 TO B(9)
        40   PRINT " T = "; T
        50   NEXT T

        1)   NOTHING
        2)   ARRAY B IS NOT DIMENSIONED
        3)   THE LOOP HAS A SYNTAX ERROR
        4)   THERE IS NO END STATEMENT

TYPE YOUR ANSWER AND PUSH RETURN
```

DO YOU WISH TO LET STUDENT WRITE A
           PROGRAM AT THIS POINT?   NO

INPUT SLIDE NUMBER?   02

HOW MANY QUESTIONS ON THIS SLIDE?   1

MULTIPLE CHOICE (1) OR NUMERIC (2)
           TYPE ANSWERS?   1

HOW MANY MULTIPLE CHOICES?   4

HOW MANY TRIES ALLOWED TO ANSWER QUESTION?   2

WHAT IS THE CORRECT CHOICE, ANSWER 1-4?   1

INPUT RESPONSE TO BE PRINTED TO
CORRECT ANSWER ON TRY 1
      ?   THE PROGRAM WILL PRINT 5 VALUES

INPUT RESPONSE TO BE PRINTED TO
CORRECT ANSWER ON TRY 2
      ?   B(10) IS AUTOMATICALLY DIMENSIONED AND
          AN END IS OPTIONAL

INPUT RESPONSE TO INCORRECT ANSWER 2?
      ?   ARRAY B IS AUTOMATICALLY DIMENSIONED AS B(10)

INPUT RESPONSE TO INCORRECT ANSWER 3
      ?   CONSTANTS OR VARIABLES ARE LEGAL SYNTAX

INPUT RESPONSE TO INCORRECT ANSWER 4
      ?   END STATEMENTS ARE OPTIONAL IN BASIC

RETURN TO AUDIO TUTORING AT THIS POINT
              IN THE LESSON?   NO

IS THERE ANY MORE TO THIS LESSON?   NO

Figure 3.7   Continued.

3.3.4 AVCAT

This is an acronym for Audio Visual Computer Aided Tutor. This is a multimedia teaching system based on the use of a minicomputer that is able to support up to 20 individual audio–visual teaching terminals (Goodwood Data Systems, 1980). Figure 5.2 (chapter 5) shows a typical student workstation.

The terminals are quite sophisticated devices. Each contains two rear projection random–access slide–image projectors. The screens upon which they project their images are touch sensitive, thereby enabling students to interact with the system by means of simple pointing operations. Student responses may also be input using a special keypad. The slide projectors each have a capacity for 80 slides. The audio unit associated with the system can store up to 200 messages having an accumulated playing time of 45 minutes. The system uses a special indexing/addressing scheme that enables a random search at 100 times the normal playing speed. When using the system, the student simply enters the pre-prepared slide trays and an audiotape into the system and then invokes a lesson by pressing appropriate buttons on the terminal's keypad (see figure 5.3).

The important feature of the AVCAT system is that the author requires no knowledge of computer technology or programming. Lesson preparation is fairly straightforward since there are facilities to enable the production of new items and the editing of older material. Facilities also exist to permit the introduction of slides, preparation of audiotapes and the entry of branching programs, see section 5.2.2, part (e).

Lessons may contain up to 200 randomly accessible items. Each of these may consist of an audio message accompanied by one or two slide images. The items used in a lesson may be any of five basic types:

(1) instructional - which presents information to the student,
(2) multichoice option - to which the student replies using any of four option keys (labelled A through D) on the keyboard,
(3) numeric question - to which the student responds by entering a numeric value,
(4) touch response - which requires the student to reply by touching an appropriate part of a slide image with his/her finger, and
(5) reinforcement/remedial units - designed to give additional information to a student following a response to a question.

The author prepares a lesson by entering appropriate values on to a specially designed coding form. These are then keyed into the computer system by means of a teletype or visual display unit. An illustration of the lesson preparation form used by the AVCAT author is presented in figure 3.8.

In this example the author is specifying the following instructional strategy. First, slide 2 is presented on the left-hand projector and slide 3 on the right-hand one. These together constitute instructional frames, as indicated by the I contained in column 2, line 1 of the coding form. When this interaction concludes, the right-hand image is replaced by slide 4. Then slides 3 and 5 are presented along with a multiple-choice question (M). The student is given 25 seconds to respond, after which time control passes to line 7 of the program.

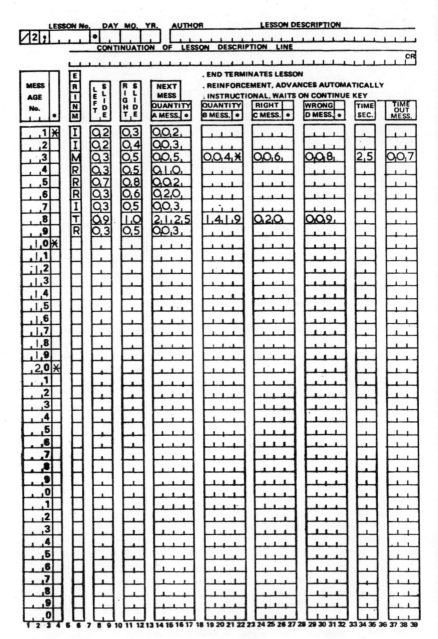

Figure 3.8   An AVCAT multimedia lesson coding form.
(Courtesy of Goodward Data Systems.)

Following the multiple-choice question specified in line 3, the associated remediation and reinforcement units are defined (flagged with an R in lines 4, 5 and 6). Notice that in line 8 the author is specifying that a touch response (T) is required.

The AVCAT approach to multimedia authoring is a reasonable one when there are only a limited number of interaction devices and instructional resources available for lesson preparation and response gathering. However, in more complex systems that have a wider range of peripherals for student input (see figure 1.4), it is unlikely that the coding form approach would be as easy to implement.

3.3.5 STAF - Science Teachers Authoring Facility

This language was originally developed as part of the UK's National Development Programme in Computer Assisted Learning during the period 1974-1977 (Ayscough, 1976a; 1976b; 1977a; 1977b). Although the system was developed mainly for chemists, its facilities are also applicable to the writing of CAL programs in other subject areas. STAF has proved to be highly portable and has been implemented on mainframes, minicomputers and a variety of different microcomputer systems. Both BASIC and FORTRAN have been used for the underlying software, but the FORTRAN version has been the most versatile. The STAF system was updated in 1982. The updated version (Ayscough and Butcher, 1983) retains the original definitions of the language which now provides an extensive range of facilities for authors and permits development of a wide range of individual styles. A very important advantage of the way in which STAF is implemented is that full use may be made of the powerful facilities of FORTRAN for performing computations. Thus, although the language was primarily developed for tutorial purposes it can also be employed for simulation and modelling techniques within the tutorial dialogue if this is desired.

The STAF system has two parts. The first allows teaching programs in the STAF language to be created, validated and modified by teachers. The second interprets these teaching programs and conducts an interactive dialogue with a student at a terminal (see figure 1.5). A response file containing selected student responses and author's comments can be set up if required, for subsequent comparison of responses or assessment of the teaching program.

A STAF program consists of a sequence of nodes - a node is the smallest independent part of a STAF CAI program. Each node has a structure similar to that shown in figure 3.9

NODE LABEL
TEXT
AUTHOR COMMENT

RESPONSE MATCHING
    (a) match type + label
    (b) anticipated responses
        and routings

Figure 3.9   Basic structure of a STAF program node.

A node label is used to identify the node; it also determines whether
or not information from that node is to be sent to a response file.
Everything following the node label (until a command character is
encountered) is regarded as text that is to be output at the student
terminal. For example, the ↑ character causes the text that follows
it to be sent to the response file – until a second ↑ is encountered;
the material between the two ↑ symbols constitutes an author comment.
Student response matching is achieved by specifying (1) the type of
match and its level, (2) the anticipated responses that are to be
accepted or rejected and, (3) the action to be taken when a match
occurs or is unsuccessful. Decimal digits within the matching criteria
specification can be used to control how exactly the match is to be
made: the greater the digit, the closer the matching has to be.
Standard digits are used to disallow the following features: extra
words (4), wrong order of words (2), extra letters in a word (1). A
match is not made unless it complies with the anticipated response at
the required level. Digits are added to increase the strictness of the
matching; only 7 requires an exact match of student input and
anticipated response. For example, in the following node:

> #B55;0*
> WHAT IS HEAT A FORM OF?
> @7 ENERGY /C80; /C75;

the label is #B55;0* and the text is 'WHAT IS HEAT A FORM OF?'. The
third line in the node is the response matching command and option.
The symbol @ means 'if the student input is' while the second symbol
(the decimal digit 7) specifies a very strict match, requiring an
exact correspondence of all characters. Both /C80 and /C75 are routing
parameters. The response matching part of the above node thus states:
if the student input is exactly the word ENERGY then go to node C80,
otherwise, go to node C75.

A simple illustration of a STAF CAI program is presented in figure
3.10. This program contains ten nodes of which A10 and A50 contain
both text and response matching parts, and illustrate the use of
different matching options. Node A10 asks the student 'What is the
capital city of the United States?' and then compares his/her response '
for an exact match with WASHINGTON. If successful, a jump is made to
node A20 (a reinforcement node). If the reply contained WASHNTN a
jump is made to node A30, otherwise to A40. From nodes A20, A30 and
A40 control then passes to node A50 - the next question node. In reply to
the second question, an exact match is expected for NEW YORK; a
different routing is followed if the reply was one of the other five
most populous cities (CHICAGO ... DETROIT) or any other form of reply.
The special subroutine $TM in node A99 terminates execution; the
physical end of the program is marked by two consecutive # symbols.

```
#A10; 0*
 WHAT IS THE CAPITAL CITY OF THE UNITED STATES ?
 @7WASHINGTON\A20;  @0WASHNTN\A30;   \A40;
#A20; 0*
 THATS RIGHT.  \A50;
#A30; 0*
 YES - BUT IT IS SPELT WASHINGTON.  \A50;
#A40; 0*
 NO, WASHINGTON.   \A50;
#A50; 0*
 WHICH UNITED STATES CITY HAS THE LARGEST POPULATION ?
 @1NEW YORK\A60;
 @0CHICAGO$LOSANGS$PHILA$HOUSTN$DETROIT\A70; \A80;
#A60; 0*
 YES - POPULATION 7. 48 MILLION.   \A99;
#A70; 0*
 NO, THIS IS ONE OF THE MOST POPULOUS CITIES, BUT \A90;
#A80; 0*
 NOT EVEN CLOSE.   \A90;
#A90; 0*
 NEW YORK HAS THE LARGEST POPULATION.  \A99;
#A99; 0*
 PROGRAM ENDS.  \$TM; *
##
```

Figure 3.10   A simple STAF CAI program.

STAF also provides counters which can store information or number
responses, keep scores of correct answers or control routing to
subsequent nodes. They also provide a simple calculating language for
use by the author in conjunction with subroutines. Many STAF
subroutines are available, enabling the author to use FORTRAN
functions (for example, SQRT, EXP, SIN), generate random numbers or
keep a record of the time spent in particular nodes. They enable the
construction of structured STAF programs using sub-files which can
also invoke special FORTRAN or BASIC subroutines. These subroutines
can thus enhance the calculating power of STAF to almost anything
conceivable for processing numerical input, simulation of experiments,
performance of special functions available in systems libraries or use
of graphics.

STAF has been extensively used within many UK universities and polytechnics for writing courseware for teaching chemistry (Ayscough, 1977a). We have also been investigating its use for the teaching of a variety of subjects at school level using microcomputer systems. The results of this work are described elsewhere (Wilford and Barker, 1983).

3.3.6 CICERO

CICERO is an authoring system that has been developed by the UK's Open University in order to generate tutorial CAL (Jones and O'Shea, 1982; Lockwood and Cooper, 1980). The courseware produced by CICERO provides students with diagnostic feedback and remedial help and can also be used as a revision tool. CICERO tutorials can be accessed at any of the Open University study centres by means of interactive terminals connected to a remote computer through the public switched telephone network.

A section of a typical student dialogue with a CICERO tutorial package is illustrated in figure 3.11. Prior to the segment that is shown, some initial 'profile' questions have already been asked; the purpose of these was to establish the student's familiarity with the material to be presented. In the diagram, the student's input to the courseware is circled; a number following a response indicates a confidence rating for that answer.

The system is adaptive in the sense that textual material (normally in the form of questions) is presented to students by the computer, the student makes a response and the computer's next presentation then depends on the student's answer. CICERO, like most other authoring systems, achieves its adaptive quality by using 'frames' of information and multiple choice questions.

Two important aspects of the CICERO system that the Open University were interested in studying were (1) evaluation of effectiveness, and (2) student take up. It was thought that (a) positive and supportive student comment, and (b) continued student use of the tutorial material could be used as reasonable measures of worth. Consequently, each of these items was used to assess the merits of CICERO courseware. Student comments could be gathered through the system itself by means of an electronic mail facility. Similarly, since the system keeps complete records of the use of all tutorials, these could be used to help in the assessment of the courseware on an item by item basis. Unfortunately, the CICERO evaluations that have been made (Jones and O'Shea, 1982; Lockwood and Cooper, 1980) do not provide any conclusive evidence in favour of the added value gained from computer based tutorials, in the type of environment in which they were employed by the Open University.

Concept ONE.
METHODS OF STUDY.

Your performance on this concept is definitely not good enough.
You are not confident enough when you are right!!
At least you are not too confident when you are wrong.
Let's see what help CICERO can give you...
Try a few more questions.

Try this question on methods...

Which of the following best describes the cross-sectional approach?
  A) Studies individuals through time, taking measurements at periodic intervals.
  B) Studies a few individuals in depth.
  C) Studies a particular group of individuals at one time.
  D) Studies several different groups of individuals through time.
  E) Studies individuals in a controlled laboratory environment.
(+ A)

You missed the correct answer, (C)
Remember, the cross-sectional approach takes a cross-section of the population (often
a particular age group) and then compares it with another cross-section (a different
age group perhaps) to see the difference between the two. (In this case the difference
that age makes.)

Would you like brief explanation of any of the wrong option(s)?
(+ YES)

Type in the letters of the option(s) you want explained.
(+ D)

D represents a combination of the cross-sectional and the longitudinal approaches.
It is often known as the convergence approach.
Would you like to have a question on the three main methods now?
(+ YES)

Figure 3.11   A typical CICERO tutorial dialogue.
(Courtesy of the Open University.)

3.3.7 ACL – Author Command Language
All   organisations   are   dependent   upon   effective   and   efficient
administration   for their smooth running. The 'office' is the accepted
place   where   administration   and   planning   is   normally   undertaken.
Because of their importance, training in office skills and procedures
is an important consideration for most organisations. It is   easy   to
see   that   this   is   an   area   where   computer   based   training   could
effectively be employed.

One large training company that has   realised   the   potential   of   the
computer   in   this   area   is Speedwriting/Speedtyping Ltd (1983). This

company has developed a minicomputer based system (using a DEC 11/34)
for teaching a variety of office skills, particularly, speedwriting
and speedtyping.

Speedwriting is a shorthand method based on the ordinary letters of
the alphabet. It was developed in the 1920s by Emma Dearborn in
response to demands for an easier shorthand system. The motivation for
its development arose because many people were unable to master
conventional   symbol   shorthands such as Pitman and Gregg. The
speedwriting system that was developed was based on ordinary
alphabetic letters and is now taught in most languages throughout the
world. It is now a recognised office skill.

In a controlled experiment to investigate this technique, the UK's
Royal Air Force reported dramatic savings in learning time (Edwards,
1979). They were able to reduce shorthand training time from 16 weeks
to 8 weeks, improve average speeds from 80 words per minute to 100
words per minute and improve the pass rate from 70% to 90%. The
critical factor from the viewpoint of the investigators was time; a
saving of eight weeks on a course represented a considerable financial
benefit.

Having learned the theory of the speedwriting shorthand method it is
essential that a student is able to transcribe shorthand notes on to a
typewriter or word processing (Simons, 1981) system. Conventional
shorthand theory takes approximately 18 weeks to learn, during which
time, the student is easily able to master the basic keyboard skills
necessary. However, at Speedwriting Ltd, the shorthand theory stage is
completed in just four weeks.

Over the years the company has used various audio–visual devices in
their keyboard skills training but have never felt that they were more
than reasonably attractive training aids. Consequently, Speedwriting
decided that they required a CAL system which would:

> (1) display information,
> (2) test the students' understanding of the information,
> (3) provide multiple–choice question formats, fill in
>   missing words and answer true/false questions,
> (4) record the students' responses,
> (5) route the student forward or backward through the
>   course material depending upon his/her response, and
> (6) analyse group records to make certain that the
>   display of information was itself not the cause of
>   any student errors.

The software development – including the authoring system – was
contracted out to a software house (Syadon Limited). The Author
Command Language (ACL) that was developed helps the student in two
areas: speed and accuracy. Students work at Lyme 4003 interactive

video terminals and are required to type exercises within certain time limits and error ranges. The exercise which the student attempts and an analysis of his/her performance are then displayed on the VDU screen. Depending upon this performance (and the criteria specified by the author) the student would be moved forward or, if unsuccessful, backward for extra practice or other remedial action.

The system also offers many benefits for the instructors. At least one third of an instructor's time is spent on tasks (mainly management) that are not directly related to the teaching of the course. These management functions include:

> registration of students,
> preparation of progress reports,
> marking and assessment, and
> preparation and evaluation of lessons.

Within the ACL system the computer takes over the duties of 'course manager'. When a new group of students is about to begin the course the registration program is used to enter their basic details. This information is then updated by the computer as the student progresses through the course. Simple interactive dialogues can then be used to transfer a student's records from one class to another, register the student on another course programme and modify the student's stored details.

Another important management program is that which provides the student print-out facility. A printed copy of the student's detailed progress report can be requested for evaluation and summary. The print-out gives details of the dates of attendance, the exercises that have been attempted and the results that have been obtained, both in terms of words/minute and the number of errors made. By further analysis these errors can be separated into categories and the type of remedial drill exercises needed can then be determined. The error categories include: wrong character or word, added character or word and transposed characters and words.

One of the reasons for the success of the CAL system is the simplicity of the author language which consists of only 12 easily understood commands. These simple commands and an explanation of their function is given in table 3.1 (Labinger, 1980). For every lesson, there is a file of 'frames' and a file of author commands. The students see the frames but never see any of the author commands. A section of a lesson written in ACL is presented in figure 3.12. The CAL program is shown on the left-hand side of the diagram and the frames that are to be used in conjunction with this code are depicted on the right.

The structure of the statements from which the program is constructed is fairly straightforward. Statements consist of one or more keywords with user selected variables and/or constants interspersed between

them. Labels, when present in a statement, appear on the extreme left–
hand side and are separated from the immediately following keyword   by
one or more spaces. Most of the keywords used in the program listed in
figure   3.12   are   presented (along with a description of the function
they perform) in table 3.1. A brief description of the   way   in   which
the program operates is given below.

Table 3.1   Command Keywords used in ACL

Command	Use
DISPLAY	Display a frame of information or instructions
RETAIN	Add a second frame to the screen without removing the first
SET	This command has a calculating function. The computer is told to convert its raw material, such as time taken to type a drill, into words per minute, or to add a number to an error count
READ	To alert the system that the student's work must be read and timed
ANALYSE	Compares the student's work with the model copy of the exercise
STORE	Commands the computer to record the results of the student's effort in its memory
COUNT	This counts the number of attempts at an exercise which were needed by the student before the target results were achieved. This is used for evaluating progress and level of difficulty
PREPARE	Insertion of student's results into a feedback frame
INFORM	Inform the student of the above results
GOTO	To move the student forward or backward in the course depending upon the results of his/her efforts
CALL TUTOR	Alerts the Tutor to a particular student who is in need of assistance
EXIT	When the student has finished the lesson with satisfactory results the computer moves on to the next lesson

In   line   2   the value of the variable 'attempts' is set to zero; this
variable is used to record the number of times   the   student   attempts
the training task. The DISPLAY statement in line 3 then causes frame 1
to be displayed on the VDU screen; the RETAIN statement then allows
the second frame to be overlayed onto the   first,   that   is,   the   two
appear   on the screen simultaneously, as soon as the DISPLAY statement
in line 5 is executed. Once the   student   starts   to   type,   the   READ
statement   causes   the system to record the time taken for the student
to type the three lines of text contained   in   frame   2.   The   STROKES
command   causes   the   computer   to   calculate   the student's speed (in
words/minute) to be calculated. If this   is   less   than   ten,   control

branches to the statement labelled 'many' – causing frame 8 to be displayed – with a subsequent branch to the point 'retry'. Provided the student's typing speed is acceptable, the material that has been typed is then analysed for five categories of error (see line 10). The results of the analysis are then stored (line 11) in the student record file. In line 12 the total number of errors is calculated and the result examined by the series of IF statements contained in lines 17 through 20, branches then being made to points that provide appropriate diagnostic or reinforcement messages.

```
CPR - *** Speedwriting -- Syadon *** - C001-02D  9-MAY-83 10:08


 1 -                    ;lesson 2D   acl
 2 - begin:   SET attempts TO 0
 3 - retry:   DISPLAY 1:1:1:-1
 4 -          RETAIN
 5 -          DISPLAY 2:3:3:-1
 6 -          FLUSH INPUT
 7 -          READ time:4:3:3:360
 8 -          STROKES chars
 9 -          IF (chars .LT. 10)  GOTO many
10 -          ANALYSE 1 2 [cat1:cat2:cat3:cat4:cat5] 120
11 -          STORE ::time:cat1:cat2:cat3:cat4:cat5
12 -          SET errs TO (cat1+cat2+cat3+cat4+cat5)
13 -          IF (errs .GT. 20)  GOTO many
14 -          COUNT attempts
15 -          PREPARE errs
16 -          RETAIN
17 -          IF (errs .EQ. 0)        GOTO end
18 -          IF (errs .EQ. 1)        GOTO loop
19 -          IF (errs .LE. 3)        GOTO next
20 -          IF (attempts .LE. 3)    GOTO here
21 -          INFORM 6:14:1:0
22 -          GOTO exit
23 - loop:    DISPLAY 4:14:1:0
24 -          GOTO exit
25 - next:    INFORM 5:14:1:0
26 -          GOTO exit
27 - here:    INFORM 7:14:1:0
28 -          GOTO retry
29 - end:     DISPLAY 3:14:1:0
30 -          GOTO exit
31 - many:    DISPLAY 8:-1:1:0
32 -          GOTO retry
33 - exit:    EXIT
```

Figure 3.12 Format of an ACL training program and its associated instructional frames.
(Courtesy of Speedwriting/Speedtyping.)

```
<- FRAME 01 ->                    ; lesson 2D

1                     Copy the following exactly:   (START type STOP)
```

```
<- FRAME 02 ->

1          jus jar lus slus jus jar lus slus jus jar lus slus
2          saul had a full slass jus; saul had a full slass jus;
3          a suard had a jaffa salad; a suard had a jaffa salad;
```

```
<- FRAME 03 ->

1          Well done! An error-free piece of work.  Press Next Frame.
```

```
<- FRAME 04 ->

1          Well done! Just one error on this exercise is very sood.
2          Press Next Frame.
```

```
<- FRAME 05 ->

1          On this exercise you have made %D mistakes.  Check that
2          you can spot them.  Then press Next Frame.
```

```
<- FRAME 06 ->

1          You have made %D mistakes on this attempt.  Slow down to achieve
2          a sood level of accuracy.  Now for your next exercise.  Go on.
```

```
<- FRAME 07 ->

1          You have made %D mistakes this time.  Try asain to produce a
2          perfect copy.   Press Next Frame.
```

```
<- FRAME 08 ->

1          You have made far too many errors for this to be considered
2          a serious attempt.  Try asain.  Press Next Frame.
```

Figure 3.12   Continued.
(Courtesy of Speedwriting/Speedtyping.)

The lesson shown in figure 3.12 is aimed at improving the student's
typing accuracy. This lesson is one of 22 that constitute a three part
course organised as follows:

Part 1:	Basic keyboard skills	(lessons 1–12)
Part 2:	Dexterity skills	(lessons 12–16)
Part 3:	Speed development	(lessons 17–22)

The Speedwriting/Speedtyping authoring system (ACL) provides a very useful example of the way in which computer assisted learning can be employed in a commercial training situation. Some further examples of similar systems will be described later in the book.

3.4 LANGUAGES AVAILABLE ON MICROCOMPUTERS

The low cost of microcomputer systems now enables CAI and CAL to be used in areas which were hitherto difficult to explore using the kinds of system described in the previous sections. The new areas of interest include primary and secondary education as well as special schools for the physically and mentally handicapped. The home environment also provides another outlet for this approach to learning. The widespread availability of microcomputers could indeed mean that they might become an important medium for CAI instruction. In view of this, there has been renewed interest in the development of simple authoring systems. This has resulted in many attempts to make author languages available on micros. Some of these languages allow only lesson delivery mode with actual authoring being done on larger machines. This approach may be used to provide low–cost delivery of quality courseware. However, a totally micro–based system (authoring and delivery) is often more desirable for those who wish to develop their own materials locally. In this section we describe some of the current approaches to author language provision on micros.

3.4.1 PILOT

This author language was developed in the early 1970s by John Starkweather in the USA. Since its original formulation (as the PILOT–73 standard) and development on an Intel 8080 system, many new implementations have become available – TINY PILOT, PILOT/P, COMMON PILOT, APPLE PILOT, PET PILOT and so on. Each of these is described and documented in the computing literature (Keyser, 1979; Gerhold and Kheriaty, 1980; Mundie, 1980; Kamp and Gomberg, 1980; Conlon, 1984). Some of the more appealing features of the language include the following:

(1) several ad hoc standards exist (for example, COMMON PILOT) so that this could form the basis for a unified standard;
(2) it is available on a large number of microcomputers such as the TRS–80, PET, APPLE, Intel, Motorola, etc. It is also available on a number of minicomputers;
(3) a number of programming languages (PASCAL, FORTRAN, BASIC) act as hosts which support PILOT interpreters;
(4) it has a relatively small number of commands (about 10) so that it is easy to learn and implement;
(5) there is a large amount of courseware available; and
(6) courseware exchange schemes exist to facilitate the interchange of materials (PILOT Exchange, 1981; Wood, 1981).

A brief introduction to PILOT was presented in chapter 2 (see section
2.4.3). An illustrative CAI program written in this language was given
in figure 2.9. PILOT permits the construction of dialogue-orientated
lessons. The language allows the author to create a variety of CAI
strategies through the use of very simple commands such as:

T: to type text on the VDU screen,
A: to accept an answer from the student,
M: to perform a matching operation,
J: to jump to another section of the program,
R: to enable program annotation (remarks),
C: to compute a value.

Other, more sophisticated commands, are also available (Conlon, 1984).

Because of the limitation of pure text as a teaching medium, many
attempts have been made to exploit sound and visual images as
ancillary learning media. Consequently, several non-standard
extensions to PILOT are currently being implemented. Thus, on versions
of PILOT used on the APPLE microcomputer there are additional
commands:

S: ‹pitch› ‹duration›
G: ‹description›

for sound generation and plotting graphics (Conlon, 1984). We are
currently examining the feasibility of adding extensions to PILOT that
will facilitate the incorporation of audio-visual media (slide
projectors, tape recorders, etc) and a number of different kinds of
interaction device – light pen, joystick, hand-print terminal and
special units for the handicapped (Barker, 1982a; 1982b; 1983b).

3.4.2 MICROTEXT
This is a frame-orientated authoring system currently being developed
by the National Physical Laboratory in the United Kingdom (Bevan and
Watson, 1982). MICROTEXT is a microcomputer implementation of a
dialogue programming language called EDUTEXT (Watson and Bevan, 1980;
National Physical Laboratory, 1982). The MICROTEXT system comprises a
simple but very powerful author language combined with a wide range of
author aids. Material to be presented can quickly be edited and
reorganised, and its use can be controlled and monitored by the
testing and tracing facilities that are provided. MICROTEXT can be
used for almost any interactive application which presents text to the
user and prompts for a reply. Commands can be incorporated to generate
graphs and charts automatically, and to control special hardware such
as clocks, timers, slide projectors and video tape recorders.
MICROTEXT packages are stored as ordinary text which is independent of
any particular hardware, so that dialogues are portable between
machines with equivalent facilities. Teaching material can be prepared
on conventional word processing equipment since facilities exist to

transfer files between different computing systems.

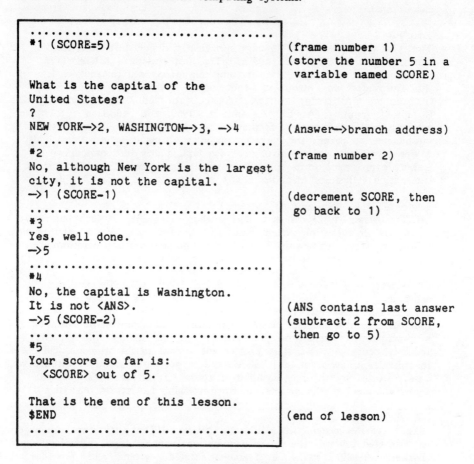

```
.....................................
#1 (SCORE=5)                              (frame number 1)
                                          (store the number 5 in a
                                           variable named SCORE)
What is the capital of the
United States?
?
NEW YORK—>2, WASHINGTON—>3, —>4           (Answer—>branch address)
.....................................
#2                                        (frame number 2)
No, although New York is the largest
city, it is not the capital.
—>1 (SCORE-1)                             (decrement SCORE, then
.....................................      go back to 1)
#3
Yes, well done.
—>5
.....................................
#4
No, the capital is Washington.
It is not <ANS>.                          (ANS contains last answer
—>5 (SCORE-2)                             (subtract 2 from SCORE,
.....................................      then go to 5)
#5
Your score so far is:
  <SCORE> out of 5.

That is the end of this lesson.
$END                                      (end of lesson)
.....................................
```

Figure 3.13 Format of a MICROTEXT CAI program.
(Courtesy of the National Physical Laboratory.)

Two versions of MICROTEXT currently exist; one of these runs on the Commodore PET series of computers while the other is designed for use on the BBC microcomputer (Commodore Business Machines, 1980; British Broadcasting Corporation, 1982). Versions of MICROTEXT for other micro–systems are currently under development. The format of a simple lesson written in this language is depicted in figure 3.13. In this example, MICROTEXT will display the text of the first frame and then wait for the student to answer the question. If the answer is NEW YORK control passes to frame 2, if WASHINGTON to frame 3, while, if any other answer is given, a branch is made (by default) to frame 4. Frames 2, 3, and, 4 all branch on to another frame without waiting for any further user input. The lesson terminates when the $END command is encountered.

3.4.3 PASS

This is an authoring language specifically designed for multimedia training systems (DELTAK, 1981). The host system, MICRO/DV, incorporates text, audio, video and computer based instruction. It thus provides an integrated four-media training facility. PASS (Professional Authoring Software System) runs on a stand-alone APPLE II microcomputer (APPLE Computers, 1980). In addition to the conventional authoring facilities it also provides appropriate mechanisms to permit the operation of a multimedia controller. This device facilitates the control of video tape, video disc, audio tape and slide-projection units. Similar systems have been described by International Business Machines (1981) and Brandt and Knapp (1979).

3.4.4 MCSD - Modular CAI System Delft

MCSD (Mast, 1982) is not an author language as such but really represents an authoring system based upon the use of a mainframe computer (for courseware development) and a series of microcomputers (for lesson delivery). It is thus a hybrid system.

Courseware is developed and tested on an IBM 370/158 mainframe computer using a special author language called PLANIT (Frye, 1970). Once lessons have been developed they are compiled into a machine independent intermediate code. This is then transferred using a minicomputer system to the target micros. Special interpreters, resident within these, then present the lessons to the students. The interpreters are written in PASCAL and so are transportable. Student data collected by the micros during a course of instruction are passed back (via tape) to the mainframe for processing and result reporting.

3.4.5 MUMEDALA

Like the PASS system, MUMEDALA (MUlti MEDia Authoring LAnguage) is orientated towards the use of conventional audio-visual technology (Barker, 1983b). It is a frame-orientated system and provides facilities for displaying instructional material on several channels simultaneously. It differs from conventional CAI systems in that it emphasises the use of a wide variety of interaction devices (see figure 5.27).

From the point of view of the author there are three general modes of interaction: frame creation, lesson creation and system interrogation. When in the first of these modes, the author creates a series of numbered VDU frames. These may belong to any of five primitive classes: instructional, remedial, reinforcing, testing and help. Once created and numbered, the frames are stored in a local data base (and possibly archived on a remote computer system). The VDU frames may be supported by ancillary sound and graphic units or diversions to on-line equipment.

When the frame creation session terminates, the author enters lesson creation mode. During this part of the authoring process the author specifies the order in which frames are to be presented and the way in which ancillary resources are to be controlled in order to support the learning process. Once a lesson becomes operational the author may enter the third mode - system interrogation. Using this mode of interaction it is possible to determine the progress being made by individual students and the way in which the instructional resources are being used. A more detailed description of the design features and architecture of the MUMEDALA system is presented in chapter 5.

3.4.6 CYCLOPS
This is an audio-visual presentation system developed by the UK's Open University (Read, 1978). It uses a domestic television receiver and audio-cassette unit as a means of presenting graphic/sonic information to students who are studying at home.

The CYCLOPS unit is a microprocessor based system that plugs directly into an ordinary TV set. It then uses the CRT screen of the TV to display graphic information obtained from a tape held within its built-in audio-cassette unit. At the same time a sound commentary is presented. This is played to the student via the TV's loudspeaker system.

The graphic information is stored on the audio-tape in the form of computer programs. These occupy one of the two available tracks. The microprocessor embedded within the CYCLOPS unit reads the program channel and converts the stored instructions into images for display on the TV screen. The second channel on the tape carries the sound commentary that accompanies the graphic display.

The authoring station (or production studio) contains a conventional visual display unit (for text input), a TV camera and digitising tablet (to enable the input of graphic material), and a TV receiver for information display. Altogether, there are four ways in which graphic material can be created: (1) by typing in characters through the ASCII [1] keyboard, these are stored in a computer file and then relayed to the TV screen; (2) via the TV camera which is used to photograph material, the resultant picture is then decomposed into small squares and stored in the computer file; (3) by means of the digitising tablet; and (4) by writing programs in a special graphics language.

The author prepares materials with the aid of a computer system, there is no author language as such. A sound commentary is recorded on one

---

[1]   This is an acronym for American Standard Code for Information Interchange; it is a coding system employed by the majority of computer systems (Lamb, 1983).

of the tracks of the tape; the graphical information (as computer
programs) is then added to the other track. The sound information is
synchronised with the visual information so that a fully coordinated
presentation is obtained. When complete, the tape is sent to the
student who inserts it into the CYCLOPS unit attached to his/her TV
set. Instruction can then commence. This technique obviously offers
one solution to the problem of disseminating courseware material (see
section 2.6).

3.5 AUTHOR LANGUAGE EVALUATION

As has happened in the past, the future development of CAI courseware
is likely to continue in two distinct directions. Conventional
programming languages (PASCAL, BASIC, APL and others) will continue to
be used. There is also likely to be renewed interest in the use of
author languages, particularly for use with microcomputer systems.
Indeed, several new languages of this type have recently been reported
in the literature. If the popularity of this approach increases, a
number of problems may need to be addressed. One of the most important
of these will be that of author language evaluation.

Unfortunately, there is not an extensive amount of published material
available (either guidelines or results) on the objective evaluation
of author languages for CAI. This state of affairs probably exists
because of the complex nature of the tasks involved and the number of
facets that need to be considered. There are at least ten major
factors that should figure prominently in any evaluative study. These
are summarised below:

   (1) THE AUTHOR'S VIEW
       Is it easy to use?

       Does it provide the facilities that are required without
       the need for undue effort on the part of the author?

       Does it provide adequate monitoring facilities?

       Is it possible to modify/update materials easily in the
       light of experience with them?

   (2) THE STUDENT'S VIEW
       Does it permit the generation of highly individualised
       instructional schemes tailored to the particular needs
       of each student?

       Do these stimulate interest, improve understanding and
       allow active participation in the learning process?

(3) EFFECTIVENESS
Does the author language permit improved author
productivity and enhanced student learning?

(4) COST FACTORS
For the job that it does, how expensive is it to (a)
produce the tools for instruction (the supporting media)
and (b) develop the courseware?

(5) AVAILABILITY
How accessible is the language (and the system in
which it is likely to be embedded) to those who
wish to use it?

(6) PORTABILITY
Can the language easily be made available on other
machines?   That is, can it be moved from one computer
to another without difficulty?

(7) EXTENSIBILITY
How easily can the language be extended to accommodate
new features and new facilities?

(8) TECHNICAL FEATURES
What instructional modes are permitted?

What types of communication media are supported?

(9) DOCUMENTATION AND TECHNICAL SUPPORT
Is the author language adequately documented, that is,
does a language reference manual exist?

Does the language supplier provide adequate technical
support in the event of software errors arising?

(10) COURSEWARE AVAILABILITY
Does the author language supplier also supply a range
of off–the–shelf courseware units?

Is there a network of courseware exchange centres
available to facilitate software exchange?

In an attempt to obtain an objective assessment of some of the
previously listed author languages we have examined an extensive
number of reports and research papers. The majority of these devote
only minor attention to the problem of assessing authoring tools. Most
of the evaluations only enabled us to arrive at qualitative views on
whether such languages are useful or not. For example, with respect to
TUTOR, Hody and Avner (1978) comment: 'As the PLATO community
increased in size, commands and new features were added to TUTOR in

response both to user requests and to data   from   student   and   author
interactions.   The   resulting   language   is   now   rather   complex   and
difficult to master completely.' They then go on to cite the views   of
one   of   the many PLATO users: 'To learn the first steps in TUTOR – how
to set up drill and practice lessons for instance – is unusually easy.
To do anything complex, however, requires you to learn the bulk of the
TUTOR language.'

In a slightly contrasting way, Davies   et   al.   (1977)   have   written:
'TUTOR is useful for a diversity of purposes. It is simple enough that
it   can   be   used   by   elementary school students and by inexperienced
teachers,   yet   it   provides   enough   power   to   allow   sophisticated
programming that takes advantage of the large CDC machine to which all
terminals   are   linked.' Some evaluations of the PLATO system (Jenkins
and Dankert, 1981) completely ignore this aspect of system evaluation.

Other author languages have been evaluated in   an   analogous   fashion.
Thus,   some   years   ago,   Lower   and   Arsenault   (1972)   performed   a
functional evaluation of COURSEWRITER III. Their results are cited   in
a   later   work   when   Lower   (1977)   writes: 'Because it has failed to
evolve with the needs and practices of CAI,   it   is   now   regarded   as
somewhat obsolete and in my view is certainly not adequate for general
purpose   CAI.' This criticism of COURSEWRITER is also supported by the
findings of Yobb (1977).

The   lack   of   objective   assessment   of   languages   available   on
microcomputers   is much more apparent, probably because they have only
recently started to become widely available. At present,   PILOT   seems
to   be   the one which is most commonly used. About this language Lower
(1977) has written: 'Although PILOT will no   doubt   be   popular   among
computer hobbyists, I do not regard the language as a good model for a
future   CAI   authoring   language.   It   seems   likely   that   the   rapid
development of hardware technology will soon eliminate   the   need   for
such a limited language.'

An   attempt   to   evaluate the merits of PILOT objectively as an author
language has been made by Barker and Singh (1983). They   conducted   an
experiment that was designed to expose a variety of potential users to
the   language;   the   views   of   the various user populations were then
solicited by means of   a   questionnaire.   Of   the   four   test   groups
involved, only two reported that they found PILOT easy to use; both of
these groups had had significant previous experience of computers.

From   what   has   been   said above, it is easy to see that the problem of
evaluation is not insignificant. Furthermore, as systems   become   more
complex   (with   respect   to   both   the interactions and the roles they
support), the problem is not likely to get easier. In the   long   term,
popularity   may   prove   to be the best evaluative measure, at least in
the context of micro–systems.

3.6 CONCLUSION

In this chapter a number of author languages (running on small, medium and large computers) have been briefly described. We do not claim that the treatment we have presented is in any way comprehensive. Instead, our objective has been to give our readers an indication of some of the types of facility that are likely to be encountered when systems of this type are used. The problems of author language evaluation have also been briefly outlined. Unfortunately, this topic is so immense that only the surface has been scratched.

In this chapter we have suggested that author languages should include facilities for the provision of multimedia CAL. Because of its growing importance this is a topic to which we return in subsequent sections of this book.

3.7 BIBLIOGRAPHY

Aird, C.L., Comments on computer assisted instruction, The Arabian Journal of Science and Engineering, 2(1), 51–53, 1976.

APPLE Computer, APPLE II – The DOS Manual, Disk Operating System, Cupertino, CA, 1980.

Aston, M., New technologies for education, Computer Age, 4, 67–69, 1980.

Atherton, R., The new languages (PASCAL, COMAL), Computer Bulletin, Series II, (29), 21–22, 1981.

Ayscough, P.B., Computer assisted learning – boon or burden? Chemistry in Britain, 12, 348–352, 1976a.

Ayscough, P.B., Computer assisted learning in chemistry: an exercise in evaluation, Computers and Education, 1, 47–53, 1976b.

Ayscough, P.B., CALCHEM Final Report, Department of Physical Chemistry, University of Leeds, 1977a.

Ayscough, P.B., CALCHEMistry, British Journal of Educational Technology, 8, 201–213, 1977b.

Ayscough, P.B., STAF Author Guide – A Guide to the Use of the STAF System and Language in Computer Assisted Learning, Department of Physical Chemistry, University of Leeds, 1981.

Ayscough, P.B. and Butcher, P.G., STAF2 Reference Manual, Department of Physical Chemistry, University of Leeds, 1983.

Barker, P.G., The computer as an audio–visual resource, Computers and Education, 3, 23–34, 1979.

Barker, P.G., A CAI interface for the disabled, Working Paper, Interactive Systems Research Group, Department of Computer Science, Teesside Polytechnic, County Cleveland, 1982a.

Barker, P.G., Data base interaction using a hand print terminal, International Journal of Man–Machine Studies, 17, 435–458, 1982b.

Barker, P.G., Data bases and data centres, in Computers in Analytical Chemistry, 366–391, Pergamon Press (Volume 6 in Pergamon Series in Analytical Chemistry), Oxford, 1983a.

Barker, P.G., MUMEDALA – an approach to multimedia authoring, in Proceedings of the Fourth Canadian Instructional Technology Conference, Winnipeg, Canada, October 19–22, 317–324, National Research Council of Canada, Ottawa, 1983b.

Barker, P.G. and Singh, R., A practical introduction to authoring for computer assisted instruction. Part II – PILOT, British Journal of Educational Technology, 14, 15–41, 1983.

Barker, P.G. and Yeates, H., Problems associated with multimedia data bases, British Journal of Educational Technology, 12, 158–175, 1981.

Bevan, N. and Watson, R., MICROTEXT Reference Manual, (V2.0C Preliminary Edition), Division of Information Technology and Computing, National Physical Laboratory, Teddington, 1982.

Bitzer, D.L., The wide world of computer based education, Advances in Computers, 15, 239–281, 1976.

Brahan, J.W. and Godfrey, D., A marriage of convenience: Videotex and computer assisted learning, Computers and Education, 6, 33–38, 1982.

Brahan, J.W., Henneker, W.H. and Hlady, A.M., NATAL–74 – concept to reality, in Proceedings of the Third Canadian Symposium on Instructional Technology, Vancouver, February 27–29, 230–240, 1980.

Brandt, R.C. and Knapp, B.H., Video computer authoring system, University of Utah, UT, 1979.

British Broadcasting Corporation, The BBC Microcomputer User Guide, (written by J. Coll and edited by D. Allen), London, 1982.

Bunderson, C.V., COURSEWARE, in Computer Based Instruction: A State-of-the-Art Assessment, 91–125, Academic Press, New York, NY, 1981.

Bunderson, C.V., Gibbons, A.S., Olsen, J.B. and Kearsley, G.P., Work Models: Beyond Instructional Objectives, Instructional Science, 10, 205–215, 1981.

Carbonell, J.R., AI in CAI: an artifical intelligence approach to computer assisted instruction, IEEE Transactiona on Man–Machine Systems, MMS–11(4), 190–202, 1970.

Christensen, B.R., A Short Survey of COMAL–80, State Teachers College, Tonder, Denmark, 1981.

Clocksin, W.F. and Mellish, C.S., Programming in PROLOG, Springer–Verlag, Heidelberg, 1981.

Commodore Business Machines, PET Series 8000 Users's Guide, Publication No. 320894, Commodore Business Machines, Santa Clara, CA, 1980.

Conlon, T., PILOT – The Language and How to Use it, Prentice–Hall International, Englewood Cliffs, NJ, 1984.

Davies, R.B., Dugdale, S., Kibbey, S. and Weaver, C., Representing knowledge about mathematics for computer aided teaching. Part II – The diversity of roles that a computer can play in assisting learning, in Machine Intelligence, 8, edited by E.W. Elcock and D. Michie, 387–421, Edinburgh University Press, Edinburgh, 1977.

DELTAK, Delta Vision – Computer Enhanced Multimedia Training Systems, product specification no. 9P2404A, DELTAK, Oak Brook, IL, 1981.

Digital Equipment Corporation, DECAL – Enhancing the Art of Teaching, Digital Equipment Corporation, Educational Products Group, Maynard, MA, 1980.

Edwards, B., Office Skills, Training and the Computer, Speedwriting/ Speedtyping, London, 1979.

Ferguson, R., PROLOG – a step toward the ultimate computer language, Byte: The Small Systems Journal, 6(11), 384–399, 1981.

Former, R., Author support requirements of a computer based instructional system, Educational Technology, 18–19, 1973.

Francis, L., PLATO IV Terminal Peripheral Devices, MTC Report No. 9, Computer Based Education Research Laboratory, University of Illinois, Urbana, IL, 1976.

Frye, C.H., PLANIT Author's Guide and PLANIT Language Reference Manual, System Development Corporation, Santa Monica, CA, 1970.

Gerhold, G. and Kheriaty, L., Microcomputers in classrooms, Computer Age, (3), 21–22; (4), 19–22; (5), 22–27, 1980.

Ghesquiere, J.R., Davies, C.R. and Thompson, C.A., Introduction to TUTOR, Computer–Based Education Research Laboratory, University of Illinois, Urbana, IL, 1975.

Goldberg, A., Educational uses of a Dynabook, Computers and Education, 3, 247–266, 1979.

Goodwood Data Systems, LEKTROMEDIA AVCAT System, Product Description and Technical Specifications, Goodwood Data Systems, Ontario, 1980.

Henry, R.D. and Howard, J.A., SAL – a simple author language for a minicomputer assisted instruction system, Journal of Computer Based Instruction, 3, 107–114, 1977.

Hody, G.L. and Avner, R.A., The PLATO System: An Evaluative Description, in Information Technology in Health Science Education, 143–177, Plenum Press, New York, NY, 1978.

Hofstetter, F.T., The meaning of PLATO at the University of Delaware, in Computer Assisted Learning – Scope, Progress and Limitations, Proceedings of the IFIP TC3 Working Conference on CAL, Roehampton, 3rd–7th September, 1979, (edited by R. Lewis, and E.D. Tagg), 123–124, North Holland, Amsterdam, 1980.

Hoskyns, J., Educational Prospectus, Hoskyns, London, 1980.

Hoy, R.E. and Wang, A.C., Index to Computer Based Learning, Educational Technology Publications, Englewood Cliffs, NJ, 1973.

International Business Machines, COURSEWRITER III for System/360 – Version 2 – Application Description, Form: H20–0587–0, IBM Corporation, White Plains, NY, 1969.

International Business Machines, Instructional Strategies Utilising a Computer Based Instructional Language, Form: GE20–0539–1, IBM Corporation, White Plains, NY, 1976.

International Business Machines, Interactive Instructional System – General Information Manual, Form: GH20–1895–1, IBM Corporation, White Plains, NY, 1977.

International Business Machines, Barclaycard Staff Learn From Their Computer, LINK, (80), 16–17, Form: 24–7824, 1978.

International Business Machines, Videodisc Enhances Customer Engineer's Education Investment, Customer Newsletter, 81–07, 1981.

Jenkins, T.M. and Dankert, E.J., Results of a three–month PLATO   trial in terms of utilisation and student attitudes, Educational Technology, 44–47, 1981.

Jones, A. and O'Shea, T., Barriers to the use of computer assisted learning, British Journal of Educational Technology, 13, 207–217, 1982.

Kahn, K., Three interactions between AI and education, in Machine Intelligence, 8, (edited by E.W. Elcock and D. Michie), 422–429, Edinburgh University Press, Edinburgh, 1977.

Kamp, M. and Gomberg, D., PET PILOT Teacher's Manual, Commodore Business Machines, Santa Clara, CA, 1980.

Kay, A., SMALLTALK, in Proceedings of the IFIP Workshop on Methodology of Interaction, Seillac, France, 1979, edited by R.A. Guedj et al., 7–11, North Holland, Amsterdam, 1980.

Kay, A. and Goldberg, A., Personal dynamic media, IEEE Computer, 10, 31–41, 1977.

Kearsley, G.P., Some facts about CAI: a quantitative analysis of the 1976 index to computer based instruction, Journal of Computer Based Instruction, 3, 34–41, 1976.

Keyser, E., Microcomputers and PILOT: a response, AEDS Monitor, 22–23, 1979.

Labinger, M., A Day in the Life of a Computer Teacher, Speedwriting/ Speedtyping, London, 1980.

Lamb, J., Mixed standards strike computers dumb, New Scientist, 98(1360), 636–637, 1983.

Lockwood, F. and Cooper, A., CICERO: computer assisted learning within an Open University Course, Teaching at a Distance, (17), 69–77, 1980.

Lower, S.K., Maxi authoring languages in the era of the mini, Journal of Computer Based Instruction, 3(4), 115–122, 1977.

Lower, S.K., IPS: a new authoring language for computer assisted instruction, Journal of Computer Based Instruction, 6(4), 119–124, 1980.

Lower, S.K., A Guide to the IPS Authoring Language for Computer Assisted Instruction, (Version 5), Department of Chemistry, Simon Fraser University, Burnaby, British Colombia, 1981.

Lower, S.K. and Arsenault, G., A functional evaluation of COURSEWRITER III, paper presented at the Summer Simulation Conference, San Diego, CA, 1972.

Lower, S.K., Gerhold, G., Smith, S.G., Johnson, K.J. and Moore, J.W., Computer assisted instruction in chemistry, Journal of Chemical Education, 56(4), 219–227, 1979.

Mast, C. van der, A portable program to present courseware on microcomputers, Computers and Education, 6, 39–44, 1982.

MITRE Corporation, An Overview of the TICCIT Program, Report No. M76–44, MITRE Corporation, Bedford, MA, 1976.

Modular Computer Systems, SIMPLER – Computer Based Education System, European Special Systems Product Bulletin, No. EHQ1000000PBN00, Modular Computer Systems, Fort Lauderdale, FL, 1981.

Mundie, D., PILOT/P: implementing a high level language in a hurry, BYTE: The Small Systems Journal, 5(7), 154–170, 1980.

National Physical Laboratory, EDUTEXT: A System for Generating and Presenting Computer Dialogues, Division of Information Technology and Computing, National Physical Laboratory, Teddington, 1982.

Osin, L., SMITH: how to produce CAI courses without programming, International Journal of Man–Machine Studies, 8, 207–241, 1976.

Papert, S., Teaching Children Thinking, LOGO Memo No. 2, Artificial Intelligence Laboratory, Massachusetts Institute of Technology, Cambridge, MA, 1971.

Pashkin, E.N., Analysis of Contemporary Computer Assisted Instruction Systems, Matematika i Kibernetika, (4), 52–64, 1979.

PILOT Exchange, Mason City, IA, 1981.

Rappaport, W. and Olenbush, A.E., Tailor–made teaching through TICCIT, MITRE MATRIX, 8(4), Mitre Corporation, Bedford, MA, 1975.

Read, G.A., CYCLOPS – An Audio–Visual System – A Brief Description, The Open University Press, Milton Keynes, 1978.

Sherwood, B.A., The TUTOR Language, Computer–Based Education Research Laboratory, University of Illinois, Urbana, IL, 1974.

Simons, G.L., Introducing Word Processing, NCC Publications, The National Computing Centre, Manchester, 1981.

Speedwriting/Speedtyping, London, 1983.

Stifle, J., The PLATO IV Student Terminal, CERL Report No. X–15, Computer–Based Education Research Laboratory, University of Illinois, Urbana, IL, 1974.

UNIVAC Computer Systems, ASET - Author System for Education and Training - CAI Instructional Technology Text, Publication No. UP5754, UNIVAC Computer Systems, 1975a.

UNIVAC Computer Systems, ASET Author Guide, Publication No. UP5785, UNIVAC Computer Systems, 1975b.

Watson, R.S. and Bevan, N., EDUTEXT - A High Level Author Language for Computer Assisted Instruction, National Physical Laboratory, Teddington, 1980.

Wilford, J. and Barker, P.G., An Investigation into the Use of STAF for Teaching in a School Environment, Working Paper, Interactive Systems Research Group, Department of Computer Science, Teesside Polytechnic, County Cleveland, 1983.

Wood, A., Interactive text handling and the superiority of PILOT, Educational Computing, 2(10), 63–65, 1981.

Yobb, G., PILOT, Creative Computing, 57–63, 1977.

Zadeh, L.A., Fuzzy sets, Information and Control, 8, 338–353, 1965.

Zadeh, L.A., A Fuzzy algorithmic approach to the definition of complex or imprecise concepts, International Journal of Man–Machine Studies, 8, 249–291, 1976.

Zinn, K.L., A Comparative Study of Languages for Programming Interactive Use of Computers in Instruction, Final EDUCOM Report under ONR contract N00014–68–C–256, 1969a.

Zinn, K.L., Interactive Programming Languages Adapted for Instructional Use of Computers, paper presented at the International Symposium on Man–Machine Systems, Cambridge, MA, 1969b.

Zinn, K.L., Requirements for Programming Languages in Computer Based Instructional Systems, The British Computer Society Yearbook, 89–98, London, 1971–72.

Further Reading

Rothwell, J., (editor), Authoring Systems, NCC CBT Library Series, Module 2, National Computing Centre, Manchester, 1983.

Chapter 4

MULTIMEDIA CAL

4.1 INTRODUCTION

Over the last few years there has been an increasing awareness of the limitations of stand-alone computers as instructional aids. Consequently, there has been a growing interest in those areas of CAL and CBT in which additional devices are interfaced to a computer in order to support and extend its instructional capability. Generally, this approach to computer based instruction is referred to as multimedia CAL. Because of its importance it has been made the subject of the present chapter. We commence by explaining, in more detail, the meaning of the term multimedia CAL and why it is so important. Then, the principles of interfacing are outlined and some examples of interfacing are presented. The final section of this chapter then describes a simple microcomputer based multimedia workstation that has been used for CAL applications in both a college and an industrial training environment.

4.1.1 What is Multimedia CAL?

As we have discussed earlier (see section 2.2.4) designers of instructional material have a wide variety of media available with which to implement their ideas. Table 4.1 lists a small selection of these. For any particular educational application each instructional medium will have its own particular advantages – and disadvantages. Furthermore, media will also differ in a number of important ways. For example, there will be differences with respect to (1) bandwidth for information transfer, (2) interactivity, (3) effectiveness, (4) intelligence, and (5) cost. When a single medium is to be used for instruction (see figure 4.1A), factors (1) through (5) can often be used in order to determine which is the most appropriate.

In contrast to the single–medium approach to instruction, an integrated multimedia system is one in which several different presentational channels are used (either simultaneously or in sequence) in order to implement a particular instructional strategy. This arrangement is shown schematically in figure 4.1B. Naturally, because of its versatility, the computer can act both as a presentational medium and as a controller of other media. This arrangement is shown in figure 4.1C. Equipment that is arranged in this fashion is said to constitute a multimedia CAL environment.

Table 4.1   Some Instructional Media

Teachers and lecturers
Books (text books, workbooks, PI texts, manuals, etc.
Slide projectors
Video tape recorders
Video disc
Educational TV and radio
Tape recorders
Training rigs and simulators
Robotic devices
Computers
Recent microelectronic devices
     – speech synthesis units
     – speech and sound recognition
     – image generation equipment
     – image and scene analysis devices
etc

A major motivation for the development of multimedia teaching equipment is the potential it offers for the production of very high bandwidths for information transfer. This is achieved through the use of a variety of communication channels – textual, sonic, graphic, tactile, and so on. In most situations these are all simultaneously available both to present information to students and, depending upon channel directionality, monitor their responses to the various learning situations that are generated. Of course, by using the computer in a suitable way (see figure 4.1C), it becomes possible to optimise information flow. That is, where options are available, it is possible for the computer to automatically select the most appropriate communication channel to use based upon (1) the type of material being presented and, (2) the nature of the student's background and ability.

(A)   Use of a single medium

(B)   Use of several media

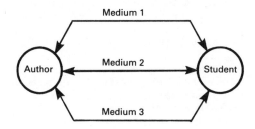

(C)   Use of a computer: multimedia CAL

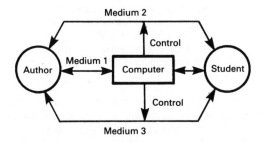

Figure 4.1   Single and multimedia approaches to education.

The origins of multimedia CAL lie in much of the fundamental CAI
research   that   was   conducted   in the USA in the early 1960s. Systems
such as SDC's (System Development Corporation) CLASS (Coulson, 1962a),
TRW's (Thompson Ramo Wooldridge) MENTOR (Chapman and Carpenter,
1962) and the University of Illinois' PLATO (Bitzer et al., 1962) equipment
incorporated many of the   instructional   devices   that   are   described
later in this chapter.   Thus, both CLASS and PLATO employed random
access slide projection techniques as a means of relaying   information
to   students.   Similarly,   the   MENTOR   system   used   a   variety   of

presentational alternatives, visual stimuli could originate from still frames, motion pictures, drawings, animation, text, charts and graphs (intermixed in any desired order); likewise, auditory stimulation could be achieved through speech, music, tones or any other suitable sound effect.

Because of the very favourable types of learning environment that can be provided, many of the more recently developed CAL systems tend to utilise the multimedia approach to instruction. This can be seen in the later versions of PLATO (Bitzer, 1976) and within systems such as CYCLOPS, TICCIT and AVCAT. Each of these was briefly outlined in chapter 3 during the discussion of author languages for CAL. The AVCAT system (which is based upon the use of a small minicomputer) is described in more detail in the following chapter.

The advent of the microcomputer has meant that it has become possible to implement a relatively low cost approach to CAL. Micros are therefore being used increasingly as the control element within multimedia CAL systems. Many commercial packages for microcomputers are now becoming available. Micro—PLATO and MicroTICCIT are two such examples. The latter (Backen, 1983) is a superset of previous TICCIT systems (see section 3.3.1). It is an integrated hardware/software system to author, deliver and manage computer assisted instruction. The system is hosted on the latest Data General Microeclipse systems and uses IBM Personal Computers that are linked through a local area network. These have colour displays and act as intelligent workstations for authors and students. System configurations range from single stand—alone machines to large networks. MicroTICCIT integrates the multimedia needs of modern instructional technology by incorporating the following facilities:

> high quality colour graphics
> video disc and video tape
> computer generated overlays combined with video
> random access digital stored audio
> student interaction via touch or light pen
> user—friendly, menu driven authoring system (called ADAPT)
> rapid graphics entry via the graphics digitiser
> and a family of graphics editors
> author support software and student management
> support for extended panel trainers

MicroTICCIT's sophistication and availability are particularly well suited to CAI applications requiring simulation. This is reflected by current MicroTICCIT applications which include US Navy pilot and aircrew training, operator and maintainer training for military and telecommunications applications as well as college and university level teaching. An illustration of the role of multimedia CAL in naval and maritime training is given in chapter 5.

When multimedia CAL systems are designed and constructed it is imperative to have available suitable techniques for interconnecting the computer system to the instructional devices that it is to control. This interconnection task is achieved through the use of either standard or specially designed interfaces. Interfacing is a topic which we discuss in the following section.

4.1.2 Principles of Interfacing

In general, the term interfacing is taken to mean those design and constructional tasks that have to be undertaken in order to facilitate the interconnection of two or more pieces of equipment. Sometimes the interfacing task is quite simple and will involve no more than connecting a special cable to each of the devices concerned. However, in more advanced situations, interfacing will often involve the creation of a special hardware, software or hardware/software unit known as an interface. Such a unit enables the smooth flow of signals, material, or, energy from one device to another. The role of an interface is illustrated schematically in figure 4.2.

(A)   Basic function of an interface

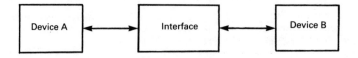

(B)   An interface for CAL applications

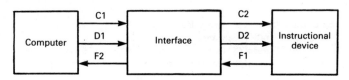

C1, C2   Control signals
F1, F2   Feedback signals
D1, D2   Display information

Figure 4.2   Device interconnection via the use of interfaces.

Devices of different kinds often have widely dissimilar types of external connection facility. The purpose of the interface is therefore to 'smooth out' and resolve these differences. It will do this in such a way that each device 'appears' to be connected to one or more partners with which it is compatible. The interface may, for example, change the voltage level of signals, alter the speed of information flow or modify the organisation of the data in various ways. Obviously, the exact nature and function of the interface will depend upon the details of the application it is to serve. A more detailed discussion of interfacing is given elsewhere (Barker, 1983a; Stone, 1982).

When it is required to connect a computer system to an instructional device, the interface is likely to have to support three basic types of information flow (see figure 4.2B). First, it may be required to pass across control information, this enables the computer to influence the way in which the instructional device operates. Second, there may be a requirement to send display information (or instructional material) to the device for presentation to the user. Third, feedback information may need to be returned from the instructional device to the computer; this may take the form of signals that describe the operating conditions of the attached device (for example, error codes, indications of machine status, etc), alternatively, it may be special data that is used to describe the user's mode of interaction with the device (such as, touch screen coordinate pairs or details of the points of contact of a light pen).

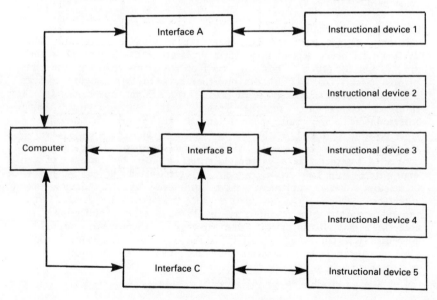

Figure 4.3   Typical interface organisation for multimedia CAL.

For multimedia CAL a number of different types of interface will probably be required. Figure 4.3 gives a schematic illustration of a typical arrangement. Each of the interfaces A and C control only one

external device. In contrast, interface B controls a cluster of three
devices. Its design and mode of operation will therefore probably be
much more sophisticated than those of A and C.

From the point of view of the architecture of a microcomputer system
(see figure 1.3), two general techniques may be used to connect micros
to external devices such as slide projectors, video discs, tape
recorders, and so on. The interconnection is normally achieved either
(1) by the use of the external I/O communication ports provided by the
computer, or (2) by means of memory mapping techniques. Each of these
methods will be briefly described in section 4.2 and will be
illustrated by appropriate examples. However, before describing these
interfacing methods it would be worthwhile outlining some of the more
important general characteristics of computer interfaces.

Interface Characteristics
When discussing the nature of the interfaces that are used to connect
instructional devices to computers, a number of different factors need
to be taken into consideration. Some of these are briefly described
below. The treatment in this section is not exhaustive. Its purpose is
only to serve as a guide to some of the points that need to be
considered.

(a) Physical Considerations
The physical nature of the link that exists between two (or more)
devices will often depend upon their proximity, that is how close they
are to each other. Thus, if each of the items reside on the same
printed circuit board (PCB), the interface between them might consist
only of copper tracks. These will run from one device (via any
interface components) to the others. If the devices being
interconnected are quite separate (and distant) from each other then
it is possible that each will need to make available some form of
electrical socket or special type of edge connector. These must be
connected together (via any required interface unit) by means of an
appropriate run of cable which is terminated at each end with
connectors that complement those provided by the devices being
interfaced. Obviously, the nature of the cable that is used will
depend upon the type of interface involved. In some applications the
interface may utilise optical fibre cabling; in others cabling may be
dispensed with in favour of an infra-red or high frequency acoustic
link. A great deal of attention must be given to the physical aspects
of interfacing in order to produce interfaces that are safe and
ergonomically acceptable to their users.

(b) Signal Types and Levels
The electrical signals used in computer interface work fall broadly
into two basic types: digital and analogue. Digital signalling
involves the use of a discrete number of signal levels, usually two,
corresponding to the presence or absence of a particular voltage level
or current flow. Most of the output ports on microcomputers are

digital   and   will   very   often   be   TTL   (transistor–transistor   logic)
compatible (Witten, 1980a). TTL interfaces employ two signal levels:

Level 1:   0.0–0.8 volt
Level 2:   2.4–5.0 volts

Of course, other signalling conventions will   probably   use   different
voltage   levels,   such   as   the   +12 and   −12 volt signalling used in the
RS–232–C interface (see below). Analogue signals differ   from   digital
ones   in   that   they   show a continuous variation in magnitude between
some predefined lower and upper limit. Thus an   analogue   signal   that
has   0 and 15 volts as its range could take on any value between these
limits. The electrical output from a microphone or the signals fed   to
a   loudspeaker are analogue in nature and usually consist of a complex
combination of many different waveforms. An understanding   of   signals
of this type is important when interfacing sound recognition and sound
generation equipment to a computer. Other examples of analogue signals
include   the   RF input to a home TV set and the data that is recorded,
stored and transmitted within video systems (Sippl   and   Dahl,   1981).
Interconversions   between   analogue   and   digital   signals   is   often
necessary in many interfacing situations. Transformations of this type
are easily performed through the use of special   types   of   integrated
circuit   known   as   A/D   and   D/A   convertors.   Use   of these is often
necessary   for   speech   processing   and   video   applications   of   the
computer.

(c)   Standard and Non–standard Interfaces
Computer   interfaces   are often classified as being either standard or
non–standard.   A   standard   interface   is   one   whose   structure,
constitution and mode of operation has been defined and agreed upon by
a national (or international) standards organisation (for example ANSI
–   American   National   Standards   Institute;   or   ISO   –   International
Standards   Organisation).   The   defining   specifications   of   such   a
standard are universally accepted, that is, all those who use it agree
to   abide   by   the conventions that ·it recommends. Typical examples of
commonly used standards include:

(1) the RS–232–C interface (Stone, 1982),
(2) the IEEE–488 interface bus (Fisher and Jensen, 1980),
(3) the S–100/IEEE–696 bus   (Bursky, 1980;
Libes and Garetz, 1981; Poe and Goodwin, 1979),
(4) the IEEE–802 Local Area Network Standard   (Saal, 1981; 1983).

Some of these will be referred to again in section 4.2.

Non–standard interfaces fall broadly into two   categories: (1)   those
produced by individual manufacturers to facilitate the interconnection
of their own equipment; and (2) special purpose interfaces designed to
meet   some   specific   interfacing   requirement   for which no available
interface exists. Examples illustrating the design of this latter type

ICAL-F*

of interface will be presented in sections 4.2.1 and 4.2.2.

(d)   Serial and Parallel Interfaces
Data and information may be transmitted through digital interfaces   in
either   of two formats: serial and parallel. A serial interface is one
in which all the bits (binary digits) of information within a   message
follow   each   other   in succession along the signal line. The RS–232–C
interface mentioned above is   an   example   of   a   serial   transmission
system.

In   a   parallel   interface the information bits being transmitted each
flow   simultaneously   through   the   interface. This   is   achieved   by
allocating to each bit its own unique signal line. A group of parallel
data   flow   lines   used   in this fashion is often referred to as a bus
(see section 1.1.2). The number of signal lines available for parallel
transmission is often referred to as the interface (or bus) width. The
majority of the more   popular   parallel   interfaces   are   designed   to
enable   either   8   or   16   bits   of   information   to be simultaneously
transmitted. The IEEE–488 interface is an example of one which enables
the parallel transmission of eight data bits (that   is,   one   byte   of
information).   Another   example   of   an   8–bit   data   bus is the S–100
interface. Each of these is quite extensively   used   in   microcomputer
interfacing operations.

Where there is a requirement for it, the interconversion of serial and
parallel   data   formats can usually be quite easily achieved. A number
of integrated circuits are now available which perform these types   of
signal   transformation. In   situations   where   there   is   a choice, a
parallel interface is to be preferred since it will usually be able to
transmit data at a much higher rate.

(e)   Data Transfer Speed
The speed at which an interface is able to transmit data   will   depend
upon   a   number   of   factors, for example the way in which it has been
constructed, whether it is serial or parallel and the   types   of   data
conversion   that   may   be   required (Barker, 1982a; 1983b). In digital
systems, transmission speeds are often measured in terms of the number
of bits per second that pass through   the   interface. This   is   often
referred to as its baud rate. Transmission speeds can vary from as low
as   300   bits/second to as high as several megabits/second. Obviously,
where large volumes of data are to   be   transmitted,   the   higher   the
transmission   rate   the   faster   the   data   gets moved. The effects of
transmission   speed   can   be   very   noticeable,   for   example   when
replenishing   the   screen   of   a   VDU   with   new   information. Thus,
completely changing the contents of a 80 x   24   character   VDU   screen
would   take 64 seconds using a 300 baud serial interface compared with
only 9.8 seconds when a 19,600 baud connection is used.

The speed of an interface is related   to   its   capacity   for   carrying
information.   In analogue systems the information carrying capacity of

an interface is often referred to as its bandwidth. This is defined as
the range of analogue signal frequencies it is able to transmit. The
larger the bandwidth the more information it can carry, and hence, the
greater its speed, for example in its ability to transmit image or
sound data.

(f) Hybrid Interfaces
Sometimes an interface must carry a wide variety of different signal
types, for example digital data for a computer VDU screen, video
images and, perhaps, voice data as well. Consequently, it is not
always possible to describe interfaces purely as digital or analogue.
Indeed, various combinations of each of these are often used in many
interfacing situations. As we shall see later, several of the
multimedia workstations described in the next chapter depend quite
critically upon the availability of complex hybrid interfaces.

4.2   INTERFACING TO MICROCOMPUTERS

One of the major differences between microcomputers and other types of
interactive computing system is the ease with which the end-user is
able to add on (or interface) additional local peripheral devices.
These 'add-ons' may take the form of standard I/O devices (printers,
tape cassettes, flexible discs, etc) or they may be special purpose
units such as a light pen, tracker ball, mouse, function keypad or
slide projector. Although some of these devices may also be interfaced
to a mainframe (or minicomputer) VDU the problems involved are usually
far more complex than those encountered when micros are used.

In this section we are going to discuss some approaches to interfacing
instructional devices to microcomputers. The discussion does not
centre around any particular micro. Instead, an attempt is made to
discuss the topic of interfacing in a computer independent way, as far
as this is possible. When using a microcomputer for instructional
applications it is important to realise that it is feasible to operate
it in either of two ways. Its most common mode of operation will
undoubtedly be as a stand-alone computing device. The alternative mode
of operation involves its use as an intelligent terminal that is
connected − either directly or indirectly − to a distributed computing
system (Barker, 1982b). In this chapter we shall be primarily
concerned with the former of these modes of operation. Some aspects of
microcomputer usage as an intelligent terminal within a computer
network will be presented in chapter 5.

The discussion of interfacing contained in the remainder of this
section is orientated towards the use of input/output ports and memory
mapping techniques. In order to enable devices to be attached by these
methods the host microcomputer must provide a variety of different
interface ports. Figure 4.4 gives a schematic representation of a rear
view of a typical microcomputer unit. It illustrates the various types
of interface port that a micro is likely to provide in order to permit

the attachment of additional peripherals and other kinds of device.

The ports shown in this diagram may be subdivided into three broad groups. First, there are those that provide for the attachment of the micro's support peripherals – such as a printer, a flexible/hard disc storage unit, a tape cassette, a graphics tablet and so on; in the diagram, these are labelled P1 through P5. Second, there are those ports that provide access to some of the microcomputer's internal communication buses; these allow for memory expansion (both RAM and ROM) as well as access to the computer's address and data buses (these ports are labelled ME, AB and DB in figure 4.4); some microcomputers also provide a facility to enable additional processors to be 'plugged in' thereby permitting faster processing speeds to be achieved and/or a wider range of facilities to be offered. Third, there will be a set of standard interface ports that enable the microcomputer to be connected to other devices that are able to provide matching/complementary facilities.

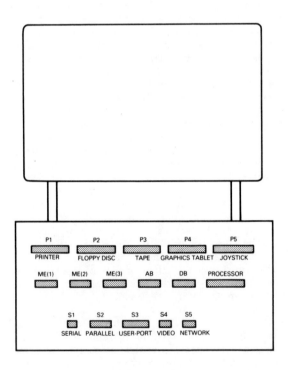

Figure 4.4   Rear view of microcomputer showing interface ports.

In figure 4.4 the set of standard interfaces are labelled S1 through
S5. Amongst these will usually be included: (1) a serial interface
(the RS–232–C is commonly used); (2) a parallel interface (here, the
IEEE–488 or S–100 standards are quite common); (3) a facility to
enable the end–user to interface his/her own applications orientated
devices to the computer (often called a userport or applications–
port); (4) connections to enable an external video monitor to be
driven; and (5) facilities that permit the microcomputer to be
directly attached to a (local area) computer network (Barker, 1982b;
1983a).

All of the interfacing examples described in sections 4.2.1 through
4.2.5 depend upon using the microcomputer's input/output ports as the
primary means of device connection. In contrast, the MUMEDALA system
(described in chapter 5) uses memory mapping as its basic mechanism
for the attachment of ancillary instructional equipment. Because of
the importance of each of these approaches to device interfacing a
further description is presented below. This will serve as a
preparation for (1) the material to be covered in the remainder of
this chapter, and (2) the description of MUMEDALA presented in the
following chapter.

(A) Using the Microcomputer's Standard Input/Output Ports
In the majority of microcomputer systems the standard I/O ports are
memory mapped into the micro's address space. That is, each of the
available ports will be assigned either an absolute or symbolic
address. This address then forms the basis by which data is
transmitted to or obtained from any of the devices attached to the
computer's input/output ports. The computer programmer is able to
initiate data transmission via these ports by means of a set of port
manipulation commands. These commands are usually special cases of two
general instructions that permit the contents of the computer's memory
to be inspected or altered. The format of these commands might be

        GET A,X   ;inspect contents of memory
        PUT A,Y   ;alter memory contents

or, in some microcomputer systems, the alternative command keywords
PEEK and POKE might be used:

        PEEK A,X   ;inspect contents of memory
        POKE A,Y   ;alter memory contents

Each of the above instructions uses the letter A to represent the
address value of the memory location involved in the operation. The
GET (or PEEK) command causes the contents of this location to be
copied into the variable X. Similarly, the PUT (or POKE) command
causes the value of the variable Y to be copied into the specified
memory location. Of course, where it is appropriate, absolute (rather
than symbolic) values may be used in each of these commands. For

example:

GET 37261,JACK   ;copy contents of memory location 37261
                         ;to the variable JACK
PUT 42589,112   ;alter contents of memory location 42589
                         ;to the value 112

It is easy to see how these commands may be used to provide a simple
mechanism to facilitate data transfer through the microcomputer's I/O
ports – provided their addresses are known.

The microcomputer's RS–232–C port provides facilities to enable a byte
of information (in bit serial form) to be transmitted to, and/or
received from, an external device. These operations may be effected by
commands of the form

PUT RS232,X   ;send value of X to the RS–232 port
GET RS232,Y   ;get value of Y from the RS–232 port

in which RS232 is the symbolic address of the RS–232–C serial
communication port.

Before data bytes can be handled by the port it will need to be
configured. In other words, unless default values are employed, the
user will need to specify the values of the port's operating
characteristics, such as its line speed, parity, number of framing
bits, and so on. For most purposes the microcomputer's default values
can be used and so any further discussion of RS–232–C port
configuration will not be necessary here. When it is required to
change the mode of operation of this port, adequate details will
usually be provided in the microcomputer's operating manual.

Notice that the signal levels of the RS–232–C port are not TTL
compatible. If this compatibility is required it is possible to employ
special purpose integrated circuits to convert from RS–232–C to TTL
signal levels and vice versa (Stone, 1982). Another limitation of this
port is worth mentioning; normally, unless special additional
circuitry is used, only one external device can be attached to the RS–
232–C port. For this reason, some micros provide several ports of this
type, thereby enabling multiple device connection. Further details on
the RS–232–C port and its more recent counterparts (the RS–422 and RS–
423) are given by Stone (1982).

The IEEE–488 port provides facilities to enable a byte of information
(in bit parallel form) to be transmitted to (or fetched from) a device
attached to this interface. This port permits several devices to be
connected to the microcomputer in parallel, each of which must have an
associated (unique) device number in order to identify it.
Consequently, the I/O command for this interface must contain extra
information – the device number of the unit involved in the data

transfer operation. Some typical commands for this port might be

    PUT IEEE,3,X   ;send value of X to device 3 on the IEEE port
    GET IEEE,7,Y   ;obtain value of Y from device 7

where IEEE is the symbolic address of the port. When interfacing devices to this port the user must arrange for the device to be allocated a unique identification number which it will need to recognise (and respond to) when transmitted over the bus. Further details of the IEEE communications port are provided elsewhere (Fisher and Jensen, 1980; Stone, 1982).

From the point of view of interfacing end–user equipment to a microcomputer, the userport probably offers the easiest solution for many of the simpler applications. The user–port usually provides eight TTL compatible I/O pins along with several others that offer special communications functions. These special functions are likely to include facilities for serial shift in/out of data, monitoring interrupts, transmitting timing (or clock) signals and handshaking of data between the microcomputer and its externally connected devices. Of course, not all of these facilities need to be used. The majority of applications will normally only involve use of the eight parallel I/O pins and it is these with which the following discussion is concerned. Further details on the other facilities and the way in which they are used are given elsewhere (Camp et al., 1979; Foster, 1981).

A schematic representation of a very simple userport is presented in figure 4.5. It has two of the computer's memory locations (or registers) associated with it. One of these (called the data direction register or DDR) is used to hold bit values that specify, for each I/O line, the required directionality of the data flow between the computer and the external device. A value of 0 indicates that the line is being used for input and a value of 1 indicates that it is being used for output. Thus, in figure 4.5, lines 0, 3 and 6 are being used for input while lines 1, 2, 4, 5 and 7 are being used for the output of data. Once the user port has been configured (by writing an appropriate value into the DDR), data is either sent to and/or received from external devices by either writing values into or reading them from the port's data register. Suppose that the two addresses needed to configure and use the userport are denoted symbolically by DDR (data direction register) and DR (data register). Provided that the microcomputer system has appropriately assigned absolute values for these symbolic addresses, manipulation of the userport becomes quite a simple process. Thus, the simple commands

    PUT DDR,X   ;configure the DDR with value X
    PUT DR,Y   ;send value of Y to the userport
    GET DR,Z   ;get value of Z from the userport

are all that are needed in order to perform a wide variety of control operations with devices that are attached to the userport.

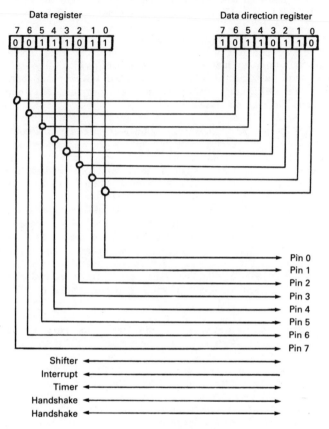

Figure 4.5   Organisation of a microcomputer applications port.

In order to illustrate how these commands may be used, imagine that the eight pins of the userport are connected (via appropriate interface circuits) to a set of switches that control the on/off status of a series of lamps (see figure 4.6A). The external circuitry is designed in such a way that writing a 1 value to a user-port line turns a lamp on while writing a 0 value to such a line turns it off. The commands needed to illuminate the lamps according to the pattern indicated in figure 4.6A might be as follows:

```
PUT DDR,255      ;configure the DDR, all lines for output
PUT DR,169       ;write pattern 10101001 to userport
```

(A)   Control of electric lamps

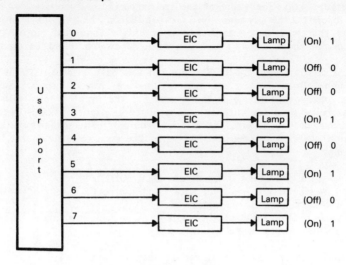

(B)   External interface circuit (EIC) used for lamp control

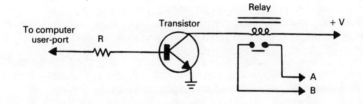

(C)   Sensing the status of a signal line

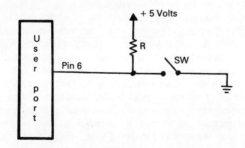

Figure 4.6   Use of a microcomputer's userport.

A circuit suitable for switching the lamps (or other devices) is shown
in figure 4.6B. The value of the resistance (R) and voltage (V) needed
to operate the system will depend upon the type of transistor and
relay that is used. Points A and B would be connected into the lamp
circuit in the same way as a conventional switch might be used.

In a similar way, the GET command can be used to determine the status
of signal lines that are attached to pins of the userport. Suppose
that userport line 6 is to be used for the input of data (all other
lines being used for output) – as depicted in figure 4.6C. Once the
port has been configured, it is then required to determine whether the
switch (SW) is open or closed. The code to achieve this might be
simply:

        PUT DDR,191   ;configure DDR 10111111
        GET DR,X   ;get data from userport

Analysis of the value of the variable X would now enable the status of
the switch setting to be determined.

From the above examples it can be seen that the userport can easily be
used for (1) controlling external devices (through its on/off
switching capability); and (2) sensing the status of an external
device (through the analysis of an appropriate feedback signal line).
The principles involved in using the userport will be illustrated in
some of the following sections in which we describe its use for the
control of some actual instructional devices (a tape recorder and
slide projector).

Naturally, one of the major limitations of the microcomputer's
userport is the restriction placed on the number of devices that can
be attached to it. This limitation can be overcome by adding
additional external circuitry (Barker, 1982c). An alternative method
of device control is through the use of memory mapping techniques, the
principles of which are described below.

(B) Using the Micro's Address and Data Buses – Memory Mapping
Many of the peripherals attached to modern microcomputers are
interfaced into the system by means of memory mapping techniques. That
is, some of the computer's address space values are not used for
referencing real memory. Instead, they are used to reference
peripheral devices which then act like 'apparent' memory locations.
Memory mapping thus involves allocating to each peripheral one or more
unused (or sacrificed) memory addresses, to which the peripheral must
respond when requested to do so. This mode of device interfacing is
implemented in such a way that data flow operations involving the
peripheral appear to be exactly the same as those involving
conventional memory. As was mentioned earlier, commands are available
(GET/PUT or PEEK/POKE) which permit any of the computer's memory
locations to be read and, in the case of read/write memory, altered.

These same commands can also be used to control data flow between the
computer and memory mapped peripherals. Thus, the two commands

> PUT AD1,X   ;send data to peripheral
> GET AD2,Y   ;obtain data from peripheral

might be used to transmit data (the value of byte X) and obtain data
(the value of byte Y) from peripherals that are interfaced into the
system at addresses AD1 and AD2 respectively.

In the same way that standard peripheral devices might be memory
mapped into the system, so too can other external end–user devices.
However, in order to do this the user must have access to the
computer's address bus, data bus and read/write signal lines (see
figure 4.4). Provided these are available, the way in which an
external device might utilise them is depicted schematically in figure
4.7.

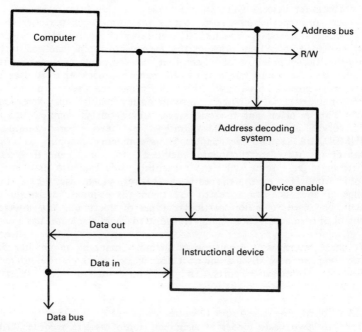

Figure 4.7   Device interfacing by means of memory mapping.

This diagram shows how an external device might be interconnected to
the computer's address and data buses. The address bus is
unidirectional. This means that information (in the form of address
values) flows from the computer's CPU along the bus to each of the
devices or items connected to it. In contrast, the data bus is

bidirectional so that information (in the form of data values) can flow either from the computer to its attached units or from these back to the computer. The direction of this data flow is controlled by the status of the read/write signal line.

From the point of view of external device control the most important interface in figure 4.7 is probably the address decoding system. This has the responsibility of continually monitoring the address bus lines and inspecting the address values that the computer is transmitting. When it recognises any of the external device's addresses it sends a signal (called a device enable signal) to the device. The purpose of this is simply to inform the device that either (1) the data being sent over the data bus is intended for it; or (2) it has to transmit some data to the computer. The external device uses the signal level on the R/W line in order to determine which of these alternatives is required.

Memory mapping is a useful way of adding additional external devices to a computer system since it overcomes the chief limitation of using a user or applications port, that is the number of peripherals that can be simultaneously attached. The number of external devices that can be added to a system using the memory mapping method is limited only by the number of addresses that the computer can make available. Thus, if the micro has a spare 4K memory block that it does not use, then it is possible to utilise this in order to add up to 4096 additional external devices, provided they require only one address each. This is often not the case since, where fairly complex equipment is involved, a range of addresses might be used. For example, the MUMEDALA system (see chapter 5) uses memory mapping as a means of connecting its instructional devices to a general purpose microcomputer. Some of the teaching aids that are used are fairly sophisticated (for example, speech synthesiser, video disc, etc) and a range of addresses are allocated to them. Individual addresses can then be used to action particular types of operation, any associated control information then being transmitted over the data bus.

We shall return to a discussion of memory mapping in chapter 5. In the meantime we now discuss some of the ways in which the microcomputer's standard interface ports might be utilised for interfacing instructional devices.

4.2.1   Controlling an Audio Cassette
There are two basic modes of using an audio cassette recorder within a CAI environment. The first of these involves situations in which sounds generated by the student are recorded for subsequent analysis. The second mode of usage involves relaying some previously recorded sonic material to the student in order to aid a learning process. Each of these modes of usage are depicted schematically in figure 4.8.

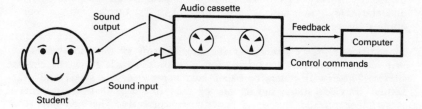

(A)   Use of an audio recorder for CAI

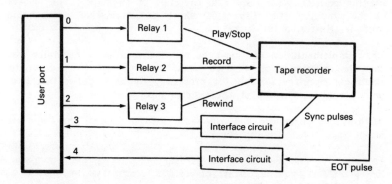

(B)   Control signals and feedback signals

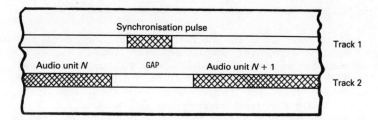

(C)   Tape synchronisation pulses

Figure 4.8   Computer control of an audio cassette player.

Once the audio recorder has been switched on and a tape inserted, computer control of the device can be effected by activation of one or more relays connected in parallel with the audio recorder's manual control buttons. The electrical connections necessary to accomplish this can usually be achieved by direct wiring of the relay contacts to the manual switches or by means of the recorder's external remote controller socket. Figure 4.8B shows a typical 3-relay control system and the way in which this might be connected to a computer's application port.

In addition to relay operation, computer control of the audio cassette will also involve watching for feedback signals from the cassette player. These will generally be of two types – device status and tape status. Device status signals can be used to check that the recorder is switched on and that it is functioning correctly. The two important tape status indicators are the end-of-tape signal (EOT) and the tape author's synchronisation pulses. The latter will have been added to the tape in order that the computer can (1) automatically locate particular pieces of audio material, and (2) calculate the current playing position with respect to the start of the tape. The location of the synchronisation ('sync' for short) pulses relative to the audio units is illustrated in figure 4.8C.

The implementation of this type of control strategy naturally assumes that the recorder is of the two track (stereo) variety and contains electronic circuitry suitable for processing the sync pulses that have been placed on track 2 of the cassette tape.

Within the courseware, the commands used to control the audio recorder might take the following form:

```
PUT  X,1        ;start player
PUT  X,0        ;stop player
PUT  X,4        ;rewind tape
PUT  X,3        ;record student message
GET  X,Y        ;get recorder status
```

In each of these commands the first parameter X represents the address of the microcomputer's applications port. Each of the PUT commands then close one or more of the relays that are attached to this port. The GET statement enables the feedback signals from the cassette to be monitored. When the recorder detects a synchronisation pulse, it is assumed that the external circuitry sets the status of pin 3 of the user port to logical 1. It then holds it in this status long enough to be detected by the program. Similarly, detection of the EOT signal from the tape recorder is assumed to place computer input pin 4 into a logical 1 state. By analysing the value of the variable Y (subsequent to a GET statement) the position of the tape can be determined (by counting the sync pulses) and an end-of-tape condition detected when it arises.

Several approaches to this type of control of an audio cassette
recorder have been described in the literature, in the majority of
which technical details of the circuits involved will be found (Kenny
and Davies, 1979; Tandberg, 1983).

4.2.2 Controlling Slide Projectors
Graphical illustrations provide an important way of presenting
information to students. Pictorial images should therefore play an
important part in all CAL systems. There are two basic ways in which
images may be made available to students: first, they may be generated
on some form of CRT screen by means of computer software; second,
images stored on an external medium may be selectively shown to the
student. Slide projection techniques fall into this second category.

The use of slide projectors and associated techniques (such as
microfiche, closed–loop filmstrips, freeze–frame video, etc) provide
an important method of projecting high resolution static images for
many CAL applications in which pictorial support is necessary. Slides
have one major advantage over the other (related) media listed above.
Namely, they provide a relatively simple and inexpensive medium in
which individual images (or frames) may be slightly modified or
completely changed with minimal effort. For this reason, slide based
techniques for pictorial presentations are likely to remain an
important part of CAL systems for some time to come (Kenny and Davies,
1979; Barker, 1982c).

Currently there is a wide variety of slide projection equipment
available from a number of different manufacturers. Overall, this
equipment may be subdivided into two broad categories: those that
operate in a purely sequential fashion (both forwards and backwards),
and those that provide random access to images. Interfacing each of
these types of projector to a computer system is usually a simple
matter. In both cases the easiest way of achieving computer control is
to make the computer imitate the action of the projector's remote
control unit (see figure 4.9). This is undoubtedly simpler in the case
of a sequential slide projector.

The control activity associated with the operation of a manual remote
control keypad for a sequential projector can easily be imitated by
using two relays. These can be made to mimic the action of the
controller's 'forward' and 'backward' buttons (see figure 4.9A). The
electronic circuits and userport interfacing requirements are exactly
analogous to those described in the previous sections (see figures
4.8B and 4.6B). However, the software requirements are somewhat
different from those described for audio cassette control. In order to
mimic the action of the manual controller, the control program must
generate a 'square wave pulse' similar to that shown below.
Essentially, this is the electronic equivalent of a manual key
depression of one of the remote controller's function buttons.

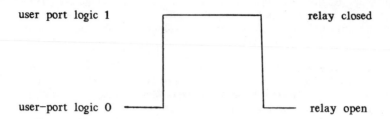

Assuming that the address of the user/applications port is X and that the relays for forward and backward control of the projector are interfaced into port pins 0 and 1 respectively, then the program statements needed to generate these pulses might be

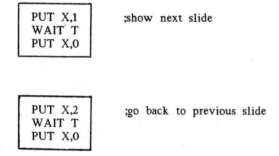

where T, the value of the waiting period, will vary from projector to projector and is best determined experimentally.

Control of a random access projector (Barker 1982d; 1982e) is slightly more difficult than that of a sequential access one since the former must be given the slide number of the image it is to display. A typical selector device for manually achieving this type of control is depicted in figure 4.9B (Kodak, 1980). This consists of two multi-way rotary switches. One of these is used to select the 'tens digit' of the slide number while the other is used to specify the 'units digit'. In figure 4.9B the settings of the selector correspond to selection of slide 57. Again, interfaces suitable for connecting this type of device to a microcomputer must emulate the action of their associated manual controllers. The design of an interface suitable for controlling the projector illustrated in figure 4.9B has been described by Barker (1982c; 1982d; 1982e).

(A) Sequential access to slides

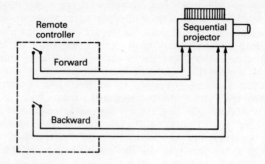

(B) Random access to individual slides

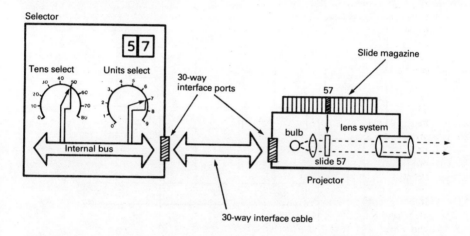

Connections for switches other than 50 and 7 have been omitted for clarity

Figure 4.9 Remote control units for slide projector operation.

The design and construction of computer interfaces for random access projectors can be a difficult problem since they can place considerable demand on the I/O port of the host microcomputer. Thus, in the example described above, each selector switch requires four input lines fot its emulation. Together, they require the use of all eight I/O lines of the microcomputer output port. This is a severe limitation if other devices also need to use this for I/O activity. Should the need arise to control a significant number of random access projectors then another limitation of the interface becomes apparent. For multiple projector control an appropriate addressing scheme would need to be introduced. The computer output port cannot be used because this is dedicated to the transfer of switch selection data. The microcomputer address bus, however, can be used to provide one solution to this problem. By equipping each projector with an address decoder/latch enable circuit (see figure 4.7) it becomes possible to memory map the projectors onto the address space of the computer. The microcomputer output port could then be used as a common external data bus from which slide selection data is strobed by the projector whose identification is sent over the address bus. Alternatively, the microcomputer's internal bidirectional data bus could be used to transmit the slide selection data. Such an arrangement is illustrated schematically in figure 4.10. When using this approach to projector control a statement of the form PUT X,Y could then be used to request that slide Y be displayed on the projector whose address is X. Memory mapping of projectors onto unused memory addresses could thus be used to provide sufficient expansion capability to support any reasonable number of slide projectors.

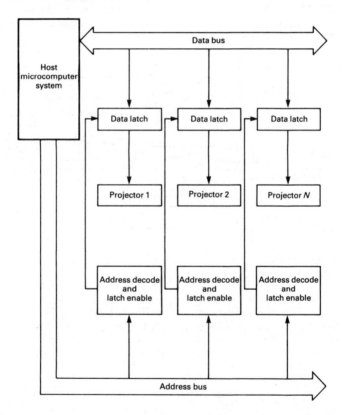

Figure 4.10   Memory mapped random access slide projectors.

4.2.3   Controlling Video Devices

Currently, there are two important types of video device that need to be considered for CAL applications. First, there are the various types of video cassette recorder (or VCR); then, there are optical video disc systems. Each of these have been used (in various combinations, both together and alone) in order to implement different types of interactive video. This approach to instruction attempts to combine the presentational powers of video with the control logic of CAL.

At present, systems involving video cassette recorders (Davies and Kenny, 1980; Laurillard, 1982; Copeland, 1983) have the advantage that teachers and authors are more easily (and less expensively) able to prepare the video material to be used for instruction. However, unless a random access VCR is available (Bryce and Stewart, 1982) this medium is much slower than video disc for many important types of instructional strategy and application. Video tape, of course, is also a less robust medium than disc. A typical VCR based CAL system (Laurillard, 1982) is illustrated in figure 4.11. The hardware is standard video (VHS) and microcomputer equipment connected by way of a special interface board with associated control software.

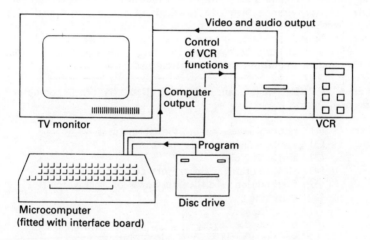

Figure 4.11   Computer control of a video cassette recorder.

Circuit descriptions and programming details for controlling this type of system may be found in a number of technical manuals, journals and research reports (VonFeldt, 1979; Hallgren, 1980; Schwartz, 1980; Bryce and Stewart, 1982).

Notice that in the system depicted in figure 4.11 the control software for the microcomputer is stored on a magnetic flexible disc. Of course, there is no reason why this should not be stored on the video tape along with the audio and video instructional material. Indeed,

several   interactive   VCR based systems are now adopting this approach
(Kane et al., 1980).

As we indicated at the beginning of this section, video disc systems
are able to offer a number of advantages over video tape for certain
types of instructional application (Bunderson, 1980; Hon, 1982; Bryce
and Stewart, 1983a; 1983b). Interfacing video discs to computer
systems is no more difficult than is the case with   VCRs. Indeed, in
many cases it is much simpler since many of the commercially available
systems now   come supplied with a standard interface that facilitates
attachment to   a   computer.   A   typical video disc player and its
interface connections are depicted in figure 4.12 (Philips, 1982a;
1982b). The special feature of this player is   the teletext   encoder
that   it contains. This enables teletext graphic codes (generated by a
computer) to be superimposed on video images being retrieved from   the
disc.

Computer   communication   with   the   video   disc   (and   vice   versa) is
achieved via the bidirectional RS–232–C serial   interface   port.   The
video disc   player is linked to a teletext TV monitor by means of the
TV signal output connection. All the   functions   that   the   player   is
capable of   providing   may   be invoked by stored operational programs
running within an   attached   computer system. This is achieved by
sending a   suitable   string of control characters to the player's RS–
232–C port and, if need be, waiting for an acknowledgement to indicate
that the control operation has been performed.

The main facilities   that   can   be   controlled   by   the   computer   are
summarised below:

   (1)   random access to individual pictures
   (2)   freeze–frame on any picture
   (3)   single stepping
   (4)   slow motion – either forwards or backwards
   (5)   fast motion – either forwards or backwards
   (6)   searching
   (7)   indexing
   (8)   teletext overlaying
   (9)   special effects (audio/video mute, etc)

In   addition,   the   player has a built–in memory that is able to store
two frame numbers; these are referred to as the   ordinary   memory   (M)
and   the   auto–stop   memory   (AS).   Special   commands are available to
change the values held in these memories. When values   are   stored   in
these   two   memory locations some interesting effects can be achieved,
for example, (1) auto stopping, (2) repetition, and (3) frame
skipping. In   the   first case, the video player will enter into still
mode whenever it encounters the picture number value that is contained
in the auto–stop memory.

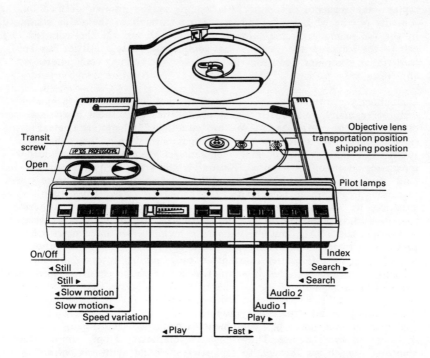

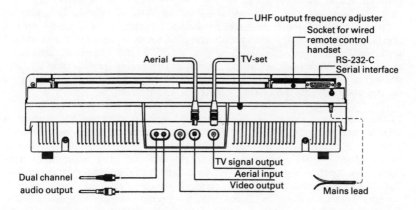

Figure 4.12   Video disc facilities and interface ports.
(Courtesy of Philips.)

In example (2), whenever a repeat command is issued, the player will replay the sequence of frames commencing at the number defined by the contents of the M memory and proceeding through to the value contained in the AS memory. Frame skipping (example 3)) can also be achieved by using the appropriate video disc commands. These facilities can· be used under computer control to achieve a variety of interesting animation effects.

Undoubtedly, interactive video systems that are based on the use of discs offer many more instructional possibilities than those based on tape. This is particularly so in situations where: (1) teletext signals (Reis, 1976) must also be incorporated within the display space, and (2) video mixing (of images from several discs) using screen segmentation is required. Naturally, there is a price to be paid for the convenience of additional facilities such as these – increased programming complexity (Barker, 1983c). In this type of situation it would be expected that a number of high level authoring tools would be available to aid the courseware author. Unfortunately, none of the CAL author languages which we have described in the previous chapters of this book provide a fully satisfactory solution to all of the difficulties inherent in programming interactive video systems. Consequently, this is a problem to which we return again in the following chapter.

4.2.4 Using Sound Processing Equipment

This broad category of equipment covers a tremendous number of different types of device. They range in complexity from simple tape recording machines through to sophisticated sound synthesis chips. In general, sound processing equipment may be taken to mean any device that is used for the production and/or analysis of sound. This may be intelligible sound (such as spoken words, music, bird song, etc), special effects (for example engine sounds, alarm bells and other sonic indicators) or noise (like coughs, shuffles and sneezes). Sound is a very important ancillary medium for aiding instruction within a computer based environment. Undoubtedly, most interest at present is in the speech/voice processing area (Witten, 1980b).

Fundamentally, there are two possible ways in which CAL authors would like to utilise voice processing equipment for instructional purposes. First, to generate sonic messages which can be relayed to the student (Underwood, 1981). Second, to analyse and recognise utterances that have been spoken by the student (Ainsworth, 1976; Underwood, 1977). To varying extents, a variety of equipment to meet each of these needs is currently available (Costronics, 1979; Frantz and Wiggins, 1982; Anderson, 1981; Lancaster, 1981; Bunn and Haigh, 1982; Levinson and Shipley, 1980; Scott Instruments, 1982; Stuart Systems, 1981; Marsden, 1982).

The generation of speech (see figure 4.13A) is undoubtedly much easier to achieve than its recognition (see figure 4.13B). There are two basic ways in which spoken messages may be created: (1) retrieval of pre-recorded material (digital or analogue) from a storage medium, and (2) dynamic synthesis. In the first of these, the computer driven system simply has to retrieve the message segments from the storage medium (audiotape, audiodisc or read only memory), transform them in an appropriate way and then concatenate them to produce the final spoken message sequence. Naturally, one of the major problems associated with any system based upon storing message segments is the limitations placed on the size of the vocabulary that can be used. For this reason, techniques based upon method (2) – dynamic synthesis – are to be preferred. Usually, systems that employ this approach (the formant synthesis method) create synthetic speech by using the basic structural units (referred to as phonemes) from which all spoken words may be constructed. In addition, special rules are often used for adding pitch, inflection, stress and timing. Using this approach, there is no limit to the vocabulary that can be generated, provided it is possible to formulate the phoneme structure of the constituent words.

(A)   Speech generation

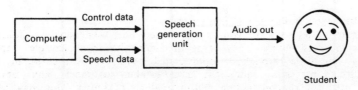

(B)   Speech recognition

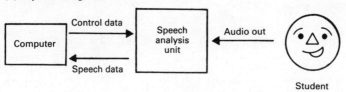

Figure 4.13   Speech processing equipment.

An example of the way in which a speech synthesiser of this variety (Wideband, 1981) may be interfaced to a computer applications port is illustrated in figure 4.14.

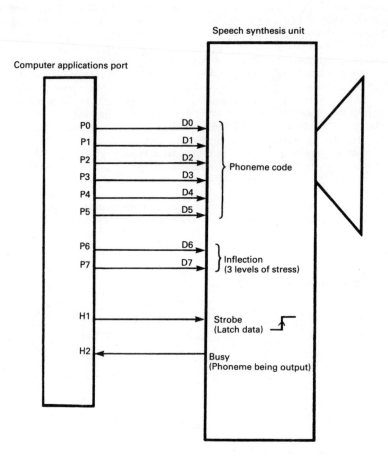

Figure 4.14 Interfacing a speech synthesis unit to a computer.

This system uses the eight I/O pins of the port as a data bus in order to pass across speech data to the synthesiser. It also employs two additional (handshaking) lines (H1 and H2) so that the computer can control the way in which the speech unit operates. One of these (H1) is used to synchronise the passage of data from the computer to the synthesiser. The other line (H2) provides feedback information; the computer can use this to sense the status of the speech unit. This may be in either of two states: ready or busy. In the ready state the synthesiser will accept data from the data bus when told to do so by the computer (by means of the strobe signal line, H1). When in the busy state the synthesiser will not accept data from the bus because it is actively in the process of generating and outputting the phoneme that was specified by the data value previously on the data bus. In a situation such as this, the computer must wait until synthesis is complete before sending another phoneme code to the synthesiser.

Of the eight data lines, six are used to specify a phoneme code (their values being 0 through 63 decimal – there being 64 in all). Two of the data lines (D6 and D7) are used to specify up to three levels of stress (0–3*64). The amount of stress to use with any given phoneme in particular situations is best determined by experiment.

The way in which this system operates is best illustrated by means of an example. Suppose it is required to program the synthesiser in such a way that it generates the word 'HELLO'. The phonemes from which this word is constructed are shown below, along with their decimal codes (Wideband, 1981).

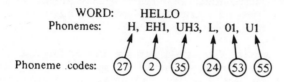

WORD: HELLO
Phonemes: H, EH1, UH3, L, 01, U1

Phoneme codes: 27 2 35 24 53 55

We now make the following assumptions: (1) these codes are stored as successive element values of an array variable called P, and (2) the (memory mapped) address of the computer's application port is A and the addresses of the handshaking lines are H1 and H2. Using these values, one possible program for generating the word 'HELLO' might be

```
10   PUT H1, 0          ;set H1 low
20   FOR I=1 TO 6
30   PUT A, P(I)        ;put phoneme code on bus
40   PUT H1, 1          ;set H1 high to latch data
50   PUT H1, 0          ;return H1 to low state
60   GET H2, X          ;test synthesiser status
70   IF X=0 THEN 60     ;if busy then wait
80   NEXT I             ;process next phoneme
```

Two points are worth mentioning about the above program. Data is only latched into the speech synthesiser during the rising edge of a signal transition on the H1 line (see program statements 40 and 50). Once the speech synthesiser has started to generate a phoneme its status must be tested (program statements 60 and 70) in order to ensure that another phoneme code is not dispatched to it prematurely. The synthesiser indicates its status by setting line H2 low (logic 0) when it is busy and high (logic 1) when it is ready to accept data from the data bus.

Within education, speech generation equipment of the type outlined above has probably been used more effectively (particularly with disabled and handicapped students) than has the complementary technique of speech recognition, mainly because the problems involved are less complex and the equipment that is needed is not as costly.

Recognition of normal human speech is an extremely complicated process and even the latest automatic techniques are very far from being able to deal with the extensive vocabulary, variations in pronounciation and disjointed syntax that are likely to occur in any conversation between people. In view of this, only limited progress has been made towards the realisation of really successful (and low cost) systems based on the use of speech input.

The various approaches that have been used for implementing speech recognition may be subdivided into three basic categories: (1) isolated word recognition (Bunn and Haigh, 1982; Stuart Systems, 1981), (2) connected (or continuous) speech recognisers (Peckham et al., 1982), and (3) speech understanding systems (Levinson and Shipley, 1980; Erman et al., 1980).

Systems operating within category (1) attempt to recognise a single word that is contained within some previously specified vocabulary. This is achieved by pattern matching. Appropriate characteristics of the spoken word (such as formant frequencies) are compared with previously stored values for the set of words contained in the vocabulary. 'Training' is often used so that, for a particular speaker, the system can construct an optimal average parameter set for each of the words being considered. Overall word recognition accuracy using this approach usually depends upon a number of factors, such as vocabulary size, word similarity, number of speakers and whether or not training is used. Accuracies of between 95% and 96% are quite commonplace, although figures as high as 99.8% have been achieved with some systems (Witten, 1980b).

Connected speech recognisers, category (2) above, attempt to recognise every word in a spoken message string. These systems use both pattern matching techniques (for identification of the constituent words) and syntax rules in order to aid message recognition. This type of speech analysis is much more difficult than the previous one because of (a) the longer message strings involved; (b) difficulties associated with locating the separating boundaries between words and phonemes; and (c) the way in which the acoustic characteristics of sounds and words depend upon the context in which they are spoken. There is an extensive amount of real-time speech processing involved with systems of this type. Because of this, they usually require the incorporation of powerful microcomputers and/or minicomputers into their design (Peckham et al., 1982; Peckham, 1983).

Speech understanding systems (Levinson and Shipley, 1980, Erman et al., 1980) differ from the previous two categories in that they attempt to mimic the human capability of understanding the intent of a message rather than recognising every word within it. This goal is achieved by using a wide range of syntactic and semantic rules. In addition, supplementary information (articulatory, lexical, phonetic and task orientated) from a variety of other sources is used to augment these. An important component of this type of system is a mechanism to generate and test hypotheses about the spoken message.

The majority of speech recognition systems of types (2) and (3) have been developed mainly for research use. However, some are now starting to appear within commercial applications. For instructional purposes, most use has been made of devices that fall into category (1). Thus, the 'Voice Based Learning System' distributed by Scott Instruments (1982) uses simple word/phrase recognition as the basis for student interaction. This approach is also used by many other inexpensive recognition systems (Stuart Systems, 1981). In the latter, training must be used in order to get anything like reasonable recognition accuracy. Unfortunately, good systems are at present very expensive.

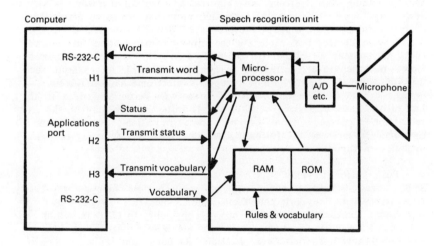

Figure 4.15   Speech recognition unit for CAL applications.

From the point of view of educational applications, a speech recognition unit (SRU) similar to that illustrated in figure 4.15 would serve a number of useful purposes, for example aural multiple choice selection, computer interaction by the disabled, etc. It is essentially an isolated–word/simple–phrase recognition system. Its mode of operation is as follows. Prior to use in a particular dialogue situation, the computer to which it is attached passes across a phonetic description of the word (or phrase) vocabulary from which spoken messages are to be recognised. The internal logic of the SRU then analyses the utterance spoken by the student and passes back to the controlling computer an indication of the word/phrase that was spoken. Should the SRU fail to recognise the spoken message, an appropriate status indication would be passed back to the computer. It is important to note that this system does not involve the use of any training dialogue. For realistic applications of speech recognition within CAL the need for any form of training activity must be eliminated or, at worst, disguised.

Before concluding this section it is important to emphasise the fact that the use of pre-recorded speech (as employed in audiotape, video tape, video disc, and so on) is now a well-established instructional technique, both with and without computer control. Unfortunately, the use of the spoken word as a means of implementing human/computer communication in CAL systems is less well established. However, in the future this medium is likely to play an increasingly important role within computer based multimedia instructional systems.

4.2.5 Adding Special Interaction Aids
We conclude this section on interfacing for multimedia CAL by describing some other simple interaction aids that are often employed in instructional environments. Most of the material presented below deals with devices that facilitate the input of information/data from the CAL student (or author) to the computer. Of course, information flow in the reverse direction is equally important, for example the use of display lights, dials, gauges, electromechanical/robotic devices and so on. The importance of these will become apparent in the last of the cases discussed – the use of training rigs. Because of the restrictions imposed upon us by space limitations, the discussion contained in most of the following sections will be essentially of an overview nature.

(a)   Push–button Devices
The ideas behind the use of push–button arrays are fairly straightforward. They originate from the types of keypad used to implement those simple multiple choice approaches to CAL in which only a limited number of student responses are allowed. In figure 4.6C we illustrated how a computer's application I/O port could be used to sense the status of an external switch, whether open or closed. This basic circuit can easily be extended to include more than one switch (or push–button). The upper limit to the number of simple push–button switches that can be added using this method of interfacing will be determined by the number of I/O pins available on the applications port, for most computers this will be eight. Suppose it was required to construct a push–button selector that made available six switches. The layout and designations of these switches might be similar to that depicted in figure 4.16A.

(A) Simple CAL keypad for multiple choice selection

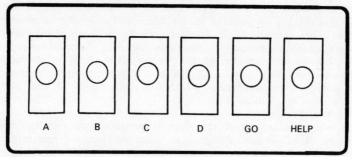

(B) Circuit arrangement for using push button switches

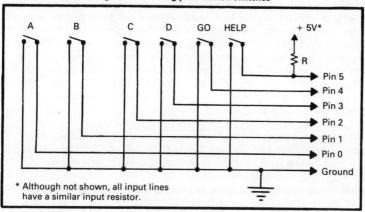

(C) Frame format for multiple choice CAL

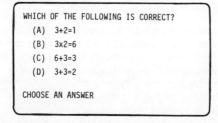

Figure 4.16   Use of push–button switches for CAL applications.

The buttons have been labelled A, B, C, D, GO and HELP. The significance of the way in which the keys have been labelled will become apparent later. Based upon the single switch circuit that was discussed previously (see figure 4.6C) it is now a simple matter to formulate a wiring diagram to enable the interfacing of the above six switches. One possibility is illustrated in figure 4.16B. This shows the relationship between the applications port I/O pin numbering and the labelling of the switches on the keypad. Given this information, a courseware program running in the microcomputer can sense the status of the push-buttons and detect whether or not any of them have been pressed and, if so, which one(s).

With a primitive keypad of this type it becomes very easy to implement elementary CAL systems based upon menu selection (or multiple choice) operations. The simplest approach to realising this technique involves presenting the student with a list of options in tabular form on a CRT screen, or sonically using a tape recorder or speech synthesis system. The student then selects (by pressing the appropriate button) the option which is most relevant to the situation in which he/she happens to be. As an example, consider the CRT frame shown in figure 4.16C. This depicts a four-item menu associated with an instructional sequence used for teaching introductory arithmetical concepts. The 'one-out-of-four' selection mechanism implied by this multiple choice question can easily be implemented using the push-button array outlined above (see figure 4.16A). The significance of the six buttons would now be as follows:

GO   – 'turns pages' of the electronic instructional text
so that the student receives the next CRT frame only
when it is required; instruction thus proceeds at a
learner controlled pace,

HELP   – enables the student to request additional assistance or
remedial information associated with the CRT frame
currently being displayed,

A,B,C,D   – are the option keys that enable the student to respond
to the multiple choice questions or which enable the
selection of a particular instructional pathway – where
a choice is given.

Many simple microcomputer based CAL systems have been constructed using this approach. The major drawbacks to this type of system are (1) the mechanical nature of the push-buttons, and (2) the input limitations imposed by having so few switches.

(b) Touch Pad Systems
Touch sensitive keyboards consist of an array of metallic contact areas that are distributed over some non-conducting surface. These areas form part of an electrical circuit that is strongly influenced by the electrical storage capacity of the human body. Consequently, when one or more of the contact areas is touched, changes are produced

in the electrical state of the circuits of which they form a part. Through appropriate circuit design it is possible to correlate these changes with the actual switches that have been selected and touched by the keyboard user.

Because they contain no moving parts, can be made more reliable and are often more robust than conventional keyboards, their use offers many attractions. However, the greatest benefit probably lies in the fact that they can be designed and fabricated in such a way as to permit a less complex human-machine interface to be created. This enables keyboards to be made more ergonomically acceptable and, at the same time, more directly orientated towards the type of application for which they are to be used, aids for the disabled and computer assisted learning are two important cases. The system depicted in figure 4.17 (Barker, 1981) is one which may be used in a wide variety of CAL applications. It is particularly attractive in situations where the keypad is required to exhibit high resistance to mechanical shock and immunity to a wide range of adverse environmental factors – liquid spillage, dirt/dust penetration, and so on. An added advantage lies in the fact that it is easy to use. The detailed technical description of the system shown in figure 4.17 is given elsewhere (Barker, 1981).

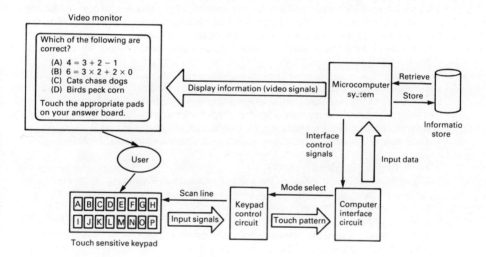

Figure 4.17   Using a touch sensitive keypad in a CAL environment.

Touch pad systems provide an extremely useful means of facilitating student interaction with CAL systems. This is particularly so in the case of handicapped and disabled students since key shapes and sizes can be designed and fabricated to meet particular needs.

(c)   Using Light Pens

Light pens provide yet another means of enabling student interaction with a VDU/microcomputer based CAL system. This mode of interaction, in contrast to the previous two, involves a 'pointing operation' rather than a keystroke or touching action. Devices of this type contain a special light detection system that reacts to areas of brightness on the CRT screen. These are created as a result of displaying alphanumeric characters, special graphic symbols and images at various screen locations. To use the pen for input the user holds it close to the CRT screen and points it at a particular spot of light. The software and hardware interface circuitry of the light pen then enables its position to be determined – either as (X,Y) coordinates or as a row/column combination. Courseware designed for use in conjunction with a light pen can therefore be written to ascertain which part of the screen the user is pointing to.

Further details about light pens and the way they are used are given elsewhere (Shepherd, 1982; Laurie, 1982; Loomis, 1976; Webster and Young, 1978; Lilja, 1983; Newman and Sproull, 1973).

(d)   Touch Sensitive Screens

Like light pens, this type of peripheral provides a mechanism for students to input information to a computer by means of a pointing operation. One of the first touch sensitive screens to be used for educational applications was that developed for use in conjunction with the PLATO computer based learning system (Bitzer et al., 1962; Bitzer, 1976).

For CAL applications, touch screens are useful both in their own right and when they are incorporated into more sophisticated CAL units. For example, many commercial video disc systems now utilise this type of control mechanism in order to facilitate facile end-user interaction with screen pointing operations (Cameron Communications, 1983).

(e)   Using a Graphics Tablet

A graphics tablet is essentially a high resolution (typically 0.01 cm) digitising device, the operation of which depends upon either (1) the use of some form of pressure sensitive surface (Stavely, 1981; Summagraphics, 1980; Newman and Sproull, 1973), or (2) the mechanical movement of a pair of accurate potentiometers (Flowers, 1983; Newman and Sproull, 1973).

Graphics tablets provide facilities that enable students to interact with CAL courseware by means of static pre-prepared diagrams, pictures and horizontal and vertical menus. In addition they permit interaction to take place through the creation of simple sketches. Each of these techniques may be used to create quite effective and novel CAL strategies. For example, a computer controlled voice synthesis unit might be used to request a student to select and position a particular pre-prepared diagram on the digitisation surface of the tablet. The student would then be asked to recognise and identify (by means of pointing or 'pecking' operations) various items on the sheet. Similarly, using a slightly different strategy, the student might be told to place a plain sheet of paper on the drawing surface and subsequently be asked to draw certain objects (for example a square, a triangle, etc). The computer would then analyse these and then make appropriate comments on the student's efforts. As we have outlined above, there are many areas within CAL where graphics tablets can be used to achieve many different and useful modes of instructional interaction with a computer. Of course, this type of device can also be employed as an aid to the courseware author. Some approaches to this mode of using a graphics tablet will be briefly outlined in the following chapter.

(f) Interaction using Hand Print Terminals
Hand print terminals provide a typical example of an intelligent peripheral device. They are referred to as an intelligent device since each one contains its own built-in microprocessor system. This enables this type of device to perform a significant amount of local processing on input data before it is transmitted to a host computer. In many ways the mode of operation of a hand print terminal is similar to that of the graphics tablet described in the previous section. It consists of a pressure sensitive surface upon which the user prints alphabetic and numeric characters. As they are printed, they are recognised by the built-in microprocessor. The code for each character, along with details of its position (row and column position respectively) are then transmitted by way of a serial interface to the host computer, which uses this information to interpret the messages that the student or CAL author is entering. Although free format data entry may be used, interaction with a CAL system is often facilitated if pre-printed forms are employed (Barker, 1982f; Barker et al., 1984).

Hand print terminals provide a useful means of student/author interaction with CAL systems, particularly where the volume of information to be input is quite small. However, for many users, having to print all input messages is both tedious and unnatural. In view of this, hand-written text would provide a better medium of communication than does printed text. Although considerable progress has been made towards the realisation of this input technique (Pecht and Ramm, 1982) it is still not sufficiently advanced to allow its easy application for use in computer assisted learning situations.

(g) Other Types of I/O Device
Many other types of device are often used to provide input and output facilities within a CAL interaction environment. Typical examples include: mice, turtles, joysticks, steering wheels and tracker balls. Each of these types of device is adequately described in the computing literature (Newman and Sproull, 1973; Warfield, 1983; Bidmead, 1984; Roper, 1983; Ciarcia, 1979; Schofield, 1984; Barker, 1984; Andrews,

1983). Many of these are often used in implementing gaming and simulation systems, being used to provide the means by which the student interacts with the underlying courseware (Allison, 1980). The turtle is a particularly important device since it is used in conjunction with the LOGO programming language (Roper, 1983), in which the student controls the two dimensional movement of a toy robot (the turtle) by means of statements entered through a keyboard. Using LOGO, students can cause the turtle to move around and produce drawings on a piece of paper. The use of a LOGO workstation is described in more detail in the following chapter.

(h) Interfacing to Training Rigs
Many forms of training involve using a variety of different types of specialised equipment, for example flight simulators, working models of engines or process plant, laboratory measuring equipment, word processing systems, special keyboards, and so on. Generally, the term 'training rig' is often used to describe this type of instructional aid. There are three basic reasons why computers are utilised within training rigs. First, the complexity of the equipment may dictate that a computer must be used in order to control and coordinate its activity. Second, a computer must be employed since without one the equipment/teaching system would not be feasible. Third, it may be important that the equipment is interfaced to a computer in order to produce a computer based training system, in preference to a conventional one. Aeroplane flight simulators represent a classic example of the first of these categories. The submarine simulation system described in the following chapter provides another example of this class. An example of the second category is the use of computerised manikins for interactive training in cardiopulmonary resuscitation (Hon, 1982). The attachment of laboratory instruments (such as microscopes, electronic balances, digital voltmeters, etc) for training purposes provides an example of the third category of equipment (Barker, 1983a). The application of computers to keyboard training skills described in section 3.3.7 also provides an example of the third category.

The effective utilisation of computers in the context outlined in this section often requires the development of complex hardware interfaces and the production of very sophisticated control programs. Some approaches to solving some of the problems encountered in this mode of CAL are briefly outlined in chapter 5.

4.3 INTEGRATION OF RESOURCES – A MULTIMEDIA CAL UNIT

In order to provide an illustration of the way in which multimedia CAL is implemented, we now describe a simple CAL workstation that incorporates some of the ideas, techniques and principles discussed in the previous sections of this chapter. The system described is one which has been used extensively for teaching and training in both academic and industrial environments (Kenny and Davies, 1979; Yeates,

1981). The discussion that follows is divided into three sections
which describe the workstation construction; courseware design and
implementation; and system evaluation. Further examples of
workstations for CAL are then described in chapter 5.

4.3.1 Workstation Construction

The basic structure of the workstation and the components from which
it is constructed are illustrated in figure 4.18. There are four
important hardware items: the microcomputer, its associated disc unit,
a tape/slide unit and an interface system.

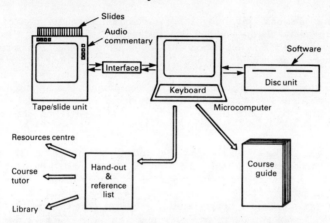

Figure 4.18   Microcomputer based multimedia CAL unit.

The microcomputer has a conventional keyboard, processing unit and low
resolution CRT screen. A number of interface ports are available which
may be used to connect other devices to it. The disc unit (containing
all the teaching software) is linked to the computer by means of its
standard IEEE-488 interface. The external interface for controlling
the tape/slide equipment utilises the computer's application port for
its mode of interconnection. As its name suggests, the tape/slide unit
provides facilities for (1) the projection of 35 mm slides, and (2)
the presentation of an audio commentary. Both the slide projection and
the audio commentary are controlled by the computer through the
connecting interface shown in figure 4.18.

The principles of operation of the interface have been described
earlier. It contains three relays. One of these controls the on/off
status of the audiocassette within the tape/slide unit, the second
initiates forward motion of the slide carousel while the third
provides a feedback mechanism for the computer, by providing a
suitable signal on one of the application port's I/O pins each time a
synchronisation pulse on the audio tape is detected.

The courseware controls the overall activity of the system as a result
of a student's interaction with it. This interaction takes place by
way of the keyboard, which may be used to enter (1) simple responses
to multiple choice questions presented on the CRT screen, and (2)
basic control commands such as STOP, HELP, CONTINUE, and so on. All
instructions to the student are issued textually with the use of the
CRT screen and the course guide. The tape/slide unit is used primarily
to provide graphic and sonic support for the learning material
presented through the CRT display. Further details of the courseware
are presented in section 4.3.2.

Teaching sessions involving the workstation normally proceed in the
following way. Before commencing instruction, the student 'sets up'
the system by (1) switching on the power supply, and (2) inserting the
courseware disc, audio tape and slide carousel into their appropriate
positions within the teaching unit. The student then enters his/her
course registration details into the computer, these are needed to
enable written progress reports to be produced for inspection by the
course director. Once the keyboard entry of registration details has
been completed, instruction can take place.

During the course of instruction the student is required to (1) watch
the microcomputer screen and read textual frames that are presented
upon it, (2) look at the slide images being displayed, (3) listen to
their supporting audio commentary, (4) refer to material contained
within the workbook, library and/or resources centre, and (5) answer
multiple choice questions presented on the CRT screen. These
activities can be amalgamated in various ways in order to create quite
sophisticated instructional encounters for the student. During these
encounters substantial information flow takes place between the
student and his/her interaction environment. The channels involved are
summarised in figure 4.19.

4.3.2 Courseware Design and Implementation
Courseware for the CAL system will normally consist of a number of
different items: computer software (stored on a flexible disc), a
course guide, a hand-out and a reference list. The two latter items
can be used to provide details of supportive learning
materials/resources not directly connected to, or in the vicinity of,
the teaching system. Thus, after a study session at the workstation a
student might be directed to (1) use an item of ancillary equipment
held in a communal resource centre, (2) partake of a consultation and
discussion with a course tutor or, (3) consult appropriate reading
material in a library. The course guide (or workbook) may be used to
provide students with a set of course notes and also specify details
of the study strategies that are to be used. It can thus form the
student's overall guide to the teaching system and the course.

The role played by the major courseware items and the mechanisms involved in their design and preparation are described in more detail below.

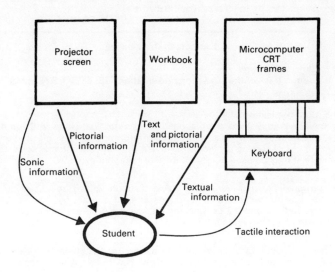

Figure 4.19   Student interaction with and information flow for the multimedia CAL unit.

(a)   Script Preparation and Audio Recording

The tape/slide equipment shown in figure 4.18 is responsible for providing a facility to enable the presentation of high quality graphic images (described in the next section) along with the accompanying narration used to explain the pictorial information that they contain. Preparation of the audio tape for use in the tape/slide unit involves two stages. First, the spoken narrative must be recorded onto one of the tracks of a blank twin-track tape cassette cartridge. Second, the synchronisation pulses (used by the computer for control purposes) must be added to the other track.

Adding synchronisation pulses is fairly easy since most tape/slide units contain a 'pulse' button. This allows a marker pulse to be put on track 2 of the audio tape each time this button is pressed. Consequently, the courseware producer now only has to sit and listen to the previously recorded commentary and press the pulse button at each point on the tape that it is required to add a pulse.

Prior to recording the audio commentary on the tape it was necessary to prepare a written script for the narrator to use, a section of such a script is illustrated in figure 4.20. The most convenient way of doing this is undoubtedly by means of a computer based word processing system (possibly running within the workstation itself when this is operating in authoring mode). This provides an easy means of modifying and reprinting versions of the manuscript without the need to involve a typist. Once the final version of the audio script is agreed upon it may be given to the narrator for recording.

Example of Draft Script

Slide 0.5 (Blue background)
This is the sound track of the tape-slide presentation "TELETEXT SYSTEMS".°

Slide 1 (Title slide)°

Slide 1.5 (Communication)
During their everyday lives people need to communicate one with another. The purpose of communication is to disseminate information. This information may be used as a means of solving problems or for carrying on conventional social discourse. Alternatively, it may be used purely for its entertainment value.°

Slide 2
People communicate in a variety of ways: through talking and listening, through writing, by drawing pictures and diagrams and, of course, by reading. Very often listening to a radio broadcast or watching a television programme can constitute very effective methods of receiving information.°

Slide 2.5
Communication is the transmission of information from a source to a destination via a suitable communication channel. It can be a one-way or two-way process.°

Slide 3
A newspaper, a book or a television programme each represent a unidirectional or one-way means of communication. The author of a newspaper article or of a book has little opportunity of interacting with the recipient of the information that he dispatches.°

Slide 4
Two-way or bi-directional communication involves information flow between the originator of the information and its recipient. For example, a conventional conversation between two people, either face to face or via a telephone system, are examples of bi-directional communication. In this mode of communication the media used to convey information need not be the same. The third example shown in the slide, mode C, illustrates how two different channels may be used to carry information between those involved in the communication process.°

Slide 4.5 (Now turn to the computer screen).°*

Legend: °   Slide change
          *   Wait 4 seconds

Figure 4.20   Section of an audio script.

(b)   Slide Production and Projection
Slides may be produced from material that originates from a variety of different sources, for example original artwork produced by the courseware team, live shots taken on location, material extracted from books, newspapers, journals, magazines, and so on. Materials that cannot be adequately reproduced as slides may instead be entered, in an appropriate way, into the lesson workbook. Obviously, it is most

convenient if all the slides are of the same type (in our system we use those of the 35 mm variety). All slides should be mounted in plastic mounts (for robustness), numbered sequentially and then stored ready for use in a suitable storage magazine (the equipment we have requires the use of a circular carousel). The numbers assigned to the slides provide a useful means of reordering them if ever they get out of sequence; they are also used to coordinate the slide display and the audio narration (see figure 4.20).

Details of the slide projection technique used in our CAL unit are given in figure 4.21. Image display is based upon the use of a back projection method, that is slides are projected from behind the viewing screen. This enables the student to look at the slides in the same way as he/she looks at the CRT screen of the microcomputer. The student viewing area for the slides measures about 25 cm x 25 cm.

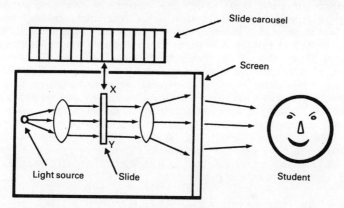

Figure 4.21   The slide projection system.

The slide storage magazine (a carousel) fits conveniently on top of the projection unit (see figure 4.21). This provides an easy means of mounting and dismounting sets of slides. Once mounted on the tape/slide unit the carousel may be rotated (under computer control) in an anticlockwise direction about a vertical axis. As the carousel advances through the slide sequence, the slide immediately above the entry hatch drops down (under the force of gravity) into the projection position – denoted by XY in figure 4.21. After being displayed, the slide is automatically pushed back up into the carousel, which is then rotated again ready for the next slide to drop in and be displayed.

Because of the mechanical movement to which slides are subjected, they sometimes wear, become jammed and thus damaged. In order to avoid inconveniences due to problems of this sort it is useful to keep duplicate copies of slides so that damaged ones can easily be replaced.

(c)   The Function and Design of the Workbook
Workbooks, in general, play an important role in CAL training schemes.
Their major uses are:

(1) To introduce a topic and thus reduce the amount of textual
information required on the computer screen.
(2) To specify general and learning objectives.
(3) To provide additional text and diagrams that expand upon
information presented by other media used in the course.
(4) To introduce the student to books and other reference material
relevant to the lesson.
(5) To provide 'take away' documentation for the course.

As   well as providing students with a set of course notes (item (5)) a
guidebook can also be used to   contain   additional   reinforcement   and
remediation   material   that,   for   one   reason   or   another, cannot be
directly incorporated into the system as   a   computer   based   resource
(items   (1)   and   (3)).   Indeed,   the workbook can become an important
element of the learning environment if its contents are   appropriately
integrated   into   the   main   teaching   strategy   of   the CAL unit. For
example, most of our courseware units make available a HELP   facility.
That   is,   the student is allowed to press a special button or type in
the command HELP when he/she requires extra help or more detailed
explanations   about   certain   topics. When a help request is made, the
additional information required by the student may be presented on the
CRT screen or, alternatively,   the   student   may   be   directed   to   an
appropriate   section   of   the   guidebook.   Once   the   material   in   the
guidebook has been consulted, the student would normally continue with
his/her computer based instruction.

Because of its   importance,   considerable   effort   must   be   put   into
workbook/guidebook   design.   Naturally,   it   has   to   be   designed   in
conjunction with the other teaching resources   and   not   in   isolation
from them.   Normally, one or two members of the courseware team are
delegated the responsibility for coordinating its   production.   As   in
the   case   of the script for the audio narrative, much of the material
for the workbook (and   artwork   used   for   slide   production)   can   be
prepared   with   the   use   of   word   processing equipment. This offers an
extremely useful approach for those situations where updating (perhaps
due   to   technical   obsolescence)   needs   to   take   place   at   regular
intervals.

(d)   Microcomputer Frame Design
A typical example of a microcomputer CRT frame display is presented in
figure   4.22. It is an example of an initial frame that is used (1) to
enable course registration details to be entered, and (2) to   provide
basic   instructions   to   the user relating to certain procedures to be
followed.

Like that shown in figure 4.22, most of the CRT frames used in our system are used to display textual information. The text display may possibly be augmented by using a variety of different text, background and border colours, provided the microcomputer CRT is able to provide suitable facilities to support these effects. Similarly, if it is able to handle teletext graphics characters then it also becomes possible to generate simple pictorial frames.

```
NAME:

COURSE:

  PRESS ADVANCE ON THE TAPE/SLIDE UNIT

  PRESS PLAY ON THE TAPE/SLIDE UNIT


  WATCH THE SLIDES ....

  LISTEN TO THE TAPE RECORDING ....


  YOU'LL BE ASKED QUESTIONS ABOUT WHAT YOU
  SEE AND HEAR ......
```

Figure 4.22   A microcomputer CRT frame.

Normally, the material to be displayed on the CRT screen (that is, the frame content) is specified by the courseware author by means of a CRT frame design chart. An example of such a chart is presented in figure 4.23. These charts not only define frame content but, through appropriate annotation, can be used to specify other details relating to the display of the frame, hold time, any special sound effects, colouring details, a pointer to the section of software code that is responsible for producing it, and so on.

Once all the frames for a particular lesson section are completed they can be passed to the software engineer (or programmer) who is responsible for producing the microcomputer instructions that will be used to produce the frame display on the CRT screen. Usually a programming language (for example BASIC or FORTRAN) or an authoring facility (such as PILOT or MICROTEXT) would be employed for the coding of frames (Barker and Singh, 1983).

(e) Software Production
In principle, the construction of the CAL unit depicted in figure 4.18 could be centred around any of the currently available microcomputer systems. Obviously, an important factor likely to significantly influence the choice made will be the availability of suitable languages for software development. Most microcomputers nowadays come

supplied with a version of BASIC as a standard software item. In many
cases an author language such as PILOT or MICROTEXT can usually be
purchased for a small additional cost, these are particularly easy to
incorporate into the micro if it is fitted with a standard operating
system (see section 1.1.3). One or other of the above development
tools must be used to convert the CAL frame design charts (see figure
4.23) into an executable CAL program. Details of the way in which
these systems are used and the facilities they offer have already been
presented in chapters 2 and 3. In our implementation of the multimedia
CAL unit (Yeates, 1981) all the teaching programs were coded in BASIC
since this was the only language available with the microcomputer
system that we employed. BASIC was found to be a very easy–to–use
language and so, after an initial learning period, it provided a
simple, rapid and effective way of coding the CAL frames.

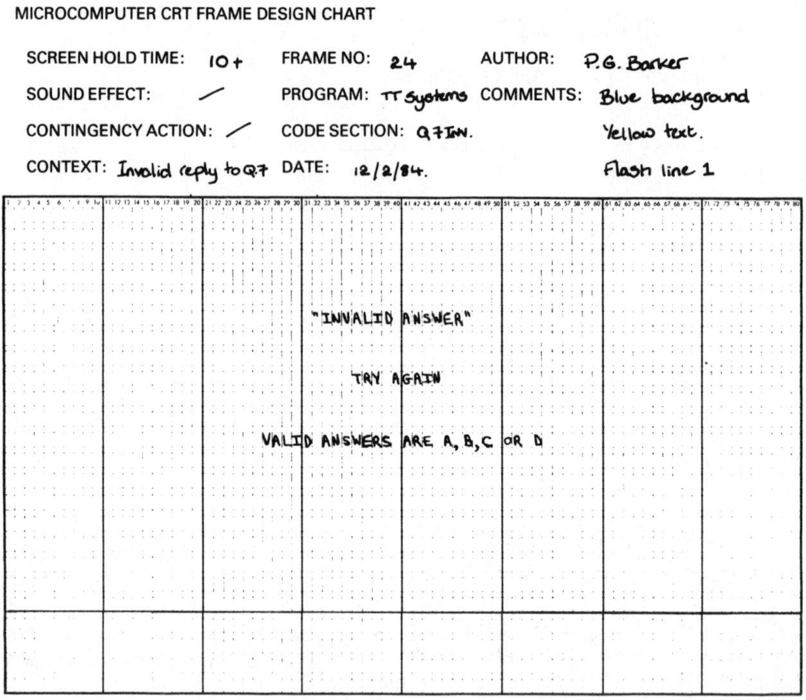

MICROCOMPUTER CRT FRAME DESIGN CHART

SCREEN HOLD TIME: 10+   FRAME NO: 24   AUTHOR: P.G. Barker

SOUND EFFECT: ╱   PROGRAM: TT Systems COMMENTS: Blue background

CONTINGENCY ACTION: ╱   CODE SECTION: Q7Iw.   Yellow text.

CONTEXT: Invalid reply to Q7 DATE: 12/2/84.   Flash line 1

```
                          "INVALID ANSWER"

                              TRY AGAIN

                    VALID ANSWERS ARE A, B, C OR D
```

Figure 4.23   CAL frame layout chart for microcomputer CRT screens.

Whenever possible, and no matter what language is used, the courseware
must be appropriately structured and documented so that it is easy to
maintain and modify. This will become necessary when errors are
detected and when changes are needed as a consequence of experience

gained with it. Of course, once the software has been developed it must be fully checked and tested before it is released for use by students.

4.3.3 System Evaluation

When evaluating a CAL based system there are a number of important factors that need to be considered. These fall into three basic categories: (1) financial aspects, (2) ergonomic considerations, and (3) teaching effectiveness. Each of these is briefly outlined below.

(a) Financial Aspects

The costs incurred in building and operating a CAL system originate from three major sources: (1) components and construction, (2) operating overheads, and (3) courseware development. The CAL unit illustrated in figure 4.18 was constructed from readily available low cost equipment. Indeed, its cost of construction was less than $5000. In general, operational costs are not significantly higher than those for other types of teaching equipment. The only substantial outlay of a recurring nature is likely to be the cost of taking out a maintenance contract for the computer equipment, if this is deemed to be necessary. The reliability of modern microcomputer systems makes the need for this questionable. Because of the many different resources involved, courseware development costs can become quite substantial. Undoubtedly, the major cost contribution here is that associated with the design and writing of the software for the system. Naturally, this can be minimised through the use of authoring facilities, standard libraries of code and aids to automate the generation of code. During the development of our system we were not greatly concerned with the financial aspects of the project since our main interest was in investigating its potential as an instructional tool.

(b) Ergonomic Considerations

There are two basic factors which need to be considered in this area — ease of use of the system and end-user satisfaction with it. Essentially, three categories of user are likely to directly interact with the system. First, there will be students who will use it in learning/teaching mode. Second, there will be authors who will require to use the system in authoring mode in order to develop courseware. Finally, there will be teachers who will supervise the use of the system and who will also need to interrogate it in order to extract course statistics. In order to gain some overall indication of end-user satisfaction with our system we performed an experiment in which we exposed a number of students, teachers and authors to a teaching programme that we had developed. We then solicited their views by means of a questionnaire.

The design of the questionnaire was based upon an assessment procedure described by a British Library Research and Development team (Hills et al., 1977). Our questionnaire consisted of 17 questions that were designed to assess:

(1) the amount of notetaking undertaken by the user;
(2) views on the amount of information presented in the time available;
(3) the pace of the information presented – in the beginning, middle and at the end of the presentation;
(4) views on the length of the presentation;
(5) the level of interest experienced in the presentation at the beginning, middle and end;
(6) amount of satisfaction in being given the opportunity to see the presentation;
(7) views on the usefulness of the presentation;
(8) views on the effectiveness of the presentation as a method of learning;
(9) the amount of difficulty experienced with the information presented;
(10) the legibility of the slides used;
(11) views on whether the content of the slides supplemented the commentary;
(12) the quality of the commentary;
(13) views on the ease of understanding of the questions posed by the computer;
(14) ease or difficulty in following instructions on the use of the equipment;
(15) the amount of information contained in the workbook;
(16) familiarity with the subject matter before using the learning package;
(17) comments on how to improve the system and suggestions for possible application areas.

The results of our analysis of the questionnaires revealed a consenus view that the multimedia CAL unit could indeed form the basis of a worthwhile and easy to use instructional system. However, some of the courseware authors who were involved in the investigation did express some concern about the lack of a high level authoring facility for the workstation.

(c) Teaching Effectiveness
Various quantitative studies have been conducted in order to prove and substantiate the effectiveness of multimedia instructional techniques. The effectiveness of the approach that we have been describing in this section has been demonstrated by some investigations performed by Kenny and Schmulian (1979). They conducted a series of controlled tests using groups of medical students who were instructed (in a given topic) using (1) conventional lecturing/tutorial techniques, and (2) a CAL based system similar to that illustrated in figure 4.18. Their measurements supported the general view that this CAL based approach provides a useful and effective medium of instruction.

In order to assess how effectively our system could be used to disseminate technical information to students, we conducted a series of pre–tests and post–tests (Yeates, 1981). The method adopted was as follows:

(1) prepare a data bank of slide material on a given subject;
(2) test student with randomly selected questions based upon the material held in the data bank and record his/her answers – this constitutes the pre–test;
(3) present the student with the course of instruction;
(4) test the student with randomly selected questions from the data bank and record his/her answers – this constitutes the post–test;
(5) compare the results of steps (4) and (2) in order to see if there is any significant difference;
(6) repeat for the next member of the sample population.

Our results indicated that, after interaction with the CAL unit, students were indeed more knowledgeable about the topic of instruction, having gained substantially higher scores in the post-test than were obtained in the pre–test. Thus, the system does impart information to students, that is, it is capable of being used for teaching. Of course, whether or not it is as effective as other techniques when cost considerations are also taken into account still remains to be seen. Further controlled experiments would need to be performed in order to investigate and confirm this.

4.4 CONCLUSION

Multimedia CAL requires a diverse range of widely different communication channels for its implementation. In this chapter we have given considerable attention to this topic, particularly the mechanisms and basic equipment necessary to implement this approach to instructional technology. Because of their importance, this chapter has concentrated on (1) explaining what is meant by the term multimedia CAL, (2) describing some of the media available, (3) outlining the basic interfacing principles involved in using these other media for CAL applications, and (4) showing how some of these resources can be integrated together to form a very simple multimedia CAL workstation.

In chapter 5 we describe some of the ways in which the techniques outlined in this chapter have been applied to the construction of a variety of different multimedia CAL workstations for use in academic, commercial, maritime and industrial training situations.

4.5 BIBLIOGRAPHY

Ainsworth, W.A., Mechanisms of Speech Recognition, Pergamon, Oxford, 1976.

Allison, D., On future fantasy games, Recreational Computing, 9(1), 27–29, 1980.

Anderson, J.C., An extremely low cost computer voice response system, Byte: The Small Systems Journal, 6(2), 36–43, 1981.

Andrews, E.W., Track–ball interfacing techniques for microprocessors, Byte: The Small Systems Journal, 8(12), 234–242, 1983.

Backen, D., MicroTICCIT comes to UK, CALNEWS, 10–11, Council for Educational Technology, London, 1983.

Barker, P.G., Experiments with a touch sensitive keyboard, Electronics and Computing Monthly, 1(7), 20–24, 1981.

Barker, P.G., Data transfer between micros, Electronics and Computing Monthly, 2(5), 21–25; 46–49, 1982a.

Barker, P.G., Computer networks, Wireless World, 88(1563) 74–78, 1982b.

Barker, P.G., Computer interfaces for slide projectors, Electronics and Computing Monthly, 2(3), 18–22; 34, 1982c.

Barker, P.G., Computer control of a random access slide projector, Microprocessing and Microprogramming, 10, 261–271, 1982d.

Barker, P.G., Computer control of projectors, Wireless World, 88(1554), 86–87, 1982e.

Barker, P.G., Data base interaction using a hand print terminal, International Journal of Man–Machine Studies, 17, 435–458, 1982f.

Barker, P.G., Computers in Analytical Chemistry, Chapter 6, 223–260, Pergamon, Oxford, 1983a.

Barker, P.G., Timing data transfer, Wireless World, 89(1569), 44–48, 1983b.

Barker, P.G., Video disc programming for interactive video, Wireless World, 89(1574), 44–48, 1983c.

Barker, P.G., Using a Steering Wheel System as an Input Device in an Interactive Workstation, Interactive Systems Research Group, Department of Computer Science, Teesside Polytechnic, County Cleveland, 1984.

Barker, P.G., and Singh, R., A practical introduction to authoring for computer assisted instruction. Part 2: PILOT, British Journal of Educational Technology, 14(3), 15–41, 1983.

Barker, P.G., Najah, M. and Roper, J.S., User Experiences with a MICROPAD, Journal of Microcomputer Applications, Academic Press, 7, 19–39, 1984.

Bidmead, C., Of mice and menus, Practical Computing, 7(1), 88–90, 1984.

Bitzer, D.L., The wide world of computer based education, Advances in Computers, 15, 239–281, 1976.

Bitzer, D.L., Braunfeld, P.G. and Lichtenberger, W.W., PLATO–II: a multiple–student, computer controlled, automatic teaching device, in Programmed Learning and Computer Based Instruction, edited by J.E. Coulson, 205–216, John Wiley, New York, NY, 1962.

Bryce, C.F.A. and Stewart, A.M., Improved Computer Aided Instruction by the Use of Interfaced Random–Access Audio–Visual Equipment, Report on Research Project No. P/24/1, Dundee College of Technology, Dundee, 1982.

Bryce, C.F.A. and Stewart, A., How to use video discs in medical education, (Part 1), Medical Teacher, 5(1), 6–10, 1983a.

Bryce, C.F.A. and Stewart, A., How to use video discs in medical education, (Part 2), Medical Teacher, 5(2), 57–59, 1983b.

Bunderson, C.V., Instructional strategies for videodisc courseware: the McGraw–Hill disc, Journal of Educational Technology Systems, 8(3), 207–210, 1980.

Bunn, P. and Haigh, S., Application note: spoken word recognition with a real–time spectrum analyser, Journal of Microcomputer Applications, 5, 173–181, 1982.

Bursky, D., The S–100 Bus Handbook, Hayden, Rochelle Park, NJ, 1980.

Cameron Communications, INTERACT Touch Screen Video Terminal, Product Specification, Cameron Communications, Glasgow, 1983.

Camp, R.C., Smay, T.A. and Triska, C.J., Microprocessor Systems Engineering, Matrix, Portland, OR, 1979.

Chapman, R.L. and Carpenter, J.T., Computer techniques in instruction, in Programmed Learning and Computer Based Instruction, edited by J.E. Coulson, 240–253, John Wiley, New York, NY, 1962.

Ciarcia, S., Joystick interfaces, Byte: The Small Systems Journal, 4(9), 10–18, 1979.

Copeland, P., An interactive video system for education and training, British Journal of Educational Technology, 14(1), 59–65, 1983.

Costronics, Microspeech system, Wireless World, 85(1518), 39, 1979.

Coulson, J.E., A computer–based laboratory for research and development in education, in Programmed Learning and Computer Based Instruction, edited by J.E. Coulson, 191–204, John Wiley, New York, NY, 1962a.

Davies, P.D. and Kenny, G.N.C., Micro control of a video cassette lecture, Medical Education, 14, 196–198, 1980.

Erman, L.D., Hayes–Roth, F., Lesser, V.R. and Reddy, D.R., The Hearsay–II speech understanding system: integrating knowledge to resolve uncertainty, ACM Computing Surveys, 12(2), 213–253, 1980.

Fisher, E., and Jensen, C.W., PET and the IEEE–488 BUS (GPIB), Osborne/McGraw Hill, Berkeley, CA, 1980.

Flowers, J.C., BBC/ATOM graphics digitiser, Practical Computing, 6(3), 100–103, 1983.

Foster, C.C., Real–Time Programming – Neglected Topics, Addison–Wesley, Reading, MA, 1981.

Frantz, G.A. and Wiggins, R.H., Speech synthesis – design case history: Speak & Spell learns to talk, IEEE Spectrum, 19(2), 45–49, 1982.

Hallgren, R.C., Interactive control of a videocassette recorder with a personal computer, Byte: The Small Systems Journal, 5, 116–134, 1980.

Hills, P.J., Lincoln, L. and Turner, L.P., Evaluation of Tape/Slide Guides for Library Instruction, British Library Research and Development Report No. 5378–HC, 1977.

Hon, D., Interactive training in cardiopulmonary resuscitation, Byte: The Small Systems Journal, 7(6), 108–138, 1982.

Kane, G.R., Leonard, W.F. and Nashburg, R.E., CAVI – a microcomputer based tool to enhance flexible paced learning, in Frontiers in Education Conference Proceedings, Houston, Texas, October 20–22, 1980, edited by L.P. Grayson and J.M. Biedenbach, 160–166, IEEE, New York, NY, 1980.

Kenny, G.N.C. and Davies, P.D., The use of a microcomputer in anaesthetic teaching, Anaesthesia, 34, 583–585, 1979.

Kenny, G.N.C. and Schmulian, C., Computer assisted learning in the teaching of anaesthesia, Anaesthesia, 34, 159–162, 1979.

Kodak, Kodak Carousel S-RA2000 Slide Projector Manual, Publication No. 0-96312-478, Kodak, West Germany, 1980.

Lancaster, M., Practical systems for speech synthesis, Practical Computing, 4(11), 112–114, 1981.

Laurie, N., ARFON light pen, Practical Computing, 5(5), 69, 1982.

Laurillard, D.M., The potential of interactive video, Journal of Educational Television, 8(3), 173–180, 1982.

Levinson, S.E. and Shipley, K.L., A conversational-mode airline information and reservation system using speech input and output, The Bell Technical Journal, 59(1), 119–137, 1980.

Libes, S. and Garetz, M., Interfacing to S-100/IEEE-696 Microcomputers, Osborne/McGraw Hill, Berkeley, CA, 1981.

Lilja, D.J., Build a light pen for the APPLE II, Byte: The Small Systems Journal, 8(6), 395–406, 1983.

Loomis, S., Let there be light pens, Byte: The Small Systems Journal, 1(5), 26–30, 1976.

Marsden, P., A voice emerges from the wilderness, Practical Computing, 5(10), 116–123, 1982.

Newman, W.M. and Sproull, R.F., Principles of Interactive Computer Graphics, McGraw-Hill, New York, NY, 1973.

Pecht, J. and Ramm, I., Recognition of hand-written characters using the DAP, ICL Technical Journal, 3(2), 199–217, 1982.

Peckham, J., The LOGOS continuous speech recognition system, Computer Bulletin, Series II, (35), 2–3, 1983.

Peckham, J., Green, J., Canning, J. and Stephens, P., LOGOS – a real time hardware continuous speech recognition system, in Proceedings of the International Conference on Acoustics, Speech and Signal Processing, Publication No. CH-1746-7/82/0000-0863, 863–866, IEEE, 1982.

Philips, Philips VP705 Professional Laservision – Operating Instructions, Publication No. PRD 4044, Philips, 1982a.

Philips, Philips VP705 Professional Laservision – Product Specification, Publication No. PRD 4042, Philips, 1982b.

Poe, E.C. and Goodwin, J.C., The S-100 and Other Micro Buses, (Second Edition), Howard W. Sams, Indianapolis, IN, 1979.

Reis, C.W.B., (editor), Specification of standards for broadcast teletext signals, IBA Technical Review, (2), Technical Reference Book, 76–89, (3rd Edition), 1976.

Roper, C., French flock to computer centre, New Scientist, 97(1344), 358–361, 1983.

Saal, H.J., Local area networks: possibilities for personal computers, Byte: The Small Systems Journal, 6(10), 92–112, 1981.

Saal, H.J., Local area networks: an update on microcomputers in the office, Byte: The Small Systems Journal, 8(5), 60–79, 1983.

Schofield, J., Joysticks and games controllers, Practical Computing, 7(1), 92–93, 1984.

Schwartz, M.D., Integrating CAI and video tape, Creative Computing, 116–117, 1980.

Scott Instruments, Voice Based Learning System, Product Description, Scott Instruments, Denton, TX, 1982.

Shepherd, M., A light pen for microcomputers, Wireless World, 88(1588), 30–32, 1982.

Sippl, C.J. and Dahl, F., Video Computers: How to Select, Mix, and Operate Personal Computers and Home Video Systems, Prentice–Hall, Englewood Cliffs, NJ, 1981.

Stavely, D.J., A high–quality low–cost graphics tablet, Hewlett–Packard Journal, 32(1), 15–24, 1981.

Stone, H.S., Microcomputer Interfacing, Addison–Wesley, Reading, MA, 1982.

Stuart Systems, 'Big Ears' SR1 Speech Recognition Unit, User Manual, Stuart Systems, Brentwood, 1981.

Summagraphics, BIT PAD ONE User's Manual, Summagraphics, Fairfield, CT, 1980.

Tandberg, TCCR-530 – Computer Controlled Cassette Recorder Characteristics and Applications, Tandberg, Kjeller, Norway, 1983.

Underwood, M.J., Machines that understand speech, The Radio and Electronic Engineer, 47, 368–376, 1977.

Underwood, M.J., Giving the computer a voice, ICL   Technical   Journal, 2(3), 253-270, 1981.

VonFeldt, J.R., A description of the DAVID interactive instructional television system and its application to post high school education of the deaf, in Proceedings of the Conference on Interactive Videodisc and Media Storage Technology in Education and Training, February 27-28, 7-15, Society for Applied Learning Technology, Warrington, VA, 1979.

Warfield, R.W., The new interface technology: an introduction to windows and mice, Byte: The Small Systems Journal, 8(12), 218-230, 1983.

Webster, J. and Young, J., Add a $3 light pen to your video display, Byte: The Small Systems Journal, 3(5), 52-58, 1978.

Wideband, SPEAKEASY Speech Synthesiser Reference Manual, Wideband, Royston, 1981.

Witten, I.H., Communicating with Microcomputers, An Introduction to the Technology of Man–Computer Communication, Academic Press, London, 1980a.

Witten, I.H., Speech Communication, Chapter 5 in Communicating with Microcomputers: An Introduction to the Technology of Man–Computer Communication, Academic Press, London, 1980b.

Yeates, H., Some Experiments in Man–Machine Interaction Relevant to Computer Assisted Learning, M.Sc. Thesis, University of Durham, 1981.

Further Reading

Coulson, J.E., (editor), Programmed Learning and Computer Based Instruction, Proceedings of the Conference on Application of Digital Computers to Automated Instruction, October 10-12, 1961, John Wiley, New York, NY, 1962b.

Duke, J., Interactive Video: Implications for Education and Training, Working Paper No. 22, Council for Educational Technology, London, 1983.

Hawkridge, D., New Information Technology in Education, Croom Helm, London, 1983.

Jamison, D., Suppes, P. and Wells, S., The Effectiveness of Alternative Instructional Media: A Survey, Review of Educational Research, 44(1), 1-67, 1974.

Chapter 5

APPROACHES TO
MULTIMEDIA CAL

5.1 INTRODUCTION

In the last chapter we gave a brief introduction to the concepts underlying multimedia CAL. Essentially, this instructional technique involves using several channels of instruction (either simultaneously or in succession) in order to optimise the efficiency of a learning task. The coordination and control problems which are normally encountered within systems of this type are quite significant. Consequently, the aid of a computer is of paramount importance (see figure 4.1C).

We concluded the last chapter by describing how a variety of different resources could be brought together to form a sophisticated learner controlled interaction environment (figure 4.18). Configurations of equipment of this type now form the basis of many different kinds of CAL workstation. Because of their importance a large part of this chapter (section 5.2) is devoted to a description of some practical approaches to workstation fabrication. The examples chosen range in complexity from simple CAL units (similar to that described in section 4.3) through to advanced simulation equipment of the type used for training pilots, navigators and process control operatives. Most of the workstations we have included in our discussion are currently being employed for commercial and industrial training applications. Utilisation of this type of equipment within conventional educational

environments is less well established at the moment. However, the
demand for this approach to learning is likely to increase in future
years as the benefits it offers are more widely realised.

Unfortunately, when resources are brought together in the way outlined
above, significant problems arise, mainly because of the complexity of
the systems produced. These problems originate from four basic
sources, namely

(1) the production of suitable hardware interfaces to
    enable device attachment,
(2) the formulation of appropriate software routines
    for controlling the attached devices,
(3) the generation of courseware that makes effective
    use of the resources available, and
(4) the difficulties associated with managing and
    maintaining these complex systems.

The principles of interfacing were discussed in some detail in the
last chapter, as were the basic ideas necessary for the development of
device control software. The ease of courseware production will depend
upon two major factors: (1) the types of resource that the workstation
utilises, and (2) the availability of suitable software development
tools; usually a special purpose author language will be required
(Philips, 1983; Barker, 1984a). The problems of managing complex
workstations are, in principle, no different from those associated
with the management and control of other types of computer terminal,
other than the additional difficulties of maintaining controls and
checks on the special purpose learning resources that are needed. In
some situations it may be necessary to implement special procedures
that ensure their security.

The extent to which the problems listed above inhibit progress with
multimedia CAL based teaching will often depend upon the type of
approach that is used for equipment acquisition. Generally, two routes
are available. First, in-house development; second, the utilisation of
a turnkey system. The first of these is the more difficult since it
involves designing and building the teaching equipment, and the
courseware that goes with it. The easier solution is undoubtedly to
purchase the equipment and courseware as an operational (turnkey)
system from a specialist supplier who is actively involved in the
professional development of workstations for educational applications.
The latter approach certainly minimises the effects of the problems
outlined earlier, even though it may be more expensive. In the
discussion that follows, examples of both turnkey and in-house systems
will be used to illustrate the different approaches to the realisation
of multimedia CAL.

5.2   APPLICATIONS OF MULTIMEDIA CAL - SOME CASE STUDIES

Given a pool of instructional resources there are usually very many ways in which they may be utilised in order to produce a lesson or courseware unit. Indeed, we have found that many organisations tend to develop instructional strategies based upon resource combinations that they feel (either intuitively or through experience) best suit their training needs. Consequently, in the discussion we present below, no hard and fast guidelines for combining resources will be given. Instead, we describe some of what has been done and leave the reader to decide whether or not particular approaches are relevant to their own training situations.

5.2.1 Texaco's TOPCAT Computer Assisted Training System

The TOPCAT system represents a novel, low-cost experimental venture that was undertaken at a time of severe financial stringency in the shipping industry. It comprises a training system that utilises inexpensive microcomputers in the role of interactive instructors at sea (Anderson, 1982; King, 1981; 1982). After two years of successful operation on merchant ships of the Texaco fleet it had reduced training costs while, at the same time, substantially improving the level of training involved. This was achieved by using the microcomputers in conjunction with a large library of existing MAVIS (Maritime Audio Visual Instructional System) audio-visual materials. The TOPCAT system has undoubtedly introduced a significant change in the methodology of marine training and provides yet another example of the importance of the microcomputer as an audio-visual resource.

TOPCAT is an acronym for Texaco Onboard Programme of Computer Assisted Training. Each ship in the fleet is provided with the following basic equipment:

(1) a microcomputer having 32 Kbytes of RAM,
(2) a compatible tape cassette recorder for the storage of computer programs, and
(3) a MAVIS audio-visual projector unit - fitted with a special internal logic board.

The audio-visual materials are contained in a continuous-loop 16 mm filmstrip and magnetic audio tape that are permanently synchronised in a single cartridge which contains up to 250 single frame 16 mm visuals. The audio capacity of the tape is either 18 or 36 minutes depending on the playing speed used. The viewing unit (see figure 5.1) for the graphic materials consists of a back projection system having a screen size of 136 mm x 184 mm; headphones can be used if required (VISCAT, 1983).

The equipment actually used on ships employed magnetic tape for courseware storage rather than discs. This did not provide any significant disadvantages for the teaching systems involved. The internal logic board (referred to in (3) above) is needed in order to provide the interface between the computer and the MAVIS unit.

Figure 5.1   Basic TOPCAT training system.
(Courtesy of Texaco.)

TOPCAT Training Programs
Some examples of the courseware units that have been produced for use in onboard training situations are listed in table 5.1.

Table 5.1   Examples of Shipboard Training Programs

> Cargo Pumping and Loading – mainly simulations
> Planning and Critical Path Analysis – Management
> Inert Gas Operation and Maintenance
> Safety Equipment Maintenance
> Power Failure (simulated operational malfunctions)
> Welding Techniques
> Firefighting Simulations
> Control Systems (Theory, operation and maintenance)
> Budgetary Control
> Cadet Training
> Electrical Engineering
>   (Theory, operation and maintenance of equipment)
> General Engineering
> Catering Topics

In addition to their use on board ship, they are also widely used in a number of marine and technical colleges. The instructional strategies that these programs embody fall into four basic categories: (1) question and answer, (2) simulation, (3) gaming, and ' (4) working models. The latter are based on the use of accurate methematical models of various parts of the ship (or its equipment); they are used both to train novices and as an aid in real problem solving situations. Most of the training programs also include a guidebook as an integral part of the teaching resources. These are regarded as essential media for background reading of basic principles. This booklet also contains text that would otherwise necessarily be displayed on the VDU screen of the computer.

As an example of the types of training for which TOPCAT is used, one of the programs listed in table 5.1 will be described in more detail. We have selected the firefighting program. It employs gaming and simulation techniques and is currently widely used throughout the shipping industry (VISCAT, 1983). The program provides an exercise in the use of fire extinguishers, the object of which is to select and use the appropriate extinguisher on simulated fires generated by the computer. It also aims to encourage the frequent maintenance of extinguishers and teach the standard colours of extinguisher types.

The computer generates a scenario where the student must extinguish three fires within a set time, given a large selection of extinguishers of varying types. The program is suitable for the inexperienced in fire-fighting techniques and for those seeking a refresher course in fire control.

The VDU of the computer displays a plan view of a section of the ship's accommodation and generates at random three fires: one material, one oil-based and one electrical. The student has to find the fires, collect the correct extinguisher and use it. Each action takes a particular amount of 'game time'. The program emphasises that fires must be brought under control as quickly as possible before they have a chance to spread. There is also a probability that an extinguisher will fail to operate correctly – to simulate poor maintenance or operation. At the end of the game a complete analysis of the student's performance is given and attention is drawn to all incidents that occurred.

In the past, difficulty was experienced with the passive distance-learning aids (such as the MAVIS audio–visual programmes) in that there was no real measurement of the student's understanding and retention of the information presented. The use of computer assessment in the TOPCAT system enables these difficulties to be overcome. The use of the projector link also introduced an added dimension to computer aided training in that it enabled the display of colour photographs and complicated diagrams, which enhanced the computer's own graphical capabilities. This added interactive visual element has resulted in the significant library of MAVIS audio–visual programmes being used to much greater effect within the Texaco fleet.

For the future, many improvements to the TOPCAT system are currently being planned. It is intended that the interaction between the audio–visual projector and the computer should be replaced by video disc technology which will enable rapid access to thousands of still pictures. We have introduced readers to this type of technology earlier in the book and present further examples of its use later in this chapter.

5.2.2 The AVCAT System

Like TOPCAT, the Audio Visual Computer Aided Tutor (AVCAT) also employs slides and audio recordings as the major instructional media within the student workstation. In view of this, existing sequential tape/slide training material can easily be modified to operate with AVCAT. Of course, the effectiveness of such material is greatly enhanced by the highly interactive features of the system.

An overview of the AVCAT system was presented earlier (in section 3.3.4) during our discussion of authoring systems. The material presented there will be used to supplement the present discussion. In this section we now concentrate on two major aspects of AVCAT: (1) a more detailed description of the workstation, and (2) an outline of some of the application areas for which this system is currently being employed. Before undertaking these tasks we give below a summary of the main features of AVCAT:

(1) a powerful interactive student workstation;
(2) student response by simple keypad or touch screen;
(3) lesson delivery by audio and visual means;
(4) very high resolution with full colour visuals;
(5) full branching capability;
(6) no computer expertise required for lesson preparation;
(7) only conventional audio–visual techniques and materials used;
(8) the system has a student assessment capability;
(9) AVCAT can be linked and operated with other large systems such as PLATO, etc.

The instructional material is composed from blocks of instructional audio messages and their supporting pictorial images, with questions at the end of each block to assess the student's progress. The audio messages and the branching instructional programme are stored on standard C90 audio cassette. The visual content of the lesson is held on 35 mm slides. Both the audio and slide delivery subsystems are both rapid random access devices enabling efficient branching to take place.

The AVCAT Workstation
The student workstation (see figure 5.2) comprises:

  (1) a microprocessor based controller;
  (2) a simple keypad; and
  (3) one or two touch sensitive screens.

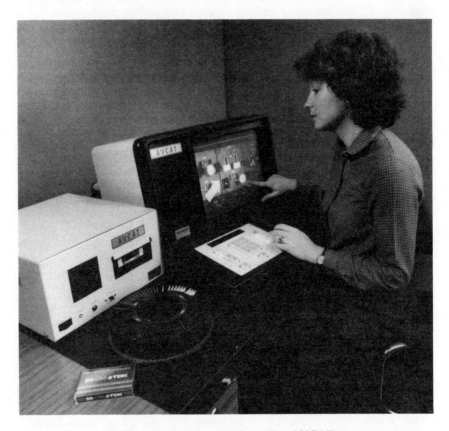

Figure 5.2 The workstation used in the AVCAT system.
(Courtesy of Goodwood Data Systems.)

Student actions are prompted by means of messages that appear on the single line display located on the keypad unit and by selective illumination of the various keys available on the keypad (see figure 5.3). The different message types, modes of interaction and other features of the workstation are briefly outlined below.

(a)   Message Types and Modes of Student Interaction
The factual material is delivered in one of two message types:

      (1)   instructional messages (I)
      (2)   reinforcement messages (R)

In the I–type, the audio message is delivered and the student is then
required to press a button on the keypad when he/she is ready to
proceed, in order to progress through the lesson. With the R–type
message the controller progresses automatically to the next item after
completing current message delivery. As we discussed in section 3.3.4,
question messages have three main types:

      (1)   numerical   (N)
      (2)   multi–choice (using keypad entry) (M)
      (3)   touch (via the projector screens) (T)

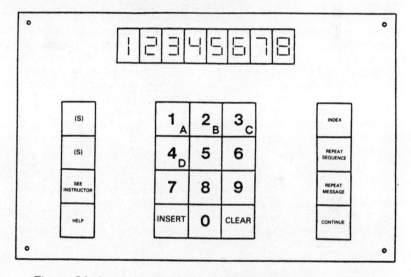

Figure 5.3 Arrangement of the AVCAT keyboard and display.
(Courtesy of Goodwood Data Systems.)

An N–type numerical question requires the student to enter a number
using the keypad. For a multi–choice question (M–type), the student is
given four options from which to select a correct answer – by pressing
one of the four illuminated keys (A, B, C, D) on the keypad.
Associated with each response option is an audio message and sometimes
a remedial slide. The 'correct' response message is usually a
congratulatory R–type reply to the student which then automatically
progresses the student on to the next item. The 'wrong' response
message may be a series of I–type items giving the student the correct
answer and reasons for his/her error; alternatively, they may be

further clues followed by a restatement of the question.

In the touch (T) question group the student is prompted to make responses by touching the slide image screen. Touch questions may be of four basic types:

(1) multi-choice touch (MT)
(2) quadrant (QT)
(3) specific entity (ST)
(4) vertical (VT)

MT-type questions utilise four (1 inch square) areas of the screen to indicate likely responses. Associated with each area is an appropriate audio message, as with the M-type items described above. One of the areas is the correct response, the other three being incorrect. If the student touches any other part of the screen a prompt is issued, requesting that the touch operation be repeated. For the ST-type questions the 'correct' response is obtained by touching the screen within the boundaries of a single rectangle. The size and position of the rectangle is defined by the lesson author. A response outside the designated area is judged to be wrong. The quadrant (QT) question type is essentially a multi-choice format in which the screen is divided into four quadrants and the student is invited to make a selection by touching anywhere within the appropriate quadrant. Vertical (VT-type) questions depend on the use of slide images that contain reference material in the top half of the image; the lower half is then divided into four horizontal strips that are used for multi-choice touch responses.

(b) Time-out Facilities
On all questions a time limit (up to 99 seconds) can be set, after this time has elapsed the student will be 'timed out' and an appropriate (author specified) audio message delivered. The question is normally re-presented at this stage and the student then requested to carry on with the lesson.

(c) Student Assessment
At the end of a lesson the student is presented with an assessment of his/her performance on the keypad display. This is expressed in terms of (1) time taken to complete the course, and (2) the score attained.

(d) Lesson Delivery – Slave Mode
The power and flexibility of the AVCAT student workstation has been recognised by users of other CAL systems, such as PLATO. AVCAT terminals have been added to such installations in order to enhance the student interface, by enabling audio messages and detailed slide images to be presented to complement the information on the host system's VDU terminals.

(e) Lesson Authoring
A major advantage of AVCAT is that no knowledge of computer
programming is required for courseware preparation. Authors need only
be expert in their subject material and in instructional techniques.
Another significant advantage lies in the fact that any student
workstation can become an authoring terminal by the addition of a
special authoring unit (see figure 5.4). Keyed entries to the machine
are then made either on the student's keypad (which in author mode has
secondary key functions), or through a dumb terminal plugged into the
controller's communication port.

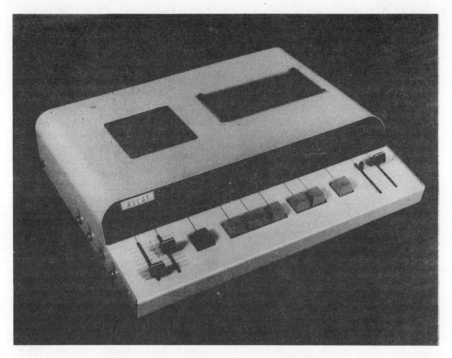

Figure 5.4 AVCAT authoring station.
(Courtesy of Goodwood Data Systems.)

As with any system of programmed learning, each lesson is developed
using accepted principles of programmed instruction. That is, a series
of instructional and tutorial messages are developed; these are each
supported by appropriate visual material, to develop a concept or
teaching point; this sequence is then followed by suitably designed
criteria questions. Therefore, in preparing courseware, the
appropriate slides are produced, the script written and the branching
table entries worked out and entered on a pro—forma coding sheet
similar to that depicted in figure 3.8. Having prepared the lesson

off-line   the   material can be loaded into AVCAT. This is a three-pass
process with the following stages:

(1)   addressing the tape,
(2)   recording the audio messages, and
(3)   recording the branching table.

In the first stage, the controller lays down an address track   on   one
half   of   the   blank tape cassette for subsequent use by the system in
cross referencing the lesson material. The next step is to record   the
audio   messages;   during   this step the author is prompted by messages
which appear on the keypad display. The AVCAT software requests   the
author   to   enter his/her identification, a lesson title reference and
the date. It then asks whether an audio or a branching table is to   be
recorded. A single key entry (A or B) is then used to specify which is
required.   If   the 'A' option is selected the prompt message 'REC MESS
1' appears on the keypad display; various keys on the   authoring   unit
are   then   used   to control the recording process and to log the start
and message markers. Message 1 is recorded and on completion a further
prompt ('REC MESS 2') is issued and the next   message   recorded.   This
process   is   repeated   until   all   the messages have been put onto the
tape. The branching table data (as defined in the   prepared   pro-forma
shown   in   figure   3.8) is then entered using the keypad. The selected
slides are presented on the slide image screen and,   in   the   case   of
touch   questions,   the   author   is prompted to touch the screen at the
points where responses are required.

(f)   Editing
Editing is really an extension of the authoring mode   and   is   equally
simple   to   perform. In the edit mode, however, instead of the machine
stepping through the messages sequentially, the system asks the author
to specify 'NEXT MESSAGE' to be edited after   completing   the   current
edit.   In   this way the author can jump at random through the material
to be edited.

AVCAT Applications
The AVCAT system represents   a   completely   general   purpose   teaching
device   that   can   be   applied   to a wide range of subject matter. The
system is particularly useful where the visual   content   demands   high
fidelity   and   good   detailed definition. In these situations the high
quality slide image out-performs the most sophisticated computer based
graphic systems. There   are   several   hundred   workstations   installed
across   Canada   (and   other   countries)   in   universities,   colleges,
industry,   government   and   military   institutions.   Some   of   the
applications   for   which   this system is employed are briefly outlined
below.

(a)   Airlines – Flight Crew Training
AVCAT is in use with   several   airlines   for   conversion   training   of
flight crew personnel (Tickle, 1983). Indeed, one of the largest users

of this system is Air Canada where it is used in Montreal and Toronto for flight crew training (Goodwood Data Systems, 1979; Freckleton, 1983). Air Canada's flight operations training has made extensive use of computer assisted training since the early 1970s. Their ground school now uses the system exclusively, thereby completely replacing former classroom methods. Some examples of Air Canada's repertoire of lessons are presented in table 5.2.

Table 5.2   Examples of AVCAT Courseware for Flight Crew Training

Flight Operations	5 lessons	17 hours
Boeing 747 Conversion	15 lessons	68 hours
Lockhead 1011 Conversion	31 lessons	137 hours
Douglas DC-8	15 lessons	75 hours
Boeing B-727 Conversion	28 lessons	130 hours
Douglas DC-9 Conversion	24 lessons	83 hours

In this table the left hand-column gives the course name, the central column specifies the number of lessons and the right-hand column indicates the total instructional time involved.

The high resolution slide image visuals are particularly effective for flight crew training since the full details of the various control panels can be presented to the student. Also, since an aircraft manufacturer provides an AV package for each type of aircraft (usually based on sequential tape/slide techniques), course preparation for delivery on the AVCAT system is very simple, since the slides and many of the audio messages already exist. Therefore, the course preparation task becomes one of rearranging this material into a branching interactive CAL lesson.

The operator advantages of CAL in this field are considerable. Traditionally, in a conversion programme, a class of from 12 to 16 pilots would have been brought in from their various operating bases. The first stages of the course would be as a class with an instructor lecturing using various visual aids, followed by written tests. The final stages would be the flight simulator which would only accommodate two of the class at any time. The remaining class members would therefore be sitting around waiting their turn in the simulator which obviously represented a loss to the operators and a degree of frustration to the pilots. Using AVCAT, however, pilots now undergo the 'lecture/test' part of the course at their normal operating base during their non-flying time; each at his own pace. The self-assessment facility allows the students to tutor themselves to the required pass level and they can then be scheduled on to the simulator at a mutually convenient time to complete the course.

One of the criticisms of this CAL approach to procedure training was that while detailed lessons could be delivered on individual equipment panels, orientation within the overall cockpit was often inadequately covered. This problem was overcome by an arrangement similar to that illustrated in figure 5.5. The AVCAT terminal was placed within a cockpit mock-up constructed from translucent photographic panels. Detailed lessons on the functions of the individual items of equipment could then be presented on the AVCAT terminal and the siting of those items within the cockpit could be indicated by rear illumination of the appropriate photographic panel on the mock-up. This concept produces a highly cost-effective procedure trainer enabling pilots to achieve enhanced familiarity with the cockpit layout prior to going into the simulator, thereby optimising simulator utilisation.

Figure 5.5 An AVCAT training rig.

(b) Medical Applications
AVCAT has been successfully applied within the area of medical training (Tickle, 1983). Two areas of application are cardiology and the study of skin-related diseases. Each of these is briefly described below.

In the cardiology application, the audio channel of AVCAT is utilised not simply for delivering instructional messages but also for recorded stethoscope sounds. Students can therefore be taught the audio cues which assist in the diagnosis of a wide range of heart conditions. At the same time, photographic slides of the appropriate sections of the heart and other visual symptoms can be displayed to the student and a series of fully interactive lessons can be delivered. The touch screen of AVCAT is used in this application to allow the student to point out abnormalities and also to present a torso so that the student can be asked to indicate where the stethoscope should be placed.

With skin-related diseases visual symptoms are naturally essential to diagnosis. High quality photographic slide images are therefore of particular value since a doctor under training (particularly in the Western World) will not necessarily have first-hand experience of many rare skin-related diseases. A series of AVCAT lessons can provide an accurate photographic record of such cases which occur. They can then also be used to deliver interactive tuition.

Other medical application training areas include haematology and bacteriology where microscope slides are photographed for use in AVCAT lesson modules. General physiology and skeletal tuition are other areas which are presented to great effect. The rapid and low-cost updating of the visual information for medical applications is a further reason for the popularity of this system in medical schools.

(c)   Engineering Applications
AVCAT has been used in many applications that involve machine shop training. A number of modules have been prepared which deal with the applications of various types of machinery, their functions and utilisation. These extend to detailed lessons on how to program and operate sophisticated numerically controlled machines and robots. Companies using computer controlled machinery are training new employees in the use of this new technology with self-teach courses.

Manufacturers of complex machinery are using AVCAT for self-study interactive training packages. This is of particular value for organisations that export equipment. In this situation the end-user may be thousands of miles away; customer training could thus involve sending skilled personnel to train the user – obviously, an expensive and often inconvenient exercise. In such applications the audio messages are recorded in the client's native language thereby enhancing the lesson material by making it more useable and acceptable to the workforce.

5.2.3   The AIDE Training and Guidance System
AIDE is an acronym for Automated Instruction, Direction and Exercise. The system was built for the US Naval Training Centre by the University of Southern California (Towne, 1979). It is a multimedia instructional system which was originally developed in order to fulfil

two important functions: (1) job training, and (2) job performance aiding. Essentially, the equipment consists of a computer controlled trainer/simulator/job support system that is built from readily available hardware components and which utilises custom written software and a multimedia storage system (images and text). The latter contains instructional information relating to the target equipment with which trainees are to become familiar.

The major hardware elements of AIDE are as follows:

(1) a small computer (microprocessor CPU, random access memory and mass disc storage);

(2) a 9-inch CRT (16 lines x 64 characters): displays words, lists, names, etc;

(3) a micrographics unit: displays colour photographs under computer control − this can be either a 35 mm random access slide projector or a colour microfiche unit;

(4) a sonic touch−pen for user inputs;

(5) a small hard−copy printer; and

(6) a voice synthesis unit.

Figure 5.6 shows a front view of the AIDE system as seen by the user. A 'command menu' is positioned below the CRT screen. This is a removable card labelled with the commands to which AIDE will respond when appropriate menu points are touched by the sonic pen. These allow the student to:

(1) select modes of instruction (assistance, instruction, drill)

(2) obtain any available information about the purpose, theory of operation, or location of any section of the target equipment for which the student is being trained;

(3) view either a photograph of functional diagram of a section of the target equipment; and

(4) exit from the AIDE system.

The majority of student inputs and responses are made by touching the sonic pen to individual items listed on the CRT, or to particular positions within an image being displayed on the micrographics screen. As we describe below, this enables the trainee to operate, disassemble and interact with AIDE regarding the instructional material that he/she wishes to have access to.

Training and Aiding Capabilities of AIDE
The system provides three basic modes of operation, namely,

(1) job assistance,

(2) instruction, and

(3) drill and exercise.

Each of these three modes is available for each of three general topics:

    (a)   target equipment configuration,
    (b)   equipment set-ups (operating and maintenance), and
    (c)   troubleshooting.

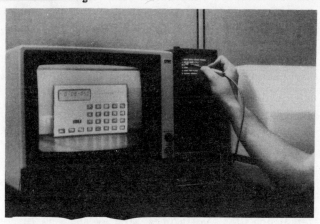

Figure 5.6 Front view of the AIDE system.
(Courtesy of University of Southern California.)

The nine resulting types of student-AIDE interactions are produced from a single bank of instructional information and graphic representations. This material, under the control of appropriate software routines, permits the following types of operation to be performed:

    (1)   present a picture of sub-element X,
    (2)   present text which explains the purpose of X,
    (3)   present a functional diagram of X,
    (4)   present a picture which shows where X is located,
    (5)   determine which part of X the user just touched with the pen,
    (6)   display a listing of switch settings for mode M,
    (7)   show the front panel set-up in mode M, and
    (8)   show indicator I reading normal.

In these operations, X denotes one of the components of the target equipment with which the data base deals, M represents a mode of usage of that equipment and I signifies an indicator panel.

The most fundamental topic addressed by AIDE is equipment configuration; it is concerned with the ability of a technician to (1) locate and identify physical elements in an item of equipment or system, and (2) understand the functions of the elements. For equipment set-up, the data base contains the names of the operational and maintenance modes, their required control settings and images of

the appropriate front panels in each state (these may include test
equipment set–ups). When used for troubleshooting, the software
routines operate in cooperation with the technician to locate a
malfunction; in this mode AIDE presents details of tests to perform,
how to perform them and symptoms to look for.

The AIDE Data Base
The objective of AIDE is to offer rich and detailed education and
training. The data base must, therefore, be extensive. For an
individual item of equipment (for example a radar repeater) the data
base might contain in excess of 1000 images. Of these, one quarter
would be taken directly from the technical manual, one half from the
actual equipment, and one quarter taken from specially prepared
diagrams and text. Both slides and microfiche may be used for storing
the pictorial information. From what has been said here it is easy to
see that a very substantial volume of photographic work is involved.
For expensive operational systems the cost incurred is acceptable when
compared with the cost of using either the actual equipment or a
special purpose simulator for training purposes.

When formulating the instructional strategy and data base structure
the author must provide both a physical and a functional breakdown of
the target equipment and also a cross reference between the two. If it
is thought to be useful, the author may also expand the target
equipment into any units that are deemed to be necessary for improved
understanding. Photographs of the physical layout of components and a
photograph of each diagram in the functional hierarchy must then be
provided. The author must also supply pages of written explanations to
describe the purpose and operation of those subelements are to be
included in the training programme. The information supplied by the
CAL author is not designed specifically for assistance, instruction or
drill. Instead, the monitor program within the workstation handles all
retrieval operations and presentation of the supplied material
according to the requirements of the user.

The mechanism of data base retrieval is interesting and proceeds as
follows: the user touches the sonic pen to an appropriate subsection
of each photograph (see figure 5.7). This produces XY–coordinates for
use in the data base retrieval software. This procedure allows the
user to search through either of the previously described hierarchies
by touching the area of interest on the currently projected image.

Each time AIDE responds to a retrieval request it presents a close–up
image of the subsection selected. Thus, in figure 5.7, when the
technician touches 'FRONT VIEW' on the uppermost image (A), a view of
the card rack front is displayed (B) along with two additional images
(not shown in the diagram) – a colour photograph and a labelled
drawing. If the technician then touches the menu selection point
located above board A2 on the labelled drawing then a diagram showing

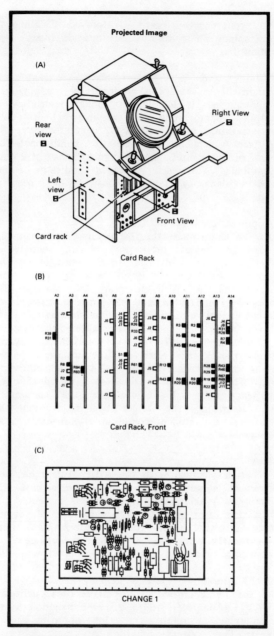

Figure 5.7 AIDE's hierarchical access strategy to stored images. (Courtesy of University of Southern California.)

the component layout for this board is displayed (C) along with three other images – a colour photograph, a part location index and a pin number designation list.

On-the-job training and job performance assessment for equipment operation and maintenance set-ups is produced by supplying names of controls, setting names, mode names, mode descriptions (required control settings) and photographs of the panel(s) in each mode. Troubleshooting training and aiding is generated by AIDE from a troubleshooting 'tree' which specifies a detailed, conditional, fault-isolation approach of the content expert, photographs of normal and abnormal symptoms for each involved indicator (including test equipment) and explanatory text to assist in performing and interpreting tests.

Instructional Approach used by AIDE
It is difficult to characterise the instructional approach employed during the teaching phases in terms of any single well-known technique. AIDE uses Socratic dialogue in the sense of its responding to user initiated requests. However, it is also heavily orientated towards the methods of Web learning (Norman, 1976), that is, it initially provides a gross, fundamental structure of knowledge about a topic which is successively elaborated with increasing detail and wealth of information. For performance aiding, the system functions primarily as an information retrieval system, with the advantage that both data base structure and retrieval functions are consistent from one application to the next, and are not the responsibility of the content expert. The approach used here is called the 'generative' approach (Rigney and Towne, 1974); it allows the content expert to concentrate on describing the target system without also being required to formulate student-computer dialogue, instructional schemes, and so on.

Future Directions
Much of the experience gained with the AIDE system has been put to use in a more advanced system called EEMT (Electronic Equipment Maintenance Trainer). A sketch of this system is presented in figure 5.8. The workstation incorporates both a video disc player (for image storage) and touch sensitive panels (for user interaction). The EEMT workstation is currently being used and further developed for training applications involving naval and military personel (Towne, 1983).

5.2.4   The CAVIS Interactive Video System
The principles of VCR based CAL have been outlined previously in section 5.2.3. CAVIS (Computer Audio Visual Instruction System) is a practical commercial example of this approach to instruction (Copeland, 1983). The system provides a teaching facility that integrates the use of video cassette pictures, text, videotex and animation, and presents these on a single television screen with supporting sound effects. Materials which originate from film, slide

and video tape can be transferred to the system for use in an
instructional process. In addition, a variety of computer based
techniques are available to enable the teacher to author text and
diagrams and also control the way in which the instructional resources
are used.

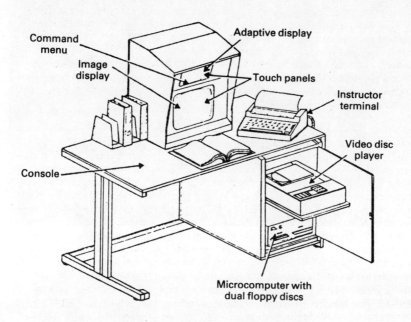

Figure 5.8 The EEMT workstation.

The disposition of the components that comprise the full CAVIS
workstation is indicated in figure 5.9. The complete workstation
includes a VCR, a student keypad (extreme left), a pair of headphones,
a TV display monitor (centre back), the author's keyboard (centre
front) and a microcomputer unit that is fitted with a magnetic disc
storage system (extreme right). The video cassette stores the audio
and video information and the magnetic disc stores all the text and
diagrams. In addition, the latter also contains the control software.
This is responsible for handling the overall operation of the system
and also guides the direction in which learning progresses as a result
of student interaction with the system.

Modes of Use
The CAVIS workstation may be used in either of two operating modes –
one for the student and one for the instructor. In teaching mode (see
figure 5.10) the student has access to a simple keypad which is used
to enter responses to questions presented on the screen or by a spoken
narrative. The keypad also enables the student to inspect the index of

CAVIS courseware and to skip, recap or search to any particular point of interest.

Figure 5.9 Components of the CAVIS workstation.
(Courtesy of SCICON.)

The instructor has access to a full alphanumeric colour coded keyboard and screen editing facilities. These enable pages of text and/or videotex graphics to be recorded and saved on the magnetic disc. They also permit subsequent revision of stored pages. No knowledge of computers or typing skills are assumed. Whenever it is appropriate, CAVIS issues guidance and help messages in order to assist authoring and editing. A section of the CAVIS (editor) help facility is illustrated in figure 5.11.

A page of information corresponds to one complete screenful (as seen in figure 5.11). Each magnetic disc can store up to 200 pages of material. Retrieval of any one of these pages – either within the presentation of courseware (during teaching mode), or during editing – is within 0.5 second. This facility therefore allows slow animation to be presented.

Figure 5.10 Student interaction with the CAVIS system.
(Courtesy of SCICON.)

During lesson development the CAL presentation can be programmed to adapt to student responses with text and also with branching video sequences. In addition the multimedia capabilities of CAVIS enable the author to use text, video pictures, text overlaid on video pictures and videotex pictures. Dynamic diagrams can also be presented in a sequence and combination that makes the delivery of information most effective. As an authoring aid, a special magnetic disc containing an analysis facility is supplied so that student's responses, viewing patterns and video cassette performance can be checked. Thus, using this evaluation facility, accumulated records can be processed to provide a detailed analysis of how a number of students studied specific courseware. This enables teaching material to be checked sequence by sequence for deficiencies. Using the editing and authoring facilities, deficient courseware can be quickly and repeatedly recycled until a defined performance level is achieved.

CAVIS Applications

The commercial development and distribution of CAVIS for industrial training applications has been handled by a British organisation called SCICON (Robinson, 1983), a subsidiary of a large multinational company called BP International. Within the latter organisation, the CAVIS system has been used extensively (throughout Europe) for teaching subjects ranging from accountancy and budgetary control to oil refinery operations and safety at work. The teaching efficiency of CAVIS is regarded as being in the range 80–100 per cent mastery of content.

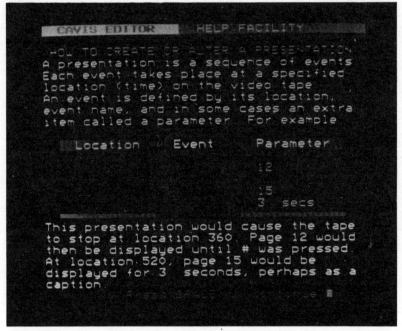

Figure 5.11 The CAVIS trainer's HELP facility.
(Courtesy of SCICON.)

Within the petrochemicals industry there are three important factors which influence the requirement for the continuous training and retraining of staff: (1) the ongoing development of new products, (2) the continual need to introduce new manufacturing and production units, and (3) rapidly changing technology. Unfortunately, organising group training for production shift operators and maintenance workers is often difficult or impossible due to low manning levels (Lenaerts, 1983). Training must therefore be limited to individuals or very small groups during slack hours; CAVIS was found to be ideally suited to this approach to training.

Several teaching programmes were developed in order to train operators
in (1) start-up procedures for new production units, and (2) operating
techniques for existing plant. Other programmes were devoted to safety
items. In one case, 80 field mechanics were retrained in using
portable gas detectors. Although most of the trainees had been using
these detectors for several years, they admitted to having learned
critical principles which they misunderstood before. Furthermore, the
training programme was carried out without interrupting daily
maintenance schedules.

Because of the initial success of the CAVIS system, several European
divisions of BP International are now developing systems for (1) the
training of production operators for process and critical procedures,
(2) teaching process safety principles, (3) teaching safety and
personel protective equipment use, and (4) skills training. In
addition, several other organisations (such as British Nuclear Fuels
and International Paints) are also starting to use CAVIS for their
internal training requirements.

5.2.5   The IVIS Interactive Video Information System
Computer technology is playing an increasingly important role in
modern society. Indeed, demand for computer equipment continues to
grow quite rapidly as a result of (1) the expansion of computing
techniques into many new areas of application, and (2) the
introduction of more powerful technology into existing ones. Each of
these activities create training problems. In case (1) there may be a
requirement to use existing inexperienced and non-technical staff to
operate and control the new equipment. In case (2), when a new system
is introduced experienced technical staff may need to be retrained.
Computer manufacturers are therefore presented with significant
training problems when they develop new equipment.

Training techniques are thus an important consideration for computer
manufacturers. Two aspects need to be considered: the training of
their own staff, and educating and training their customer's staff. As
new products are developed the computer manufacturer's staff will need
to be trained in a variety of skills, such as sales promotion, product
facilities, equipment servicing, etc. Similarly, as customers purchase
new products they will need to be trained to use these. A variety of
customer and staff training techniques are used to achieve these
educational objectives: customised courses, seminars, training
manuals, lecture/lab courses and computer based training. Within the
latter category, interactive video is becoming an extremly important
instructional tool. Because of this, we provide (in the following case
study) descriptions of two slightly different ways in which this
instructional technology is being used to implement customer and staff
training procedures by computer manufacturers.

IVIS is an Interactive Video Information System which was developed by
Digital Equipment Corporation (Powell, 1984) in order to meet some of

the training requirements of both its own staff and those of its customers. Figure 5.12 shows a picture of the IVIS multimedia workstation. It consists of a keyboard, high resolution colour CRT display, a pair of headphones (and/or audio speakers), a video disc player and a microcomputer system.

Figure 5.12   The IVIS multimedia workstation.
(Courtesy of Digital Equipment Corporation.)

The video images presented on the display monitor can be dynamic or still frame; one of two selectable external video sources is accepted for display – possible sources being video disc, video tape, video camera or other live video output. Two audio channels are available. They can be employed singly, alternately, in stereo or as four monophonic channels. For listening students can use a pair of speakers or a headset (in situations where free sound could be disturbing to others). Depending on the lesson material being presented, the audio could consist of narration, a life–like conversation, special sound effects, music or any combination of these. The CRT monitor allows bit–map text and graphics to be displayed alone on the screen, or they may be overlaid onto dynamic and still frame natural video images. The resolution of the bit–mapped text and graphics is 960 (horizontal) by 240 (vertical) displayable pixels. In order to enhance definition between overlays and an underlying video image, drop shadowing can be applied to both text and graphics with a width of from 1 to 15 pixels. Virtually any kind of graph, tabulation, labelling, geometric shape and pictorial overlay can be created. The overlays can be in any simultaneous combination of eight colours selected from a range of 256.

Digital Equipment Corporation have been using the IVIS system for some
time and have made several comparisons of its performance. Their
experiences with their own personnel have shown that IVIS trained
students learn up to 53% faster – and with better retention – than
students trained by conventional methods.

5.2.6   IBM's Guided Learning Centre

As we mentioned in the previous section, customer training is an
important service provided by computer manufacturers for their
clients. Computer based techniques (combined with interactive video)
are being used increasingly to fulfil these requirements. The approach
used by International Business Machines (IBM) for customer training
illustrates the use of an open learning arrangement in which students
attend a 'Guided Learning Centre' at times when it is most convenient
for them to come (International Business Machines, 1982).

The Guided Learning Centre is a carefully structured educational
environment in which participants learn, at their own pace, under the
guidance of an education administrator. The operation of the centre is
the responsibility of the administrator who enrols customers on the
required course, shows them how the centre operates, provides the
right materials and records the participants' progress at each stage.
IBM have found this approach to training to be quite successful. Its
success depends upon:

(1) specially created performance based, self-paced texts,
(2) interactive video disc modules which support the text and
    test the participant's comprehension of the subject matter,
(3) hands-on practical sessions at a terminal giving real
    experience of problem solving, and
(d) practical support given to participants by the education
    administrator.

When students arrive at the centre they are assigned individual areas
where they can work in privacy on their own course modules, at their
own pace. At times the material will direct the students to perform an
exercise at a display station or to view a video segment which may
introduce, summarise or supplement the written material. When this
occurs, the student will go to an adjacent display or video station.
After completing the activity, the student might proceed to the
printer to obtain any output from the exercise, go to the reference
library or return to the assigned study area. The diagram shown in
figure 5.13 illustrates the student flow within the centre.

A Guided Learning Centre course is composed of a series of modules.
Each module is self-contained; that is, the module booklet contains
the student's objectives and text for that module, directions to
complete the module, examples, exercises and progress checks or
examinations. Each student covers topics step-by-step and can regulate
the pace and depth of learning. Material may be recapped or repeated

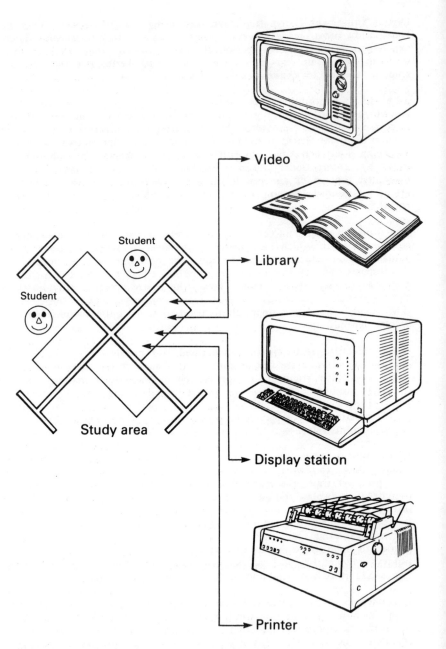

Figure 5.13 The multimedia facilities of a Guided Learning Centre.
(Courtesy of IBM.)

until a satisfactory level of understanding has been reached. This learning method undoubtedly encourages a high level of comprehension. The materials used in Guided Learning Centre education are designed to allow the study of a single concept, give immediate practice of that concept, and provide the student with the results of the practice. The practice may consist of coding a program, following an instruction with the aid of video disc or audio tape, or completing an exercise at a terminal. In each case the student is actively involved in the learning process.

The multimedia approach used in the Guided Learning Centre bears some similarity to that described previously in section 4.3. However, it is somewhat different from that outlined in the previous section since it places greater emphasis on the use of a much wider range of learning resources. Bearing in mind the nature of the tasks for which the students are being trained, this is undoubtedly a more realistic training technique, mainly because of the fact that in an actual situation a staff member would be required to access information from many different sources in order to solve a particular problem.

5.2.7   Using Simulation Systems for Training

The topic of simulation packages was briefly introduced earlier in section 2.5.2(e). As a general concept, simulation is widely accepted as a method for training persons in jobs where correct response in difficult situations is vital. The best-known field of simulator training is for aircraft pilots (Freckleton, 1983), but the range of applications is rapidly expanding. Most modern simulators operate under control of a computer, having the dynamic behaviour of the simulated system implemented as software modules. A fundamental requirement of the simulator is that it should bring the person to be trained as close to the real job situation as is possible. This often requires the production of sophisticated audio and visual effects as well as the provision of a training environment that closely imitates that which would be encountered in an operational system. Some of the more advanced simulator systems thus represent extremely good examples of multimedia CAL applications. In the following sections we describe two examples of advanced simulation systems, both of which are orientated towards the training of maritime personnel.

(1)   The CASSIM Simulator

CASSIM is an acronym for CArdiff Ship SIMulator, a training and research tool developed by the Department of Maritime Studies at the University of Wales (Cardiff) in the United Kingdom (McCallum and Rawson, 1981). The range of functions for which it is employed is summarised in figure 5.14. In addition to its research applications it is also used to train the crews of large tankers, for an outlay which is only 3-10% of the cost of using an actual ship. The arrows within the figure depict the interrelationship between the teaching and research applications of the simulator.

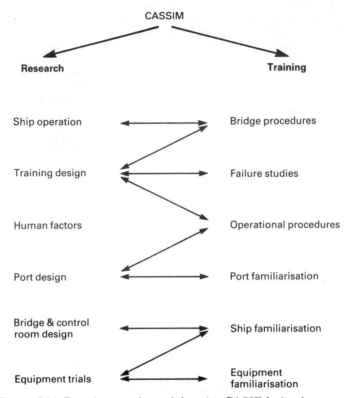

Figure 5.14 Functions performed by the CASSIM simulator.
(Courtesy of University of Wales.)

CASSIM is housed in a purpose built building, the layout of which is illustrated in figure 5.15. The simulator consists of a bridge, an instructor station and two computers. The bridge structure (measuring 4 m wide by 5 m long) is mounted on a large vibrating platform in order to simulate the effects of the propellor. The presence of propellor induced vibrations has been identified as an important sensory cue to ship's officers. The bridge and window (supplied by Racal Decca Systems and Simulators Ltd) is used for crew control and operation of the visual scene. The simulator is supplied with three projectors giving a total horizontal field of view of 120 degrees. Facilities have been incorporated into the building to allow for a further two output channels, giving a field of view of 200 degrees in the horizontal plane and 30 degrees in the vertical plane. Bridge instrumentation includes a steering pedestal with auto pilot and manual wheel, a 16 inch radar display, engine telegraph, VHF radiotelephone, navigation lights control panel, whistle controls and a chart table. The visual scene is affected by bridge commands and may

also be altered by the instructor or research controller, who, as far
as the bridge team is concerned represents the outside world. The
instructor is able to (1) induce fog or other ships into the visual
scene, (2) talk to the bridge using internal and external
communication systems, and (3) introduce navigational equipment or
engine failures. Engine and rudder commands are fed to the motion
computer which contains the manoeuvring equations of a range of
different ships. The bridge instruments and visual system alter in
response to the computerised ship motion.

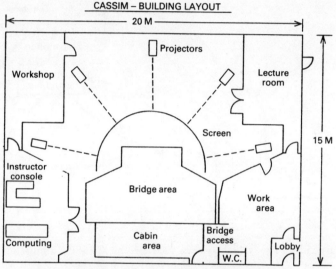

Figure 5.15 Layout of the CASSIM simulator.
(Courtesy of University of Wales.)

The motion computer (a Kongsberg 5500 supplied by Racal) is
interlinked with a visual scene computer (a DEC PDP 11/34) which
controls the visual scene viewed from the bridge. The data base for
the simulator is stored on discs and is produced from maps, charts,
drawings and photographs of the area, using a digitiser. Different
simulation exercises are developed for different training requirements
and features such as light houses, tankers and other ships are
produced separately and added as required. The area covered by the
data base is thus unlimited and very many complex visual scenes can be
produced. The change of scene as the 'ship' changes position or
heading is achieved by transferring new picture material from the
backing store of the computer into its working store. The backing
store employs two discs: one for storing a library of models of ships,
buoys, jetties and buildings; and, another for the topographical model
of a particular exercise area. Spare discs hold extensions to the area
and disc changes can be made during an exercise in order to extend its
scope.

The underlying visual system of the CASSIM simulator was developed by Marconi Radar System (UK) under the trade name Tepigen (Marconi, 1982). It is illustrated schematically in figure 5.16. Television pictures are produced by direct generation from video signals, without the need for any intermediate stages, such as using photographs or models. The pictures are then back projected onto a cylindrical screen. The visual system permits a high degree of realism to be brought into bridge training schemes.

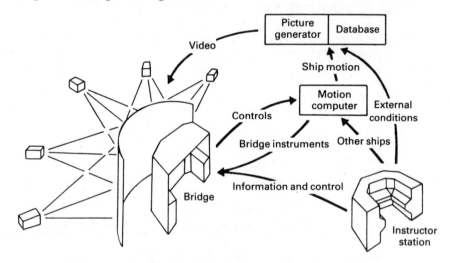

Figure 5.16   The visual system used in the CASSIM simulator.
(Courtesy of University of Wales.)

Using this system, training can be provided for a wide variety of vessels ranging from a general cargo ship (of say, 18,000 tonnes displacement) through to a very large crude oil carrier. Research activity using CASSIM is currently orientated towards studying port design and operation which includes an investigation of channel configurations, jetty sitings, design of navigational aiding systems and a study of tug operations. Simulation systems such as CASSIM provide invaluable tools to aid both research and training since they introduce considerable cost savings into what would otherwise be a significant educational budget.

(b) A Submarine Simulator System
In many training situations it often costs a great deal more to construct a real operational system (to dedicate to training) than it does to build a simulator counterpart. This is particularly true in many types of military and naval training applications where it is very difficult to set up exercises that involve realistic combat situations. An additional advantage of using a simulator lies in the fact that the risks to trainees and operational equipment are greatly

reduced.   A   growing   trend, made possible through the availability of
low cost microcomputers, is the   concept   of   'part   task'   simulation
whereby a   complex   task   is broken down into part tasks each of which
only forms a part of the overall training objective. This technique is
now employed in the design of a number of advanced   training
simulators.   Typical   of   such advanced equipment is that developed by
Ferranti Computer Systems (UK) to enable the cost   effective   training
of   submarine   crews   (Ferranti,   1981).   A plan and photograph of the
indoor submarine simulator are presented in   figures   5.17   and   5.18,
respectively.

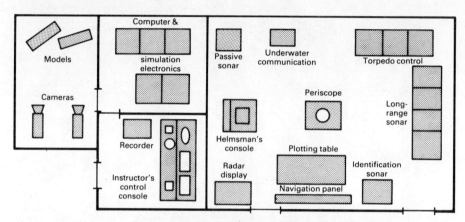

Figure 5.17   Equipment layout for a submarine simulator.
(Courtesy of Ferranti.)

Within   this   training   rig the periscope simulation uses a television
system in which each target ship image   is   derived   from   a   separate
model   and camera channel. The models provide the necessary detail and
realism to enable very effective training in ship   recognition   to   be
achieved.   The   images are seen against a computer generated landscape
of sea and sky – the shade of each varying with the distance (becoming
lighter at the horizon). Ships can be shown with realistic   bow   waves
and stern wash, each of which can be varied with speed. Positioning of
ships   in   the   field of view is entirely electronic and controlled by
the computer to   give   a   composite   representation   in   which   range,
bearing, aspect   and   speed are correctly synchronised with sonar and
radar effects in the indoor trainer.   The   model   is   free   to   rotate
through   360 degrees allowing any aspect of the target to be presented
to the trainee. Entirely realistic obscuration   of   distant   ships   by
nearer   ships   is   provided   and   ships   are correctly positioned with
respect to the horizon.

Within the repertoire of exercises, all aspects   of   torpedo   training
are   included,   for   example   their   selection,   setting, guidance and
homing. The synthetic seascape for visual target   simulation   includes

foreground wave representation (which is responsive to sea state and periscope height) and visibility simulation (for dusk and night time conditions). Debrief facilities include a recording of the whole or strategic parts of the exercises for subsequent replay on the closed circuit television equipment. Replay techniques include the use of both 'frame freeze' and 'fast run' strategies as a means of analysing trainees' performances.

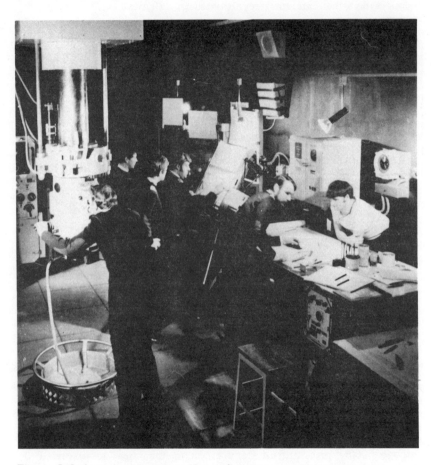

Figure 5.18 Actual appearance of a submarine simulation system.
(Courtesy of Ferranti.)

5.2.8   LOGO Learning Centres

LOGO is essentially a special purpose, procedural, high level programming language. It originated from the Massachusetts Institute of Technology (MIT) and was developed by Seymour Papert in the 1960s. During its development the language was significantly influenced by the ideas of the Swiss educational theorist Jean Piaget (Roper, 1983). The language was developed for the specific purpose of 'making computers make sense to children'. LOGO seeks to develop cognitive and linguistic skills as children use the computer to draw pictures, solve puzzles, play games and generate music. The underlying theory behind this approach to learning is that experimenting with programs is likely to achieve two things: (1) it will give the child a feeling of control over the computer; and (2) it will develop intellectual structures (in a young mind) that are firmly based on a feeling for mathematical concepts.

As we mentioned earlier in section 4.2.5(g), one of the most attractive and well known features of LOGO is its turtle graphics (Abelson and diSessa, 1981). Indeed, most of the educational applications of LOGO have nearly all focussed on this aspect of the language. The attractive feature of turtle graphics is that children simultaneously acquire skills in programming, geometry and art. The turtle is a small object that is able to draw pictures as it moves around under the student's control. Student control of the turtle is accomplished by means of a series of simple English-like commands (such as FORWARD N, LEFT N, and so on) which are typed into a host computer by means of a conventional keyboard system – sometimes purpose built keyboards are used in which the keys are labelled with the LOGO command keywords. There is a variety of different types of turtle, some are small mechanical toy robots that are connected to the computer by means of an appropriate interface system (see figures 5.19 and 5.20) while others are screen and plotter based (Williams, 1982; Ciarcia, 1982).

Figure 5.19 shows a typical LOGO learning environment which consists of a microcomputer keyboard, a CRT screen and a small mechanical turtle to which is attached a pen. The turtle is connected to the host microcomputer by means of an interface box. The latter contains a microprocessor whose function is to interpret command characters sent to it from the LOGO computer by way of a standard I/O interface. In addition to converting these command characters into basic control operations for the turtle, this microprocessor also has the responsibility of sending back (to the host computer) various sorts of acknowledgement signal as each operation is completed. Some turtles have a 'touch sensitive nose' that enables them to generate feedback signals when they collide with another object. This provides the student with a facility for negotiating the robot in obscure conditions (in the dark or within a covered maze.

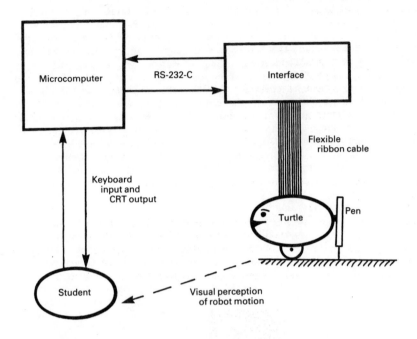

Figure 5.19 Interaction and feedback in a LOGO learning centre.

The keyboard provides the means of controlling the turtle. It enables the student to type sequences of commands of the following form:

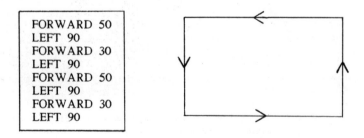

```
FORWARD 50
LEFT 90
FORWARD 30
LEFT 90
FORWARD 50
LEFT 90
FORWARD 30
LEFT 90
```

in order to make the turtle draw out a rectangle of size 50 x 30.

Similarly, the sequence

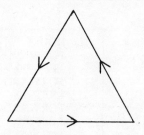

```
FORWARD 40
LEFT 120
FORWARD 40
LEFT 120
FORWARD 40
LEFT 120
```

would cause the turtle to produce an equilateral triangle of side 40 units.

The numeric value associated with the FORWARD command represents the distance that the turtle is to move in the direction in which it is currently pointing; the value associated with the LEFT command specifies (in degrees) the magnitude of the anticlockwise rotation that the turtle is to make when it is instructed to change direction.

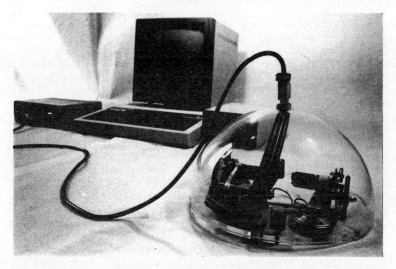

Figure 5.20   A mechanical turtle for use with LOGO.
(Courtesy of Jessop Microelectronics.)

Sequences of commands can be combined together to form a program which may be stored in the computer's memory. For example, the list of commands:

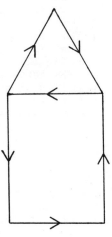

```
TO: HOUSE
    FORWARD 50
    LEFT 90
    FORWARD 40
    LEFT 90
    FORWARD 50
    LEFT 90
    FORWARD 40
    RIGHT 120
    FORWARD 40
    RIGHT 120
    FORWARD 40
    RIGHT 120
    PENUP
    FORWARD 40
    LEFT 90
END
```

constitutes a simple program called HOUSE. Each time the student now types the command HOUSE, the program of that name would be executed, causing the turtle to draw a house starting at the position on the drawing surface at which it is currently located. By suitably moving the turtle the student could progress towards using the program to produce a street or even a village of houses. Of course, it is possible to introduce variables to represent distances and rotation, thereby enabling students to generate houses of different shapes, sizes and colours by means of a single LOGO program.

Applications of LOGO
At present the greatest demand for LOGO learning environments tends to originate from conventional educational institutions. The areas of application that have been most widely explored relate to the teaching of mathematics and science. It has also been used extensively as a communication aid and research tool for instructional studies with handicapped children.

Within the context of mathematics teaching, LOGO environments have been utilised for the provision of instructional aid for both teachers and students. For example, Du Boulay and Howe (1982) conducted an experiment which attempted to use LOGO to improve the mathematical skills of student teachers, by providing them with a LOGO environment that enabled them to explore troublesome maths topics. Unfortunately, the results of their experiments were inconclusive in that the trainee teachers did not show any overall marked improvement in their mathematical ability. Undoubtedly, greater success has been achieved when younger children are introduced to mathematics using the LOGO approach (Papert, 1980; Abelson and diSessa, 1981). Indeed, once a child has used LOGO to discover new ways of thinking about mathematics, this new way of thinking continues to produce beneficial results, even if the child is no longer exposed to the language (Kildall and Thornburg, 1983).

Within science, LOGO has been employed for the teaching of Newtonian physics (using a dyna-turtle), orbital motion, robot control, maze solving strategies, music and a host of other topics. Generally, for teaching within the physical sciences, LOGO is useful since it can be used to construct 'microworlds' (Papert, 1980; Lawler, 1982) in which bodies obey different natural laws. By exploring these artificial microworlds, children can develop better intuitions about the properties of their own corner of the universe. Through the use of appropriate CRT animation techniques (for example, sprite graphics – see section 5.3.4), LOGO can be used to create powerful and stimulating microworlds. These can be constructed by combining the effects of both static and dynamic imagery. The dynamic images consist of many moving objects (sprites) of different size, colour and shape that move in front of extremely colourful and vivid static background (or backdrop) scenes. The BEACH microworld of Lawler (1982) illustrates the power of this technique.

As well as being used for conventional instructional applications, LOGO has been widely investigated as a tool for teaching the handicapped (Emanuel and Wier, 1976; Geoffrion, 1983). The language has been used to devise a series of learning environments individually adapted to the specific needs of each handicapped person involved. For example, in Emanuel and Weir's work (1976) with an autistic seven-year-old child, a special button box was designed, each button being labelled with a simple drawing to indicate its function. By pushing appropriate buttons the handicapped child was able to instruct the computer to move the turtle, make it hoot or raise/lower its drawing head. The positive effects of the child's experiences with the LOGO turtle on his ability to communicate were quite dramatic. In another situation (Geoffrion, 1983), a special input device was constructed in order to enable a non-vocal cerebral-palsied teenager to draw pictures using the LOGO language. The input device consisted of a rod which was attached to a special helmet worn by the student. Through this device he could use simple head movements to enter picture drawing commands into the computer which then enabled him (through LOGO procedures) to generate quite sophisticated graphic patterns. LOGO has had a significant impact upon teaching and research in this area of education. Undoubtedly, it will continue to do so as the cost of special microelectronic aids for the handicapped continues to decline.

Conclusion
Many useful approaches to CAL and CBT have been implemented through
the use of a simple CRT screen and keyboard combination. However, as
the value of truly multimedia instruction is more widely realised,
there is likely to be a significant movement towards the development
of learning centres (or workstations) able to cater for the
requirements inherent in this approach. Within this section we have
given some typical examples of the type of situation wherein this
technique may be used to add realism and excitement to learning and
training processes.

5.3   SOME APPROACHES TO MULTIMEDIA AUTHORING

In the previous section we outlined a number of different approaches
to the provision of multimedia CAL and CBT environments. Within
systems of this type the control of:

> (1) the available resources,
> (2) the teaching processes, and
> (3) student interaction,

will each depend quite critically upon the availability of suitable
programming facilities to enable courseware production. Any
programming tool that is used for workstation control must contain the
necessary (and appropriate) linguistic primitives needed to achieve
the control requirements listed above. Many of the author languages
outlined in chapter 3 were unsuitable for use in this type of
environment. However, some of them (such as TUTOR and MUMEDALA)
were able to provide many, if not all of the required programming
facilities. Because of the importance of software development
techniques for multimedia workstations, the remainder of this chapter
is devoted to a description of some current approaches to providing
authoring facilities for the production of courseware for this type of
application.

5.3.1   MicroTICCIT, Micro–PLATO and PHILVAS
We describe here three current approaches to CAL authoring systems for
multimedia CAL. Two of these (MicroTICCIT and Micro–PLATO) have
evolved as a result of many years experience with established computer
based training systems. The third (PHILVAS) is a more recent
development that has arisen as a consequence of the growing need for
an easier means of authoring courseware for teaching systems based
upon the use of interactive video. Each of the systems listed above
will be briefly outlined in the following sections.

(a)   MicroTICCIT
The MicroTICCIT system has developed as a result of ongoing research
and the application of modern microcomputer technology to an earlier
CBT product that was introduced over ten years ago (TICCIT – see
section 3.3.1). TICCIT is a fairly well established system currently

being used in a number of higher educational establishments throughtout North America. For example, Brigham Young University (Utah), Pheonix College (Arizona) and the Northern Virginia Community College all use this system. At the latter institution a 128 terminal TICCIT configuration was installed in 1972 and has since been used to teach significant elements of the mathematics, English and science programmes using an open-learning approach – with TICCIT handling all the assessment and grading. In addition, the multimedia aspects of TICCIT have been successfully employed within a 'fundamentals of music course' which uses both the audio and the graphic capabilities of the system. The introduction of MicroTICCIT represents a more flexible approach to the provision of CBT than could be achieved by TICCIT itself (Hazeltine Corporation, 1983). It uses off-the-shelf hardware systems in order to provide training systems containing from two to sixty-four workstations that may be configured in either a centralised or distributed network fashion. Undoubtedly, two of the most attractive features of this system are (1) the powerful workstation facilities that are provided and (2) the ADAPT authoring system that allows the easy and efficient production of high quality courseware by authors of all skill levels, through its ability to tailor its mode of operation to the experience of the authors who use it. These two important features of this CBT system are discussed in more detail below.

(i)   The MicroTICCIT Workstation

The workstation is depicted in figure 5.21; it is designed for use by students, instructors, courseware developers and training administrators. It consists of a personal computer, a colour monitor, a detached keyboard with an integral instructional keypad and special function keys, a light pen, and a high-speed communications link to the system's host computer. The display supports flicker-free presentations of computer-generated text and graphics and is fully compatible with video tape and video disc. Under author control, up to seven foreground colours and four background colours can be selected for use in the creation of each frame of computer-generated text and graphics. These colours may be selected from a palette of 4096. In addition, an option is available to allow computer-generated displays to overlay motion and still-frame video from video disc. This capability allows unprecedented freedom for courseware authors to take advantage of the special attributes of each medium for training.

The keyboard is the commonest mode of interaction for all users of the system. Each keyboard includes an alphanumeric keypad, an editing keypad and a special function keypad designed to give students easy access to instructional units (OBJECTIVE, RULE, EXAMPLE, PRACTICE and HELP). The keyboard also includes programmable function keys which can be used to define as many as 33 special characters or symbols unique to a particular training application.

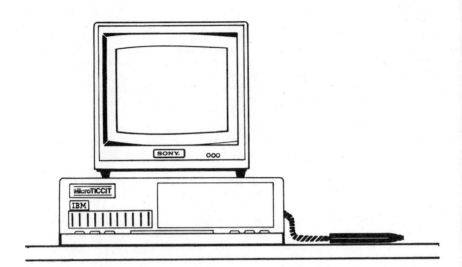

Figure 5.21 The MicroTICCIT workstation.
(Courtesy of Hazeltine Corporation.)

The standard workstation may be expanded in various ways by the
addition of different options which (if necessary) may be interfaced
into the system using the I/O interface ports available on the
microcomputer. Some of these options include a touch sensitive
transparent screen overlay to support finger contact response; a
random access audio system to provide sonic messages to support visual
presentations; a video disc overlay option; and the ability to
interface panel mock-ups and other auxiliary training devices to the
system.

(ii) The ADAPT Authoring Facility
The authoring system used with MicroTICCIT is called ADAPT. This is
an easy-to-learn courseware development tool that enables authors to
produce very·effective courseware after only a few hours of on-line
training. It is able to achieve this because the system elicits all
required inputs from the author (through menus and prompts) and then
makes use of program generation facilities to produce the courseware
for all common authoring tasks. For those who are more experienced,
the menus and prompts used for novice authors can be by-passed – in
favour of a direct coding approach. The operation of the system is
aided by the provision of an optional built-in teaching model and on-
line help facility for all authoring functions.

ADAPT is a multi-level authoring system that may be entered at a variety of levels depending on the ability of the author and the instructional design requirements of the material being authored (Mudrick and Stone, 1983). The ability of this authoring tool to 'adapt' its user interface to suit the experience of the user represents a very important approach to author language design, particularly in those situations where skilled and experienced authors represent a rare commodity. The four levels of entry into the ADAPT system are depicted in figure 5.22 which represents a two-dimensional matrix of authoring expertise plotted against instructional design model.

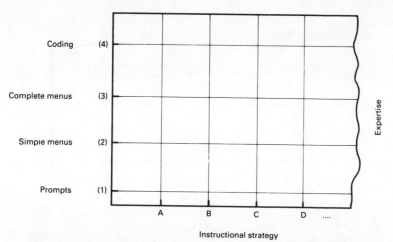

Figure 5.22 Two dimensions of courseware authoring: expertise and strategy.

Along one axis are levels of editor format, based upon those outlined above. Along the other axis are various instructional design presentation strategies for developing lessons for particular classes of instructional objective (for example concept classification, rule using, simulations, linear procedures, branching procedures, etc) plus the option to have no embedded strategy. When creating a lesson file, the author selects the point on this matrix that represents his/her current need – the intersection of the desired authoring level and the appropriate instructional strategy. As can be seen from figure 5.22, there are four levels of entry eveilable, ranging from level 1 (the lowest) to level 4 (the highest). Level 1 (for the novice author) is a prompt-driven format in which the author is led through the authoring process by means of questions (prompts). These prompts cover a limited set of options for the beginning author to consider. The author provides the data required for these prompts by answering yes/no questions and by typing English-like data statements. When the author no longer needs to be led step-by-step entry to level 2 is possible.

This abandons the prompts and directly presents the same limited set
of options through simple menus. An example of a typical level 2 menu
is shown in figure 5.23A. Level 3 (for the intermediate author)
presents the full set of options through complete menus. Some of the
options at this level may require the author to supply data in a coded
syntax. Figure 5.23B shows the level 3 version of the level 2 menu
shown in figure 5.23A. Level 4 (for the advanced author) corresponds
to programming using the author language facility (TAL) – with all its
complete capabilities and flexibility. At this level the author
creates program code by writing statements in their required syntactic
form. Some menu facilities are also available at this level should the
author choose to use them.

(A) Level 2 Menu

```
┌─────────────────────────────────────────────┐
│ ┌─────────────────────────────────────────┐ │
│ │ Additions  to  the  Display             │ │
│ └─────────────────────────────────────────┘ │
│                                               │
│   Answer checking .................. Exists   │
│   Graphic .......................... Exists   │
│   Video ............................ None     │
│   Audio ............................ None     │
│   Time limit (in seconds) ......... 10        │
│   Remarks .......................... None     │
│                                               │
└─────────────────────────────────────────────┘
```

(B) Level 3 Menu

```
┌─────────────────────────────────────────────┐
│ ┌─────────────────────────────────────────┐ │
│ │ Additions  to  the  Display             │ │
│ └─────────────────────────────────────────┘ │
│   Remarks .......................... Exist    │
│   DISPLAY CONSTRUCTION:                        │
│     Clear screen before display?... Yes        │
│     Palette ........................ System    │
│     Variable display data ......... Exists     │
│     Graphic ........................ None       │
│     Motion ......................... None       │
│     Video .......................... Exists    │
│     Audio .......................... None       │
│     Timeout (seconds) ............. None        │
│   RESPONSE ANALYSIS:                            │
│     Branch table ................... Seen      │
│     Answer checking ............... Exists     │
└─────────────────────────────────────────────┘
```

Figure 5.23   ADAPT – authoring by menu.
(Courtesy of Hazeltine Corporation.)

ADAPT lessons are created as a series of screen displays. The authoring of each screen is enhanced through the use of two components: (1) the display page; and (2) the 'additions' menu. The display page is a clear screen on which the author may type directly all text (in the desired position and colour) that will unconditionally appear on the student screen. The additions menu is a listing of options by which the author can modify the display. At ADAPT level 2 these options include answer checking, graphics, video and audio sequences (including the overlaying of text/graphics on the video frames), and a time limit (see figure 5.23A). Further options are available at level 3, such as graphical animation (motion), colour palette and conditional text data based upon the run-time environment, (see figure 5.23B). At level 4 the display page for unconditional text remains the same, but the additions to the display are accomplished through the use of specific programming commands which the author inserts in command sections following the display page. For example, graphics are provided through GRAPHIC commands, answer checking through COMPARE commands and conditional text data is displayed by means of the SHOW commands.

The large amount of training required before authors can efficiently produce usable multimedia courseware has always been a problem with authoring languages in the past. Consequently, an advanced authoring system like ADAPT is a potential solution to some of the problems encountered by those involved in the development of CBT courseware. Such a system can overcome a lack of programming aptitude among authors by removing the need for programming. A great deal of the instructional material can be input by personnel lacking programming skills or experience. Material requiring these skills can then be left to those authors able to input them. In a similar way, ADAPT can overcome the lack of CBT design expertise by providing built-in instructional models that help ensure that the on-line material is fully consistent with the most effective teaching and learning strategies available. Similar models are used in the stand-alone PLATO systems described in the following section.

(b) Micro-PLATO
A review of the PLATO computer based learning system has been given elsewhere (Bitzer, 1976; Barker, 1979). Originally, PLATO instruction was only available through special multimedia terminals attached to a large time-sharing mainframe computer. However, now that powerful low-cost microsystems are available there is an increasing demand for 'Stand-Alone PLATO', a version of the system designed to run on microcomputer based hardware. Two types of workstation are involved, one to enable the author to generate the courseware and another to enable students to access it. The relationship between the author station and the student stations is depicted in figure 5.24.

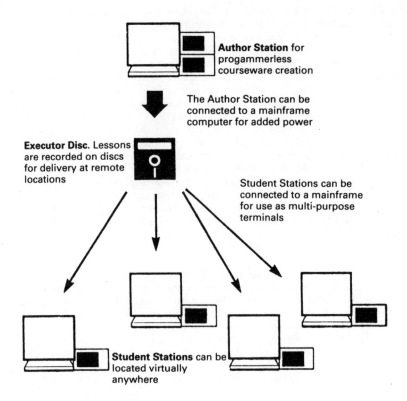

Figure 5.24 Workstations for Stand-Alone PLATO
(Courtesy of Control Data Corporation.)

The system's author station makes it possible for someone without a
knowledge of computer programming to create courseware quickly and
easily. It is totally independent of a mainframe computer but can be
connected to one when necessary, either for use as a multi-purpose
time sharing terminal or for use of central PLATO. The author
workstation thus contains two flexible disc drives. One of these is
used to hold a disc containing the courseware creation software; the
other contains a disc on to which the lesson is recorded. Courses
recorded on to disc using the author station are subsequently used on
the system's student stations.

The student station is similar to the author station except that it
contains only one disc drive. The keyboard provides standard
alphanumeric and mode–dependent special function keys. The screen
supports a 512 x 512 graphics capability and can be fitted with a 16 x
16 array touch panel option.

As with the MicroTICCIT system described in the previous section, there are two approaches to authoring multimedia courseware for PLATO systems: by means of its authoring language (TUTOR) or through the use of parameter driven instructional models. An brief description of the TUTOR language was given in section 3.2.3. The remainder of this section is therefore devoted to an overview of some of PLATO's author application models which provide a mechanism for the programmerless authoring of courseware (Control Data Corporation, 1983).

In order to create lessons the author simply inserts an author application model disc into the primary flexible disc drive on the author station. The author disc contains an editor that takes the author step-by-step through the process of lesson creation. As it is created, the lesson material is recorded on the executor disc (see figure 5.24). Once created, the lesson can be delivered by placing this executor disc into the single flexible disc drive on the student station. Examples of typical author application models include:

(1) the tutorial lesson model,
(2) the drill and practice model,
(3) the situation simulation model, and
(4) the certification testing model.

Tutorial lessons are primarily informational in content and are designed to enable trainees to absorb the information at their own rate. Some testing can be incorporated into the lesson in order to determine readiness for the next stage of the lesson. Drill and practice units are essentially testing modules. They enable both the student and the instructor to keep track of the student's progress. Lessons involving situation simulation enable trainees to experience work-like situations without the expense and risks of actually using production equipment. The certification testing module permits easy creation and administration of tests to certify mastery in areas where an individual's performance must be of the highest standards.

In order to provide some insight into the nature of PLATO's author application models, two of them (the tutorial lesson model and the situation simulation model) will be described in more detail. Figure 5.25A shows a flow chart that represents one of the many different alternatives for controlling student branching using the tutorial lesson model. The model utilises the following basic steps:

Step 1: The student is given a brief introduction to the topic.
Step 2: An index is displayed allowing the student to choose specific topics of interest.
Step 3: Having chosen a topic the student is shown the relevant information.
Step 4: The student is asked a question to test comprehension of the lesson material.

Step 5: If the answer is correct the student is told
to go on to the next topic; if not, the student
is advised to review the lesson material.

The tutorial lesson model allows the author to create simple tutorial lessons. Once an initial key depression has been made, prompts on the screen lead the author step–by–step through the creation of each display. Tutorial lessons created using this model can include the following features: text and graphics; indexes to allow students to concentrate on specific lesson areas; a variety of question types such as multiple choice, true or false, short answers or touch choice; answer judging with feedback; and branching specified by the author, as illustrated in figure 5.25A.

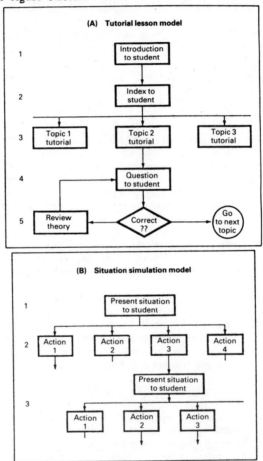

Figure 5.25 Examples of PLATO author application models.
(Courtesy of Control Data Corporation.)

The situation simulation model (see figure 5.25b) allows the author to create simulation lessons with multiple paths. Each student's path is determined by the choice made in response to situations presented in the lesson. In figure 5.25B the following steps are involved:

Step 1: The student is presented with a situation
        such as might happen in a workplace. A
        number of possible responses are listed.
Step 2: The student chooses one of the responses.
Step 3: The result of the student's choice is
        announced, the new situation is described and
        a new set of possible responses listed.   The
        process is repeated as often as necessary.

As in the case of the other application models, authoring is by means of prompting from the system and so is well suited to novice authors.

Through the use of the types of model described above, it is possible to dispense with the need for advanced programming ability on the part of the author. Indeed, by taking the author step-by-step through the process of courseware creation, the Micro-PLATO author station eliminates the need for any extensive computer background. In principle, anyone who can design a training course should also be able to construct an equivalent computer based lesson using the Stand-Alone PLATO system.

(c) PHILVAS
PHILVAS is an acronym for PHilips Interactive Laser Vision Authoring System. This interactive software package has been specially designed to simplify the tasks associated with preparing programs for the control of instructional interactive video disc equipment of the type that was discussed earlier in section 4.2.3 (figure 4.12). In the discussion that follows it is assumed that the reader is familiar with the material presented in this earlier section.

The PHILVAS system consists of a number of program modules. Included amongst these are:

(1) the supervisor
(2) the manager
(3) the program editor
(4) the teletext editor
(5) the simulator
(6) the compressor
(7) the ALLVA author language

The supervisor is the overall control module; it provides the user's initial entry into the system and also gives access to all the other constituent parts. The manager helps the author to organise and administer the coarseware units that are produced; it can be used to

provide access control, make changes to passwords and titles, and
move/copy/rename/list/remove   sections of courseware. The program
editor provides the means by which the author builds the fragments of
courseware that will ultimately form the final instructional program.
Similarly, the teletext editor enables the author to create and update
teletext frames using the TV interface. As soon as courseware has been
produced, the simulator then allows the author to test a complete
lesson (or part of it). Finally, the compressor is a special program
module used to produce a compact version of the courseware suitable
for storage on an optical video disc (or other storage medium). The
courseware author communicates and controls the   multimedia   resources
provided by the interactive video system by means of a special author
language called ALLVA (Author Language for Laser Vision Applications).
The remainder of this section deals only with the latter aspect of the
PHILVAS system.

ALLVA statements (see table 5.3) each begin with a unique keyword
which (with certain exceptions) may be preceded by a picture number
and followed by data items or other keywords. When a picture number
comes before a keyword the specified picture is retrieved from the
video disc before the command following it is actioned. However, when
a picture number occurs within a pair of PLAY and ENDPLAY statements
it means: wait until that picture number is reached and then   do   what
the statement says. A section of an interactive video control program
written in ALLVA is shown below.

```
12000   PLAY
        SWITCH ON VIDEO, REMOTE
        ERASE TEXT
13000   TEXT FRAME1
14000   SOUND BEEP
15000   ENDPLAY
```

This code would cause the video player to retrieve picture number
12000 and start showing the animation commencing at that frame in a
forward direction. The video and remote control keypad are then each
switched on and any text on the TV screen is erased. When picture
number 13000 is reached the text fragment named FRAME1 is retrieved
and then superimposed over whatever is on the TV screen. It is assumed
that FRAME1 has been previously created and formatted using the
teletext editor subsystem (item (4) above). When picture number   14000
is reached, a tone is sounded and, finally, animation is stopped as
soon as frame 15000 has been shown.

Table 5.3 Table of ALLVA Statements.
(Courtesy of Philips.)

Statement	Operand Format	Descriptive Comments
* BREAK	ON {<Cc> ! <Vs>} TO <Fp>	define an interrupt facility
* DECREMENT	<Vn> [BY <VCn>]	decrement a numeric variable
* DIGIT	[<Vn>] [UPTO <Cd>]	wait for single digit input (and assign)
* DISABLE	BREAK	cancels the BREAK statement
* DO	<Fp>	execute a named program fragment
@* ENDFORM		delimiter for the FORM statement
ENDPLAY		delimiter for the PLAY statement
@* ENDSELECT		delimiter for the SELECT statement
* ERASE	TEXT	clear text from TV screen
* EXIT	{FRAGMENT ! SELECT}	leave specified control structure
* FORM	<Ft>	enable entry of variable data
* INCREMENT	<Vn> [BY <VCn>]	increase the value of a numeric variable
* KEY	[<Vs>]:	wait for a single key depression (and assign)
MARK	POSITION	identify current position in script
* OUTPUT	<VC>	send item to host computer
* PAGE	<VCn>	select a Teletext page (range 100 - 899)
* PAUSE		stops a PLAY sequence
* PICTURE	<VCn>	retrieves a specified picture
PLAY	[{<Cn> [/2] ! [2/] <Cn>}]	start playing at specified speed and direction
* REPEAT	{FRAGMENT ! SELECT}	enables repetition of a unit
* RESUME		restart after a PAUSE statement
* RETURN	TO {PREVIOUS ! LATEST} MARK	return to marked position in a script
* SELECT	[ON {<V> ! PICTURE ! KEY}]	create a multiple choice situation
* SET	<Vn> TO {<VCn> ! PICTURE}	assignation (result = numeric value)
* SET	<Vs> TO <VCs>	assignation (result = string value)
* SOUND	BEEP	produce an audible tone
* STEP	{FORWARD ! BACKWARD}	move to the next (or previous) picture
START		start a new script
* SWITCH	{ON ! OFF} <functions>	control video functions (on or off status)
* TEXT	<Ft>	display the named text overlay fragment
* WAIT	<VCn> [SEC]	wait for the specified time interval

LEGEND: * means the statement may be used between a pair of PLAY/ENDPLAY statements
@ means no picture number allowed for this statement; all others may have picture numbers

<Fp>	denotes a program fragment	<Vs>	denotes a string variable
<Ft>	denotes a text fragment	<Vn>	denotes a numeric variable
		<Cn>	denotes a numeric constant
		<Cc>	denotes a character constant
		<Cs>	denotes a string constant
		<Cd>	denotes a digit constant

Notice that the PLAY/ENDPLAY combination of keywords is an example of an ALLVA compound statement whose function is to start and stop the animation presented on the TV screen. The values of the picture numbers that precede the keywords determine the direction of play. A parameter value following the PLAY keyword can be used to specify the speed at which the animation is presented. The following examples illustrate this.

```
11000   PLAY
  600   ENDPLAY
```
Start animation at frame 11000 and play backwards at normal speed until frame 600 is reached and then stop.

```
500   PLAY 3
800   ENDPLAY
```
Play forward at three times normal speed.

```
100   PLAY 1/2
150   WAIT 5 SEC
300   ENDPLAY
```
Play forward at half speed from frame 100 and wait for 5 seconds when frame 150 is encountered; then, resume playing at half speed until frame 300 is presented and then stop.

```
5000   PLAY 2/3
3000   ENDPLAY
```
Go to frame 5000 and start playing backwards at 2/3 normal speed until frame 3000 is reached.

Another useful compound statement is the SELECT/ENDSELECT combination. This enables the courseware author to create multiple choice situations in which the student is allowed to make one choice. Its use is illustrated by the following sections of ALLVA code.

```
SELECT                    **   Text fragment (OPTIONS)
TEXT OPTIONS              **   Choose part you want to see:
     IF 1 DO PART1        **   Part 1:  Swimming
     IF 2 DO PART2        **   Part 2:  Gliding
     IF 3 DO PART3        **   Part 3:  Sailing
                          **
                          **   Enter 1, 2 or 3
ENDSELECT
```

In the above example the teletext overlay called OPTIONS would be displayed on the TV screen. The student could then make a selection by pressing an appropriate key on the keypad. As a result of this, control would branch to that part of the program designed to handle the option selected by the student. Notice how comments (which commence with the sequence of characters **) may be used in order to improve the readability of the program and also to explain what is happening. In fact, in the code illustrated above, the comment facility is used to enable the author to indicate the textual content of the OPTIONS fragment.

The next example shows how (1) video is switched off, (2) a teletext frame (FRAME10) is displayed for 10 seconds and its contents then erased, (3) video picture 15000 is retrieved and displayed with teletext frame WHATDAY subsequently overlayed onto it, and (4) the analysis of an input is then achieved using the SELECT statement.

```
SWITCH OFF VIDEO
TEXT FRAME10
PAUSE 10 SEC
ERASE TEXT
PICTURE 15000
SWITCH ON VIDEO
TEXT WHATDAY
SELECT
    IF 1 DO MONDAY AND EXIT FRAGMENT
    IF 2 DO TUESDAY AND REPEAT FRAGMENT
    IF 3 DO WEDNESDAY
    IF 4 DO THURSDAY
    IF 5 DO FRIDAY
    IF 6 DO SATURDAY AND EXITFRAGMENT
    IF 7 EXIT SELECT **NO WORK ON SUNDAY
    IF 8 TEXT NODAY AND REPEAT SELECT
    IF 9 TEXT NODAY AND REPEAT SELECT
ENDSELECT
```

The student responds by entering a single digit from 1 to 9 to obtain his/her choice; this is done by depressing any numeric key from 1 to 9 inclusive − all other keys being inoperative.

In addition to analysing input responses for particular single digit key depressions it is also possible to test input strings which have been typed by the student. The following example illustrates this point.

```
14000   FORM QUES10
            INSERT REPLY$ FROM USER
        ENDFORM
        SELECT ON REPLY$
        IF 'YES' DO YESPART
        IF 'NO'  DO NOPART
                OTHERWISE DO INVALID
        ENDSELECT
```

In this example picture number 14000 is retrieved and displayed. A text fragment called QUES10 is then overlayed onto the TV screen on top of the video picture. The text fragment will have a substitution field into which the student has to type in a reply (either 'yes' or 'no'). The student's reply is stored in a string variable called REPLY$ and is subsequently analysed using the SELECT statement. If the value held in the string variable REPLY$ is 'YES' then the program segment called YESPART is next executed; if the value of the variable is 'NO' then the program segment NOPART is executed; if REPLY$ contains any other value then the program segment INVALID is performed.

Unfortunately, it is not possible to provide a complete description of the entire ALLVA language. Those parts that we have described have been included for the express purpose of giving the reader an indication of the types of linguistic primitive that need to be incorporated into those author languages to be used for controlling CAL workstations which employ interactive video facilities.

As a final point, it may be worthwhile briefly outlining the way in which the PHILVAS CAL author uses the teletext editor to create text and graphic frames for overlaying on to the TV screen. Essentially, a keyboard based screen editing facility is used. This employs a variety of different key–stroke combinations to (1) position text and graphic characters on the screen, and (2) generate the teletext control characters that are used to create the special effects (colour, boxing, flashing, etc) embodied in the display. This approach to teletext frame authoring can be quite effective. However, we feel it may be too complex for many categories of user. Consequently, we have been investigating an authoring methodology relies upon menu selection techniques that employing pictorial interfaces (Barker, 1984b) which are implemented by means of a high resolution digitiser (see section 4.2.5(e)). We believe that this technique may lead to a much easier authoring methodology than those based upon the use of just a keyboard/screen editing system.

5.3.2 SMALLTALK and LOGO

Although these programming systems are not normally classified as 'authoring languages' in the conventional sense, their potential importance for CAL courseware development dictates that they are each briefly mentioned in this chapter. We feel that their inclusion here is justified since they do provide mechanisms to facilitate the provision of multimedia (or multi–channel) experiences for the student terminal user.

Programming languages enable their users to control the hardware and software resources available within a computer system (see section 1.1.3). Such languages vary quite significantly in (1) what they allow their users to do, and (2) the ease with which they enable their users to achieve their desired goals. Conventional languages often involve the use of procedures (sequences of descriptive statements) that operate on information values held in various forms of static data structure (that is, a fixed organisation of data values). Some languages allow the creation and manipulation of dynamic data structures, thereby considerably enhancing their usefulness. Compared with ordinary programming systems SMALLTALK and LOGO represent significant departures from the accepted idea of a programming language, this is particularly true in the case of SMALLTALK. In the remainder of this section we provide a few descriptive comments in order to give the reader a basic introduction to each of these new tools.

(a) SMALLTALK

SMALLTALK is an interactive programming system that was designed, researched and developed during the 1970s by the Learning Research Group at the Xerox Palo Alto Research Centre in California (Byte, 1981). The language is highly graphics orientated. Ideally, it requires a high resolution CRT screen and a pointing device, such as a pen or mouse (see section 4.2.5(e)), to facilitate user interaction. Through these types of device the user can select screen information and invoke various sorts of message in order to interact with it.

In contrast to the conventional types of (procedural) language outlined above, the ideas embodied in SMALLTALK centre around the notion of an object/action metaphor (Goldberg and Robson, 1983; Ramsey and Grimes, 1983). Essentially, every element in the SMALLTALK language is an object that may communicate with other objects by sending and receiving messages. An object is a package of information along with descriptions of how it is to be manipulated. Each object has a set of variables that refers to other objects (these variables are called private variables) and a set of methods. A method is a description of a single type of manipulation of the object's information. That is, a definition of the response the object should make when it receives a particular type of message.

Each object belongs to a class. A class describes a set of objects called its instances. Each instance contains the information that distinguishes it from other instances. This information is a subset of its private variables called instance variables. The values of these variables are different from instance to instance. As new objects are created, they inherit the properties of the class from which they are generated. SMALLTALK has many predefined classes about which the system knows (kernel classes). It also allows users to define new classes (called user-defined classes). Classes may be defined in a number of different ways. One way to achieve this is through the use of a class template. An example of a class definition using this technique is shown in figure 5.26 (Althoff, 1981). This template defines a class whose name is 'Card'. An instance of this class can be used to represent a card in a game playing program.

class name	Card
superclass	Object
instance variable names	suit rank faceUp
class messages and methods	

suit: aString rank: aninteger | aCard |
  aCard ← self new. aCard setSuit: aString setRank: aninteger.
  ↑ aCard.

instance messages and methods

external
suit | | ↑ suit.
rank | | ↑ rank.
turnFaceUp | | faceUp ← true.
turnFaceDown | | faceUp ← false.
turnOver | | faceUp ← faceUp not.
IsFaceUp | | ↑ faceUp.
IsFaceDown | | ↑ faceUp not.

internal
setSuit: aString setRank: aninteger | |
  suit ← aString. rank ← aninteger. self turnFaceDown.

Figure 5.26 Class template for the class 'Card'.
(Courtesy of Byte magazine.)

Notice that class 'Card' has instance variables named 'suit', 'rank', and, 'faceUp'. A new instance of this class may be created by sending the class "Card" a message that assigns particular values to these instance variables.

Messages are described by expressions. A message–sending expression contains three parts: a receiver, a selector and arguments. The receiver is the object to which the message is sent; the selector is the symbolic name used to specify the method or operation to be performed; the arguments give the values needed in order to effect the correct manipulation of the object. Thus, in addition to enabling the creation of objects, messages also invoke certain types of activity, for example in the case of graphical objects that are used in screen animation, messages could be used to specify position, colour, direction of movement, and so on.

The primitive types of SMALLTALK object can be used as a basis for building up extremely sophisticated programs. For example, the class 'Card' might be used in conjunction with other classes (such as 'CardDeck', 'CardHand', and so on) in order to simulate a game of cards between a number of players and a dealer (Althoff, 1981; Goldberg and Robson, 1983). Message passing from one object to another could then be used to invoke the activities associated with shuffling a deck, dealing cards, returning cards to the pack, etc. This type of approach leads quite naturally into another useful SMALLTALK concept, the notion of application kits (Kay, 1977; 1980; Goldberg and Ross, 1981).

A kit is essentially a set of components and the tools necessary to manipulate these in order to produce different types of special purpose interface for particular types of application. For example, there could be a car-building kit, a poetry kit, a music kit, a painting kit, an editing kit, and so on. Some detailed descriptions of SMALLTALK application kits are given in Byte (1981). Goldberg and Ross (1981) describe a dance kit and its use for producing CRT animation (both of a dancer and of a turtle); Bowman and Flegal (1981) outline the description of 'Toolbox' – a kit which is used to help designers and artists make graphical sketches using a computer system. Through the kit approach it is possible to hide the unnecessary details of the SMALLTALK system. This greatly facilitates the interaction of novice users with the computer since they do not need to become directly involved with classes and instances. Kits thus provide a means to develop high level end-user (and application) orientated mechanisms for the utilisation of computer technology. For this reason alone, SMALLTALK would seem to have much to offer those interested in using it for CAL applications. Indeed, when this language becomes more widely available for use within CAL environments it should (through kits) provide a powerful authoring tool for implementing multimedia courseware that incorporates text, sound, static imagery and animation. Kay and Goldberg (1977) have provided an insight into what is likely to be possible in their descriptions of 'Personal Dynamic Media' and the 'Dynabook' concept (Goldberg, 1979; Kay, 1979).

The Dynabook involves the idea of a 'moldable' medium for handling information (Goldberg, 1979). That is, each type of user tailors the system to meet the requirements of his/her particular application (as discussed in kits above). The importance of SMALLTALK in the context of the Dynabook lies in the fact that it reflects the type of software support necessary to realise the concepts involved in dynamic (or reactive) communication with the computer. In hardware terms, the Dynabook is perceived of as being a hand-held, high performance computer with a high resolution display and supporting audio and visual communication paths; through appropriate network connections (see figure 1.13 for example) this could have connections to a wide range of shared (encyclopaedic) information sources. It is important to realise, however, that implementations of the Dynabook do not yet exist. Indeed, it is a futuristic multimedia communication tool. In order to give the reader some insight into its likely form and capability we conclude this section on SMALLTALK with some extracts taken from an article written by Alan Kay (1979):

THE FORM:

We visualised the personal computer of the 1980s
as a notebook sized package whose front side was a
flat–screen reflective display, like a liquid–
crystal watch face. The surface of the screen
would be sensitive to the touch of a finger or
stylus. It would contain miniature computer
circuits that could carry out millions of
instructions per second, and there would be enough
storage capacity to retain several months worth of
projects. The machine would be completely self–
contained. However, it also could be connected to
hi–fi sets to create music, to other personal
computers for group projects, and to external
information sources such as the computerised
libraries of the future. We called this visionary
computer 'Dynabook'.

THE CAPABILITY:

The next step in personal computing will probably
be do–it–yourself cartoons. It is already possible
to represent and animate stylised colour images,
applying techniques similar to those employed in
SMALLTALK. Soon after that, the first
participatory drama systems will appear. Imagine a
full–colour ... movie in which you can insert a
character representing yourself. You can be the
hero, the villain, or one of the minor characters,
with the plot controlled by decisions you make
during the course of the action. Your family or
friends can also assume roles. The story will be
the result of your combined decisions.

The artistic possibilities are tremendous,
... imagine manipulating a Shakespearean play. Or,
working with your personal computer and a music
synthesiser, you could create your own sonata ...
If your taste turns to art, your computer can
become a canvas on which you can experiment with a
realistic sunset, or the most inventive abstract
painting. With your personal computer, you can do
as much as your imagination will allow,

Imagine the potential applications of the above types of simulation
for use within education, for all subjects of the curriculum, not just
science and mathematics. How far are we towards the realisation of

some of these capabilities? Some distance yet. However, Perry (1984) describes how current technology is moving rapidly towards some of Kay's visions of the future. For example, he outlines the development of video disc games (based on filmed action) in which the player controls the sequence of events by making a series of choices. Thus, in the video disc game 'Many Roads to Murder' there are up to 16 different outcomes - depending upon the player's decisions a variety of different crimes can occur and then be solved. Included in Perry's report is a description of the Koalapad Touch Tablet - a hand-held peripheral connected to the computer with a cable. The user selects functions from a menu and draws on the tablet with a finger or stylus, creating an image that appears on the screen. The tablet can be used as a sketch pad to reproduce any image, as a custom keyboard with overlays of any combination of characters or graphics, or as a game controller. Similarly, the practical low-cost realisation of application kits is reflected in Perry's description of Commodore International's 'Magic Desk' software. This uses pictures instead of words as a menu: in order to type, a pointer is moved to a picture of a typewriter; in order to store or retrieve information, the pointer is moved to a picture of a filing cabinet and so on. From this description it is easy to see that technology is slowly moving in the direction of Kay's prediction of the future. Indeed, many microcomputers that are currently available, for example the LISA (Stobie, 1983a; 1983b;), do provide the type of graphical interfaces and software support advocated by the SMALLTALK philosophy. However, they are physically large machines; undoubtedly, it will be some time yet before a multimedia device as compact as the Dynabook will become a practical reality.

(b) LOGO

When it was first initiated, the design and development of the SMALLTALK system was greatly influenced by another language research project that was being conducted at MIT (Kay, 1977). This was Papert's LOGO project (Papert, 1980). Papert and his colleagues were attempting to devise a programming tool that could be used by children and which would (1) 'let them explore their ideas', and (2) 'teach them to become mathematicians'. We have already introduced LOGO and some of its applications in section 5.2.8 where we described the basic ideas underlying the use of LOGO learning centres. In this section we give a brief description of the language and explain its relevance to studies in multimedia CAL.

The multimedia aspects of LOGO are primarily associated with the graphical aspects of programming the turtle. The basic ideas underlying turtle graphics were summarised pictorially in figure 5.19. As we mentioned in section 5.2.8 the turtle may be implemented in either of two ways. Some systems use small mechanical motor driven robotic devices that are fitted with one or more pens. This approach to turtle implementation is illustrated by the photograph in figure 5.20. The alternative method of providing a turtle is by displaying a

turtle-like shape (usually triangular) on the CRT screen; this is
often done using sprite programming techniques (see section 5.3.4(d)).
Depending on the type of turtle that is used, a variety of different
types of graphic effect can be created. Undoubtedly, the CRT based
turtle is able to produce more spectacular graphic displays, provided
the CRT screen is of a high enough resolution and that it supports
full colour facilities. No matter which type of turtle is used, there
are undoubted learning advantages associated with each (Papert, 1980).

One of the most significant features of the LOGO language is its use
of basic English words as commands. These act as building blocks which
can be built up into more complex structures. Initially, LOGO consists
of a limited vocabulary of words which between them perform a number
of primitive functions; some of these were introduced in section 5.2.8
(LEFT, FORWARD, TO, PENUP, and END). As a student learns how to use
these commands it becomes possible for him/her to put them together in
numerous different ways in order to build up more complex structure
which, in turn, can again be defined by means of a single word. This
principal was illustrated in section 5.2.8 where we described the
steps involved in defining a simple LOGO procedure to make the turtle
draw out a sketch of a house.

The LOGO language has been used extensively as a tool for studying the
mechanisms by which students learn and to provide a computer based
medium to enable them to investigate their own ideas, particularly
those relevant to mathematical concepts. Most of the research work
that has been conducted in this area stems from the pioneering work of
Seymour Papert (1980). Since his initial work, over the last fifteen
years a number of other teaching and learning institutes have shown
considerable interest in this language – both in the USA (Byte, 1982)
and in other countries. For example, in the United Kingdom, Edinburgh
University developed many LOGO based educational projects several of
which related to the teaching of mathematics (Howe and O'Shea, 1978;
Du Boulay and Howe, 1982). Similarly, in France the Centre Mondial was
set up in Paris as a walk-in centre where 'ordinary people' might
interact with computers. Both LOGO and turtle graphics are used in an
attempt to achieve this objective (Roper, 1983).

Further details on educational applications and uses of LOGO are given
in a number of sources. For example, O'Shea and Self (1983) describe
the use of the language in the context of developing many of the
underlying relationships between artificial intelligence and computer
based learning; Watt (1982) outlines a number of application projects
that are going on in schools; and Solomon (1982) describes a number of
different learning styles associated with the task of introducing LOGO
to young children. We have already mentioned some examples of the work
that has been done or is being conducted with handicapped children
(Emanuel and Wier, 1976; Geoffrion, 1983). The interested reader is
strongly recommended to seek further information from each of these
sources.

5.3.3 MUMEDALA

MUMEDALA is an acronym for MUlti–MEDia Authoring LAnguage (Barker, 1983; 1984a; 1984c). This system was concieved of as being an experimental test vehicle that was designed to provide a framework in which to conduct those hardware, software and interfacing experiments thought to be necessary in order to produce successful solutions to the problems inherent in multimedia authoring. In this section we outline some of the more important features of the system.

(a) Design Considerations

When the requirements specification for the MUMEDALA system were originally formulated a number of items were considered to be of prime importance. Some of the more important of these design criteria are listed below. It was thought that the system must be capable of:

(1) operating both autonomously and in a networked environment;
(2) supporting a variety of human–computer interaction techniques;
(3) providing both frame and line orientated dialogues;
(4) providing good frame editing facilities;
(5) presenting animated sequences;
(6) providing highly end–user orientated interfaces, that is, it must be user friendly and easy to use;
(7) providing adequate data base support facilities for the storage of instructional material (included here is the possibility that the user may wish to create an expert system (see section 6.2.3);
(8) capturing broadcast (radio and TV) material from global distribution systems;
(9) supporting a variety of information storage media;
(10) constructing dynamic models of individual students and of using them to produce highly individualised instructional material (see Self (1979) and section 6.2.7);
(11) incorporating standards (where they exist) in order to facilitate the exchange of instructional material;
(12) producing material that can be easily modified to meet different requirements;
(13) providing an extensible environment capable of absorbing unforseen advances in technology and user requirements;
(14) being made highly reliable and being easily maintained by local technicians;
(15) permitting facile control of the learner's interaction environment.

The growing importance of both global and local area communication networks (see figure 1.13, section 6.2.4, Haefner (1980), Boutmy and Danthine (1979)) should mean that the dissemination and exchange of educational material might, in principal, be more easily accomplished in the future than it has been in the past. We therefore believe that educational workstations that are unable to exploit networking facilities of this type will be of limited applicability, particularly in situations where it is required to access archived material from a

remote   (or semi–remote) data base system. Another extremely important
design feature for the system is the requirement to be able to capture
(and, subsequently, modify and/or 'cut and snip') material transmitted
by radio and TV broadcasting networks (such as the UK's BBC   and   Open
University). Unfortunately, the problems inherent in manipulating
multimedia data bases (Barker and Yeates, 1981) impose severe
restrictions on what can currently be achieved in this context.

The storage facilities that need to be provided must cater for,
amongst others, both video and digital information. For example:
flexible and hard magnetic discs; video read and read/write stores, as
are provided by optical disc and video cassette systems; and ancillary
static image stores of the type made available through slide
collections and microfiche equipment. The introduction of a single
all–purpose storage medium (Kane et al., 1980) will undoubtedly be a
major step forward as far as multimedia instructional technology is
concerned.

Requirements in the area of modelling and the provision of a mechanism
(author language) to enable the facile control of the learner's
interaction environment were briefly outlined above. The remaining
parts of this section are now devoted to a description of some of the
work that we have conducted with respect to providing authoring
facilities to meet the requirements previously outlined.

(b)   Modes of Usage
A   schematic   illustration   of the MUMEDALA interaction environment is
presented in figure 5.27. The system is primarily a frame based one in
which CRT frames, video frames (from a VCR and/or optical   disc),
and/or slide frames are used to facilitate the output of instructional
material to the user. Users may belong to either of two broad classes:
learners   and   authors. From the point of view of the latter there are
three general modes of interaction: (1) frame generation, (2)   lesson
creation,   and   (3) system interrogation. Only CRT frames and teletext
overlay frames are generated during live on–line interaction with the
system. The other types of frame are produced externally and then pre-
loaded into the workstation or made accessible to it by way of a
suitable back–end data base and communication network.

When in frame generation mode the author creates a series of numbered
VDU frames. These may belong to any of five primitive classes:
instructional, remedial, reinforcing, testing and help. Once created
and numbered, the frames are stored in a local data base (and possibly
archived on a remote computer system). The VDU frames are supported by
ancillary sound and graphic units, off–line resources (such as
workbooks, maps, plans, etc) and diversions to on–line equipment. As
soon as some instructional frames exist the author may enter lesson
creation mode. During this part of the authoring process the author
specifies the order in which ancillary resources are to be controlled
so that they support the learning process in the most appropriate way.

When a lesson becomes operational the third mode of interaction –
system interrogation – may be invoked. Using this mode it is possible
for the teacher/author to determine the progress being made by
individual students and the way in which the instructional resources
are being used.

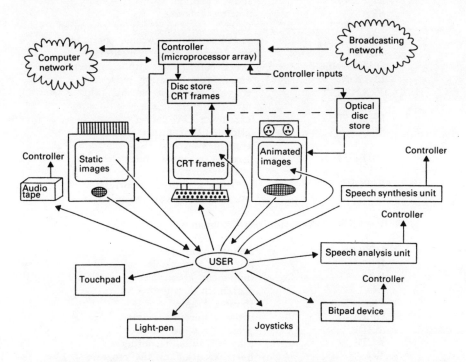

Figure 5.27   The MUMEDALA interaction environment.

The authoring facilities to achieve the above objectives are realised
through the use of a keyword based command language (Bailey, 1982).
This uses two basic types of command: direct and indirect. When the
system is loaded and executed (in authoring context) the other is
placed in direct command mode. When in this mode the author may issue
any of the MUMEDALA direct commands (see table 5.4A) to the terminal
control program. Each of these commands causes the system to pass into
other states that enable the CAI author to perform certain standard
types of operation.

Table 5.4 Summary of MUMEDALA Keywords

(A) MUMEDALA Direct Commands

CREATE	frame creation
EDIT	frame editing
DISPLAY	show a frame
ERASE	destroy a frame
CONNECT	form a link to a remote computer
SEND	send frame(s) to remote computer
FETCH	get frame(s) from computer
DISCONNECT	break connection with computer
LESSON	enter lesson creation mode
TRANSLATE	convert source statements into an executable lesson
EXECUTE	execute a CAI lesson
SET	allow author to set global control switches
INSPECT	look at a stored student/courseware record
REPORT	produce a printed report on student/courseware records

(B) MUMEDALA Indirect Commands

DEFINE	define a variable
INIT	initialise a variable
INC	increment a counter
DEC	decrement a counter
FRAME	show a frame
QFRAME	show a question frame
SLIDE	present a slide image
AUDIO	play an audio recording
WAIT	halt execution of the program
ACCEPT	await a student response
GOTO	jump to another part of program
IF	test value of variable/response
IFNOT	test value of variable/response
INFOBLOCK	define an information block
CONTROL	send control information to a peripheral device
TEST	test the status of a device
MATCH	perform a match operation
SET	set program switches or values of system variables
SPEEK	message to voice synthesiser
STOP	terminate execution of program
ANIMATION	show sequence from optical disc
MESSAGE	send a message via a device
MONITOR	set student monitoring options

An instructional unit with which a student interacts will usually
consist of a control element and the associated set of frames upon
which it operates, The control element for a lesson is defined in
terms of the indirect commands available in the MUMEDALA system.
Generally, an indirect statement will contain four basic parts: (1) a
label, (2) a command keyword, (3) an operand list, and (4) a comment
field. Of these, the label and comment field are optional. Some
commands may not require an operand, in which case this field will be
absent from the statement. The allowed command keywords are listed in
table 5.4B. The basic format of the MUMEDALA command template and
examples showing the syntax of particular commands are given
below.

<command>::=<label><command-keyword><operand-list><comment-field>

Examples:

(1) FRAME <value> [,<value>] (O:N)

(2) SLIDE <device>[,<value>] (O:N)

(3) SPEEK <device>[,<value>]

(4) ANIMATION <device>,<start>,<finish>[,<controller>] (0:1)

In the above examples, the FRAME command allows the CAI author to
cause one or more CRT frames to be displayed in succession on the CRT
screen. Progression through the sequence being caused by depression of
an appropriate key (NEXT) on the keyboard. The SLIDE command allows
one or more slides to be shown on the particular slide projector
specified by the value of the <device> parameter. The third of the
examples (SPEEK) provides an author with the facility to pass messages
to the student by means of speech synthesis equipment. In the final
example, the ANIMATION command provides for the presentation of
animated sequences (from cine, video tape or optical video disc) using
a suitable control program to monitor both the presentation device and
the student interaction with the system. Further details of the
structure of the operand lists and specifications for the parsing
algorithms used for analysing and checking the validity of individual
statements are given in the system documentation (Barker et al., 1982;
Barker and Skipper, 1982).

A MUMEDALA source program consists of a file containing a series of
commands similar to those described above. A typical program section
is shown in figure 5.28. In order to convert files of this type into
executable control units, the source program must be translated into
an appropriate target code, at present BASIC (see section 2.3.1) is
used for this purpose. This language was chosen because it is
available on most of the microcomputers which were likely to be
candidates for use in workstation construction. It therefore provided

a machine independent target code.

```
DEFINE WRONGS,RIGHTS,MARK
INIT   WRONGS = 0, MARK= 50
INIT   RIGHTS = 1    /NON-ZERO START POINT
*UNIT1
   FRAME 1
   FRAME 2,21,22
*LOOP1
   FRAME 3
*F7  QFRAME  7,14,21
   ACCEPT 57    /57 IS KEYBOARD
   IF<A>,  *REMO1
   IF<B>,  *REINO1
   IF<C>,  *HELPO1
   GOTO *LOOP1
*REMO1  FRAME 3     /REMEDIATION STEP
   FRAME 4
   FRAME 5
   INC WRONGS + 1
   GOTO *UNIT2
*REINO1  FRAME 6         /REINFORCEMENT STEP
   FRAME 2,21,23
   FRAME 7
   INC RIGHTS + 1
   GOTO *UNIT3
*HELPO1    FRAME 12
   FRAME 14
   GOTO *F7
*UNIT2   FRAME 8
      o
      o
     ETC.
*UNIT3   FRAME 14   /NEXT LEARNING UNIT
      o
      o
     ETC.
```

Figure 5.28 Section of a MUMEDALA source program.

(c)   Towards an Implementation

The   major implementation effort to date has been devoted to two basic areas: (1) the development of a command interpreter to   handle   direct commands,   and   (2)   the   design and programming of algorithms for the statement analyser to handle the direct commands.   In   case   (1),   the system   hardware is based upon an ETHERNET (Wolfberg, 1982) local area network (LAN) with (as a future development) gateway connections to   a number of remote computers. Software development for the command interpreter has been mainly concerned with the code needed to handle CRT frame creation and editing at the workstation with subsequent storage of the frames both within the workstation and in a local back-end data base connected to the LAN. In case (2), the statement analyser is now complete thereby enabling complete MUMEDALA programs to be checked for syntax and (some) semantic errors. The next stage within this project requires the development of software to handle target code generation. It will then be possible to down-load code to the workstation so that it can be used to create and control students' learning activities.

(d) System Evaluation
Some rudimentary evaluations of the basic facilities summarised in table 5.4 have been conducted using potential authors, some skilled in computer technology and others not so. Unfortunately, the results (in the latter case) were not encouraging. However, a more objective evaluation must now be performed before any major revisions to the end-user language interface are undertaken. We are currently involved in designing the experiments to enable this evaluation to be undertaken.

(e) Problem Areas
We foresee a number of problem areas with respect to the future development of the MUMEDALA system. Briefly, these relate to (1) workstation implementation, (2) the availability of a hybrid LAN system to enable the movement of both digital and video information, (3) the limitations of the authors' interface, which is still not sufficiently user friendly, and, (4) the hardware and software interfaces within the workstation are still difficult to design and implement.

We believe that many of the problems encountered in areas (1) and (4) can be overcome through appropriate use of memory mapping techniques (see section 4.2). Indeed, to this end we are designing and constructing an 'intelligent' microprocessor based address decoding unit that will enable workstation peripherals to be attached to the controlling microcomputer in a standard and consistent way. Hardware to overcome problems in area (2) is now becoming commonly available; this should minimise the difficulties associated with the combined transmission of different types of information. Finally, we anticipate that the provision of an on-line HELP facility and a suitable designed computer based training package may help alleviate problems in area (3).

(f) Conclusion
A considerable amount of research and development effort still needs to be devoted to the production of truly user-friendly authoring systems for use in a multimedia environment. Our initial investigations into the acceptability of the MUMEDALA system would suggest that this language may still be too complex for the non-

specialised user. In contrast, systems like Stand–Alone PLATO, MicroTICCIT and PHILVAS do present very 'easy to use' techniques for the production of multimedia courseware. The kinds of approach used in these systems may well provide the solution to the problems associated with the future production of coursewarefor multimedia CAL.

5.3.4 Special Techniques
Each medium used in CAL represents a distinct channel of communication. Multimedia CAL therefore derives its name from the concept of using multiple media for the communication of instructional information. That is, several channels of communication are used simultaneously, or in sequence, in order to achieve a particular pedagogic objective. This approach to CAL has been discussed at length in chapter 4.

As tools for the presentation of CAL material, CRT screens and video monitors provide very powerful display media. Through special techniques such as windowing, segmentation and overlaying, a CRT screen is able to support 'multiple channels of communication', and hence, is extremely useful for providing many novel facilities for the realisation of multimedia CAL. In the remaining parts of this chapter we briefly discuss some of the special techniques that are likely to be of value in attempting to meet the requirements of and demands for multimedia CAL.

(a) Overlay Methods
In general, overlay methods refer to techniques in which a final display image (which may be static or dynamic) is constructed by superimposing (or overlaying) two or more images (which may originate from different sources) on top of each other. Several simple applications of this technique have already been discussed both in this chapter (sections 5.2.4, 5.2.5 and 5.2.7) and in the previous one (section 4.2.3). In these examples we discussed the idea of combining teletext frames (generated by a microcomputer) with video images (retrieved from an optical disc). This approach to overlaying is summarised in figure 5.29A.

In this example, the video image(s) provide the static (or animated) background scene. Against this is presented the foreground material that is generated under computer control using the facilities provided by teletext encoder/decoder equipment.

Another example of an overlaying technique is illustrated in figure 5.29B (Bejah, 1982). Here, computer generated text and graphics (either high or low resolution) are displayed on the computer CRT screen. As they are produced, they are photographed using a video camera. The output of the camera is fed into the special effects generator (SEG); video images coming from the optical video disc are also input to this device. The SEG synchronises the signals coming from these two sources and produces a resultant output signal that

corresponds to superimposing the two images. This final overlay image
is then presented on the display monitor shown on the right–hand side
of the diagram.

(A) Teletext and video

(B) Computational graphics and video

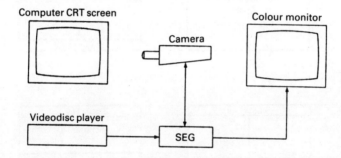

Figure 5.29   Examples of techniques for frame overlaying.

Special   effects generators can be used to achieve a variety of useful
image display strategies (for example video mixing, screen   splitting,
fading, wiping, and so on). Some of these techniques will be discussed
in   more   detail in the following section. SEGs suitable for combining
video signals from a camera and a video disc (see   figure   5.29B)   are
available commercially: A   typical   example is that supplied by Sony
(the SEG 1–A) for use in conjunction with their AVC–3250 camera (Sony,
1982).

The combination of computer generated output (digital) signals with
those   derived from a video source is an extremely important process.
It is therefore not surprising that a number of different approaches
have   been   used. Some of these employ an ancillary computer system to
perform the   function   of   the   SEG described above. This   approach
involves   three   distinct   steps. First, the digitisation of the input
video signals; second, the addition of images using digital processing

techniques; and third, the reconstruction of a resultant video signal for driving the display monitor. Other, more fundamental and less expensive techniques for the manipulation of digital CRT/video signals are also widely used. Some of these are described by Sippl and Dahl (1981) in their video–computer book.

(b) Screen Segmentation and Windowing
The basic idea underlying segmentation (or screen splitting) techniques is quite simple, the use of one single screen to support more than one logical channel of communication simultaneously. Screen segmentation thus provides a means of using a single CRT display or video monitor to present several frame images at exactly the same time. Figure 5.30 illustrates some different approaches to this technique.

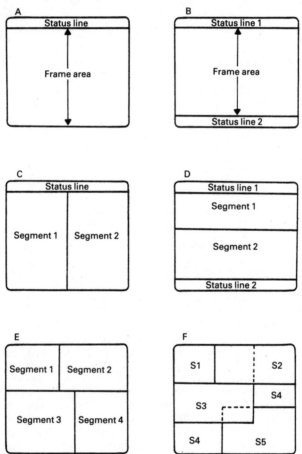

Figure 5.30 Some approaches to screen segmentation.

Example   A depicts a simple, effective and frequently used arrangement
– provision of a system status line. Systems that provide this type of
facility usually use the main frame area of the CRT as the primary
channel of communication to the user with the status line providing an
ancillary channel for error display or context specification, etc.
This technique can be used very effectively, especially when different
colours and text fonts are used to distinguish the two areas of the
screen. The MICROTEXT system described in chapter 3 uses this
approach. Actually, when in command mode, MICROTEXT uses a status
line, a header line, a command line and a frame area (compare figure
5.30B).

Other simple examples of screen splitting strategies are shown in
examples B, C and D of figure 5.30. Example B shows how two status
lines may be used to support a single main frame area. In example C a
split screen (vertical segmentation) is used to display two (half
width) frames simultaneously, each sharing a common status line.
Similarly, example D illustrates horizontal segmentation with each
segment having its own status line.

(A) Fixed segmentation (vertical screen split)

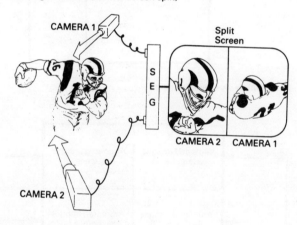

(B) Dynamic segmentation (screen wiping)

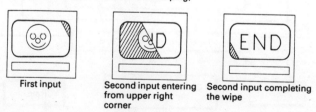

First input   Second input entering   Second input completing
                     from upper right   the wipe
                     corner

Figure 5.31 Practical examples of screen segmentation.

Some practical examples of simple screen segmentation are presented in figure 5.31. The arrangement shown in diagram A depicts fixed screen segmentation in a given (1:1) geometric ratio. It illustrates how a special effects generator can be used to mix the output from two separate video cameras and thereby show two views of the same object simultaneously. Diagram B illustrates the concept of dynamic segmentation or screen wiping. In this splitting effect the geometric ratio of the areas of the segments varies with time. Wiping is thus simply a split screen in which the line of demarcation between the two images is moving. It is possible to implement horizontal, vertical and diagonal wiping. Figure 5.31B shows the way in which a diagonal wipe (or corner insert) takes place from right to left across the screen.

(A)   A multi-function CRT display

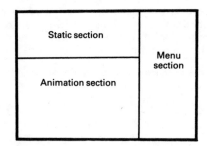

(B)   Multiple video image display

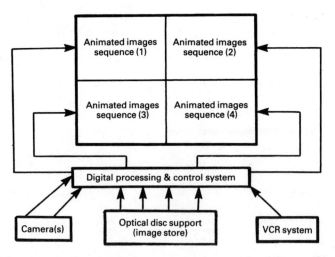

Figure 5.32   Applications of multiple screen splitting techniques.

Split screens with two segments are quite commonplace. However, situations often arise in which it is necessary to use more than two segments. Figure 5.30E illustrates one way of dividing a screen into four unequally sized segments. Some examples of circumstances that might require this type of screen splitting strategy are depicted in figure 5.32. Diagram A shows how three CRT screen areas might be used to support three distinct functions simultaneously: menu selection; static display of text or graphics; and animated display, either from a video source or as a result of high speed graphical computation. Diagram B illustrates a more sophisticated arrangement in which four animated image sequences are displayed at the same time. The position on the screen at which a particular animation channel is displayed and the source from which its display material is obtained (video disc, VCR or camera) is controlled by the software residing in the digital controller.

None of the screen segmentation techniques thus far discussed involve the concept of overlapping frames. That is, situations in which there are multiple images being displayed on the screen each 'appearing' to overlap its neighbours. This segmentation arrangement is depicted schematically in figure 5.30F. It shows how a part of segment S3 appears to lie beneath segments S1 and S2. Similarly, segment S5 has a corner that is covered by segment S3 while segment S4 appears to be partly hidden by S3 and S5. In order to achieve this apparent overlapping effect a priority is associated with each frame. Priorities may be changed dynamically by their user. Frames can therefore be brought to the forefront of the screen or taken to the background by changing their assigned priorities.

This type of display technique is often referred to as 'windowing' by some authors (Kay, 1977; Stobie, 1984). However, we prefer to refer to it as a special instance of segmentation, thereby reserving the term windowing to refer to a more specific technique which we will describe below. Many terminals and microcomputer systems are now starting to provide this type of display facility (Stobie, 1983a; 1983b). Special languages (such as SMALLTALK) or screen handling packages need to be used in order to produce and control this type of segmentation.

We conclude this section by providing a brief description of another important and often used technique – windowing. A window on to some activity is simply a viewing port for that activity. A window may occupy any fraction of a display screen. Similarly, many windows may be displayed on a single screen, in which case we prefer the term segmentation (as we discussed above).

Any window that is used to view an activity will normally have dimensional limitations placed on it by the amount of space it can occupy within the overall display area. In the discussion that follows we assume that the physical size of the window is p x q, as illustrated in figure 5.33.

270 Introducing CAL

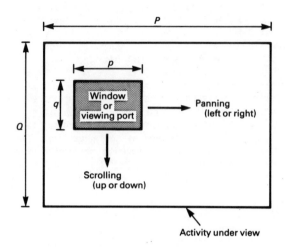

Figure 5.33   The basic principle of windowing.

This diagram shows how a viewing port may be used (under computer control) to view an activity which is logically (and/or physically) much larger than the actual window being used. A variety of operations are usually available to enable the window to gain full access to the whole of the activity under study. For example, panning left/right enables the user to move his/her field of view horizontally across the target scene; scrolling up/down allows viewing of a particular vertical strip; and zooming in/out provides the user with greater/lesser detail of the activity being observed. If a suitable spoken (or keyboard) command set is not available then a special purpose peripheral (see section 4.2.5(g)) such as a steering wheel or a set of joysticks (Perry et al, 1983) may be needed to control the windowing operations. Undoubtedly, hardware control of the window is probably most natural for the majority of CAL applications. Windowing can be used to provide a variety of useful effects within CAL simulators of the type described earlier in this chapter (see section 5.2.7).

(c) Multiple Screens
Multiple screen techniques refer to arrangments of CAL equipment in which two or more display screens are used within a given interaction environment in order to (1) physically enhance viewing bandwidth, and (2) provide greater degrees of realism in simulated situations. A typical illustration of this approach is presented in figure 5.34. This example utilises three viewing screens each independently serviced by an appropriately constructed image store.

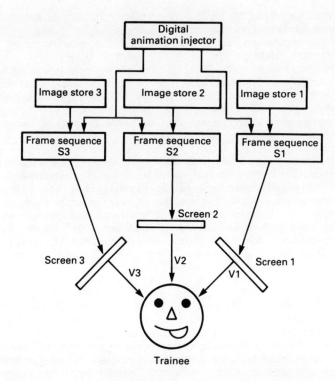

Figure 5.34   An application of multiple screen technology.

The construction of the image stores may be based upon the use of optical discs, video tape or cine materials. Typically their purpose is to provide background scenes, both static and animated. The digital animation injector (which is also connected to the frame sequencers) provides a means by which computationally generated images (or part images) may be added to those being retrieved from the image stores. This facility is useful for (1) creating randomly timed events set against a given background scene, and (2) generating the illusion of global motion of an object within the trainee's field of view. For example, an object (such as a car, aeroplane or ship) may be generated and then displayed in turn on screens 1, 2 and 3 respectively. By correctly overlapping the image over two or more screens it ·is possible to create the illusion that the object is moving horizontally from left to right across the trainee's viewing area. Using this type of equipment, a student can be subjected to very realistic training experiences. For example, consider a situation in which a student is training to be an aircraft pilot. In such a case, the screens shown in figure 5.34 would form the windows of a mock cockpit. During a training exercise the views presented to the student through the cockpit windows would be totally controlled by the software contained within the supervisory computer that is responsible for running the simulator. This would generate appropriate scenes for aircraft taxiing on the runway, taking off, various airborne manoeuvres, a crash landing situation, and so on. Other examples of this type of approach to CAL have already been described earlier in this chapter – the submarine simulator and the CASSIM marine training system (see section 5.2.7). Indeed, figure 5.16 shows a very good example of multiple image projection onto a large screen that simulates the control bridge of a ship.

Much of what was said earlier in section (b) under the discussion of screen segmentation is also relevant to multiple screen utilisation. The only major difference between the two techniques (apart from the actual number of real physical screens involved) is the facilities each provides for spatial distribution. When using multiple screens, the viewing areas may be spatially distributed in ways which simple screen segmentation does not permit. Many areas of CAL require this additional flexibility and, therefore, must have access to this technique.

(d)   Sprites
A high resolution graphics screen consists of a two–dimensional array of pixels (picture elements). Each pixel may be individually controlled by means of software running within a suitable control microprocessor. In terms of pixels, typical dimensions of a screen might be 1024 x 1024, 1024 x 512, 512 x 512, etc. Screen resolution (that is, the separation between individual pixels) will obviously depend upon its physical size and can easily be calculated from its known dimensions.

Sub–arrays of pixels (usually 8 x 8 or 16 x 16) can be used to define (through their on/off status) graphics characters or shapes which can subsequently be displayed at any screen location. By writing control software that (1) generates a character at a particular screen location (x,y); (2) erases it; and then (3) relocates it at screen location (x+d, y+e) it is possible to produce the illusion of animation. Subarrays of pixels used in this way are often referred to as sprites (Larsen, 1983; Ciarcia, 1982). Because of their importance for animation programming, special hardware systems have been designed to generate them, control them and display their effects, thereby making the task of programming their activity much easier. A special type of microprocessor called a video display processor (Ciarcia, 1982) is used for these tasks. The relationship between a video display processor (VDP) and its supporting hardware is illustrated schematically in figure 5.35.

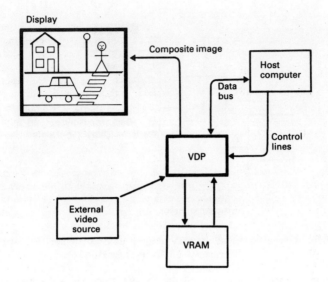

Display

VDP – Video Display Processor
VRAM – Video Random Access Memory

Figure 5.35   Video display processor for producing sprite graphics.

The composite image produced by a video display processor may be regarded as a set of overlapping display planes sandwiched together as shown in figure 5.36. In this illustration there are 32 sprite display planes, each holding one sprite, a pattern plane, a backdrop plane, and a plane for the display of input that is derived from some other external video source. The video display processor combines the multiple image sources to produce a single composite image.

In figure 5.36 sprite plane 0 is regarded as being nearest to the viewer. Objects in planes that are closest to the viewer have higher priorities of visibility than those in planes further away. When objects within two different planes attempt to occupy the same area on the screen, the object on the higher priority plane will be the one actually observed by the viewer.

The pattern plane is used for the display of text and graphics generated according to one of the allowed display modes for the processor – this plane thus functions just like a conventional display screen. The backdrop plane, being larger than any of the others, is used to form a border around the resultant image produced by the other planes; it is usually coloured (but may be transparent). The rearmost plane is that used for the display of video images produced from any other external source which is compatible, including the output from another display processor.

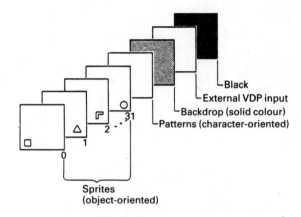

Figure 5.36   Organisation of display planes used with sprite graphics.
(Courtesy of Byte magazine.)

A sprite is essentially a video display object that has a location and
a heading (or velocity) but does not have any drawing capability
(contrast the LOGO turtle discussed in section 5.2.8). The sprite will
have a shape and a colour; usually only one colour is allowed for a
given sprite. Information about each sprite is stored in the form of a
sprite attribute table in the VRAM (video random access memory)
associated with the display processor. Figure 5.37 shows a section of
a sprite attribute table (Ciarcia, 1982).

In this example the first two attribute bytes give the (x,y)
coordinates of the sprite's screen location and the third specifies
its name. Notice that each sprite has associated with it a sprite
generator table. This contains the binary coding for the 8 x 8 pixel
array that defines the sprite shape. Each bit in the pattern
corresponds to one pixel in the displayed pattern. Whenever a 1 is
stored in a pixel's bit pattern, the sprite will be coloured (turned
on); where there is a 0, the sprite will be transparent (turned off).

Being a graphics object of a specified pattern, a sprite will appear
within its plane in a position determined by a single (x,y) coordinate
pair (see figure 5.37). Simply by changing this one set of
coordinates, the sprite can be easily and quickly moved across the
screen. Usually, a complex animated scene will consist of several
objects each moving independently. Often in order to produce the
correct visual effect a particular object within a scene may need to
be constructed from several sprites. Thus, in Ciarcia's illustration

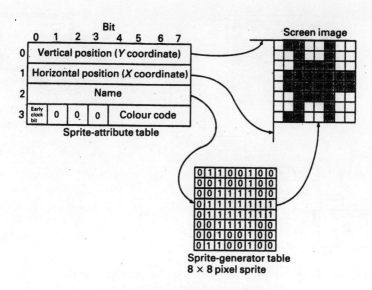

Figure 5.37   Sprite attribute and generator tables.
(Courtesy of Byte magazine.)

of an automobile motoring through hilly countryside (see figure 5.38) the objects are constructed in the following way:

motor car	sprites 2,3,4,5
tree	sprites 0, 1
clouds	sprites 6,7,8
hills	
grass	pattern plane
road	
sky	

Of course, it is important to remember that when animating an object that is composed of several sprites, the (x,y) coordinates for each of the component sprites must be altered simultaneously – by the same amount – in order to produce coordinated motion.

In order to enable the programmer to create and control sprites, appropriate facilities must exist at the software level. Two types of facility are usually provided: (1) a special purpose sprite editor; and (2) command/subroutine interfaces within a host programming language.

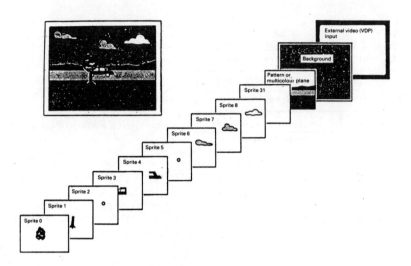

Figure 5.38   Structure of a composite sprite animation scene.
(Courtesy of Byte magazine.)

Using a sprite editor, it is possible for the user to interactively
generate sprites using a keyboard and VDU screen; they can then be
stored in a sprite library for subsequent use by programs that run in
conjunction with the video display processor. Typical editor commands
might be

EDIT

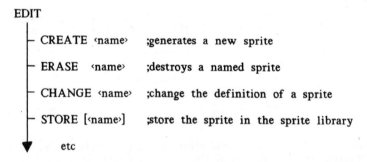

     CREATE ‹name›   ;generates a new sprite

     ERASE ‹name›   ;destroys a named sprite

     CHANGE ‹name›   ;change the definition of a sprite

     STORE [‹name›]   ;store the sprite in the sprite library

       etc

When a create command is issued, an empty sprite generator table (see
figure 5.37) is displayed on the CRT screen of the host microcomputer
(see figure 5.35). By using appropriate cursor control commands and
function keys the user can proceed to set the status (either 1 or 0)
of the bits that define each individual pixel's on/off status. Once a
sprite has been defined using this screen editing technique it can be
saved in the sprite library by issuing a save command. Sprite editors

also provide a number of other useful facilities; for example, there will usually be a series of commands to allow the creation of new sprites from existing or partially defined ones. Typically, these commands would provide for bit inversion, anding, rotation, shifting and so on.

In much the same way as the editor does, a host programming language must also provide suitable primitives to allow the dynamic creation and manipulation of sprites. These primitives must also cater for the need to be able to interrogate and change values held in the sprite attribute tables. Usually, these requirements can be met either by means of subroutine calls or through the use of special sprite manipulation commands embedded within the host programming language. Some versions of LOGO that provide sprite graphics (Ciarcia, 1982; Williams, 1982) use this approach. Examples of commands designed specifically for sprite manipulation include: MAKESHAPE, YOURNUMBER, SETSPEED, SETHEADING, FREEZE, THAW, etc. The way in which these are used is illustrated in the following simple examples:

```
TELL 0
SETSHAPE  :BOX
SETCOLOUR :GREEN
SXY       20 20
```
defines sprite 0 in terms of a predefined shape (BOX) that is stored within the sprite library; the sprite is coloured green and is

```
TELL 1
SETSHAPE  :TRIANGLE
SETCOLOUR :BLUE
SXY       30 30
```
creates sprite 1 as a blue–coloured triangle located at screen position (30,30)

```
TELL 2
SETSHAPE  :CIRCLE
SETCOLOUR :YELLOW
SXY       50 50
```
creates sprite 2 as a yellow circle located at screen position (50,50)

These sprites would appear at fixed screen locations – as shown schematically in figure 5.39. However, by assigning to each one a velocity and a direction in which to travel, it would be possible to

make them move about the screen in various ways, thereby producing
simple animation effects. From this example it is easy to see how,
through sprite technology, a whole new range of interesting animation
techniques can now be provided. Naturally, these will be of
substantial benefit to the CAL courseware designer provided that their
advantages (and limitations) are realised.

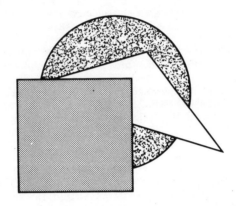

Figure 5.39   Static display of overlapping coloured sprites.

5.4   CONCLUSION

Of the six chapters contained in this book chapters 4 and 5 are
undoubtedly the longest. They have each been dedicated to various
aspects of multimedia CAL. Chapter 4 presented the underlying ideas
and techniques needed to support this mode of computer based
instruction; the chapter was concluded with an introductory discussion
of CAL workstations.

The present chapter has carried on from where the previous one
finished – the workstation idea. In this chapter we have considered a
number of different approaches to the provision of advanced CAL
workstations, training rigs, and, simulators – the ultimate in
multimedia CAL. These advanced types of workstation require the
development of (1) quite complex software, and (2) the appropriate
support tools and techniques necessary to produce this. A large
section of this chapter has therefore been devoted to a description of
(1) authoring facilities for multimedia CAL, and (2) some of the
special types of hardware now becoming available for use in this area.

Hopefully, the amount of space that we have devoted to this topic will reflect to the reader of this book the underlying importance of multimedia CAL. We believe that many new and important future developments in computer assisted learning will come as a result of activity in this area.

5.5   BIBLIOGRAPHY

Abelson, H., A beginner's guide to LOGO, Byte: The Small Systems Journal, 7(8), 88–112, 1982.

Abelson, H. and diSessa, A., Turtle Geometry: The Computer as a Medium for Exploring Mathematics, MIT Press, Cambridge, MA, 1981.

Althoff, J.C., Building data structures in the SMALLTALK–80 system, Byte: The Small System Journal, 6(8), 230–278, 1981.

Anderson, S., The TOPCAT System of Onboard Training – An Operational Perspective, Conference on Training and Distance Learning Onboard Ships, Institute of Maritime Engineers, London, 1982.

Bailey, R.W., Human Performance Engineering: A Guide for Systems Designers, Prentice–Hall, Englewood Cliffs, NJ, 1982.

Barker, P.G., The computer as an audio–visual resource, Computers and Education, 3, 23–34, 1979.

Barker, P.G., MUMEDALA – an approach to multimedia authoring, in Proceedings of the 4th Canadian Symposium on Instructional Technology, Winnipeg, October 19–21, 317–326, National Research Council of Canada, Ottawa, 1983.

Barker, P.G., MUMEDALA – an approach to multimedia authoring, British Journal of Educational Technology. 15(1), 4–13, 1984a.

Barker, P.G., Design of a Multimedia Editing Facility for the Creation of Teletext Overlay Frames for use in Interactive Video Systems, Working Paper, Interactive Systems Research Group, Department of Computer Science, Teesside Polytechnic, County Cleveland, 1984b.

Barker, P.G., MUMEDALA – an approach to multimedia authoring, Computers and Education, 8(4), 463–469, 1984c.

Barker, P.G. and Skipper, T., MUMEDALA Statement Analysis, Working Paper – Version 6.1, Interactive Systems Research Group, Department of Computer Science, Teesside Polytechnic, County Cleveland, 1982.

Barker, P.G., Skipper, T. and Singh, R., MUMEDALA – An Approach to Multimedia Authoring (System Overview), Working Paper – Version 3.3,

Interactive Systems Research Group, Department of Computer Science, Teesside Polytechnic, County Cleveland, 1982.

Barker, P.G. and Yeates, H., Problems associated with multimedia data bases, British Journal of Educational Technology, 12(2), 158–175, 1981.

Bejah, I.I., Videodiscs in education – integrating the computer and communication technologies, Byte: The Small Systems Journal, 7(6), 78–104, 1982.

Bitzer, D.L., The wide world of computer based education, Advances in Computers, 15, 239–281, 1976.

Boutmy, E.J. and Danthine, A., TELEINFORMATICS '79, North Holland, Amsterdam, 1979.

Bowman, W. and Flegal, B., Toolbox: a SMALLTALK illustration system, Byte: The Small Systems Journal, 6(8), 369–376, 1981.

Byte, SMALLTALK, Special issue of Byte: The Small Systems Journal, 6(8), 1981.

Byte, LOGO, Special Issue of Byte: The Small Systems Journal, 7(8), 1982.

Ciarcia, S., High resolution sprite–orientated colour graphics, Byte: The Small Systems Journal, 7(8), 57–80, 1982.

Control Data Corporation, PLATO Stand–Alone Author and Delivery System, Product Description Brochure No. 203–328, Control Data Corporation, Minneapolis, MN, 1983.

Copeland, P., An interactive video system for education and training, British Journal of Educational Technology, 14(1), 59–65, 1983.

Du Boulay, J.B.H. and Howe, J.A.M., LOGO building blocks: student teachers using computer based mathematics apparatus, Computers and Education, 6(1), 93–98, 1982.

Emanuel, R. and Wier, S., Catalysing communication in an autistic child in a LOGO–like learning environment, in Proceedings of the Summer Conference on Artificial Intelligence and the Simulation of Behaviour, 118–119, Edinburgh, 1976.

Ferranti, VTS – Visual Target Simulator, Leaflet No. 81/22A, Ferranti, Stockort, 1981.

Freckleton, F.C., Use of computers for Air Canada's pilot ground training, in Proceedings of the 4th Canadian Symposium on

Instructional Technology, Winnipeg, October 19–21, 131–135, National Research Council of Canada, Ottawa, 1983.

Geoffrion, L., Computer–based approaches to overcoming language handicap, Chapter 21, in World Yearbook of Education 1982/83 – Computers and Education, edited by J. Megarry, D.R.F. Walker, S. Nisbet and E. Hoyle, 215–229, Kogan Page, London, 1983.

Goldberg, A., Educational uses of a Dynabook, Computers and Education, 3(4), 247–266, 1979.

Goldberg, A. and Robson, D., SMALLTALK–80: The Language and Its Implementation, Addison–Wesley, Reading, MA, 1983.

Goldberg, A. and Ross, J., Is the SMALLTALK–80 system for children?, Byte: The Small Systems Journal, 6(8), 348–368, 1981.

Goodwood Data Systems, Lektromedia AVCAT–1 Audio Visual Computer Aided Tutor – System Description, Goodwood Data Systems, Ontario, 1979.

Haefner, K., The concept of an integrated system for information access and telecommunications (ISIT) and its impact on education in the 80's, in Information Processing 80, edited by S.H. Lavington, 973–978, North Holland, Amsterdam, 1980.

Hazeltine Corporation, MicroTICCIT – The System for Professional Trainers, Hazeltine Corporation, McLean, VA, 1983.

Howe, J.A.M. and O'Shea, T., Learning mathematics through LOGO, ACM SIGGUE Bulletin, 12(1), 1978.

International Business Machines, Guided Learning Centres – An Environment for Learning, Form: GU50–2412, Second Edition, Basingstoke, 1982.

Jessop Microelectronics, The Edinburgh Turtle, Product Description, Jessop Microelectronics, London, 1983.

Kane, G.R., Leonard, W.F. and Nashburg, R.E., CAVI – a microcomputer–based tool to enhance flexible–paced learning, in Proceedings of the 10th ASEE/IEEE Frontiers in Education Conference, edited by L.P. Grayson and J.M. Biedenbach, 160–166, IEEE, New York, NY, 1980.'

Kay, A.C., Microelectronics and the personal computer, Scientific American, 226, 230–244, 1977.

Kay, A.C., Programming your own computer, in Science Year – The World Book Science Annual, 183–195, 1979.

Kay, A.C., SMALLTALK, in Methodology of Interaction, Proceedings of the IFIP Group 5.2 Workshop, Seillac, France, 1979, edited by R.A. Guedj, P.J.W. ten Hagen, F.R.A. Hopgood, H.A. Tucker and D.A. Duce, 7–11, North Holland, Amsterdam, 1980.

Kay, A.C. and Goldberg, A., Personal dynamic media, IEEE COMPUTER, 10(3), 31–41, 1977.

Kildall, G. and Thornburg, D., Digital Research's DR LOGO, Byte: The Small Systems Journal, 8(6), 208–226, 1983.

King, J., The Design of Computer–Aided Maritime Packages, Shipboard Computer Group, Department of Maritime Studies, University of Wales, Institute of Science and Technology, Cardiff, 1981.

King, J., Applications of Small Computers to Shipboard Training, Transactions of the Royal Institution of Naval Architects, 124, 274–284, 1982.

Larsen, S.G., Sprite Graphics for the Commodore–64, Prentice–Hall, Englewood Cliffs, NJ, 1983.

Lawler, R.W., Designing computer based microworlds, Byte: The Small Systems Journal, 7(6), 138–160, 1982.

Lenaerts, L., The Use of CAVIS at BP Chemicals (Belgium), Schlededijk 50, 2730 Zwijmdrecht, Belgium, 1983.

Marconi, TEPIGEN Computer Generated Imagery Systems, Marconi Radar Systems, Leicester, 1982.

McCallum, I.R. and Rawson, A.J., The Cardiff Ship Simulator – Design Features and Operational Philosophy, in Proceedings of the 2nd International Conference on Marine Simulation (MARSIM '81), E1–1 to E1–11, New York, 1981.

Mudrick, D. and Stone, D., An Adaptive CBT Courseware Authoring to Meet the Needs of Military Authors, Personnal Communication, 1983.

Norman, D.A., Studies of Learning and Self–Contained Educational Systems (1973–1976), Technical Report No. 7601, San Diego Centre for Human Information Processing, University of California, 1976.

O'Shea, T. and Self, J., Learning and Teaching with Computers – Artificial Intelligence in Education, Harvester Press, 1983.

Papert, S., Mindstorms: Children, Computers and Powerful Ideas, Harvester Press, 1980.

Perry, J.R., Thompson, B.E., Staab, E.V., Pizer, S.M. and Johnston, R.E., Performance features of a PACS Console, IEEE Computer, 16(8), 51–56, 1983.

Perry, T., Consumer electronics, IEEE Computer, 21(1), 78–81, 1984.

Philips, PHILVAS – Philips Interactive Laser Vision Authoring System User Guide, Philips, London, 1983.

Powell, N., IVIS – The Interactive Video Information System, Conference Presentation (Authoring Systems for Interactive Video), Gatwick Airport, 1984.

Ramsey, H.R. and Grimes, J.D., Human factors in interactive computer dialogue, Chapter 2, in Annual Review of Information Science and Technology, Volume 18, edited by M.G. Williams, 29–59, American Society for Information Science, 1983.

Rigney, T.W. and Towne, D.M., Computer aided performance training for diagnostic and procedural tasks, Journal of Educational Technology Systems, 2(4), 279–304, 1974.

Robinson, C., Computer based training and interactive video, SCICON Review, Milton Keynes, 1983

Roper, C., French flock to computer centre, New Scientist, 97(1344), 358–361, 1983.

Scott, J.E., Introduction to Computer Graphics, John Wiley, New York, NY, 1982.

Self, J.A., Student models and artifical intelligence, Computers and Education, 3, 309–312, 1979.

Sippl, C.J. and Dahl, F., Video–Computers: How to Select, Mix, and Operate Personal Computers and Home Video Systems, Prentice–Hall, Englewood Cliffs, New Jersey, 1981.

Solomon, C., Introducing LOGO to children, Byte: The Small Systems Journal, 7(8), 196–208, 1982.

Sony, New York, NY, 1982.

Stobie, I., Apple's LISA, Practical Computing, 6(3), 77–80, 1983a.

Stobie, I., Using the LISA, Practical Computing, 6(8), 92–95, 1983b.

Stobie, I., VISI ON, Practical Computing, 7(2), 78–79, 1984.

Tickle, J., AVCAT – CAL Without Tears, Internal Report, Ferranti Computer Systems, Stockport, 1983.

Towne, D.M., The automated integration of training and aiding information for the operator/technician, in Proceedings of the Third Biennial Conference on Maintenance Training and Aiding, 53–63, Orlando, FL, 1979.

Towne, D.M., The Electronic Equipment Maintenance Trainer (EEMT), Behavioural Technology Laboratories, University of Southern California, Redondo Beach, CA, 1983.

VISCAT, Computer Linked Audio Visual Training System, VISCAT, Rochester, 1983.

Watt, D., LOGO in schools, Byte: The Small Systems Journal, 7(8), 116–134, 1982.

Williams, G., LOGO for the Apple II, the TI–99/4A, and the TRS–80 colour computer, Byte: The Small Systems Journal, 7(8), 230–290, 1982.

Wolfberg, N.E., (editor), The ETHERNET Handbook, Shotwell and Associates, San Francisco, CA, 1982.

Chapter 6

THE FUTURE OF CAL

6.1 INTRODUCTION

Over the last decade interest in CAL and CBT has developed enormously.
This has been mainly due to:

(1) the availability of low cost personal computers,
(2) their intrinsic ease of use,
(3) the introduction of these machines into the home,
schools, offices and virtually all other places
of work, and
(4) the realisation that computer systems do have
considerable potential as a learning and teaching
resource.

Earlier in this book (see section 2.1.3) we suggested that this rapid
growth in demand for microcomputer systems would significantly
influence the future directions in which CAL courseware development
might proceed. Indeed, figure 2.1 predicted that there is likely to be
a substantial increase in demand for courseware both for use in
teaching establishments and for applications within the home
environment. These growth areas are developing as a direct consequence
of an increasing awareness of interactive computer systems and their
capabilities (especially for education and training). Added to this,
of course, is the ability (with low cost equipment) to apply CAL in

situations and contexts where, hitherto, it has not been either
technically   or economically feasible to do so. Undoubtedly, these two
factors (awareness and decreasing cost) are responsible for a
considerable amount of the recent activity and renewed interest in
computer assisted learning. Naturally, it would be of substantial
value if we could speculate on whether or not the current wave of
interest in CAL is likely to continue into the future and, if so, what
shape and form it is likely to take.

Obviously, there are many factors that are   likely   to influence   the
future   adoption of CAL as a general instructional tool. These factors
will also have a significant effect on the ways in which it is
utilised,   where   it is employed and when it is used. In figure 6.1 we
have listed a few of the more important factors which we believe   will
effect the future form and shape of computer assisted learning. We
will briefly outline our reasons for including these and then, in the
remaining   parts of this chapter, concentrate on two specific aspects
of the future – technical trends and potential application areas.

Financial considerations are undoubtedly the controlling factor behind
the utilisation of all forms of technology – most of all CAL. At the
end of the day, in order to provide an acceptable form of education
CAL must be cost effective. This is certainly true if it is to have a
future. As we suggested above, CAL is moving closer and closer towards
fulfilling this requirement, particularly in industrial applications
if not (yet) in academic ones. In the long term we do not envisage
that the cost of hardware will negatively influence the utilisation of
CAL technology. Furthermore, although the cost of producing courseware
is still regarded as being quite high, this is likely to fall as
better courseware production systems are developed.

Ergonomic factors refer to the ease of use of the CAL equipment (for
the courseware author, the instructor and the student population) and,
of course, the users' satisfaction with it. Currently, there is much
interest in this topic. Research activity in this area covers
ergonomic aspects of both hardware and software. Some important
results have been derived from studies of general terminal systems for
office use (Bailey, 1982; Morland, 1983; Jenkin, 1982). Naturally,
many of the findings can (with some limitations) be applied to the
more specific task of CAL workstation design (Barker, 1984a). Because
of the extensive ongoing research that is currently underway in this
area, CAL systems of the future will be extremely 'user friendly' at
all levels of system interaction. Consequently, future developments
arising as a consequence of ergonomic factors will undoubtedly
influence the uptake of CAL in a positive way.

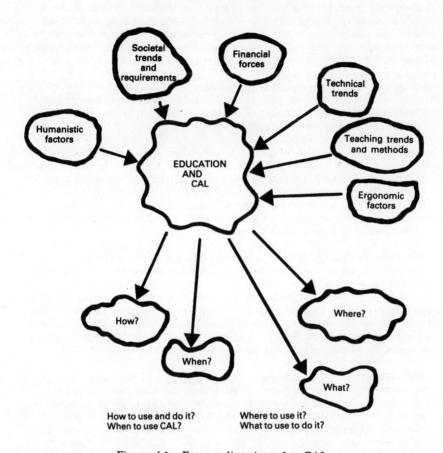

Figure 6.1   Future directions for CAL.

The computer is often regarded as a 'universal medium' or metamedium (Stonier, 1983). In principle it is thus feasible for the computer to provide a suitable medium for the implementation of virtually all teaching methods. In addition, it is important to realise that the computer can provide many teaching techniques which (in its absence) could not otherwise be made available. However, if the computer is to be widely used then it is imperative that instructional designers should be allowed to decide how it is to be used and for what purposes it should be employed. Any trend in the opposite direction (that is, when computer technology attempts to impose and dictate teaching methods) is likely to have adverse effects on the future of CAL.

Indeed, such a situation could lead to rejection of this approach to teaching.

Throughout history the form, content and mechanisms of education have been closely regulated by the societies in which people have lived. Today, two important trends must be considered. First, most societies are now very dependent upon advanced technology (particularly, computers) for all aspects of modern living. Second, all societies are becoming increasingly information based; that is, they depend upon the ongoing collection, generation, processing and dissemination of information. This latter factor was discussed in the opening chapter of this book (see section 1.2.1). Undoubtedly, the future survival of particular societies will depend upon their ability to (1) use technology in an advantageous way, and (2) design techniques that will enable their members to handle and assimilate the vast amounts of information and knowledge which (on a world-wide basis) is being generated unceasingly. In this context, the inadequacies inherent in conventional instructional methods must surely dictate a fresh approach? Thus, we may well see the future use of CAL becoming a necessity for the achievement of an effective education, particularly in the science and technology based subjects.

Applicable technology is the underlying driving force responsible for advances in many areas of human endeavour. Today, as a consequence of the (incipient) merging of computer and instructional technologies, we are beginning to see a number of routes towards the realisation of CAL systems that more closely meet the requirements and ideals of those involved in the design and construction of teaching/learning systems. As time progresses, we believe that this merging of interests will increasingly favour the future development and utilisation of CAL.

Any attempt to use computers for teaching will undoubtedly bring up the humanistic issues associated with the question of automation. This, in turn, will naturally cause people to think about whether or not it is (1) feasible, (2) desirable, and (3) ethical to automate teaching processes through the use of sophisticated (some would say intelligent) teaching machines. It is obviously difficult to assess what effects humanistic factors of this type will have on the uptake of CAL. Undoubtedly, because it does 'smell of automation' many teachers would be expected to disapprove of it – at least on the basis of job security. We can only hope that this will not be so. Firstly, because we believe that through computers it will be possible in the future to achieve richer and more effective educational techniques. Secondly, because we are certainly not aware of any situation where the adoption of CAL has resulted in any reduction in the requirement for teachers.

For obvious reasons, in this chapter we take a positive attitude towards the future of CAL. We therefore assume that when the above factors are summed the outcome will favour the overall adoption of this technology, not as a substitute for but as an aid to conventional teaching. Subsequent sections of this chapter therefore concentrate on two themes which we feel are important, namely CAL technology/techniques and CAL application areas. In the discussion that follows we outline some of those computational and instructional techniques that are most likely to influence the future of computer assisted learning. In addition, we also try to indicate the application areas where CAL is likely to be employed and how it might be used within these domains.

6.2 TECHNOLOGY AND TECHNIQUES

Technology provides the fundamental mechanisms that enable us to convert our ideas into material realisations of them, be these of a poetical, artistical, mathematical, scientific, design or engineering nature. Without technology, modern education would be very near impossible. Undoubtedly, electronic and information processing technology (Hawkridge, 1983; Barker, 1983) are today having a significant impact both on (1) the ways in which we teach (that is, instructional techniques), and (2) the nature of what is taught. As we have just hinted, techniques refer to the basic methodologies that we use in order to convert our teaching/instructional ideas and personal knowledge into useful learning procedures. These may be used to control our own learning and that of others. Obviously, technology and techniques are both closely bound to each other since new technology often provides us with new techniques, as indeed is the case with computer technology and its influence on the methods of computer assisted learning.

In the following parts of this section we identify eight important areas which are likely to play a key role in the development of future CAL systems and the instructional techniques that are embedded within them. No claim is made that the coverage in this section is in any way comprehensive; we apologise beforehand for any serious omissions.

6.2.1 Graphics
From the previous sections of this book the reader will no doubt have inferred that the term 'graphics' is used to refer to the use of various forms of static/dynamic image as a means of communicating ideas, information and knowledge. The techniques that this topic embodies are therefore of paramount importance to education in general and CAL in particular. Undoubtedly, the major reason for wanting to use graphic imagery as a teaching tool lies in the fact that this technology provides a very high bandwidth communication channel. Furthermore, through this technology it is possible to present information in ways that would otherwise be impossible. That is, certain of the teaching techniques and strategies provided by graphics facilities are unique to this medium. Of course, many added advantages can be derived from the various types of special effect that can be created. Some examples of these were discussed in section 5.3.4.

Naturally, the generation of these is critically dependent upon the availability of suitable technology and techniques to manipulate both single and multiple images. The effects that are then produced may reflect some (possibly distorted) view of reality, or else they may provide one or more of the dimensions that are used to construct an illusory experience. Both of these graphics techniques can be utilised in a variety of different ways by the CAL instructional designer. However, in order to produce the desired results the CAL courseware author will need to have available a number of basic facilities for image manipulation. Broadly, these fall into three basic categories: image creation; image capture and storage; and image processing. Often, the boundary between each of these is not sharp so that technology/techniques used in one area often overlap with those used in another.

Images for use in CAL may be of many different types and may originate from a number of sources. Typical image sources include: conventional photographs, video based materials, hand sketches/drawings, and (of growing utility) images generated by computers. Conventional photography gives rise to a range of still image types (such as slides, snapshots and illustrations for use in guidebooks) and animated material (through the use of motion film techniques). Video is becoming increasingly popular as a medium for the capture, storage and presentation of images. It is extremely valuable for capturing images that are transmitted through broadcast TV networks. These can be edited and reorganised in various ways for subsequent incorporation into many different types of instuctional unit. Hand sketching and drawing is still one of the most widely used and powerful teaching techniques available to a teacher. This may involve either preparing pictorial material before it is used, or, generating it (in real-time) during the course of instruction. Notice that the CYCLOPS system discussed in chapter 3 (section 3.4.6) provided a mechanism for the provision of sketching facilities within a distance learning situation. Computer generated images usually depend (for their creation) upon the execution of a sophisticated algorithm that generates points, lines and surfaces that are then displayed in multiple colours on either a high or low resolution CRT display. If need be, these images can be photographed in various ways in order to facilitate their long term storage, duplication and subsequent use. Clark (1981) has written a useful introduction to and overview of the technical foundations of computer image making.

Over the last decade the importance of computer generated imagery has grown considerably. Several interesting illustrations of computer generated (static) three-dimensional images have been presented and described by Resch (1974). Essentially, these images are produced using one or other of three possible approaches:

> (1) with the use of a digitised data base,
> (2) by means of a procedure-defined data base,

(3)   through the use of a user–defined data base.

The first of these approaches involves taking measurements of an
existing three–dimensional object and then processing that information
by means of an image producing algorithm. The second method uses some
digitised input to represent a three–dimensional object but the
picture itself is produced as a result of computational changes or
enhancements to the object. The third method employs a building block
technique in which primitive structures are defined once and are then
used as component parts of more complex forms. This approach forms the
underlying basis of 3–D modelling and is also widely used in animation
(Csuri, 1977).

Computer based animation techniques (Hackathorn, 1977; Levoy, 1977;
Gould and Finzer, 1981; Byte, 1982a; Booth et al., 1983) are also
becoming an extremely popular CAL tool. Within this context, animation
is the term that is generally used to describe the illusion of motion
within computer generated images. Animation effects can be produced
purely by computational means. Alternatively, they can be created by
combining images generated by an animation computer with those that
are derived from other sources (such as film or video disc). In the
first of these the computer calculates (at regular intervals) the
positions and attributes of all the objects within a particular
sequence of CRT images. The time lapse between successive computations
is made sufficiently small so that (in situations where objects within
the picture sequence must be made to move) the viewer is given the
impression of smooth movement. Sometimes, the computational
requirements are too high to enable this objective to be realised. In
these situations, individual CRT frames are photographed and then
'speeded up' during subsequent display. The second animation technique
(based on combining images from different sources) is often used as a
means of reducing the amount of computation that needs to be performed
by the animation computer. This is achieved by using other sources
(such as a second computer or a video disc) to create the static or
dynamic background effects within an image. Some examples of this
technique were discussed in chapter 5. Several of the new types of
'arcade game' (Perry, 1983) also employ this approach to create
illusions of realism within the games that they implement.

Nowadays many subjects within the curriculum require access to
sophisticated graphics facilities to enable their effective teaching
by computer assisted methods. For example, certain aspects of many
design and engineering based subjects (Computers and Education, 1981;
Grover and Zimmers, 1984) are becoming increasingly difficult to teach
without adequate graphics support. Within some subject areas, such as
geography/ cartography (Phillips, 1974; Neale, 1979), physics (Bork,
1980; McKenzie, 1978; Walrand et al., 1982), chemistry (Demaid et al.,
1981; Martin, 1982) and mathematics (Ferrari and Parenti, 1980), the
use of graphics is now more or less a standard requirement. It is very
encouraging to observe that there is also a growing demand for such

resources from within other disciplins such as drama, art, dance and physical education (Lusignan and North, 1977; Holden, 1984).

As interest and applications in this area develop, so new technical advancements are likely to follow. Future developments will undoubtedly be orientated towards making graphics resources easier to use, less expensive and more widely available. Ongoing research and development projects that will (in the future) be of relevance to the CAL user include: graphics support languages; animation languages; special hardware facilities such as video display processors (as discussed in section 5.3.4) and colour registers as used in some of the more powerful microcomputers (Fox and Waite, 1982); image analysis procedures (for example, to analyse and interpret student sketches); and devices/instruments to enable the facile input of multi-dimensional data into the computer for subsequent use in image making.

6.2.2 Games and Toys

Toys and games represent important teaching devices for students of all ages and learning ability. Provided they are suitably designed, devices of this type can be employed as an effective vehicle for skill transfer to (and development within) their user population. Often, skill transfer/development takes place in a subconscious way. That is, users of games and toys are not actively aware of the skills they are acquiring as a result of their involvement with them. Teaching mechanisms based on the use of toys, games and puzzles are very attractive from a student's point of view. This attraction stems from the high entertainment value with which devices of this type are normally associated. Consequently, they are frequently used as a basis for the realisation of many different approaches to informal learning. Because of their entertainment value, most students require very little external motivation to encourage involvement with this type of resource. Hence, instructors have available a very powerful teaching medium, provided the material and skills to be learned can be encoded into a suitable toy, game, quiz or puzzle.

Obviously, in the CAL environment we are primarily interested in gaming devices that, in one form or another, incorporate some kind of computer system. Examples of instructional resources that fall into this category include:

(a) computerised toys which, because of the logic embedded within them, can (a) react in various ways to their environment, and/or (b) be remotely controlled; the turtle described in section 5.2.8 is an example of this class of device;

(2) various forms of simple toy robot that can be programmed in different ways by its user; these are discussed in more detail in section 6.2.5;

(3) construction kits that students use in order to build toys, models and other types of equipment in which a

microcomputer system is used to implement some
form of control function;

(4) special types of microelectronic teaching aid; typical
examples of these are those developed by Texas Instruments
(for example Speak and Spell, Speak and Maths, Speak and
Read, etc) which were designed to support learning
processes in young children; these are discussed in
more detail in section 6.2.6;

(5) hardware based games, trainers, puzzles and tutoring
devices; each has a dedicated microcomputer system to
support the game it implements; computerised chess
tutors, arcade games and many home video games (such
as Ping-Pong) are examples of this category;

(6) software based games that are intended to be used on a
wide variety of general purpose microcomputers.

There is a continually increasing demand for each of the above types
of resource. However, over the last few years the greatest requirement
has undoubtedly been for software based video computer games,
particularly for use in the home (Perry and Wallich, 1983; Wiswell,
1984).

Games are essentially skilful activities in which one, two, three (or
more) people participate in a competitive way to achieve some
predefined goal. Associated with a game will be:

(1) a specification of the objective or goal to be achieved,
(2) a set of rules that must be learned and by which all
players must abide,
(3) a set of strategies that the players will develop in
order to achieve (1) within the constraints imposed
by (2), and
(4) a set of skills needed to play the game.

By careful manipulation of the above parameters the educational game
designer can produce computer based materials that are interesting to
use, entertaining, pedagogically useful and, in many cases, addictive.

The formal aspects of computer game playing, particularly those
relating to the theoretical and practical considerations underlying
the design and construction of software, are described (and
illustrated) in books devoted to this topic (Bramer, 1983; Hartnell et
al., 1983; Renko and Edwards, 1984) and in textbooks on artificial
intelligence (Jackson, 1974; Michie, 1974). The reader is referred to
these for further details. Unfortunately, in this section we can only
(1) outline the roles that the computer can play within a gaming
program, (2) provide some typical examples of games courseware, and
(3) indicate those technical developments likely to influence future
gaming environments. For further information about this fascinating
subject the reader is urged to consult the two special editions of

Byte magazine (1981; 1982b) that are devoted to games. In addition to these, the three reports authored by Perry (1983) and Perry et al. (1982) provide a useful source of information about video computer games.

As well as generating the scenario for a game there are two other basic roles that the computer may perform in a gaming environment. These are (1) participative, and (2) managerial. In the first of these the computer actually plays a part in the game and competes against the user(s). Chess playing programs are the ideal illustration of this (Flock and Silverman, 1984). In its other role, the computer simply monitors and controls the progress of the game, that is, it keeps a record of each player's score and attempts to assess how well each is performing. Computerised Ping–Pong provides one of the most well known examples of this (Perry et al., 1982). In this game two players control the motion of an electronic ball on a CRT screen by means of games paddles. Of course, in many games the computer will participate as a player, generate the scenario and manage the course of the game.

Computer games may be designed for use in either a single–user situation (Cullingford et al., 1979; Baird and Flavell, 1981; Szymanski, 1982; Miastkowski, 1984) or a multi–user environment (Wiswell, 1984; Renko, 1984). Within CAL, the broad spectrum of teaching situations that can arise means that there is ample scope for using games of each type.

An example of a (single–user) microcomputer based game that requires its player to acquire a wide range of coordination skills is the JET Simulator Electronic Trainer (JETSET) described by Szymanski (1982). This is a game that allows the player to control the flight of a jet aircraft. The CRT screen of the microcomputer acts as a simulated instrument panel and cockpit view; the keyboard is then used to provide the aeroplane control functions. The object of the game is to fly the aeroplane from one location to another without crashing. Various lessons are available within the game: take–off, manoeuvring and navigation. Once these techniques are mastered the computer can be called upon to generate flight plans for a variety of different trips. During these trips the student pilot (or game player) has to use his/her skills to overcome a variety of different types of unforeseen event. Undoubtedly, the concepts and principles built into JETSET are typical of the many other games that also fall into this single–user category, even though the themes they employ (exploration, adventure, mystery, wars and battles, etc) are likely to be different.

Because the majority of approaches to CAL have emphasised the concept of individualised instruction, a large proportion of the currently available games are similar to that described above and cater only for a single–user gaming situation. However, the number of games suitable for use with multiple users is increasing. Basically, these are of two types: (1) those designed for group participation within a classroom environment; and (2) those intended to support many simultaneous individual competitors, located locally or geographically dispersed (Wiswell, 1984). Many of the single—user games could be used to fulfil the requirements of (1), for example one student could directly interact with the game in a way that is determined by the members of a collaborative classroom group. Games for category (2) require the development of specialised input techniques to support multiple user inputs; special types of interaction device are also often necessary. However, with the technology that is currently available the implementation of these does not really present any problems.

Several authors have suggested possible ways in which current and future technology is likely to influence the development of computer games (Allison, 1980; Perry et al., 1982; Perry, 1983; 1984; Vousden, 1983; Wiswell, 1984; Audio—Visual, 1984; Byte, 1984). Some of the more important factors/requirements are listed below:

(1) use of video discs,
(2) better graphics facilities (including animation),
(3) ability to generate personalised scenarios,
(4) ability to project the players' personal identities
    into game characters,
(5) support for multiple inputs,
(6) development of special games hardware (for
    example, the geometry engine),
(7) development of more sophisticated interaction
    techniques involving sound and bio—feedback
    methods,
(8) ability to combine powerful graphics and simulation
    techniques,
(9) ability to transmit games over communications lines
    to schools and homes.

These facilities are likely to give the games designer many new dimensions with which to experiment. They will enable the production of new types of game that implement many different kinds of gaming strategy and technique. Obviously, the CAL environment will be a natural outlet for many of these.

6.2.3 Expert Systems
A considerable volume of material has been written about expert systems (Michie, 1979; 1980; Buchanan and Duda, 1983; Gevarter, 1983; IEEE, 1983; Coombs and Alty, 1984). This material amply covers the history, current state and projected future developments of this rapidly expanding field. We include a brief discussion of this topic because we feel it has significant relevance to the future of CAL. However, in view of the substantial coverage given to this subject within the references cited above, we restrict our discussion to the following three aspects: composition and structure; mechanisms of creation; and potential applications within CAL.

An expert system (ES) is essentially a specialised computer application environment designed to contain (and make available) large amounts of specialised knowledge relating to some particular subject domain. Systems of this type provide much more than just an information retrieval or data base facility, since the algorithms/heuristics embedded within their software enable logical inferences to be made. Often systems of this kind are referred to as Intelligent Knowledge Based Systems (IKBS). When the concept of expert systems was originally formulated it was intended that they should provide help, advice and guidance relevant to the solution of problems within the particular specialist areas with which they dealt, for example, medical diagnosis, machine fault finding, engineering design, mineral prospecting, and so on. Numerous examples of expert systems, covering a wide range of application domains, have been described in the literature (Gevarter, 1983).

The following basic components are fundamental to the operation of an expert system:

(1) a knowledge base,
(2) a variety of interactive dialogue units,
(3) software to permit structuring and reorganisation of the knowledge base,
(4) subject specialists (human experts),
(5) novice users and problem solvers.

The relationship between some of these building blocks is depicted schematically in the upper part of figure 6.2.

The knowledge base contains all the stored information/knowledge relating to the particular application area with which the system deals. This may be constructed from readily available hardware/software components. Alternatively, its construction may require the use of (1) special purpose hardware (especially designed to facilitate particular types of information processing and retrieval), and/or (2) sophisticated software tools (for knowledge representation and programming). The information held within the knowledge base may be derived from a variety of widely disparate sources – books, data archives, experiments, surveys, interviews and so on. Of course, most of the knowledge that is built into the system (encoded in the form of rules, frames, assertions in predicate logic, etc) is derived from human experts through computer driven 'conversations' initiated and controlled by the software contained within the dialogue units.

Dialogue units represent the hardware/software interfaces between the expert system and its different user groups. Broadly, there will be two classes of user: first, the experts from which the knowledge for the ES is derived and who enable its subsequent updating; second, other experts (and novices) who call upon the services of the ES to aid problem solving activity. Each category of user will require a particular type of interactive dialogue to facilitate interaction with the ES. At present, there is much interest in providing dialogue units based upon the use of some form of natural language understanding (Harris, 1983; Zorkoczy, 1982).

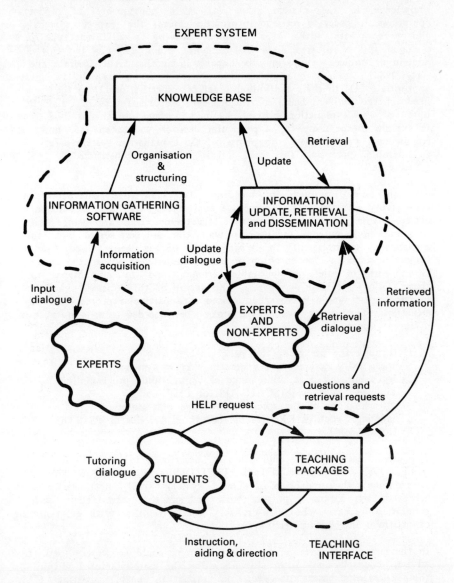

Figure 6.2   Teaching applications of expert systems.

The acquisition of information is achieved by means of input dialogues in which human specialists enumerate various facts and the different relationships that exist between them. Subsequently, this information/knowledge may be structured and reorganised in different ways to enable it to be utilised in an optimal way. Usually, reorganisation will be required as a result of the addition of new knowledge to the system, that is, as a consequence of update operations. In order to retrieve information from the expert system and/or seek its advice for problem solving a different type of dialogue unit is required. This will enable other experts in this domain or novices – who may be experts in another field (Coombs and Alty, 1984) – to pose questions to the system in a way which is most appropriate (1) to their individual level of expertise, or (2) to the needs of the problem being solved. Another important type of dialogue unit is the 'explanation system'. As its name suggests, this is used to explain to the user why a particular decision was taken or how a conclusion was derived. In principal, the explanation system offers considerable potential for use within suitably constructed CAL courseware.

The processes involved in building the knowledge base are often collectively referred to as 'knowledge engineering'. As we mentioned above, this primarily involves structuring and organising the information, knowledge and data in ways that are best suited for the application environment in which the ES is being used. Another important aspect is the encoding of expert knowledge within the system in the form of rules, decision tables, frames, and so on. Many of these rules are used to represent the nature of the decisions that a human expert would make when placed in a particular problem solving situation. The rules themselves may be encoded using a number of different approaches. For example:

(1) through the use of special packages and tools
    specifically designed for generating expert systems,
(2) by using any of a wide range of conventional programming
    languages such as PASCAL, APL or LISP, and
(3) by using one of the special knowledge representation
    languages such as KRL (frame based), PLANNER or PROLOG
    (logic based).

The use of each of these approaches is described in the literature (IEEE, 1983; Buchanan and Duda, 1983). Obviously, for use within CAL environments the production of expert systems will most easily be achieved by means of purpose–built packages that permit their facile generation by users who will probably not be familiar with programming or artificial intelligence techniques.

In the future we envisage that expert systems could be widely used to advise, counsel and tutor students using the material stored within their knowledge bases. However, in order to enable existing CAL courseware to be 'driven' by the knowledge base facility embedded within an expert system (see figure 6.2) it will be necessary to design and construct suitable software interfaces to link the two together. These will be needed in order to translate the information requirements of the teaching packages into a form that can be serviced by the support modules within the expert system.

Undoubtedly, expert systems will have an increasing impact upon education and industrial training, especially when linked to video disc and existing CAL and CBT packages. We anticipate that the use of this technology within education will allow:

(1) scarce and expensive resources (consultants/special skills, etc) to be made accessible to a wider audience,
(2) training to be decentralised without loss of quality,
(3) the in-house creation of effective distance learning and CBT packages, and
(4) an increase in the reliability and speed of training.

Probably, the most spectacular of all these developments will be the 'intelligent video' system. Produced by combining expert system and video disc technology this concept could offer an exciting new medium for use in all areas of instruction.

6.2.4 Communications
For the discussion presented in this section we use the term 'communications' to describe the wide variety of techniques that enable information to be transmitted between two or more locations by electronic means. The importance of communications technology within CAL systems stems from the opportunities it offers for the flexible interconnection of 'learning centres' (see below) in both a local and/or a global fashion. Such interconnections can be used to achieve: (1) the sharing of instructional resources; (2) access to data banks containing large volumes of encyclopaedic information; and (3) electronically mediated student-teacher and student-student interactions. Some of these possibilities are shown schematically in figure 6.3. Each of the above facilities - particularly (3) - is important in the context of distance learning (and open learning systems) since the principles they involve are independent of geographical location.

The types of learning centre involved in the interconnection strategy depicted above (see figure 6.3) are likely to show considerable variety, as will their specific service requirements. The following examples are chosen to illustrate the breadth of the spectrum of possibilities that exist:

(1) linking of a single CAL workstation (located in a home, within an office or an industrial/manufacturing site) to a more powerful remote computer system, either on a permanent or

temporary basis;
(2) the interlinking of many workstations within a CAL laboratory –
   to each other and/or to a central computing service;
(3) the interconnection of many workstations distributed
   over single or multiple sites; these may be (a) school, college
   or university campuses, or (b) one or more industrial sites
(4) the connection of geographically distributed learning centres
   (see section 5.2.6) of a similar type to enable resource sharing,
   common training standards and uniformity of training techniques
   to be achieved;
(5) combinations of any of the above; together these can produce
   highly geographically dispersed CAL systems similar to that
   depicted in figure 1.13.

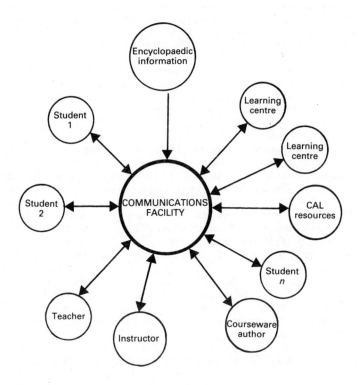

Figure 6.3   The role of communications in CAL.

Currently, communications technology exists to facilitate the
realisation of each of the above approaches to CAL system
interconnection (Boutmy and Danthine, 1979; Haefner, 1980; Barker,
1982; 1983; Bott and Robertson, 1983; Forsythe and Collins, 1983).

However, its widespread use will depend upon (1) acceptance of the new types of teaching/learning methods that this technology implies, and (2) cost effectiveness.

One of the most economic methods of transmitting educational material to a large number of geographically distributed CAL workstations is through the use of some broadcast teletext facility, similar to the UK's ORACLE and CEEFAX systems (Hawkridge, 1983; Fedida and Malik, 1979). Unfortunately, teletext systems do not provide interactive (two-way) communication media and so they have many limitations for educational use. Greater interactivity can be achieved by using videotex networks (Ball et al., 1980; Bott and Robertson, 1983), which provide a bidirectional communication ability. Typical examples of national videotex systems (and the country in which they operate) include: Antiope (France); Telidon (Canada); Captain (Japan); and Prestel (United Kingdom). The use of Prestel for promoting home education facilities for young children in the UK has been described by Fiddy and Yam (1984) – their results are discussed later in section 6.3.2.

The local coupling of CAL workstations (within a building or small campus) can be achieved extremely easily by means of local area networks (Wilkes, 1980; Stallings, 1984), of which ETHERNET (Shoch et al., 1982) is probably one of the most well known. Local networks are usually owned by a single organisation and are operated within a restricted geographical area of about one mile radius. In order to link together workstations and centres that are more geographically remote than this, the use of long-distance (or global) networks becomes necessary (Barker, 1983). Long-distance networks (regional, national, international) are normally owned by communications carriers and are operated as a public utility for their subscribers, providing a variety of services and facilities for the transmission of voice, data and video. Through the development of suitable interconnection gateways it is possible to link together both the long-distance and the local-area types of network (Schneidewind, 1983). Obviously, to facilitate the facile interconnection of workstations in a flexible way a large number of standards are necessary – the IEEE-488 and RS-232-C (which have been discussed earlier) are two simple examples. The production of standards is an ongoing activity. The recommendations contained in the recently formulated ISO-OSI (International Standards Organisation – Open Systems Interconnection) standard (Schneidewind, 1983) will undoubtedly have a favourable influence on the ease with which CAL workstations will be able to communicate on a world-wide basis (Hiltz and Turoff, 1978).

Other than through the new types of facility that they offer, the type of physical media used to construct communications networks will normally remain transparent to their user. As time progresses there is likely to be a move towards greater use of both optical fibre technology (Sandbank, 1980) and satellite transmission systems

(Martin, 1978) for the dissemination of educational material. The former will probably be used most effectively to implement local area and regional networks with the latter finding greatest application for long-distance (particularly international) networks.

Potentially, two of the most useful educational benefits likely to arise from the above developments in communications technology are (1) the more wide-spread use of electronic mail (Connell and Galbraith, 1982) for supporting teaching operations; and (2) the use of telesoftware as a means of disseminating CAL materials. Electronic mail is capable of providing many useful facilities to enable facile student–student and student–teacher interaction (see figure 6.3) that is independent of the location of either students or teachers – an ideal tool for supporting open learning systems. Telesoftware (Hedger,1978) refers to those methods used to distribute computer programs (and, of course, CAL courseware) by means of some form of broadcast videotex or teletext system (see figure 1.13). Like electronic mail, telesoftware provides an easy and economic means of effecting the widespread distribution of CAL resources. This technology therefore provides another useful tool for those involved in the implementation of open and distance learning systems. The new advances currently being made within communications technology could significantly influence the way in which educational systems are implemented. These developments could affect teaching and learning in two major ways by (1) providing easier access to a greater range of learning resources, and (2) taking learning opportunities into the local vicinities of students (for example, their homes and places of work) rather than requiring them to attend conventional centres of learning. Thus, through developments of this type, people could always have available the opportunity of learning new skills and acquiring more knowledge at any stage in their life – no matter where they live, in a city, a village or within some remote part of a country.

6.2.5 Robotics

Robotics is the general term used to describe the study of robots. The most important aspects of studies in this area include (1) how robots, robotic aids and robotised devices are designed; (2) how they are constructed and programmed; (3) their mechanisms of operation; (4) the influence of robot technology upon society; and, of course, (5) their various applications. It is this latter aspect with which we are primarily concerned – more specifically, potential applications of robots within CAL.

Essentially, a robotic device is some form of electro–mechanical entity that is specifically designed to perform a particular job function or task. It does this both autonomously and automatically, that is without any form of human intervention or operator assistance. Most often, in order to achieve these objectives, a computer is used for control purposes. This controlling computer may be embedded within the robot itself or it may be located externally to it. In the latter case there must be some form of communication link between the two.

Broadly, robots may be subdivided into two basic types: static and mobile. Those of the static variety tend to occupy a fixed location and are not designed to be moved without human aid. In contrast to these, mobile robots similar to that shown in figure 6.4 (Your Robot, 1984a) are able to move about freely from one location to another – as dictated by their environment or the task lists that they have to perform. To enable this movement within particular sorts of environment, special types of sensor have to be employed. For this purpose tactile sensors, radar and vision systems are the most frequently used.

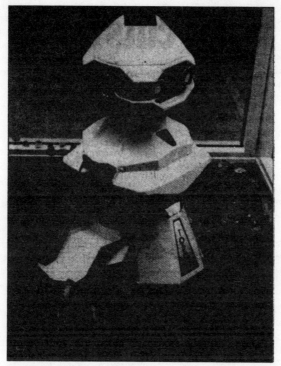

Figure 6.4   The TOPO mobile robot produced by Androbot.
(Courtesy of Your Robot.)

Robots have most often been associated with the process of industrial automation (Bagrit, 1965; Paul, 1979). That is, for the performance of certain job tasks, a human workforce is replaced by suitably designed machines. In addition to their industrial applications, robotic devices and aids are being used increasingly for many other important tasks. For example they are often incorporated into special. Aids for the disabled (Schneider et al, 1980; 1981); similarly, within teaching and learning situations they are often employed as a mechanism for helping students to develop certain types of skill. Thus, in the context of education, robot systems can also be used to aid the development of logical thinking and reasoning, and to promote a greater understanding of many different types of mathematical concept, particularly computer programming. Because of the ways in which they are able to enhance learning, 'toy robots' are becoming increasingly popular and much more commonplace in schools, colleges and within the home.

We introduced the basic ideas underlying the educational use of a simple robotic device earlier in section 5.28 when we discussed the LOGO turtle. This is a small mechanical device fitted with wheels and a drawing pen (see figures 5.19 and 5.20). The turtle is connected to its controlling computer by means of a flexible cable. By constructing suitable programs, students can make this robot move around and (by means of its pen) produce a variety of different types of drawing and artistic creation. Some other examples of toy robots include the Big Trak system (Hoffman, 1984), the BBC Buggy (Your Robot, 1984b) and the many different contestants for the IEEE Micro–Mouse maze competition (Allan, 1978; Schallon, 1978).

The Big Trak system was introduced some years ago as a toy in the form of a model army tank. This was fitted with two caterpillar tracks to enable it to move around. A keypad system was conveniently located on the turret of the tank to enable it to be programmed. Its repertoire of commands (each represented by a function key) enabled it to (1) move forwards, (2) move backwards, (3) turn right, (4) turn left, (5) stop, (6) go, and (7) repeat a stored sequence. Children could use this toy robot to enter simple control programs and then investigate the effects of these on the motion of the tank. Unfortunately, the number of commands that the system could store was quite small and so the complexity of the manoeuvres that the tank could undertake was quite limited.

The BBC Buggy is another example of an educational toy robot. It was built by the British Broadcasting Corporation to support a special series of educational TV broadcasts about robotics and computer control, as part of a nationwide computer literacy project (Mathews, 1984). It was designed to be attached to a BBC microcomputer (James, 1983) by means of an interface board and a length of twenty–way cable. During the time the educational programmes were being broadcast (and at subsequent times), demonstration software for the robot was made available to viewers through the BBC's Telesoftware Service that operates in conjunction with the CEEFAX teletext system. In many ways the BBC Buggy is similar to the LOGO turtle described in the last chapter – it has a pen that can be raised or lowered and it is programmed using simple English–like commands.

Several important examples of autonomous toy robots (such as Microbot, Charlotte and the Moonlight Special) were developed as contestants for a maze solving contest sponsored by the IEEE (Allan, 1978). These simple robotic devices had to be built to the following specification: no hard wiring or radio control; length and width not to exceed 10 inches. Contestants were required to negotiate a maze containing a single entry and a single exit. The mice listed above each contained a microprocessor system (for control purposes) and employed various sorts of optical and tactile sensor in order to locate the positions of the walls within the maze. Obviously, designing and writing the control software for negotiating the maze is quite an intellectual exercise involving a considerable amount of thought and reasoning power.

From the descriptions we have provided above it is easy to see that robot systems can provide a useful learning medium. They have been little used in the past because of their high cost and difficulty of fabrication. However, as each of these problems has been overcome, robotic devices are now becoming extremely popular both as 'add−on' units to personal computers and in the form of special purpose−toys. Devices of this type provide a useful learning medium for students of all ages and we foresee a definite future for educational robots.

6.2.6   Special Microelectronic Aids
Aids in this category can be broadly subdivided into three basic categories: (1) those involving the design of specialised equipment (mainly hardware) to produce a particular type of educational aid to fulfil a specific learning task; (2) those that are primarily software based and are designed to run on either a single type or a wide range of general purpose microcomputer systems; and (3) those that combine both hardware and software resources in various ways in order to meet the needs of those with special learning requirements. Essentially, category (3) is concerned with: (a) the design and construction of custom built workstations (as discussed in chapter 5); and (b) the production of tailor−made equipment to enable handicapped and disabled students to utilise CAL equipment. This latter category of aid is discussed in more detail in section 6.3.4. In the remainder of this section we concentrate on providing a brief description of the other two categories mentioned above, namely (1) and (2).

The most common type of microelectronic aid for CAL is probably the 'pocket calculator'. This device was originally developed to help students (and others) to perform mathematical calculations which they would otherwise find difficult. Much has been written about electronic hand−held calculators and so little more needs to be said here. However, it is worth mentioning the ways in which they are able to assist learning. First, (like larger computers) they can help many types of learning process by removing the burden of having to perform repetitive, time consuming and difficult arithmetic tasks, thus clearing the way for more creative thought processes. Second, they provide a powerful aid to those who do not have significant mathematical ability, thereby preventing a lack of such skills from affecting other studies in a detrimental way.

The hand–held calculator undoubtedly paved the route for other kinds of special–purpose hardware for teaching. Particularly well known are those manufactured by the educational division of Texas Instruments (Texas Instruments, 1983; Frantz and Wiggins, 1982). Some of these are illustrated in figures 6.5 A and B. Probably, the most well known of these learning aids are: the Little Professor, Speak & Math, Speak & Spell, Speak & Read, Speak & Write and Touch & Tell. The Little Professor was the first of the learning aids to emerge from Texas Instruments; introduced in 1976 this device was designed to teach basic arithmetic skills. Following the development of this, a second aid was produced (called the Spelling Bee) which was an electronic learning aid for teaching spelling to children; the Spelling Bee formed the basis of the Speak & Spell product which was released in 1978 (Frantz and Wiggins, 1982). The range of teaching aids available from Texas Instruments undoubtedly marks a revolution in education for children since they provide instructional aids that make learning and practising an enjoyable experience to look forward to. As their names suggest, most of these learning aids employ voice synthesis techniques to enable them to speak with a friendly, warm synthesised voice which rewards, prompts and continually encourages children to learn. Originally, these special microelectronic aids were intended to be used for teaching various skills to pre–school children. However, they are now also extensively used for teaching within many primary and elementary schools. These learning aids seem to be successful because they provide exciting and motivating experiences for children. This is achieved through the employment of different types of drill, quiz and learning game that are intriguing, challenging, educational and, above all, fun to use.

The other type of special aid that was mentioned above is that which is software or firmware orientated; teaching modules are either loaded (software) or plugged (firmware) into an existing general purpose microcomputer system. These modules each convert the micro into an instructional tool that provides a specific type of learning environment for the duration of the teaching session for which they are being used. Examples of the type of software that is available are presented in figures 6.6A and 6.6B; they are all intended to be run on a Sinclair Spectrum microcomputer (Sinclair–MacMillan, 1983). As was the case with the examples presented under category (1) above, these illustrations are of courseware intended to be used primarily for teaching elementary skills. Each of the programs has a step–by–step example section and gives correct answers after a number of incorrect attempts. In the reading programs (see figure 6.6B), vocabulary changes can be made thereby allowing each program to keep pace with the learner's development. This flexibility can also be employed

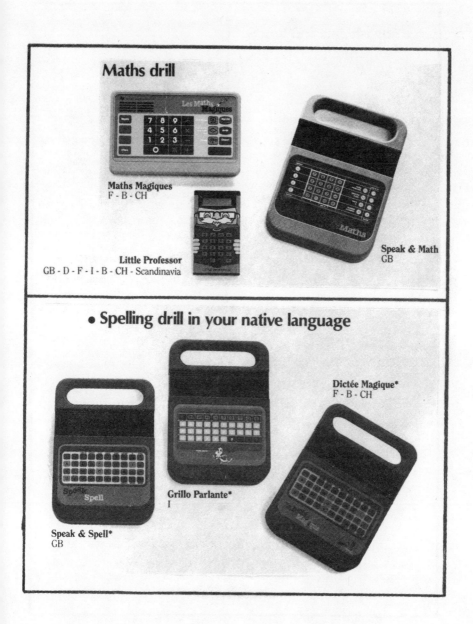

Figure 6.5A   Examples of microelectronic aids for teaching.
(Courtesy of Texas Instruments.)

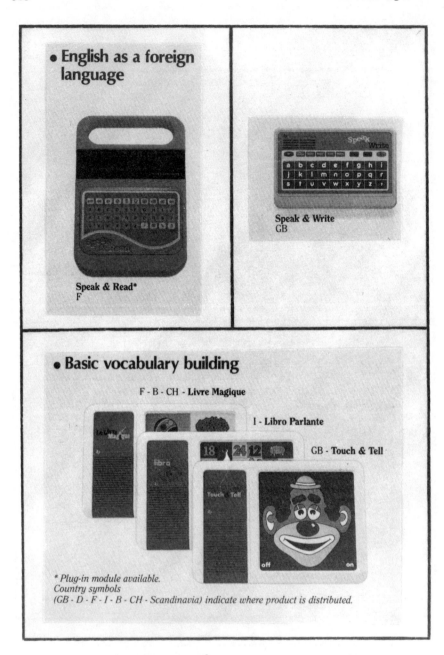

Figure 6.5B   Examples of microelectronic aids for teaching.
(Courtesy of Texas Instruments.)

Alphabet Games

Three games of letter recognition (using either upper or lower case) to help children learn the alphabet and find their way round the computer keyboard.

Alphagaps — The full alphabet is displayed, along with a second, incomplete version. The child must fill in the missing letters.

Random Rats — Press the letter key that is displayed on the gun to destroy the rats which have invaded the cellar!

Invaders — Stop little green men from landing on Earth by pressing the appropriate letter.

Early Punctuation

While an animated matchstick man marches above displayed sentences the child must decide which punctuation mark is missing and where to insert it. At the touch of a key the matchstick man drops the mark into place. After successful completion of every sentence in the exercise, light relief comes in the form of a bottle-shooting game!

The Apostrophe

As each sentence is displayed, a bird appears with a worm in its beak. The keyboard is used to move the bird and drop the worm into the correct place for the apostrophe. When ten sentences have been corrected, the Grub Game is displayed. Press the correct character to change the grub into a butterfly...before it munches through a flower!

Capital Letters

A program to teach the use of capital letters. Sentences incorporating proper nouns and sentences without opening capitals are displayed. The child inserts the correction by guiding an animated figure to the appropriate letter.

For each correct answer an apple grows on a tree. After ten correct answers the child's skills in recognising letters and using the Spectrum keyboard are needed to save the apples as they fall to the ground.

Speech Marks

A comprehensive program including sentences with one or two sets of speech marks ("inverted commas") and exercises in both direct and reported speech.

Using the Spectrum keyboard, a cursor is used to guide speech marks to the correct position. The program offers three levels of difficulty, with full examples for each section. Guide Max the mouse through a maze, after the correct completion of five sentences from each section, but beware of Persian cats!

Castle Spellerous

A spelling game with ten levels of vocabulary, including words with silent first letters, double letters and other difficult words. The Princess has been captured and carried off to Castle Spellerous. Helped by ten soldiers, the child can attempt a rescue by giving the right answers. Part of a siege tower is built for each correctly spelt word. Mistakes are costly — the wicked wizard appears as a vampire bat, turning the men into frogs, butterflies and bats!

When ten words are spelt correctly the rescue begins and the wizard takes flight.

Figure 6.6A Examples of software aids for teaching.
(Courtesy of Sinclair–Macmillan.)

Learn to Read 2

Learn to Read 2 extends the fundamental reading skills practised in the first program, as well as encouraging logical thinking. The child's vocabulary is gradually built up as new words such as "red," "green," "car," "ship" and "bus" are introduced. In addition, Learn to Read 2 features an attractive 'reward' system enabling children to see their achievements grow.

Learn to Read 3

Learn to Read 3 builds on the child's progress so far, so that he or she can gain the confidence to move on through the complex reading process. Learn to Read 3 features four different activities, all of which are colourful and lively. Further vocabulary is introduced until the child is reading more than 30 words.

Learn to Read 5

Learn to Read 5 teaches positional language – often difficult to understand and remember – by using words and phrases such as "behind" and "in front of," "inside" and "outside."

The program first demonstrates the meanings of the words using clear pictures. It then tests the child's understanding of the words in two lively games.

Cargo

Set sail around the world. Choose your ports of call – New York, Tokyo, Belem, Helsinki – then the real challenge begins! You must reach your destinations safely, weathering storms on the way. But first, load your cargo – using all your knowledge and skill. Poor loading can mean capsizing and sinking. Your rank, if not your life, is always at stake!

Survival

Discover what it is like to be an animal in the wild! Be a lion stalking your prey, escaping human hunters. Or be a hawk, mouse or even a butterfly, searching for food and avoiding predators.

Survival models the natural world and brings to life hazards that different creatures must face in their struggle to stay alive.

Magnets

With an army of small magnets you set out to conquer the powerful supermagnets of your opponent. You have one weapon – your forces of magnetic attraction and repulsion.

The strategy is simple: attract smaller magnets to build strength to repel the supermagnet. When cornered, just turn your poles on your enemy and see what happens!

Figure 6.6B   Examples of software aids for teaching.
(Courtesy of Sinclair–Macmillan.)

to cater for children of differing ability. The instructive and colourful games, which follow the successful completion of each group of sentences, provide useful practice in letter recognition and also increase familiarity with the microcomputer keyboard. Most of the programs concentrate on key scientific ideas, and through simulation of real life situations, make the learning process entertaining and enjoyable. Based on the material we have presented in this section it should be apparent that there is significant potential for the development of many different types of special microelectronic aid for teaching applications. Indeed, the scope of the possibilities that exist is limited only by our imaginations, ingenuity and, perhaps, our failure to realise the nature of the problems that remain to be solved.

6.2.7 Models and Intelligent CAI

Artificial intelligence (or AI) is probably one of those areas of current research activity that is most likely to influence the future directions of development of CAL and CAI. Indeed, this subject forms the basic backbone of many of the other topics which we have previously discussed in this chapter, namely expert systems, gaming and robotics. Generally, AI techniques are used in order to provide computer based systems with some of the decision making, problem solving and reasoning skills that would normally be associated with intelligent human behaviour. The major objectives of introducing AI techniques into CAI systems is undoubtedly to make them behave more like a human tutor might. Some of the desirable properties of a human tutor (Gable and Page, 1980), which, if possible, would be worth incorporating into an intelligent CAI system, include his/her ability to:

(1) cause the problem solving heuristics of the student to converge towards those of the tutor;
(2) learn and adopt student solution methods if they are superior;
(3) choose appropriate examples and problems for the student;
(4) recommend solution scheme choices and demonstrate how to apply techniques when the student is in need of help;
(5) work out arbitrary examples chosen by the student;
(6) adjust to different student backgrounds;
(7) measure the student's progress;
(8) review previously learned material with the student as the need arises;
(9) give immediate feedback on errors while allowing the student a free hand in deciding how to solve a problem; and
(10) (after a student solves a problem) point out more direct solutions or ones that use more recently learned theorems or techniques.

In attempting to incorporate some of the above requirements into CAL systems a variety of different types of AI technique has been employed. These include the use of special kinds of information structure (called semantic networks) and knowledge bases; gaming and simulation methods; theorem proving; conversation theory; and various forms of modelling, a few of which will be briefly outlined below.

Some of the earliest work involving advanced information structures was probably that embodied in the studies made by Carbonell (1970) and also those made by Wexler (1970). Carbonell used the semantic network approach in order to construct an interactive teaching system called SCHOLAR. This utilised a simple knowledge base as a means of controlling teaching dialogues, the object of which was to teach students about the geography of South America. In a similar way, Wexler used this type of information structure to construct a generative CAI system which dynamically generated simple instructional and remedial sequences for non-numeric subjects such as geography and biology. Undoubtedly, the basic research involved in these pioneering studies has provided many valuable ideas and techniques to aid the construction of future intelligent knowledge based CAI systems (International Journal of Man–Machine Studies, 1979; O'Shea, 1979; Sleeman and Brown, 1982).

The basic ideas underlying gaming and simulation have been discussed earlier. Gaming is probably more intimately associated with artificial intelligence than is conventional simulation. However, the application of AI concepts to the latter can lead to the production of many different forms of intelligent simulation system. Courseware based on this approach is extremely important since it not only simulates some target system (related to the topic of instruction) but, in addition, it is capable of 'reacting' to its student users. It does this in such a way that it can offer help, advice and guidance when a student has gone wrong or in situations where aid would be appropriate. The SOPHIE system for teaching students the principles of electronic circuit trouble–shooting is an example of this type of approach to intelligent simulation (Brown et al., 1975; Brown et al., 1982). Frequently, in courseware of this type it is important to utilise specially formulated theorem proving methods (Gable and Page, 1980; O'Shea, 1982). These can be used for a variety of purposes; however, their most important role is probably that of checking that the steps taken by a student (within a particular problem solving strategy) are sound and will lead to a solution.

Conversation theory is another important area that is likely to be of substantial value to the future development of CAL and CAI. The theory is based upon a system view of the learner and of knowledge. Much of the research in this area is aimed at understanding the nature of creativity and encouraging qualitative improvements in learning and learning to learn. Many of the basic ideas embodied in conversation theory have been formulated by Pask (1980; 1983). Essentially, the theory deals with the interactions that take place between people (or a single person) and a body of knowledge or experience. Pask writes: 'It is a collection of empirically tested hypotheses, not so far

falsified in any crucial respect, applicable to conversations or
kinetic transactions of a very wide ranging type; ... The transactions
concerned are typified by but not all confined to, those which take
place between a teacher and a learner, or between several students
learning about a subject matter or as participants in a design
project'. A computer based application of conversation theory (called
CASTE) has been described by Lee (1983). CASTE is an acronym for
Course Assembly System and Tutorial Environment. This system helps
instructors to assemble courses in keeping with a circular hermaneutic
approach to the structure of knowledge. It then tutors students by
allowing each to choose his/her own path through the course. The
knowledge structure upon which this system is based (called an
entailment mesh) is dynamic (that is, responds to conversations) and
embodies the topics and topic relations relevant to the domain in
which it tutors. Like knowledge engineering, conversation theory is an
invaluable tool for the development of learning systems. We are
therefore optimistic about the possibilities that each will offer in
the context of CAI.

Before concluding this section it is imperative that some mention is
made of the ways in which models are being used in the development of
intelligent CAI courseware. Models are used for a variety of different
purposes and at several different levels. They are needed in order to
provide suitable windows on to (and hence views of) the many levels of
interface that exist (and which are needed) in order to bring
learners, instructors, knowledge and computers into productive
harmony. The most important categories of model used in accomplishing
this objective are those of:

(1) the cognitive processes within the student;
(2) students and their behaviour;
(3) instruction and learning;
(4) information transfer;
(5) instructors, teachers and experts; and
(6) the concepts and procedures relevant to the universe
     of discourse that forms the object of instruction.

Bunderson (1981) has identified a subset of these which he feels is
particularly important to the future development of intelligent CAI.
His four categories include:

(1) a model to simulate a performance environment;
(2) a model of an expert performer within this environment;
     he/she must have (i) conceptual domain knowledge that permits
     an understanding of the concepts (and the interrelations
     between them) in the subject domain, and (ii) procedural
     knowledge that guides performance of relevant tasks within
     the domain;
(3) a diagnostic model of learner status; this can be compared
     with that of an expert in order to deduce an appropriate

aiding or instructional strategy which can be used to guide the student along a correct learning route; and

(4)   a prescriptive model that describes how to tutor a given individual student.

Items (2) and (3) relate very closely to the notion of student modelling – an area of research to which a large amount of effort has been devoted (Gable and Page, 1980; Koffman and Blount, 1975; Self, 1974; 1977; 1979). The basic idea underlying this work is that, for some particular universe of discourse, an intelligent CAI system should be able to (1) deduce the knowledge levels of the student (through a generative dialogue), (2) determine the desired goal state that the student wishes to arrive at (if this is possible), (3) dynamically select an optimal instructional (possibly learner controlled) pathway for that student which brings him/her to a state that is as close as possible to that which he/she is aiming for. Although we are some way from achieving these objectives, their fulfilment represents a very laudable aim for future research and development work in intelligent CAI.

6.2.8 Authoring Methods

Several of the previous sections of this book (particularly those in chapters 2 and 3) have given considerable attention to the topic of author languages. The reader will therefore realise that this type of software tool is essentially a special type of courseware generator specifically designed to ease the burden of developing software for instructional applications of the computer. No matter what advances take place in educational technology and computer programming techniques, we are confident that there will always be a role for CAL authoring systems that embrace useful, easy to use, development facilities. Hence, as far as the future is concerned the question that arises really relates to the form that author languages will take (and the facilities they will provide) rather than whether or not they will be available (and used). In view of this, the remainder of this section is used to briefly discuss five important factors that are likely to influence the design of future author languages. These are user friendliness (or ease of use); transportability issues; the growing importance of knowledge bases; ease of interfacing to other software systems; and the increasing use of multimedia instructional techniques.

It is very easy to make authoring systems available. However, it is much more difficult to motivate CAL authors into using them for courseware production. Many factors need to be considered before embarking upon the use of a particular system (if one is employed at all); the more important of these relate to how easy it is:

(1)   to understand the way in which it operates;
(2)   to assimilate the range of facilities offered;
(3)   to learn how to use it;

(4)   to communicate with it; and
(5)   to make it do what is required.

User friendliness (or ease of use) is a term that is often applied to
mean good software ergonomics; that is, designing software that   makes
using   it   a   pleasurable and satisfying experience, in the context of
the task being undertaken. There are many ways in which these
objectives   can   be   achieved.   Several   of   these   have been outlined
previously (see, for example, the   description   of   the   ADAPT   system
given   in section 5.3.1(a)). For the future it is important to improve
user friendliness by persuing three major lines of development. First,
the provision of a variety of automated aids such as mimic   facilities
containing   specialised   code   generators; techniques for constructing
models of users (both authors   and   students); and   methods   for   the
automatic   assessment of courseware effectiveness. Second, the greater
use of built-in tutors and on-line learning/aiding facilities.   Third,
a   much greater use of knowledge bases in order to improve the quality
of the human/computer   interface   involved   in   CAL   systems   (Barker,
1984b). Each of these objectives are likely to be realised through the
application   of   existing (and currently developing) techniques within
artificial intelligence.

Two of the problems that have always confronted CAL/CBT authors are
(1)   the   proliferation   of   author languages, and (2) the differences
that often exist   in   the   implementations   of   a   given   language   on
different   computers. This has often meant that courseware designed to
run on one class of machine would not (without considerable conversion
effort) run on any other. This is particularly true when attempting to
move mainframe based courseware onto a micro system. A number of
researchers   have   addressed   the   various technical issues associated
with courseware transportability (Wilson, 1982; Mast, 1982; Blandford,
1982;   Wilson   and   McCrum,   1984). Their   results   offer   reasonable
solutions   to   the   limited   (scopewise) problems that they attempt to
solve. In the long term, a far more   structured   approach   is   needed.
Ideally, CAL   authors   require   several levels of authoring tool that
together provide facilities   ranging   from   specification   through   to
implementation. These   levels,   together   with an indication of their
degree of transportability, are indicated in table 6.1.

Through   the   design   of   appropriate   software   (such   as   dialect
translators,   interconversion interfaces, etc) and the use of a common
internationally   accepted   machine   independent   code,   considerable
progress   towards   solving the transportability problem could be made.
However, as is the case in other areas of   computer   technology,   this
problem is likely to remain with us for some time into the future, for
both political and financial reasons.

Table 6.1   Portability of CAL courseware materials.

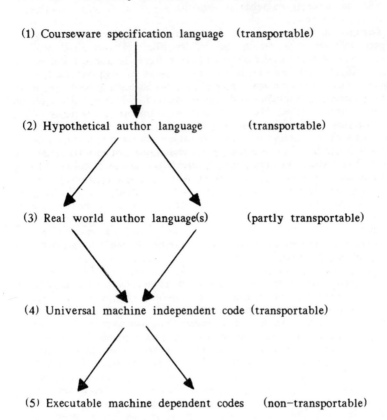

(1) Courseware specification language   (transportable)

(2) Hypothetical author language   (transportable)

(3) Real world author language(s)   (partly transportable)

(4) Universal machine independent code (transportable)

(5) Executable machine dependent codes   (non-transportable)

As we have discussed in section 6.2.3 (expert systems) the increasing availability of knowledge bases and the use of knowledge engineering techniques are each having a considerable impact on the design of computer applications systems (Barker, 1984b). It is therefore imperative that CAL and CBT systems are each able to utilise these technological developments if they are to provide realistic future approaches to education and training. For this reason the next generation of author languages must be capable of providing those facilities that are necessary (1) for constructing knowledge bases, and (2) providing access to existing ones. The authoring facility must then allow the courseware author to specify how the knowledge base is to be used to control the course of instruction. We have tried to indicate these ideas in figure 6.2. Knowledge bases provide a new and exciting dimension for those involved in author language design; we await eagerly the emergence of a system that incorporates these facilities.

It is important that the reader realises (1) that a large amount of courseware material currently exists; (2) there are many valuable types of software development tool presently available and widely used for instructional purposes (conventional programming languages, simulation packages, authoring tools, etc); and (3) the impossibility of ever being able to build an 'all embracing' authoring facility. Because of these three very important factors we feel that it is imperative that future author languages must provide a wide range of interface facilities that enable best use to be made of items (1) and (2) above. At present very few languages allow this. We hope in the future that this situation will be remedied.

Multimedia CAL has been dealt with in considerable detail in chapters 4 and 5. This is an area with which very few author languages deal in an adequate way. We believe that there is significant scope for this approach to instruction in the future – indeed, Zinn (1981) has written:

> Communication between machines and people needs careful attention. As long as the students (or other casual users) need to type on a keyboard and watch for text and numbers and simple diagrams to appear on a special screen, these machines will have a rather narrow application in training and education. However, when a user can talk to the machine and get a response in printed text as well as in spoken words and other sounds, and can see the effects of directives in the actions of equipment such as models and tools, then the computer will fit into a much larger world of learning and performance.

This quotation admirably summarises the essence and basic objectives of multimedia CAL. Throughout this book we have tried to impress upon our readers the importance of this technique. We have also attempted to point out how poorly it is catered for within so many of the currently available author languages. Let us hope that our desire for an improvement in multimedia capability will come to fruition in future authoring systems.

6.3 APPLICATION AREAS

CAL and CBT applications of the computer are today far more widespread than they were a decade ago, primarily because of the availability of personal computing resources and the prolific increase that has taken place in inexpensive microelectronic aids for teaching. There is scope for this type of instructional technology in virtually all areas of learning and training. Indeed, the possibilities that exist are far too numerous to be individually listed. Therefore, in order to provide a basic structure for the material contained in this section we consider four basic application areas: the home; academic institutions; the workplace; and those with special needs – the handicapped and disabled. As can be seen from figure 6.7, these cover a wide range of learning activities: from pre–school education (CAL in the home) through to the creation of a trained (or retrained) industrial workforce (CAL in the workplace). We do not claim that our coverage of these areas is in any way comprehensive. Our intention is only to illustrate, within the categories listed, some of the many things that are possible with this teaching technology.

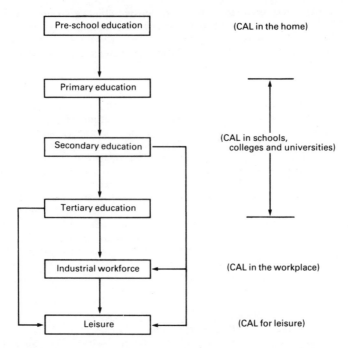

Figure 6.7   The wide spectrum of computer assisted learning.

6.3.1   CAL in the Home

Virtually all people spend at least some time in the environment of their home. It is therefore quite reasonable to assume that this setting will form the scene for a considerable amount of learning – both formal and informal. Such learning is likely to arise either as a direct or an indirect consequence of the various types of activity that normally take place within the home. Typically, these activities might include reading, watching TV, listening to the radio, using a home computer, playing games of various sorts, participating in family discussions, and partaking in a variety of other leisure interests.

Together, these possibilities provide innumerable mechanisms from which can arise an extremely complex web of learning activity. Naturally, because of an increasing presence of the computer within the home, for a large number of people CAL is likely to offer yet another extremely versatile and useful medium with which to learn. The amount of time individuals spend in their abodes will obviously vary quite considerably. Some will occupy their homes for only a relatively short period each day. For others, the period of residence may be much greater (some even being confined there). People who spend the greatest amount of time at home can be broadly subdivided into six basic groups:

(1) the very young (pre-school children);
(2) handicapped and disabled people;
(3) those who are geographically isolated;
(4) retired people;
(5) the unemployed; and
(5) those who work from their homes.

For each of these groups of people the use of computer assisted learning methods has much to offer. For example, it can be used to provide: pre-school learning (for the very young); education for leisure (for the unemployed and retired); mainstream education (for the geographically isolated); fundamental skill acquisition (for the house-bound handicapped/disabled); and new skill acquisition and skill enhancement (for those who work from home, job seekers, leisure workers and people generally). Some of these possibilities are further discussed later in this section.

The Resources
Within the modern home environment it is possible to find most of the basic components that are needed in order to (1) initiate many of the types of learning process outlined above; and (2) enable the construction of sophisticated home learning centres. Amongst the more important resources we include:

(1) a TV set for information receipt and display;
(2) a radio;
(3) a personal computer;
(4) a telephone; and (possibly)
(5) a video disc player.

Most of the above items can be used either individually or in various combinations in order to initiate and sustain a number of different approaches to learning. Several different examples of techniques for interlinking this equipment in different configurations have been described and illustrated previously (see, for example, figures 4.11 and 5.27). In the following we briefly outline some of the ways in which the above components (either alone or in combination) can be used to support CAL processes in the home.

For some time, TV and radio have provided extremely useful sources of
a great deal of educational material for use in home instruction.
Indeed, educational broadcasting is now a major concern for many radio
and TV networks. This type of home education is particularly valuable
for both (1) those who are compelled to study from within their homes
(for example, handicapped and disabled people); and (2) those who are
studying on a part-time basis during their leisure hours. In the
latter context, it is important to note the success achieved by the
United Kingdom's Open University (OU). Through the agency of the
British Broadcasting Corporation this organisation has used
educational broadcasting (both TV and radio) to relay a variety of
different courses of instruction to those whose studying is confined
to the home environment. Indeed, ever since its inception in the late
1960s, the OU has been at the forefront of those involved in
pioneering the use of educational broadcasting as a means of
implementing teaching and learning processes. Because of their
success, it is natural to assume that these media (TV and radio) will
continue to be used in the future, probably in the same ways as they
have been in the past and possibly augmented by appropriately designed
CAL study software. In addition, these media will continue to provide
a range of ancillary services that can each be usefully utilised
within home education.

Some of the most important of these ancillary service developments
include teletext and telesoftware (based on TV); and radiotext, based
on the use of radio broadcasting (Smith and Zorkoczy, 1982). As we
have described previously, telesoftware techniques can be used to
transmit CAL courseware directly into people's homes for use on their
personal microcomputers. In a similar way the OU hope that radiotext
can be employed to allow material in the form of text and graphics to
be transmitted over an unmodified VHF broadcasting network, thereby
replacing the need for producing conventionally printed materials. As
well as allowing the dissemination of audio-visual material, it is
anticipated that radiotext will also enable the delivery of computer
software to be made. Many other novel developments have arisen as a
consequence of research orientated towards the provision of ancillary
services associated with TV and radio transmission. The Open
University's CYCLOPS system (Sharples, 1982), which was described in
section 3.4.6, and the use of TV subtitling techniques for the deaf
(Hawkins and Robinson, 1979) are just two of the numerous examples
that could be cited. All of these developments have important
contributions to make towards enhancing the scope and capability of
CAL within the home.

The potential of teletext and viewdata for CAL applications in the
home environment has already been briefly outlined (see section
6.2.4). As an information dissemination aid each of these services is
of unprecedented value within home education, particularly as teletext
(at least in the UK) forms the basis for telesoftware. Future
enhancements to these services will undoubtedly benefit their

applications within CAL. In this context, possible developments of teletext that could prove extremely useful include (1) the use of a wider range of characters (including a dynamically redefinable character set) thereby giving access to additional symbolisms such as Roman, Arabic, Japanese and so on; (2) a wider range of colours; (3) the provision of simple animation; (4) a move towards greater graphics resolution; and (5) the ability to combine telesoftware and teletext techniques in order to achieve new types of information display. Similarly, viewdata services are also likely to benefit considerably from both present and future technological developments. Probably, the most significant influence will be that of cable communication facilities, which could offer the possibility of using a much greater bandwidth for the communication of viewdata materials. It is therefore likely that viewdata services might move away from the use of teletext-like frames, in favour of higher quality video based images.

Obviously, the most important resource for home CAL applications is the personal computer itself. Indeed, the most significant benefits of CAL in the home environment are unlikely to be realised until (1) every household contains a micro; and (2) each type of micro is supported by an appropriate range of courseware. Both of these requirements are starting to materialise. Basic micromputer systems are available for less than $100; these can be plugged into an existing TV set; they come equipped with a tape cassette; and each type is capable of being expanded into a more powerful system by the addition of a flexible disc, a printer, a communications modem and so on. A variety of tape (and disc) based study software is now beginning to appear in shops and stores. This caters for a wide variety of subjects ranging from elementary home matters (such as how to fill in a tax form, read a map or repair a car) through to basic mathematics and classics. Typically, this courseware is often multimedia, combining book material and reference manuals with interactive computer dialogue. Thus, in the case of the classics, the study software refers students to relevant passages in books and, by providing further comments and questions, helps to develop a much deeper appreciation of the work.

By adding an inexpensive modem to the home micro system it is possible to convert it into a terminal device that can, through a telephone network, communicate with other computers located virtually anywhere in the world. The educational possibilities that arise from this type of configuration is quite overwhelming, since the possibility of accessing courseware resident on any other computer system now becomes a practical reality.

Although it is not a critical component, perhaps one of the most exciting resources for use in home CAL applications is the video disc. This device offers enormous potential for use as a tool for home instruction. Two possibilities exist for its use: (1) coupled to a home computer; and (2) as a stand-alone intelligent interactive video unit. The first of these approaches has been described previously (see section 4.2.3). The second mode of usage is probably more novel since it allows the possibility of providing, within the home, libraries of 'electronic books' with which users can converse – by means of a keypad, by touching a screen or by simple spoken phrases. Naturally, a computer is an important part of an interactive intelligent video unit. However, in this case it is embedded within the video unit and therefore is hidden from the user. A self–contained system such as this could have many advantages (for example, portability, ease of use, etc) over systems in which a computer is connected externally. Few units of this type yet exist. We therefore eagerly await their commercial availability.

The Users
In order to provide the basis for a simple classification scheme, we listed earlier six broad categories into which we felt potential home CAL users could be grouped. Before concluding this section we must therefore briefly describe the importance of CAL within each of these categories. At the same time we will need to outline how CAL is currently being employed (if at all) and how it might be used by each of these groups in the future.

As we indicated in figure 6.7, pre–school education takes place before any formal instruction commences. It is therefore an important factor in preparing a suitable foundation upon which to build subsequent levels of education. Therefore, the use of CAL techniques might well have much to offer young children in terms of skill uptake, particularly with respect to rudimentary activities such as spelling, number concepts, composition and so on. Plausibly, the best approach to using the computer in this way is probably through the use of appealing and stimulating games that are likely to develop learning motivation within the child. This area of involvement of CAL is very new, and so much investigatory and development work needs to be undertaken. We have mentioned previously the work of Fiddy and Yam (1984) in the UK who have investigated the use of Prestel (a national viewdata service) for home education of young children in the context of numeracy and literacy. Teaching proceeded through the use of games and involved both independent usage by the children (aged 3–4 years) and family involvement, in which parents or groups of adults also took part. These researchers concluded that although there were many positive benefits associated with using a viewdata system in this way, the cost implications were restrictive. In view of this, we feel that it would be worthwhile attempting to compare the results of the above experiments with similar ones involving the use of microcomputers. Currently, there are many ongoing studies of pre–school applications of CAL. Unfortunately, the results that are available are not yet sufficiently widely established to enable the formulation of any positive policy or recommendations.

We mentioned in the previous section the use of teletext subtitling as a   means   of extending the facilities of the TV to the deaf user. This technique is just one way in which modern technology might be employed to aid the disabled CAL user. Nowadays, the availability of   adaptable microprocessor   based   equipment   (that   can   be   modified   to   meet individual requirements) means that CAL   can   offer   a   wide   range   of learning   opportunities   to   this   category of home-bound learner. The MAVIS system (which is described in section 6.3.4) provides   just   one example of the type of development that is being made which could enable disabled and handicapped people to   successfully   utilise   both educational   broadcasting and conventional CAL courseware within their own home environment. As in the case of pre-school education, this   is an   area   in   which there is currently much active specialist research taking place. This is aimed at (1) developing special purpose learning and teaching strategies for use with   this   class   of   CAL   user;   (2) reducing   the cost of providing the currently available interface aids that are needed; and (3) designing new interaction facilities in order to extend the use of CAL to those who have previously not been able to experience it. Because of the potential importance of   this   teaching method   to   this   category   of   user,   we   return   to a more extensive discussion of CAL for the disabled in section 6.3.4.

People   who   live   in   geographically   isolated   parts   of   a   country constitute another important category of home CAL user. Generally, but not   necessarily, people in this group will live in countries having a substantial land mass, relatively few people, and so a low   population density.   In   this   situation,   students   might   typically   reside   in isolated farms or in small villages having only two or three families. Very often such students are disadvantaged as a result of   not   having access to many of the conventional learning resources that students in large   towns   and   cities have available. To compensate for this, many countries (such as Canada, Australia and   Africa)   use   a   variety   of different approaches to distance education to support learners who are in an isolated region. Fortunately, computer assisted learning methods are   particularly well suited to this type of application. They may be implemented through an approach based upon a teletext   system,   direct satellite   distribution   or   specially designed learning packages that also incorporate self-study   CAL   based   materials.   Because   of   the possibilities   that   it offers, the CAL approach to distance education is actively being evaluated by many of the countries   that   face   this problem.

Many   modern societies are facing problems associated with unemployment and the need to reduce the size of the active workforce (in particular industries)   by   means   of   early   retirement.   These problems open up important potential areas of application for CAL in the context of (1) education for leisure; and (2)   education   for   re-employment   through retraining   and the subsequent acquisition of the new skills necessary to take up employment within new types of trade and profession. Although some cursory studies have been made of the relevance of CAL to these problems, little is yet known of the real contribution it could make or of its effectiveness. These areas are indeed in need of much further exploratory research.

Another large and wide–open target area for CAL applications within the home is provided by the large group of people who would like to acquire skills that they do not possess or enhance those that they already have, perhaps in order to enable them: to get a better job; to do things they would otherwise be unable to do (such as read music, play a piano, repair a TV, service a washing machine or maintain their home); or generally improve the quality of their lives through learning. Adult education and a variety of different post–experience courses have in the past provided the means by which some of these requirements have been catered for. Unfortunately, as is so often the case with this type of education many of the courses that have been available tend to be (1) of the wrong type; (2) good – but over subscribed; (3) take place at an inconvenient time; or (4) are of the correct type but at the wrong level. Obviously, there is much to be done towards improving the general opportunities for adult education, whether this is for leisure or for the pursuit of further job qualifications. Optimistically, we suggest that in the immediate future CAL may have something to offer; alternatively, in the longer term, intelligent interactive video may come to the forefront as a tool for aiding home study for these students.

6.3.2 CAL in Schools, Colleges and Universities
Within most countries of the world, schools, colleges and universities form the backbone of the majority of existing educational systems. In general, schools tend to cater for the requirements of students at the primary and secondary levels of education while colleges and universities fulfil the needs of those seeking some form of higher education. As can be seen from figure 6.7 each of these levels is dependent upon the one that precedes it. Ideally, such a system would cater for each student at every stage during his/her educational and intellectual development. Moreover, it is not unreasonable to expect that passage through such an educational system might provide an adequate preparation to enable people to lead useful and satisfying lives. Needless to say, these ideals are more often the exception than the rule.

Unfortunately, conventional education (as we have described it) has many problems and limitations. Two of the most important problems are those of continuity and completeness. Continuity is concerned with the ease and smoothness with which transitions between the levels depicted in figure 6.7 can take place. Rarely, if ever, do these take place smoothly or easily, due to a variety of reasons such as differences in student ability, syllabuses, examining standards and resource availability. Of equal importance is the problem of completeness of education. Most people would accept that conventional approaches to teaching frequently result in the emergence of students who are

incompletely   educated   and   ill-prepared   for life in a difficult and
competitive world. If education is deemed to be a preparation for   the
process of living then, in many cases, it is sadly deficient, due to a
lack   of   emphasis   and   coverage.   Perhaps   this   latter problem is a
necessary consequence of an over-packed curriculum. Of course, it   may
also   be   partly   due to an inadequate use of the available resources,
particularly the instructional capability of the computer. We are   not
suggesting   for   one moment that CAL is a panacea for all the problems
of modern education. However, we do believe that   the   seeds   of   CAL,
once   sown,   will   yield   a   harvest   of   benefits across the complete
spectrum of educational endeavour.

Historically,   most   of   the   early   research   and   development   work
involving   the   computer as an instructional resource was conducted at
university sites – notably, those   in   the   USA.   This   research   was
motivated   by   the   problems   created by having to cope with very high
student numbers. Fortunately, the research   that   was   undertaken   was
facilitated   by the availability of large (and powerful) multi-access,
time-shared computer systems. These were able to support a significant
number of computer terminals as well as many different kinds of
special   purpose   learning   centre   (such   as the PLATO terminal). The
advent of low-cost microcomputers has enabled the use of CAL and CAI
techniques to spread to other types of educational institution. Today,
many   particularly important developments are taking place at both the
secondary (Thomas, 1979; Candy and Edmunds, 1982) and   primary   (Petty
et   al., 1984; Bell, 1982) levels of education. Indeed, there has been
a spate of work in this latter area (Fiddy and Wharry, 1983) probably
because   of   (1)   the   awakening   realisation   amongst teachers of the
instructional potential of   the   computer;   (2)   the   more   widespread
availability   of resources suitable for use within this age group; and
(3) the acceptance of the computer as a job aid rather than as   a   job
threat.

Obviously,   many important questions need to be asked about the future
role of CAL within our present educational systems. By posing some   of
these   questions,   and   attempting to answer them in as constructive a
way as is possible, we hope to convince our readers of   the   positive
need   and future for CAL in all our institutions of learning. There is
no significance in the order in   which   the   following   questions   are
presented.

(a)   Is Individualised Instruction the Only Approach to CAL?
No.
There are many ways of using the computer to teach. In this book we
have been chiefly concerned with using it to create individualised CAI
schemes. An alternative strategy to this is that in which a teacher or
instructor uses the machine as an aid to support his/her teaching,   in
much   the   same way as a slide projector, a blackboard or a video tape
system might be used. When   used   in   this   fashion   the   computer   is
controlled   by the teacher (using a suitable keyboard) while the class

as a whole watches the computer output on a large TV screen or overhead projection system. This approach to teaching can often be used to advantage within all sectors of education. In colleges and universities, for example, the computer aided lecture (particularly for technical topics) is becoming more and more popular, provided that lecture theatres are equipped in such a way as to cater for this technique. Of course, in many teaching institutions this approach to computer usage may be the only one feasible, especially in situations where there is only one computer terminal (or micro) to share between a whole school or a single class.

Philips et al. (1984) have conducted an observational study of this mode of teaching within the secondary education sector. They observed 174 school lessons during which 14 teachers (from 9 schools) employed microcomputer aided teaching regularly with particular classes of students for a whole term. The subject they taught was mathematics and the lessons all involved one of three possible strategies: competitive (mainly games software); investigative (involving exploratory simulation situations); and electronic blackboard mode (using demonstrations and information display such as graph plotting, etc). They concluded from their study that: (1) computer aided teaching would be successfully adopted by a substantial number of teachers if the necessary resources were made available; and (2) the computer provided a versatile teaching aid which could be used to good effect in a number of quite different ways. The above results support our own views, namely, that this approach (the group approach) to CAL should not be underestimated as a teaching tool. Indeed, in situations where there are limited resources available it can prove to be extremely effective. Furthermore, even where individualised CAL can be used, there will usually be very many instances arising where the group teaching approach is more beneficial. Obviously, there is much research to be done in this area. Hopefully, through detailed studies (of the type described above) we will be able to formulate many new applications and teaching strategies for using this mode of CAL.

(b)   Is Computer Education Important?
Yes and No.
Obviously, the answer to this question depends upon the context in which it is posed. Basically, there are two possibilities depending upon whether reference is being made to teachers or students.

In the first case, if it is the primary intention of the teacher/instructor to use the computer purely as an instructional resource, then a minimal degree of computer education is required. Provided pre-packaged courseware is used, the only requirement on the part of a teacher is (1) a general understanding of the computer, and (2) knowledge of the practical procedures and details relating to the operation of the teaching system. Both of these aspects of computer education may be very quickly assimilated.

The other possibility, involving computer education for students, again generates two situations. First, students who are studying computer related subjects (computer specialists); second, those who are pursuing some other course of study. In the latter case, the opinion has often been voiced that such students should participate in computer awareness and appreciation courses, as part of their general education. Consequently, many institutions at both the secondary and tertiary levels of education have made considerable movement towards the provision of facilities for making this option available for those students who are interested.

The context in which we feel that computer education is most important is that of providing a trained workforce for the data processing and computer based professions. Of course, we naturally feel that CAL has much to contribute here. In the past, teachers of computer related subjects have been slow to realise the usefulness of the computer itself as a teaching medium. However, the situation is changing both at the secondary and tertiary levels of education; an increasing number of teachers are now beginning to realise the importance of and need for the use of CAL techniques. Indeed, CAL methods are now being used in a number of areas – for example: (1) programming (through drill and practice, tutorial systems, expert system usage, and simulation methods); and (2) the teaching of both elementary and more advanced hardware concepts through the use of simulation and aiding systems. Typical examples of some of the many interesting projects in this area include (1) that of Williams et al. (1983) involving the use of a simulator for teaching the internal workings of an assembler; (2) Balman's (1981) work on the computer assisted teaching of FORTRAN; (3) the computer assisted instruction system for digital engineering education developed by Bonnema and Dunworth (1978); and (4) the use of intelligent video for the provision of courses in electronics, as outlined by Wood et al. (1980). From the diverse range of projects listed here, it is easy to see that CAL has much to offer those whose interest lies in the provision of computer education for students who specialise in this field. Simulation, of course, is a particularly important topic because, in an age of rapid technological change, it offers a relatively inexpensive method for educational establishments to keep abreast with new developments without the need for substantial financial outlay.

(c) What Subjects can CAL be Applied to?
Virtually any subject.
We do not claim that CAL can be used to teach all aspects of all subject disciplines. However, within the majority of most curriculum subjects (at both basic and advanced levels) there will undoubtedly be certain parts that could adequately be taught by computer. In contrast to this, it is important to realise that certain sections of particular courses may be totally unsuitable for computerisation. Therefore, the decision of what to teach by computer and what should be taught by conventional methods is one which should always be made

by the specialist teacher, instructor or course developer.

At the university level, mathematical and science based subjects (such as physics, chemistry and medicine) were undoubtedly the first to use CAL approaches to teaching. In hot pursuit followed the engineering disciplines (electrical, mechanical, civil, etc). Currently, the use of CAL is rapidly expanding into many other areas including music (Benwood, 1984), zoology (Leiblum et al., 1984), linguistic analysis (Marshall, 1983), literary appreciation, French (Ariew, 1979), economics (Paden and Barr, 1980) and msny more (Maddison, 1982). The expansion of CAL into new subject areas within universities is likely to continue well into the future as new developments in hardware and software technology make easy the solution of what were intractable problems within many subject domains, such as character display in subjects such as Greek, Russian, Arabic and Chinese.

As was the case in university sites, the mathematics and science courses in schools were also the first to employ CAL techniques. Their use is also now spreading to other subject areas such as English (Candy and Edmunds, 1982), history, geography, music and art (Dawkins, 1980). At the lower end of the school system (primary education) the computer is now being used extensively to aid the teaching of many elementary subjects and for supporting basic skill acquisition in a number of areas – predominantly, reading, spelling, writing and early maths concepts.

At all levels within schools, colleges and universities there are three areas where CAL technology can offer substantial help: (1) the teaching of subjects that are declining because of a shortage of specialist teachers; (2) the provision of courses for minority groups which for financial reasons would otherwise not be provided; and (3) the integration of handicapped/ disabled students into conventional classroom situations. The first two of these are fairly obvious applications of CAL. However, the third is less easy to comprehend and so we discuss this topic in more detail in section 6.3.4.

(d)   Will Educational Institutions Change their Character?
It is unlikely.
Obviously, it is difficult to anticipate what influence (if any) computer technology (and hence, CAL/CAI) is going to have on the future of our educational institutions. Two major developments which might effect what they do and how they operate are (1) the extensive use of distance learning (or open learning systems); and (2) the widespread availability of portable, computer based learning terminals similar to the Dynabook described in section 5.3.2(a). Together, these resources could provide the facilities needed to enable students to learn in their own home environments thereby removing the need for them to participate in group teaching methods at conventional centres of education. Thus, in the long term we may see a movement towards the type of education provided by the United Kingdom's Open University,

particularly in higher education. However, it is less likely that such
an approach could be used at the primary and secondary levels where
there is a greater need for social interaction with a teacher and
other students.

In the immediate future (5-10 years) it is very unlikely that any
substantial changes will take place within our institutions of
learning as a result of computers. Those that do take place will be of
a very minor nature. We list below a few of the possibilities:

(1) considerable reduction in the time needed to complete courses;
(2) greater use of CAL, and hence, increased individualisation
    of instruction;
(3) a wider range of modular computer based courses;
(4) computer counselling of students with respect to correlating
    career requirements with course options;
(5) easier access to electronic data banks; via personalcomputers
    and communication networks; and
(6) a change in the role of the teacher – a shift in emphasis
    from subject expert towards a director of studies.

Educational establishments are extremely conservative in their
outlook. Thus, if they occur at all, these changes will only take
place very slowly.

(e) Will CAL be Cost Effective?
It depends.
This is a difficult question to answer since the overall cost of
setting up a CAL system will depend upon what particular organisations
are attempting to do. For example, in a teaching situation that might
involve potential damage to expensive equipment or injury to students,
the use of CAL simulation techniques could probably be easily cost
justified. On the other hand, attempting to use costly computing
equipment to perform relatively simple tasks (that could more easily
be taught using book material or a blackboard) is unlikely to prove
cost effective.

Several studies of CAL costing have been made (for example Fielden,
1974; 1975). However, as far as we are aware, no financial model for
estimating cost effectiveness · currently exists. Therefore, we would
suggest that the only way to answer this question is to consider each
situation in its own right. In doing this it is important (1) to use
the previous experience of other organisations as a basic guideline to
what is involved in costing; and (2) to remember the maxim – what is
expensive today may not necessarily be expensive tomorrow. This latter
point is very nicely illustrated in a paper by Edmunds (1980). He has
drawn up a comparison between the cost of a large IBM 650 computer
(1955 cost = $200,000) and a small (but more powerful) TI-59
calculator (1978 cost = $300). Dramatic performance and cost changes
similar to these must therefore be taken into consideration when

costing out CAL.

With respect to CAL cost effectiveness we look forward to the future optimistically. Indeed, we believe that the falling cost of hardware and software combined with the development of new teaching methods (such as student proctor systems, open terminal labs, resource sharing techniques, etc) is likely to make CAL more cost effective in the future than it has been in the past.

(f)   What about the Information Explosion?
There is no real need for concern.
In an earlier chapter of this book (see figure 1.6) we indicated that the volume of information and knowledge, at least that which is documented, appeared to grow at an exponential rate. However, we are not of the opinion that this is likely to cause any substantial problems for those involved in education, provided we are able to teach students how to:

  (1)   gain access to stored items of information;
  (2)   evaluate the worth of this information; and
  (3)   use it for solving the problems they face.

As more and more of the world's information is committed to electronic form, so it will become increasingly easier (disregarding political and financial factors) to gain access to it. This access is being achieved primarily through global communication systems similar to that depicted in figure 1.13. Used in conjunction with systems of this sort, CAL technology will undoubtedly provide an extremely useful tool for aiding the human knowledge assimilation processes associated with the rapid development of new knowledge within all areas of human endeavour.

(g)   How Desirable is the Extensive Use of CAL?
It is not.
Educational systems provide the mechanisms by which knowledge is passed from one generation to another. For better or for worse, modern society has become extremely dependent upon technology. We depend upon the motor car for travel and transport; and the radio, TV and video for much of our entertainment. Are we then likely to become dependent upon the computer for our education? Is such a situation feasible – or even desirable? We believe it could well be feasible but it is certainly not desirable.

Much of education is a 'social thing'. That is, it involves bringing people together and attempting to get them to communicate and cooperate with each other. Hopefully, by using their combined effort and resources they will successfully solve problems that they feel are either (1) worth solving for their own self–esteem or profit; or (2) of value and benefit to society as a whole. Social interaction is therefore a very important aspect of education. Will computers advance

or   destroy this type of interaction between people, perhaps replacing
it by artifical images, sounds and communication   dialogues?   We   hope
not.   Indeed, we think that it is highly unlikely – during 1984 or any
subsequent year – that computers will 'take   over'   education   through
the medium of CAL.

From   the answers to the questions that we have posed we conclude this
section   by   suggesting   that,   within   our   schools,   colleges   and
universities,   CAL   will have an indespensible (but not over–powering)
role to play. The immediate problems for   the   future   are   associated
with   ensuring   that   this   role   is   appropriately   and   adequately
fulfilled.

6.3.3   CAL in the Workplace

CAL and CBT techniques are gaining rapid and wide acceptance in many
areas   of   industry,   business   and commerce. They are also being used
quite extensively in the armed forces and   within   the   professions   –
particularly,   those   involving   engineering,   design   and   medicine.
Because their use is becoming so widespread, it is impossible   for   us
to   cover each of the above areas in any great depth. Consequently, in
this section we adopt the same strategy of presentation as we   did   in
the   previous one. That is, we pose a number of questions that we feel
are of some relevance to those who are contemplating   introducing   CAL
within   the   organisations   to   which   they belong; we then attempt to
answer these questions on the basis of the information we have   gained
as a consequence of our research experience in this area.

(a)   In What General Ways can Organisations use CAL/CBT?

Obviously, the way in which these methods are likely to be used within
any   particular   organisation   will depend upon (1) the basic function
that the organisation fulfils (for   example,   whether   it   provides   a
sales,   a   service   or   a   manufacturing   facility); (2) its aims and
objectives; (3) its internal structure; and (4) the types of (internal
and external) personnel with which it deals. In the latter context   it
is   important   to   realise   that   CAL/CBT can be used for both (1) the
training of the organisation's workforce, and (2) for the   development
and   reinforcement   of those relationships that must exist between the
organisation and the external population with which it   interacts   and
serves.

Typical   external functions for which CAL is suitable include customer
education, sales promotion, company publicity, and so on. For internal
training the computer can be employed at any of   four   broad   levels.
These   cover   its   use   with (1) supervisory, management and executive
personnel; (2) administrative and office staff; (3) employees involved
in sales promotion and publicity; and (4) technical staff.   Two   basic
types   of CBT technique will probably be required in order to meet the
training   requirements   of   these   four   classes   of   personnel:
gaming/simulation   methods   and   facilities   for   technical   skills
training. The first of these is likely   to   involve   the   use   of   the

computer to generate management games and situation scenarios in which staff have to act out a particular role, thereby providing them with an opportunity of obtaining valuable experience which will enable them to act in the most appropriate way when confronted with a similar real-life situation. The second type of training involves using the computer to train employees in particular types of skill such as machine operation, safety procedures, component assembly, machine servicing, fault finding, and so on.

In addition to the foregoing instructional uses, the computer can also be used in a variety of other applications such as (1) maintaining training records (both CAL and non-CAL) for each employee; (2) providing performance certification testing; (3) recording employee survey or questionnaire answers; and (4) testing to identify the general training needs of a given group in order to help the training organisation identify what new training must be developed.

Notice that it is important to realise that a decision to adopt CAL does not mean that existing training materials have to be discarded or even revised in any drastic way. Instead, CAL may be regarded as just another training medium to be combined with other media as appropriate.

(b)   What are the Training Problems of Industry and Commerce?
Many industries are facing a rapidly rising demand for staff training facilities. This situation arises as a result of a number of factors:

(1) the 'perishability' of information due to rapidly
    changing technologies;
(2) the lack of relevantly qualified new employees with the
    necessary skills entering the employment sector from the
    educational system;
(3) the introduction of new information processing technologies
    into an organisation often requires the development of new
    methods and procedures; staff will therefore require
    familiarisation and training in order to become acquainted
    with the new facilities;
(4) the introduction of new types of product (based upon advances
    in microelectronic and communication technologies) requires
    a significant amount of employee retraining if these products
    are to be used effectively.

Although CAL has been in use in the educational sector for some time, there are some major differences between education and training needs. Organisations in commerce and industry often have a wide geographical distribution of trainees, high turnover rates (particularly of female staff), they need to employ large numbers of part-time staff and have fragmented recruitment. Consequently, many of the problems associated with training in commercial and industrial organisations include the need to:

(1) provide comprehensive training for new staff;
(2) offer refresher training for existing staff;
(3) minimise the time an employee spends away from the job (or from home) while being trained;
(4) supply only that training which is relevant to an employee's needs and to make this available when it is required;
(5) prevent time being wasted while a student waits for a training course to be scheduled (due to fragmented recruitment); and
(6) reduce the costs associated with training arising from travel, subsistence and the cost of publishing training materials.

Increasingly, many organisations are attempting to overcome the above problems by integrating CAL techniques into their existing training programmes.

(c) What Factors are Likely to Influence the Decision to Use CAL?
The greatest potential for the use of the computer in training is its contribution to increasing the productivity of people. One of the characteristics that distinguishes training from education is the fact that training establishments are more concerned with cost-effectiveness. Thus, a major factor which influences a decision to use CAL has to do with benefits which can be quantified financially. Organisations that are involved in using CAL are also finding that cost savings, while important, are not the only benefits that can be obtained. Various other qualitative benefits (such as improved performance and standardisation of procedures) have also been attributed to CAL. A number of factors have influenced decisions to involve computers in commercial and industrial training programmes. These will be described under the following headings:

(A) financial benefits;
(B) improvements in the quality of training; and
(C) the relationship between costs and benefits.

(A) Financial Benefits
CAL tends to reduce the use of resources whose costs are increasing (for example, expenditure on those providing instruction). At the same time it tends to increase the use of computing facilities – whose costs are declining. This relationship can therefore often be used to justify a decision to use CAL. Some of the other ways in which financial benefits of CAL may be realised are discussed in paragraphs A1 through A3 below.

(A1) Use of Existing Computing Facilities at Marginal Cost
A dominant reason for adopting CAL (given by two large UK banking groups – Midland and Barclays) was a thoroughly pragmatic one, the computers were already available. These large organisations had been using computers for many years. They had spread terminal networks across geographically dispersed branches (both in the UK and worldwide) and saw the opportunity to exploit unused computing

capacity at marginal cost. For the same reason a large airline (British Airways) and a leading retail distribution organisation (Tesco) pioneered computer based training in the UK.

(A2)   Reduced Costs of Residential Training
Large organisations similar to those described above (with widely dispersed companies and branches) have achieved significant reductions in the costs of residential training. Using CAL with telecommunication links allows training to be taken to the trainee 'on the job'. This saves travelling and hotel accommodation costs for certain types of training. The need for residential and centralised training cannot be entirely eliminated by CAL. There are social objectives in some kinds of training (for example, social skills training) which cannot always satisfactorily be met using computers.

(A3)   Cost of Live Instruction
There are many ways in which the costs of live instruction could be reduced by using CAL. For example, it could be employed: (1) to reduce course length; and (2) to avoid the need to duplicate live training courses. Companies are often required to duplicate live courses as a consequence of fragmented recruitment; the high costs associated with this could easily be reduced by adopting CAL methods. Indeed, companies using CAL have reduced costs by not having unproductive trainees waiting until there are sufficient of them to start a traditional class. Nowadays there is undoubtedly a commercial incentive to reduce the labour costs of training by investment in computers. Consequently, many of the organisations who are currently using CAL view it as a form of capital investment.

(B)   Improved Performance
It is often very difficult to evaluate claims that CAL has improved training performance, mainly because very few of the organisations that are involved in CAL invest very much in controlled evaluation. However, a number of companies do report that they have observed error reduction, better on-the-job performance and a more standardised performance of staff. Two of the more important benefits of CAL (standardisation and individualisation) are discussed in B1 and B2 below.

(B1)   Standardisation
The use of CAL in geographically distributed companies has helped to bring about greater standardisation in training, documentation and procedural techniques. In areas such as banking and insurance, standard procedures often need to be rigorously applied in all branch offices throughout the organisation. Similarly, the area of emergency skills training is one in which rigorous standards need to be applied. In situations where complex tasks need to be performed, the human instructor is often unable to retain the sequence of detailed instructions in his/her head and CAL is often able to help in situations like these.

(B2)   Individualisation

Benefits other than financial ones are derived from the individual approach to instruction that CAL provides. Thus, trainees can absorb material at their own pace and in their own time (thus avoiding the constraints imposed by rigid class schedules). Furthermore, many employees involved in retraining (particularly, the more mature ones) are usually unwilling to make errors in public. Consequently, many do not participate fully in formal classroom tuition. CAL offers facilities to overcome these problems.

(C)   Cost/Benefit Relationships

In general, a CAL course may cost more to develop than a similar course based upon some other medium. It is impossible to generalise on development times for CAL courses. However, it is important to realise that the development cost is only expended once. Organisations using CAL claim savings of instructor time (for preparation and presentation) and reduced study time (for assimilation). They believe these advantages significantly affect the development costs. Because CAL frees instructors to work on new course development, more training can be provided from the same group of resources. Two major considerations with respect to cost/benefit relationships are discussed below in paragraphs C1 and C2.

(C1)   Training Equipment Costs

Much of commercial and industrial training concerns the learning of skills on specific types of equipment. The costs of this equipment are often a significant item in the training budget. Computer simulations can reduce the requirement for training equipment and can also increase the amount of available practice time. Examples of simulation case studies have been presented earlier in this book. Simulations involving the use of computer terminals have the advantage of being inherently more flexible. Thus, if there are changes in the equipment specification, these can easily be accommodated by changes in the computer software.

(C2)   Updating Training Materials

The increasing speed of technological change makes the costs of updating training materials formidable. Changes in technology will obviously bring changes in products, systems and procedures. Through the use of CAL techniques it becomes much easier for organisations to accommodate any necessary updating of training material. Indeed, many banking organisations within the UK have reported both faster and cheaper updating of their training procedures as a consequence of using computer assisted learning methods.

From the material that we have presented in this section it is easy to see that there are many benefits (not necessarily all financial) that can be realised as a result of involvement with CAL. Undoubtedly, these are likely to influence (in a positive way) an organisation's decision to utilise CAL methods for their training requirements.

(d)   What Improvements in Quality of Training might be Expected?
Cost savings, actual or potential, are a major but not the sole reason
for the decision of many organisations to use CAL. In addition to cost
factors a number of other important reasons for adopting CAL have
emerged. Qualitative benefits relating to the quality of training   are
often described in terms of

   (1)   relevance to training task;
   (2)   improved performance;
   (3)   standardisation and control of quality; and
   (4)   individualisation of instruction.

Each of (2), (3) and (4) have been described previously in section (B)
of   the   answer to the last question. It therefore only remains for us
to discuss item (i).   Many   commercial   applications   of   CAL   in   the
airline, travel, retail and banking industries (for example) are based
upon   the   need   to train large numbers of operators and clerks to use
their organisation's computer system. A summary of the types of   staff
using   CAL   is   given   in   figure   6.8.   During their training period,
operators become familiar with and adjust to the technology with which
they are working. This familiarity has been found to reduce   hostility
towards   computerisation   and,   of course, is directly relevant to the
ultimate job that the trainee will eventually perform.

Mode	CAL contribution	Examples
Problem solving	Presentation of problem situations requiring the trainee to make a series of decisions to solve a problem	Fault finding Management training Critical path analysis Management games
Apparatus simulation	Training in keyboard skills Simulation of equipment	Typing Flight simulation Radar operation Safety equipment
Business system simulation	Drill and practice on large scale business systems files and procedures	Credit card accounts Airline reservation systems Banking procedures TV rental accounts
Process modelling	Method of operation is demonstrated and the effects of changing variables are observed	Cargo pumping & loading Control systems theory, operation & maintenance All diagnostic and operating situations

Figure 6.8   Summary of computer based training applications.

(e)   What CAL Technologies are likely to be used?

Two basic media will probably be extensively used in order to implement CAL in the workplace: the computer itself (using either a micro or a terminal attached to a larger machine) and interactive video. We have previously discussed the many ways in which computers can be used to implement training processes. Obviously, when the facilities provided by a computer are combined with those of a video disc system the resultant combination can be used to produce very effective computer based training systems.

Video disc technology is currently being employed for a number of applications within the workplace: product demonstrations; low budget commercial advertising of toys, games and records; presentation of company profiles, products, processes and services; and for product launches and exhibitions. However, as can be seen from the survey data presented in figure 6.9, education and training applications of the video disc easily outrank other uses (Pioneer Video, 1983).

Type	Number [*]	Rank
Training and education	86	1
Exhibits	22	2
Simulations	21	3
Communications	20	4
Archival	14	5
Marketing	13	6
Point-of-purchase	10	7

[*] Actual application counts from a random sampling of completed video discs as of January 1982

Figure 6.9   Survey of types of interactive video disc application.
(Courtesy of Pioneer Video.)

At various points in this book we have described some possible ways in which this type of instruction could be used. As more experience is gained with this technology, so many new modes of using it become apparent. Some of these different modes have been described by Siegal, Schubin and Merrill (1980) and are summarised in figure 6.10. In this figure the ways of using interactive video have been classified according to the type of presentation involved, audience requirements, structure and method of control.

At present, the video disc is primarily still a read—only medium. However, in the immediate future the availability of a 'write—once' disc recording system now seems to be a practical reality. Naturally, this would make the optical disc a much more attractive medium for instruction than it is at the moment. This type of capability would probably mean that establishments wishing to use this medium for

teaching could now record instructional material onto their discs
themselves – thereby removing the need to be dependent upon external
organisations for this service. Authoring of courseware for
instructional applications of interactive video would, therefore, be
much easier than it is at present.

By type of presentation

- individual self-study (guided)
- group presentation tool (group driven)
- group presentation tool (presenter driven)
- point of sale presentations
- point of purchase presentations
- individual research (archival)

By audience

- dual audiences with all or some equivalent visuals, but
  different narration
- branching to accommodate the needs of varying audiences

By structure

- directed, controlled branching archival research, unstructured
  'browsing' mode
- archival research with programmed cross referencing
- still and motion visuals to support CAI

Player driven or processor driven

- all interaction via the video disc player's keypad
- all interaction via an interactive terminal
- mixed control where the processor manages the instruction
  and the viewer uses the video disc player to complement other
  training materials

Figure 6.10   Modes of using interactive video.

In the longer term we see developments in interactive video proceeding
in such a way as to facilitate two vital requirements: (1) the need to
incorporate expert systems technology (see section 6.2.3), and (2) a
movement towards the use of the optical disc as a single unifying
medium for the storage of courseware. Fulfilment of each of these
requirements will be a necessary pre–condition for the production of a
wide variety of instructional products that are based upon the concept
of intelligent interactive video.

(f)   How do Industrial Organisations get going?
Broadly speaking, industrial and commercial organisations can get into
computer–based training at three different levels. At the lowest level
an organisation could purchase the hardware and ready–made
instructional software produced by a company that specialises in the
production of training material. At the second level, a company might
opt for developing its own courseware in–house. Unless such firms

already have their own instructors who are fully conversant with appropriate development methods, this could prove difficult. In situations where companies have instructors available, the use of an authoring facility or courseware generator may be useful, these enable instructors to input their own material without the need for any previous experience of computer coding techniques. The third level of involvement is that in which an organisation buys in the hardware they require and then hires courseware development consultants to work alongside their own staff in order to develop the required training materials. Each of these three approaches can provide a useful entry method into CBT.

More and more companies are beginning to investigate the use of CAL and CBT for use within their training and retraining schemes. In some cases the involvement is only partial, being used alongside conventional training materials (Shaw et al., 1984) or for the management of training. Undoubtedly, as organisations begin to realise the utility of this training medium, so they are likely to increase their involvement with it.

6.3.4   CAL for the Handicapped and Disabled

The average student has many aids to learning. Examples of these include graphically illustrated books; charts; pictures; games; educational TV; radio; CAL and CBT; and conventional classroom contact with teachers and other students. Unfortunately, because of some physical or mental abnormality, handicapped and disabled students cannot easily make use of the same types of learning resource that 'normal' students are able to employ. This means that either (1) special types of learning resource have to be devised for the handicapped/disabled learner, and/or (2) purpose built interfaces need to be developed to enable them to utilise the same types of resource that are used by other students. Many examples of each of these approaches will be found documented in the literature (Byte, 1982c; Rush, 1982; IEEE, 1980; Schofield, 1981; IEEE, 1981).

Naturally, development work in this area is usually very difficult because of (1) the (often) unique nature of most forms of mental/physical disability; (2) the additional limitations and restrictions that these are likely to impose on conventional communication and learning processes; and (3) the high expense associated with research and development work in this area. Despite these factors, a considerable amount of research into learning aids for the handicapped/disabled has been performed, especially with microcomputer based equipment. When they first became available, it was expected that inexpensive microprocessors and microcomputers (through CAL and CAI techniques) would help alleviate some of the problems in this area. To a large extent this expectation has certainly been realised. However, a significant volume of work still remains to be done. Unfortunately, the amount of space we are able to devote to this topic, of necessity, must be limited. Consequently, our

ICAL-L*

objectives in this section are twofold. First, to give an indication
of how CAL, CAI and CBT can help those with special needs. Second, to
provide an outline of some of the many projects that have made useful
contributions in this field.

Because CAL and CAI are concerned with both communication and the
development of learning processes, this technology is able to help
handicapped and disabled students in two general ways. Thus, it is
possible for CAL techniques to be used (1) to augment deficient or
malfunctioning channels of communication or, if necessary, provide new
ones where none previously existed; and (2) to provide the fundamental
instructional strategies necessary to develop special learning aids.
Within these two areas many different types of microelectronic aid
(both hardware and software based) have been developed for use by
handicapped/disabled people. Any attempt at compiling an exhaustive
list would be impossible. The examples presented in figure 6.11 are
intended to provide only an indication of some of the many different
possibilities that exist.

Fairly general and very useful introductions to the practical
application of microcomputers to aid the handicapped have been given
by both Vanderheiden (1981) and Goldenberg (1984). Readers who are
particularly interested in this area should find these sources most
useful. Descriptions of one or two more specialised projects designed
to investigate CAL applications for the disabled have been given
earlier in this book. For example, the use of LOGO systems for
studying the communication problems of the disabled was briefly
described in section 5.2.8. This language continues to be of
substantial interest and value to those involved in research in this
area (Weir et al., 1982). Obviously, it is not possible to discuss
each of the above types of system in detail. Consequently, a few
representative examples of projects have been selected in order to
illustrate the basic principles involved in providing microcomputer
based support for CAL with disabled students. The examples that we
have chosen include Handi-Writer; Minspeak; MAVIS; and some systems
that employ speech synthesis techniques.

The Handi-Writer system (Batie, 1981) represents a simple and cost
effective approach to the provision of a communication aid for
students having certain types of physical handicap. It is based upon
the use of a standard personal computer system to which is interfaced
a special five-button control pad. The latter is responsible for
providing four cursor control commands and a print facility. The
support software for the system displays a special menu on a video
display screen. This contains predefined words, letters of the
alphabet, the decimal digits and certain command words that are used
to control the status of a workspace. This workspace is used to enable
the student to build up single words and sentences by means of
character/word selection from the display menu. These are selected by
means of a flashing cursor whose position is controlled by the

(A)   **General communication aids**

the Abilityphone *(Rush, 1982)*
the TIC Scanning Communicator *(Thomas, 1981)*
the Possum *(Schofield, 1981)*
the MAVIS system *(Schofield, 1981; Adams, 1982)*

(B)   **Speech aids**

use of pre-recorded speech: the MicroTalker *(Adams, 1982)*
use of voice synthesis equipment *(Vincent, 1982; Law et al., 1984)*
speech display systems such as VISISPEECH *(Jessop Acoustics, 1983)*
VOCAID: Texas Instruments *(Adams, 1983)*

(C)   **Reading aids**

the Kurzweil (text to speech) reading machine *(Adams, 1982)*
text enlargement — Viewscan *(Adams, 1983)*
the Optacon reading machine *(Schofield, 1981)*
speaking calculators for the blind *(Mokhoff, 1982)*

(D)   **Writing aids**

Handiwriter: a video notepad *(Batie, 1981)*
custom built typewriters
word processing systems

(E)   **Hearing aids**

teletext subtitling techniques *(Schofield, 1981)*
voice to text transcription
speech display systems

(F)   **Special purpose keyboards**

the concept keyboard *(Adams, 1983)*
pressure pad systems
the Microwriter *(Wheeler, 1980)*

(G)   **Robotic aids**

microprocessor controlled artificial limbs
computer controlled robotic arms *(Schneider et al., 1981)*

(H)   **Learning aids based on toys**

acrobatic dolls
electronic sirens and music generators *(Adams, 1983)*

(I)   **Various tactile communication devices**

brailink *(Adams, 1983)*
Optacon reading machine *(Schofield, 1981)*

(J)   **Special types of display**

flashing lights and attention getters
dynamic menu systems and moving/flashing cursors

(K)   **Specially designed communication prosthetics**

for example, the Minspeak system *(Baker, 1982)*

(L)   **Software packages of different types**

special menu selection systems
word processing packages
programming systems such as LOGO *(Weir et al., 1982)*
software based play aids
games software for the disabled *(Truxel, 1982)*

Figure 6.11   Examples of aids for the handicapped and disabled.

specially designed function keypad. As words and sentences are
constructed they are displayed on the lower half of the video display.
Although this system was not specifically designed for CAL
applications it would be extremely easy to adapt it for this purpose.

The Minspeak system is an example of a new language prosthesis
designed for people who cannot express themselves through speech or
handsigns (Baker, 1982). It consists of a specially designed keyboard,
a microcomputer and a voice synthesiser that is driven by
sentences/part-sentences that are contained within an EPROM store. A
student using a Minspeak keyboard having fewer than 50 keys can
produce many thousands of clear spoken sentences by using less than
seven key-strokes. Most keys on the keyboard are multi-purpose; each
one usually contains an image, a number, a letter of the alphabet and
a word or name. Some examples of typical keys are illustrated in
figure 6.12. The coding system used within the Minspeak system uses
sequences to define context. The easily understandable symbols on each
key represent ideas. The meaning of each key image changes according
to the sequence in which it is struck. By combining these symbols,
whole spoken sentences can be generated. The simplicity or complexity
of the symbols used on the board depends upon the individual needs and
abilities of its user. As was the case with the Handi-Writer system,
Minspeak could easily be converted for use in a CAL/CBT environment.

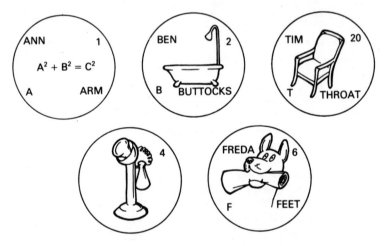

Figure 6.12   Examples of Minspeak concept keys.
(Courtesy of Byte magazine.)

The MAVIS system is an example of an aid for the handicapped that was
developed in the United Kingdom. It was researched and produced by a
man-machine interaction group working at the National Physical
Laboratory under the direction of Chris Evans (Schofield, 1981;
Howlett et al., 1981). MAVIS is an acronym for Microelectronic Audio

Visual Information System. It was designed specifically for use by severely disabled people. Contained within a suitcase, it is portable; it uses an ordinary colour TV for display, allows the attachment of an optional printer and provides several interface facilities to allow for the inter-connection of other devices. The system is illustrated schematically in figure 6.13. In designing the system it was assumed that many users would be unable to type. Hence, although a typewriter keyboard may be attached to the equipment (for those who are able to use it), a wide variety of other interaction aids may also be used. A range of games and other software exist to enable this system to be used both as a general aid for the disabled and as a medium for CAL. Results of the evaluative studies of this system for use in education are discussed by Schofield (1981).

THE MAVIS SYSTEM

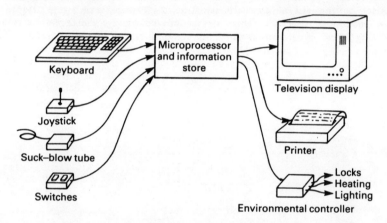

Figure 6.13   The MAVIS system for the handicapped.
(Courtesy of Heyden, London.)

Because of its decreasing cost, speech synthesis equipment (see section 4.2.4) is now becoming more commonly available, and so, is being used increasingly within microcomputer based aids for the handicapped/disabled. In view of the importance of this approach, before concluding this section we will briefly outline two CAL projects that employ this technique. The first is based at the University of Regina in Canada (Law et al., 1984); the second is located at the Open University in the United Kingdom (Vincent, 1982).

The Canadian project was launched in order to develop a CAL system for visually handicapped university students. The initial intention of the project was to devise a simple audio tool to support students taking BASIC programming assignments (see section 2.3.1) in an introductory computer science course. Subsequent extensions to this project have

enabled it to provide a convenient text processing system that allows
a blind student to create, edit and print out formatted material. The
way in which the system operates is illustrated in figure 6.14.
Essentially, as the student types in BASIC statements the voice
synthesiser unit (Votrax) 'speaks' them so that they can be checked
for correctness and, if necessary, corrected. Another extremely useful
aid associated with this project was a special device that enabled
program flowcharts to be represented in Braille. An example of a
Brailled flowchart is presented in figure 6.15. Within computer
science education, flowcharting is extensively taught as a standard
program development aid. This technique is often used as an important
stepping stone between problem analysis and program formulation. The
lack of such a facility can therefore severely inhibit the progress
made by blind persons who are learning to program. In order to
overcome this difficulty, Law et al. (1984) devised a special Braille
flowcharting process. This was based upon the use of a standard
Brailler having just a few cells per line. As can be seen from figure
6.15 the output from this device proved quite an effective way of
allowing blind programmers to construct and read flowcharts.

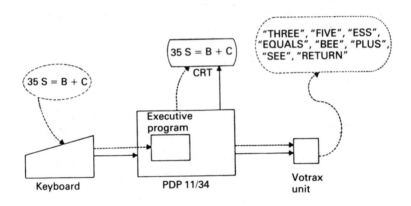

Figure 6.14   Audio support for program entry by blind students.
(Courtesy of Pergamon Press.)

The Open University's (UK) project (Vincent, 1982) involving
inexpensive voice synthesis equipment is in some ways similar to that
of the Canadian group described above. It commenced in 1979 and was
initially concerned with providing Open University blind
undergraduates with access to computing facilities. The project
started with CAL, progressed to programming in BASIC and now also
includes word-processing, information storage and retrieval. The
'talking word-processor' (based on the BBC microcomputer) is being
used for correspondence and essay writing. Another Open University

project that has just started involves the evaluation of new technological developments for disabled students in distance learning: viewdata and visual telephones for deaf students; Braille terminals for blind students; and the Microwriter for physically handicapped students.

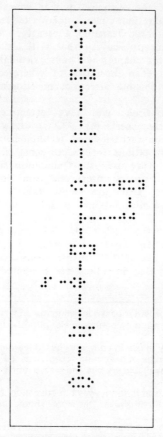

Figure 6.15   A Brailled flowchart (Law et al., 1984).
(Courtesy of Pergamon Press.)

From what we have written above it is easy to see that there is much ongoing activity with respect to the development of CAL aids for the disabled. Bearing in mind the amount of space that has been made available for this topic, attempting to do justice to the significant volume of work that has been done in this area would have been an impossible task. We hope, through the examples that we have provided, that the interested reader is motivated to delve more deeply into this subject by consulting some of the specialist in-depth material that is available (Schofield, 1981; IEEE, 1981; Adams, 1982; 1983).

6.4   CONCLUSION

Today, computers play an important role in society. They influence, quite significantly, all aspects of modern living; they are used in planning, in controlling, in manufacturing and, of course, in education. Applications of the computer within education are likely to include general administration, management of learning and various approaches to computer assisted learning. Presently, within the CAL domain there is much fervent activity that will considerably shape and mould its future. In this chapter we have tried (1) to describe some of this activity, (2) to give an indication of where this is taking place, and (3) to hint at possible directions of future progress.

Generally, within this book we have attempted to emphasise three important and fundamental aspects of CAL: courseware production and authoring tools; multimedia facilities and techniques; and the utility of special purpose workstations for use in some of the more advanced applications of CAL. We have used the foundation formed by this three-centred framework as a basis for interpreting and describing some of the many developments that are now taking place in educational computing – both in academic and non-academic environments.

In his keynote address to the UK's CAL '83 conference, Alfred Bork (University of Irvine, California) made several basic assertions about the present status of computers within education (Bork, 1984). The eight fundamental points that he raised are presented in figure 6.16.

> (1) Extremely little good computer based learning material is available in any country. Much of the material, including commercially published material, is of very poor quality.
> (2) The standards currently in use in computer based learning material are extremely low and are in great danger of becoming accepted as *the* standards.
> (3) Many of the materials available are bits and pieces rather than coherent collections of learning material.
> (4) The computer can be used in many ways in education. Philosophical discussions should not rule out certain ways. Decisions should be made on pedagogical grounds.
> (5) The training of teachers is a major weakness in our current systems. Most of the present in-service ways of training teachers are entirely inadequate to the task.
> (6) In teaching programming at any level—primary school, secondary school or college or university—the major emphasis should be on teaching good modern programming structure.
> (7) It is very unlikely that good programming courses will be taught in BASIC. BASIC should be avoided at all costs.
> (8) Authoring languages are useless in generating effective computer based learning material.

Figure 6.16   A view of the current status of CAL (Bork, 1984).

We would agree with most of the points that he raised, particularly (1) through (5). Points (6) and (7) relate more specifically to the teaching of computer science, and so they are not directly relevant to the contents of this book. However, as teachers of computer related subjects, we would also agree with the intent of these assertions.

Much of the material that we have presented in earlier sections of this book is relevant to the eighth of Bork's assertions. In view of this, we find that we are unable to completely concur with his views on authoring languages, although there may be some truth in his (admittedly unsupported) claim. It is a fact that author languages are used quite widely; whether or not they do produce effective training materials is open to investigation. As far as we are aware, nobody has yet done the experiments necessary to support or refute this claim. This would indeed be a useful venture for the future.

6.5   BIBLIOGRAPHY

Adams, J., (editor), Learning to Cope – Computers in Special Education, EMAP, London, 1982.

Adams, J., (editor), Learning to Cope – Computers in Special Education, EMAP, London, 1983.

Allan, R., Three amazing micromice: hitherto undisclosed details, IEEE Spectrum, 15(11), 62–65, 1978.

Allison, D., On future fantasy games, Recreational Computing, 9(1), 27–29, 1980.

Ariew, R., A diagnostic test for students entering a computer assisted learning curriculum in French, Computers and Education, 3(4), 331–333, 1979.

Audio–Visual, Disc adds a soundtrack to still–frame images, Audio–Visual, 65, March 1984.

Bagrit, L., The Age of Automation, (The BBC Reith Lectures 1964), Weidenfeld and Nicolson, London, 1965.

Bailey, R.W., Human Performance Engineering – A Guide for Systems Designers, Prentice–Hall, Englewood Cliffs, NJ, 1982.

Baird, A.N. and Flavell, R., A project management game, Computers and Education, 5(1), 1–18, 1980.

Baker, B., Minspeak, Byte: The Small Systems Journal, 7(9), 186–202, 1982.

Ball, A.J.S., Bochmann, G.V. and Gecsei, J., Videotex networks, IEEE Computer, 13(12), 8–14, 1980.

Balman, T., Computer assisted teaching of Fortran, Computers and Education, 5(2), 111–123, 1981.

Barker, P.G., Computer networking, Wireless World, 88(1563), 74–78, 1982.

Barker, P.G., Chapter 12 – Computer networks and the future, in Computers in Analytical Chemistry, 420–453, Pergamon, Oxford, 1983.

Barker, P.G., The Many Faces of HMI, Working Paper, Interactive Systems Research Group, Department of Computer Science, Teesside Polytechnic, County Cleveland, 1984a.

Barker, P.G., Expert Systems for CAE Workstation Design, Working Paper, Interactive Systems Research Group, Department of Computer Science, Teesside Polytechnic, County Cleveland, 1984b.

Batie, H., Handi–writer – a video notepad for the physically handicapped, Byte: The Small Systems Journal, 6(12), 474–482, 1981.

Bell, G.H., Teacher research, microcomputers and primary education, Computers and Education, 6, 235–242, 1982.

Benwood, B.C., CAL in music designed for use with a companion text, Computers and Education, 8(1), 127–132, 1984.

Blandford, C., CAL software design for transferability, Computers and Education, 6, 165–174, 1982.

Bonnema, T.R.C. and Dunworth, A., A computer assisted instruction system for digital engineering education, Computers and Education, 2(4), 279–290, 1978.

Booth, K.S., Kochanek, D.H. and Wein, M., Computers animate films and video, IEEE Spectrum, 20(2) 44–51, 1983.

Bork, A., Physics in the Irvine Educational Technology Centre, Computers and Education, 4(1), 37–57, 1980.

Bork, A., Computers and the future: education, Computers and Education, 8(1), 1–4, 1984.

Bott, G.P. and Robertson, D., Northern Ontario Distance Education Project – Educational Utilisation of Telidon Delivered by Satellite, TV Ontario, Ontario, 1983.

Boutmy, E.J. and Danthine, A., TELEINFORMATICS '79, North Holland, Amsterdam, 1979.

Bramer, M.A., (editor), Computer Game–Playing: Theory and Practice, Ellis Horwood, Chichester, 1983.

Brown, J.S., Burton, R.R. and Bell, A.G., SOPHIE: a step towards a reactive learning environment, International Journal of Man–Machine Studies, 7, 675–696, 1975.

Brown, J.S., Burton, R.R. and de Kleer, J., Pedagogical, natural language and knowledge engineering techniques in SOPHIE I, II and III, in Intelligent Tutoring Systems, edited by D. Sleeman and J.S. Brown, 227–282, Academic Press, New York, NY, 1982.

Buchanan, B.G. and Duda, R.O., Principles of rule based expert systems, Advances in Computers, Volume 22, 163–216, 1983.

Bunderson, C.V., Chapter 4 – Courseware, in Computer–Based Instruction: A State–of–the–Art Assessment, edited by H.F. O'Neil, 91–125, Academic Press, New York, NY, 1981.

Byte, Computer Games, Special edition of Byte: The Small Systems Journal, 6(12), 1981.

Byte, Graphics, Special Issue of Byte: The Small Systems Journal, 7(11), 1982a.

Byte, Games, Special edition of Byte: The Small Systems Journal, 7(12), 1982b.

Byte, Computers and the Disabled, Special Edition of Byte: The Small Systems Journal, 7(9), 1982c.

Byte, Simulation, Special Edition of Byte: The Small Systems Journal, 9(3), 1984.

Candy, L. and Edmunds, E.A., A study of the use of the computer as an aid to English teaching, International Journal of Man–Machine Studies, 16, 333–339, 1982.

Carbonell, J.R., AI in CAI: an artificial intelligence approach to computer assisted instruction, IEEE Transactions on Man–Machine Systems, MMS–11(4), 191–202, 1970.

Clark, D.R., The technical foundations of computer image making, in Computers for Imagemaking, (Audio–visual Media for Education and Research, Volume 2), edited by D.R. Clark, 1–28, Pergamon, Oxford, 1981.

Computers and Education, Computer graphics in engineering education, special edition of Computers and Education, 5(4), 165–275, 1981.

Connell, S. and Galbraith, I.A., The Electronic Mail Handbook – A Revolution in Business Communications, Kogan–Page, London, 1982.

Coombs, M. and Alty, J., Expert systems: an alternative paradigm, International Journal of Man–Machine Studies, 20, 21–43, 1984.

Csuri, C.A., 3–D Computer animation, Advances in Computers, 16, 1–53, 1977.

Cullingford, G., Mawdesley, M.J. and Davies, P., Some experiences with computer based games in civil engineering teaching, Computers and Education, 3(7), 159–164, 1979.

Dawkins, C.H.H., Computers in the classroom, CALNEWS, (14), 5–6, 1980.

Demaid, A., Butcher, P.G. and Verrier, J., Understanding phase diagrams. An example of the integration of interactive graphics into a CAL authoring system, Computers and Education, 6(1), 133–140, 1981.

Edmunds, E.A., Where next in computer aided learning?, British Journal of Educational Technology, 11(2), 97–104, 1980.

Fedida, S. and Malik, R., The Viewdata Revolution, Halstead Press, New York, NY, 1979.

Ferrari, G. and Parenti, L., A teaching experience with the use of a computer: Fourier series, Computers and Education, 4(4), 275–286, 1980.

Fiddy, P. and Wharry, D., Micros in Early Education, Longman, London, 1983.

Fiddy, P. and Yam, L., Prestel and home education for young children, Computers and Education, 8(1), 209–212, 1984.

Fielden, J., The financial evaluation of computer assisted learning projects, International Journal of Mathematical Education in Science and Technology, 5(3), 625–630, 1974.

Fielden, J., An Approach to Measuring the Cost of Computer Assisted Learning, Technical Report No. 9, National Development Programme for Computer Assisted Learning, London, 1975.

Flock, E. and Silverman, J., SPOC – the chess master, Byte: The Small Systems Journal, 9(3), 288–294, 1984.

Forsythe, K. and Collins, V., British Columbia – Higher Education and the Integration of New Technology, OECD Case Study, Knowledge Network, Victoria, British Columbia, 1983.

Fox, D. and Waite, M., Computer animation with colour registers, Byte: The Small Systems Journal, 7(11), 194–214, 1982.

Frantz, G.A. and Wiggins, R.H., Design case history: Speak & Spell learns to talk, IEEE Computer, 19(2), 45–49, 1982.

Gable, A. and Page, C.V., The use of artificial intelligence techniques in computer assisted instruction: an overview, International Journal of Man–Machine Studies, 17(3), 259–282, 1980.

Gevarter, W.B., Expert systems: limited but powerful, IEEE Spectrum, 20(8), 39–45, 1983.

Goldenberg, E.P., Computers, Education and Special Needs, Addison–Wesley, Reading , MA, 1984.

Gould, L. and Finzer, W., A study of TRIP: a computer system for animating time–rate distance problems, Proceedings of the IFIP World Conference on Computers in Education (WCCE–81), Lausanne, North Holland, Amsterdam, 1981.

Grover, M.P. and Zimmers, E.W., CAD/CAM – Computer Aided Design and Manufacture, Prentice–Hall, Englewood Cliffs, NJ,, 1984.

Hackathorn, R.J., ANIMA–II: a 3–D colour animation system, Computer Graphics, 11(2), 54–64, 1977.

Haefner, K., The concept of an integrated system for information access and telecommunications (ISIT) and its impact on education in the 80's, in Information Processing 80, edited by S.H. Lavington, 973–978, North Holland, Amsterdam, 1980.

Harris, L.R., The advantages of natural language programming, in Designing for Human–Computer Communication, edited by M.E. Sime and M.J. Coombs, 73–85, Academic Press, New York, NY, 1983.

Hartnell, T., Gee, S.M. and James, M., Games BBC Computers Play, Addison Wesley, Reading, MA, 1983.

Hawkins, W.R. and Robinson, R.N., The development and use of an electronic keyboard for television subtitling by Palantype, International Journal of Man–Machine Studies, 11, 701–710, 1979.

Hawkridge, D., New Information Technology in Education, Croom Helm, London, 1983.

Hedger, J., Telesoftware – home computing via Teletext, Wireless World, 84(1515), 61–64, 1978.

Hiltz, S.R. and Turoff, M., The Network Nation – Human Communication via Computer, Addison–Wesley, Reading, MA, 1978.

Hoffman, E., Big Trak gets brains on board, Practical Robotics, 39–50, September/October, 1984.

Howlett, J.M., Evans, C.R., Bevan, N., Folkard, T.J. and Penn, R.F., MAVIS: A Microprocessor driven audio/visual information system for the handicapped, International Journal of Man–Machine Studies, 14, 29–37, 1981.

Holden, G., Chalk board's powerpad and Leonardo's library, Byte: The Small Systems Journal, 9(3), 268–272, 1984.

IEEE, Proceedings of the IEEE Computer Society Workshop on: The Application of Personal Computing to Aid the Handicapped, IEEE Publication No. 80CH1596-6, The APL Report, April 2nd–3rd, Laurel, Maryland, 1980.

IEEE, Computing and the Handicapped, special issue of IEEE Computer, 14(1), 1981.

IEEE, Various authors on knowledge representation, in IEEE Computer, 16(10), 1983.

International Journal of Man–Machine Studies, Intelligent CAI, special issue of International Journal of Man–Machine Studies, 11(1), 1–145, 1979.

Jackson, P.C., Introduction to Artificial Intelligence, Chapter 4, 117–167, Petrocelli, New York, NY, 1974.

James, M., The BBC Micro – An Expert Guide, Granada, London, 1983.

Jenkin, J.M., Some principles of screen design and software for their support, Computers and Education, 6, 25–31, Pergamon, 1982.

Jessop Acoustics, VISISPEECH, Jessop Acoustics, London, 1983.

Koffman, G.B. and Blount, S.G., Artificial intelligence and automatic programming in CAI, Artificial Intelligence Journal, 6, 215–234, 1975.

Law, A.G., Maguire, R.B., Sabo, D.F.G. and Shuparski, B.M., Computer voice support for visually handicapped students, Computers and Education, 8(1), 35–39, 1984.

Lee, H.M., The practice of conversation theory: understanding and encouraging innovation, in Proceedings of the Fourth Canadian Symposium on Instructional Technology, 538–541, National Research Council of Canada, Ottawa, 1983.

Leiblum, M.D., van Haarlem, R. and Huisman, W.H.T., Computer based learning in a university zoology course, Computers and Education, 8(1) 155–158, 1984.

Levoy, M., A colour animation system based on the multiplane technique, Computer Graphics, 11(2), 65–71, 1977.

Lusignan, S. and North, J.S., Computing in the Humanities, Proceedings of the Third International Conference on Computing in the Humaniti University of Waterloo, Ontario, 1977.

Maddison, J., Information Technology and Education – An Annotated Guide to Printed, Audio–Visual and Multimedia Resources, The C_r University Press, Milton Keynes, 1982.

Marshall, S., Computer aided instruction in the skills of linguistic analysis, Computers and Education, 7(1), 25–32, 1983.

Martin, J., Communications Satellite Systems, Prentice–Hall, Englewood Cliffs, NJ, 1978.

Martin, J.S., Teaching descriptive inorganic chemistry at first year university using high resolution graphics, in ADCIS '82 Conference Proceedings, 361, Association for the Development of Computer–Based Instructional Systems, Western Washington University, Bellingham, WA, 1982.

Mast, C. van der, A portable program to present courseware on microcomputers, Computers and Education, 6(1), 39–44 Pergamon, 1982.

Mathews, P., The 'Robot Programme' previewed, Your Robot, 1(3), 8–9, 1984.

McKenzie, J., Interactive computer graphics for undergraduate science teaching, Computers and Education, 2(1), 25–48, 1978.

Miastkowski, S., Microsoft flight simulator, Byte: The Small Systems Journal, 9(3), 224–232, 1984.

Michie, D., On Machine Intelligence, Edinburgh University Press, Edinburgh, 1974.

Michie, D., (editor), Expert Systems in the Micro Electronic Age, Edinburgh University Press, Edinburgh, 1979.

Michie, D., Expert Systems, The Computer Journal, 23(4), 369–376, 1980.

Mokhoff, N., Solid state speech synthesis expanding, IEEE Spectrum 19(2), page 49, 1982.

Morland, D.V., Human factors guidelines for terminal interface design, Communications of the ACM, 26(7), 484–494, 1983.

Neale, S.G., The development and use of a mapping package for sixth form geography students, Computers and Education, 3(4), 367–380, 1979.

O'Shea, T., Self Improving Teaching Systems: An Application of Artificial Intelligence to Computer Assisted Instruction, Interdisciplinary Systems Research No. 67, Birkhauser Verlag, Basel, 1979.

O'Shea, T., A self–improving quadratic tutor, in Intelligent Tutoring Systems, edited by D. Sleeman and J.S. Brown, 309–336, Academic Press, New York, NY, 1982.

Paden, D.W. and Barr, M.D., Computer assisted instruction in an elementary college economics course, Computers and Education, 4(4), 259–268, 1980.

Pask, G., Developments in conversation theory – part 1, International Journal of Man–Machine Studies, 13, 357–411, 1980.

Pask, G., A computer based knowledge representation: an application of conversation theory, in Proceedings of the Fourth Canadian Symposium on Instructional Technology, 125–129, National Research Council of Canada, Ottawa, 1983.

Paul, R., Robots, models, and automation, IEEE Computer, 12(7), 19–27, 1979.

Perry, T.S., Video games: the next wave, IEEE Spectrum, 20(12), 52–59, 1983.

Perry, T.S., Consumer electronics, IEEE Spectrum, 21(1), 78–81, 1984.

Perry, T.S., Truxal, C. and Wallich, P., Video games: the electronic big bang, IEEE Spectrum, 19(12), 20–33, 1982.

Perry, T.S. and Wallich, P., Design case history: the Atari video computer system, IEEE Spectrum, 20(3), 45–51, 1983.

Petty, J., Burkhardt, H., Fraser, R. and Stewart, J., Micros in the primary curriculum: the ITMA approach, Computers and Education, 8(1), 189–195, 1984.

Philips, R.J., Burkhardt, H., Coupland, J., Fraser, R. and Ridgway, J., The future of the microcomputer as a classroom aid: an emprical approach to crystal gazing, Computers and Education, 8(1), 173–177, 1984.

Phillips, R.L., Computer graphics in urban and environmental systems, Proceedings of the IEEE, 62(4), 437–452, 1974.

Pioneer Video, 5150 E Pacific Coast Highway, Long Beach, California, USA, August 1983.

Renko, H., The Secret of Arendarvon Castle – A Complete Microworld Adventure for the APPLE-II, Addison Wesley, Reading, MA, 1984.

Renko, H. and Edwards, S., Crazy Games for Your Commodore-64, Addison Wesley, Reading, MA, 1984.

Resch, R.D., Portfolio of shaded computer images, Proceedings of the IEEE, 62(4), 496–502, 1974.

Rush, W.L., The Abilityphone, Byte: The Small Systems Journal, 7(9), 240–246, 1982.

Sandbank, C.P., (editor), Optical Fibre Communication Systems, John Wiley, New York, NY, 1980.

Schallon, J., Robot mice draw crowds, TV coverage at NCC, IEEE Computer, 11(7), page 130, 1978.

Schneider, W., Schmeisser, G. and Seamone, W., A computer aided robotic arm/worktable system for the high level quadriplegic, IEEE Computer, 14(1), 41–47, 1981.

Schneider, W., Seamone, W. and Schmeisser, G., A microprocessor controlled robotic arm allows self-feeding for a quadriplegic, in Proceedings of the IEEE Computer Society Workshop on The Application of Personal Computing to Aid the Handicapped, Laurel, Maryland, April 2–3, 31–36, IEEE, New York, NY, 1980.

Schneidewind, N., Interconnecting local networks to long-distance Networks, IEEE Computer, 16(9), 15–24, 1983.

Schofield, J., Microcomputer-based Aids for the Disabled, Heyden, London, 1981.

Self, J.A., Student models in computer aided instruction, International Journal of Man-Machine Studies, 6, 261–276, 1974.

Self, J.A., A state-space model for automatic instruction, Computers and Education, 1, 199–205, 1977.

Self, J.A., Student models and artificial intelligence, Computers and Education, 3, 309–312, 1979.

Sharples, M., CYCLOPS – A Case Study in the Design of User–Friendly Educational Technology, Report No. 23, Computer Assisted Learning Research Group, The Open University, Milton Keynes, 1982.

Shaw, K.A., Swallow, S.J. and Chapman, P., A use of microcomputers in training at ICI, Computers and Education, 8(1), 179–181, 1984.

Shoch, J.F., Dalal, Y.K., Redell, D.D. and Crane, R.C., Evolution of the ETHERNET local computer network, IEEE Computer, 15(8), 10–27, 1982.

Siegal, E., Schubin, M. and Merrill, P., Videodiscs: the Technology, the Applications and the Future, Van Nostrand, Reinhold, New York, NY, 1980.

Sinclair–Macmillan Educational Software, Sinclair Research, Camberley, 1983.

Sleeman, D. and Brown, J.S., (editors), Intelligent Tutoring Systems, Academic Press, New York, NY, 1982.

Smith, P. and Zorkoczy, P.I., Radiotext, Report No. 30, Computer Assisted Learning Research Group, The Open University, Milton Keynes, 1982.

Stallings, W., Local Networks: An Introduction, Collier Macmillan, West Drayton, 1984.

Stonier, T., The Wealth of Information – A Profile of the Post – Industrial Economy, Methuen, London, 1983.

Szymanski, E., JETSET, Byte: The Small Systems Journal, 7(11), 272–327, 1982.

Texas Instruments, Houston, TX, 1983.

Thomas, A., Communication devices for the nonvocal disabled, IEEE Computer, 14(1), 25–29, 1981.

Thomas, D.B., The effectiveness of CAI in secondary schools, AEDS Journal, Spring 1979.

Truxel, C., Video games aid the brain injured, IEEE Spectrum, 19(12), page 49, 1982.

Vanderheiden, G., Practical application of microcomputers to aid the handicapped, IEEE Computer, 14(1), 54–61, 1981.

Vincent, T., Computer assisted support for blind students. The use of a microcomputer linked voice synthesiser, Computers and Education, 6(1), 55–60, 1982.

Vousden, E., S4C meets the space invaders, Television Weekly, page 22, 30th September 1983.

Walrand, J., Blanquet, G. and Cardinael, G., One dimensional collision: an interactive graphics program, Computers and Education, 6(4), 369–372, 1982.

Weir, S., Russell, S.J. and Valente, J.A., LOGO: an approach to educating disabled children, Byte: The Small Systems Journal, 7(9), 342–360, 1982.

Wexler, J.D., Information networks in generative computer assisted instruction, IEEE Transactions on Man–Machine Systems, MMS–11(4), 181–190, 1970.

Wheeler, P.S., The Microwriter as an educational aid, British Journal of Educational Technology, 11(3), 161–169, 1980.

Wilkes, M.V., The impact of wide–band local area communication systems on distributed computing, IEEE Computer, 13(9), 22–25, 1980.

Williams, M.H., Pote, G.R. and Brooks, P.J., A simulator for teaching the internal workings of an assembler, Computers and Education, 7(1), 55–64, 1983.

Wilson, R.N., A cost effective approach to the production of portable CAL software, IUCC Bulletin, 5, 36–41, 1982.

Wilson, R.N. and McCrum, E., Use of a modular design in the production of portable CAL software: a case study, Computers and Education, 8(2), 229–237, 1984.

Wiswell, P., Video worlds, OMNI, 56–58; 99–100, January 1984.

Wood, K.W., Ohlsen, W.D., Bergeson, H.E. and Mason, G.W., An electronics course using an intelligent video format – a progress report, Computers and Education, 4(1), 59–66, 1980.

Your Robot, Introducing TOPO, Your Robot, 1(2), 12–13, 1984a.

Your Robot, Economatics' BBC Buggy, Your Robot, 1(1), 10–11, 1984b.

Zinn, K.L., Chapter 8 – Computer based instruction in Europe and Japan, in Computer–Based Instruction – A State–of–the–Art Assessment, edited by H.F. O'Neil, 231–249, Academic Press, New York, NY, 1981.

Zorkoczy, P., Information Technology, An Introduction, Pitman, London, 1982.

Further Reading

Dean, C. and Whitlock, Q., A Handbook of Computer Based Training, Kogan Page, London, 1983.

Hawkeridge, D., New Information Technology in Education, Croom Helm, London, 1983.

Maddison, J., Information Technology and Education – An Annotated Guide to Printed Audio Visual and Multimedia Resources, The Open University Press, Milton Keynes, 1982.

O'Neil, H.F., (editor), Computer–Based Instruction: A State–of–the–Art Assessment, Academic Press, New York, NY, 1981.

Schofield, J., Microcomputer–Based Aids for the Disabled, Heyden, London, 1981.

Sleeman, D. and Brown, J.S., (editors), Intelligent Tutoring Systems, Academic Press, New York, NY, 1982.

GLOSSARY OF TERMS

ACCESS TIME
The time taken following instruction before reading from, or writing
to, a location in memory takes place. The access time can vary between
nanoseconds for a register in a fast processor, seconds for a magnetic
tape deck, or even longer for some mass stores. The reading and
writing access times are not necessarily equal for a particular device
or class of devices.

ACCUMULATOR
A REGISTER in which the results of an arithmetic or logic operation is
stored.

ACOUSTIC COUPLER
A device which translates the audible sounds carried by a telephone
into the digital signals used by a computer (and vice versa). By these
means a computer can be linked to another computer through the
telephone system. A similar job is performed by a MODEM.

ADDRESS
An identification for a register, location in storage, or other data
source or destination; the identification may be a name, label or
number.

AFFECTIVE DOMAIN
The area of human learning that deals with feelings, attitudes and
beliefs.

359

ALGORITHM
A clearly defined series of steps which will provide a solution to the
problem for which it has been designed. Computer PROGRAMS employ
algorithms to enable the computer to solve problems.

ALU
Arithmetic–logic unit. That part of the CENTRAL PROCESSING UNIT
which performs arithmetical and logical operations.

ANALOGUE
A quantity which varies continuously like time or temperature, not
discretely like the number of books in a library or fingers on a hand
(which are DIGITAL). We can measure an analogue quantity like time
by the movement of hands across a conventional clock face (analogue) or
by digits on a modern electronic watch (digital).

ANIMATION
The process whereby the computer repeatedly plots a picture on the
screen so that the impression of movement of the picture is given.

ANSI
American National Standards Institute. Among its areas of
responsibility lies the specification of some of the high level
programming languages, including COBOL and FORTRAN.

ARRAY
A technique for storing and manipulating information in the computer's
memory. It is similar in concept to a list or chart on paper.

ARTIFICIAL INTELLIGENCE
Some computer programs perform tasks in such a way that if a human
were to do the same thing, their behaviour would be described as
intelligent. For example, programs can 'learn' from experience; play
championship chess, converse in 'natural–sounding' English, prove
theorems in geometry. (See also the Turing Test for machine
intelligence.)

ASCII
American Standard Code for Information Interchange. This was
established by ANSI in 1963. It is one of the standard ways of
representing alphanumeric characters in BINARY code, where specific
binary patterns correspond to particular alphanumerics.

ASSEMBLER LANGUAGE
A low level computer language which uses simple mnemonics instead of
ordinary words to make the computer execute simple tasks. It is harder
to write in than a high level language, and is mostly used to control
INPUT, OUTPUT and DISC operations and to do animated GRAPHICS.

AUTHOR LANGUAGE
A very high level programming language designed to enable people
without much experience or skill to write instructional programs. Some
writers use it to refer only to specialized CAI languages like PILOT,
PLATO and COURSEWRITER which tend to encourage a specific style of
programming. Others use it more generally to include advanced and
conversational languages like LOGO.

BACKPLANE
A piece of the computer chassis into which printed circuit boards slot
and which provides extension for the circuits with other system
elements, for example a BUS.

BANDWIDTH
Width of a frequency band of a communication channel. Usually
expressed in cps (cycles per second) or hertz.

BAR CODING
A code consisting of vertical bars of varying width and spacing which can
be read by a LIGHT PEN attached to a computer. They are also known
as zebra codes because of their appearance. Bar coded labels are now
used on most grocery products for use with automated check-outs.
Computer PROGRAMS can be turned into bar codes and distributed in the
form of 'books' which can be 'read' into the computer using a light
pen.

BASIC
Beginners All-purpose Symbolic Instruction Code. A language which
converts the instructions contained in the PROGRAM to a form which the
computer can read and obey. It is the most widely used language for
MICROCOMPUTERS.

BATCH PROCESSING
A system of computer operation where no interaction with the user is
required. This allows the computer to concentrate all its power on one
PROGRAM until it is completed. Hence it is fast for the machine and
useful in survey and research work but of limited value in the
practice of education where INTERACTIVE use is generally preferable.

BAUD
The capacity of a digital communication channel is measured in bauds.
The number of bauds specifies the rate at which information will pass
down that line. Synonymous with bits per second.

BAUDOT
Just as ASCII is a standard code for computers; Baudot is the standard
code for telegraph and telex communications. In Baudot five bits
represent one character (ASCII uses eight).

BINARY
In general a binary choice offers only two alternatives: 1 or 0, 'on' or 'off', black or white. Binary numbers are expressed as powers of 2, unlike our usual counting system which is based on powers of 10. For example, 9 would be represented as 1001 in binary code. Deep down all computers work in binary.

BINARY CODED DECIMAL (BCD)
A type of notation in which each decimal digit is identified by a group of 1s and 0s.

BIT
Short for BINARY digit. Represented in the computer as a 1 or 0 ('on' or 'off').

BLOCK DIAGRAM
A diagram of a system, instrument, computer or program in which selected portions are represented by annotated boxes and interconnected lines.

BRANCH
1. (n) A sequence of instructions executed as a result of a decision instruction. 2. (v) To depart from the usual sequence of executing instructions in a computer; synonymous with jump or transfer.

BUG
An error in a PROGRAM or, more generally, in the logical processes leading to it.

BUS
Information travels from one part of a computer system to another by means of a bus, sometimes called a trunk on larger computers. A bus is a set of connections which enable the hardware components of a system to link or INTERFACE. (See figure 1.3.)

BYTE
A unit of MEMORY in which the computer can store one character, or piece of information. Thus a computer with 32K bytes of memory can store 32,000 characters, which is about six pages of this book. (See also K.)

CAI
See COMPUTER AIDED INSTRUCTION.

CAL
See COMPUTER ASSISTED LEARNING.

CARD FRAME
Or card cage. A skeletal chassis with slots for PRINTED CIRCUIT BOARDS (which are also called cards).

CENTRAL PROCESSING UNIT (CPU)
The unit of a computing system containing the circuits that calculate and perform logic decisions based on a man—made program of operating instructions.

CHANNEL
A communication channel or input/output channel is often synonymous with terms like data path, circuit and line, that is, an electronic path along which signals can be carried, typically between a PERIPHERAL and a CPU.

CHARACTER
One of a set of elementary symbols acceptable to a data processing system for reading, writing or storing.

CHIP
A small piece of silicon on which has been printed an integrated electrical circuit capable of processing and/or storing information. Its small size has enabled MICROCOMPUTERS to be developed. (See MICROPROCESSOR.)

CLEAR
To put a storage or memory device into a state denoting zero or blank.

CLOCK
The rate at which a computer performs operations is controlled internally by a clock. This is an electronic circuit or group of electronic components which generate a set of control signals. Each set of control signals will initiate an action on the part of the CENTRAL PROCESSING UNIT.

CML
See COMPUTER MANAGED LEARNING.

COBOL
A HIGH LEVEL programming language used for commercial data processing applications of the computer. COBOL is an acronym for COmmon Business Orientated Language.

CODE
The actual instructions which comprise the PROGRAM. The terms 'programming' and 'coding' are often used interchangeably.

COGNITIVE DOMAIN
The area of human learning that involves thinking, reasoning and problem solving activities.

ICAL-M

COMPILER
A PROGRAM inside the computer which converts a complete program written in HIGH LEVEL LANGUAGE into the MACHINE CODE version which the computer can execute.

COMPUTER
A machine which processes information electronically. (See also MAINFRAME, MINICOMPUTER and MICROCOMPUTER.)

COMPUTER AIDED (or ASSISTED) INSTRUCTION (CAI)
Where computers are used to guide the user through a prescribed course of learning and testing. The computer assumes the role of teacher, asking questions and assessing the user's responses.

COMPUTER ASSISTED (or AIDED) LEARNING (CAL)
Where teaching and learning in any part of the curriculum are aided by some application of the computer. The role of the computer can be as a teaching aid, or it can be more student-centred. The latter approach is becoming more significant with the spread of MICROCOMPUTERS.

COMPUTER BASED LEARNING (CBL)
See COMPUTER-ASSISTED LEARNING.

COMPUTER LITERACY
Often used generally to indicate awareness of computers and appreciation of their power and limitations. By analogy with book literacy it may denote skills like KEYBOARD familiarity, screen reading and information retrieval. Some writers use the term to mean the ability to use or even to program a computer.

COMPUTER MANAGED INSTRUCTION
Equivalent in meaning to CML.

COMPUTER MANAGED LEARNING (CML)
The use of the computer to monitor, analyse and report on student's learning in an individualized curriculum.

CONFIGURATION
A collection of hardware, software and options that together form an arrangement for a computer system.

CONTENT-FREE CML
A CML system which can be used with any subject matter.

CONTEXT-FREE CML
A CML system which can be used in some way to support any method of learning.

COURSEWARE
Educational material comprising SOFTWARE, DOCUMENTATION and other MEDIA resources. Some writers use the term more specifically to mean COMPUTER-AIDED INSTRUCTION (CAI) materials.

CP/M
An OPERATING SYSTEM that has been adopted in one form or another on numerous microcomputers – often with name changes to disguise the origins. It was originally developed by Digital Research in 1976, and is now a mature and widely available system. It is the OPERATING SYSTEM which broadly determines whether a particular SOFTWARE package will run on your computer. If you have CP/M there are many off-the-shelf packages available to you.

CPU
See CENTRAL PROCESSING UNIT.

CRT (Cathode ray tube)
A cathode ray tube is used to provide the display in most types of visual display unit. It is of the same type as used in TV sets, which is why a TV set can sometimes be used as a display monitor of a terminal. Another display option is the gas-discharge sometimes called the PLASMA DISPLAY.

CURSOR
A symbol (sometimes flashing) which appears on the screen to show where the next character put in to the KEYBOARD will appear.

DAISYWHEEL
A removable print element in the shape of a disc with characters on the end of stalks radiating from an external hub giving the appearance of a flower. This can be attached to any computer and represents a good compromise between cost, speed and print quality.

DATA
(1) Information; especially information that can be processed by the computer; (2) a representation of facts, concepts or instructions in a formalised manner suitable for communication, interpretation or processing by humans or by automatic means.

DATA BANK
This is a collection of DATA in various forms, usually collected for use in education.

DATA BASE
An organised collection of DATA, usually for analysis by a computer.

DATA BASE MANAGEMENT SYSTEM
A set of PROGRAMS to allow the establishment, sorting and searching of
a DATA BASE stored in the computer. It usually also provides a
procedure for producing reports and may have calculating facilities.

DATA PROCESSING
One of the major roles performed by a computer. It makes use of the
computer's power to handle and compare information and is
educationally most useful in information retrieval.

DEBUG
The process of removing BUGS (errors) from PROGRAMS. Seymour Papert
and others have drawn attention to the heuristic value of debugging as
a process which helps in problem solving.

DECISION RULES
The rules, written by a CML system designer or a CML user, which
govern the generation of individualized feedback in a CML system.

DECODER
A gadget which translates the code used to transmit data (eg as
broadcast television) into the code used by the computer.

DEDICATED
Describes a computer which is designed for only one application, such
as those that are found in washing machines.

DIALECT
A variant of a computer LANGUAGE. All too often different
manufacturers offer slightly different versions of a language, which
leads to a lack of PORTABILITY. This is a particularly serious problem
with BASIC.

DIGITAL
Relating to numbers (see ANALOGUE). Modern electronic devices usually
operate on digital principles. Computers basically depend on
representing information and instructions as a series of 1s and 0s
(see BIT).

DIGITISER
A device connected to the computer which can detect and record the
position of a pointer as a digital code. This facility can be used to
record map outlines and engineering drawings for subsequent use by a
computer PROGRAM.

DIODE
An electronic device used to permit current flow in one direction and
to inhibit current flow in the opposite direction.

DIRECT ACCESS
Ability to extract required data immediately from memory, regardless of its location. As opposed to SEQUENTIAL or serial access which proceeds in a simple predetermined sequence associated with storage on magnetic tapes.

DISC
See FLOPPY DISC and HARD DISC.

DISC DRIVE
A device which enables the computer to store and retrieve information on DISC. Disc drives may be single–sided or double–sided and can 'read' and 'write' information in varying densities (usually either 'single' or 'double' density).

DOCUMENTATION
The written materials which accompany a computer PROGRAM and instruct the user in its use. It provides additional information such as background details and ways in which the use of the program can be extended.

DOWNLOAD
The process of transferring PROGRAMS or DATA from one computer directly into the MEMORY of another, usually smaller, computer. It can be done by telephone (using an ACOUSTIC COUPLER) or by TELESOFTWARE (using appropriate DECODERS).

DUMP
To copy the contents of all or part of a storage, usually from a CENTRAL PROCESSING UNIT into external storage.

EBCDIC
Extended Binary Coded Decimal Interchange Code. One of the two principal character codes, the other being ASCII. EBCDIC is an IBM contribution to standardisation. The EBCDIC code allows for more control characters and special graphics symbols than does ASCII.

EDGE CONNECTOR
The means by which PRINTED CIRCUIT BOARDS slot together (or INTERFACE with each other) to form more complex systems.

EDITING
The process of altering text, DATA or PROGRAMS by the insertion and deletion of characters from the KEYBOARD. Editing programs are useful for WORD PROCESSING, for revising and debugging programs and for DATA BASE MANAGEMENT.

ELECTRONIC OFFICE
The use of computers and microelectronic devices to perform office functions such as WORD PROCESSING, DATA BASE MANAGEMENT and accounting and copying. It also includes the transfer of documents between offices by telecommunications.

EPROM
Erasable Programmable Read Only Memory. A long term memory that under special conditions can be rewritten.

ERROR MESSAGE
A message produced by the computer system when it detects an error made by the user. These are often cryptic and can be discouraging to the novice user.

EXECUTE
To perform a data processing routine or program, based on machine language instructions.

FIELD
Area of data in a record; or area with standard format in some storage unit such as a DISC, to which information of a given type is assigned.

FILE
A collection of related records; eg in inventory control, one line of an invoice forms an item, a complete invoice forms a record, and the complete set of such records forms a file.

FIRMWARE
Intermediate between HARDWARE and SOFTWARE. It is the name given to the connections that can be made on a semi-permanent basis within the computer. The term is also used for PROGRAMS that are distributed as a plug-in memory unit.

FLIP-FLOP
A circuit or device containing active elements capable of assuming either one of two stable states at a given time.

FLOPPY DISC
A thin flexible disc, coated with magnetic particles, used to store DATA and PROGRAMS. It is contained within a protective paper sleeve within which it revolves. 'Standard' discs are 8 inches in diameter and the more common 'mini' disc is 5 1/4 inches. A mini disc could hold around 15 to 20 pages of this book.

FLOWCHART
A graphic representation for the definition, analysis, or solution of a problem in which symbols are used to represent operations, data flow and equipment.

FORTRAN
The earliest HIGH LEVEL LANGUAGE, FORmula TRANslation is still widely used on MAINFRAME computers for scientific applications.

FRAME
In CAL applications the term frame refers to a single screenful of information in textual, diagrammatic or pictorial form.

FRAME GRABBER
A PROGRAM which 'grabs' information from a television camera and turns it into a form which can be displayed by a computer.

FUNCTION KEY
A key on a keyboard which calls up a function. Functions can be activated by pressing a 'CONTROL' key and another alphanumeric key at the same time in a defined code key sequence.

GAMES PADDLE
A rotating knob, similar to a volume control on a radio. It is used instead of the KEYBOARD to feed information into the computer. For example, the paddles can be used like joysticks to draw pictures or to control the movement of objects on the screen, eg a Space Invader or a droplet of oil in a simulated physics experiment.

GATE
One of the fundamental units of the microprocessor; when it carries a charge it will prevent a current passing, and when the charge has been released the current is able to flow. The use of this device is fundamental to all the processes in the computer.

GOTO
A statement used freely in BASIC programming which sends control to another part of the PROGRAM. It is considered by purists to indicate a lack of structure in the design of the program and is used as an argument for replacing BASIC with more structured languages.

GRAPHICS
Computers can draw pictures and diagrams as well as text on the screen. RESOLUTION varies according to the MEMORY available. MICRO-COMPUTERS usually offer LOW or MEDIUM RESOLUTION GRAPHICS.

HANDSHAKING
Refers to communication between two parts of a system, typically a terminal and the central processor. It means that the receiving end is confirming that it has, in fact, received something.

HANDS-ON
The direct interaction with the computer by the user, normally by means of the KEYBOARD.

HARD COPY
A printed copy of machine output, eg printed reports, listings documents, etc.

HARD DISC
External computer MEMORY with greater capacity than a FLOPPY DISC (50 to 5000 times as much). Hard disc units are more expensive than floppy disc drives and the discs cannot usually be removed. WINCHESTER hard discs are small sealed units often used with MICROCOMPUTERS.

HARDWARE
The computer equipment and its associated PERIPHERALS which comprise a computer system (as opposed to the SOFTWARE which tells it what to do).

HIGH LEVEL LANGUAGE
See PROGRAMMING LANGUAGE.

HIGHLIGHTING
A process which causes some of the characters on the computer display screen to stand out. Typically it involves causing some characters to be lit with greater intensity or level of brightness than others. Only some microcomputers have this capacity.

HIGH RESOLUTION GRAPHICS
GRAPHICS which are resolved to individual picture cells of about 500 down by 500 across so that the individual cells are difficult to distinguish. This gives really convincing curves and lines, and can produce a crude 'photographic' image. They use a lot of MEMORY and processing power.

HOUSEKEEPING
Operations in a routine which do not contribute directly to the solution of a problem but do contribute directly to the execution of a program by the computer.

IMAGE SCAN
A generic term for devices that work on shapes, for example input devices that accept handwritten characters.

INFORMATICS
A term that is used to describe all aspects of the processing of information by machine. It is thought to be a more precise definition than computing which refers back to the times when the major use of the computer was for mathematical computation.

INFORMATION TECHNOLOGY
The technology which surrounds the storage, processing, retrieval, and dissemination of information (see DATA BASE, VIDEOTEX, WORD PROCESSING).

INPUT
General term used to describe information/data that is fed into a computer; also refers to any means of achieving this.

INSTRUCTION
A statement that calls for a specific computer operation.

INSTRUCTIONAL SYSTEMS DESIGN
A generic term for the procedures involved in constructing learning activities which comprise a solution to a set of learning problems. Any type of media or learning approach may be used so long as the principles and techniques generally accepted as the 'systems approach' are employed. The approach generally employs: (1) written documentation specifying learning outcomes, (2) selection and creation of learning activities to match and accomplish learning outcomes, and (3) utilisation of feedback to improve the learning activities.

INTELLIGENT TERMINAL
Instead of a terminal having a simple typewriter or display screen without processing power, the practice has increasingly developed of incorporating cheap microprocessors within the terminal system to provide greater processing capability.

INTERACTIVE
A style of computing in which the user and the program interact with each other as opposed to BATCH PROCESSING. The difference is like that between a telephone and correspondence by mail. Most CAL is now interactive, though batch processing is still used for administrative applications like timetabling and marks processing.

INTERFACE
A piece of equipment which enables computers and/or PERIPHERALS to be connected to each other.

INTERRUPT
A break in the normal flow of processing. The normal job flow can be resumed from that point at a later time. An interrupt is usually caused by a signal from an external source, eg a terminal unit.

ITERATE
To repeat automatically, under program control, the same series of processing steps until a predetermined stop or branch condition is reached; to LOOP.

JOYSTICK
A normally vertical lever which can be tilted in any direction. When provided on a computer system, it usually moves the cursor around the screen.

ICAL—M*

LCD DISPLAY
Display utilising liquid crystal technology.

LED DISPLAY
Display utilising light–emitting diodes.

K
Short for Kilo, but in computer circles actually just over a   thousand
(K=1024).   When used to describe a computer's memory (as in '32K RAM')
it means a kilobyte. (See also BYTE.)

KEYBOARD
A set of keys, similar to those on an electric typewriter, which
enables the user to communicate directly with the computer.

KEYPAD
A set of keys, similar to those on a calculator.

LANDSAT
A series of survey satellites capable of transmitting digital data
about radiation from the earth in four different wavebands. It is
possible to process this data by computer to produce simulated
photographs of quite high resolution.

LANGUAGE
See PROGRAMMING LANGUAGE.

LEARNING CYCLE
The cycle of learning frequently encountered in CML. Successive steps
are to select a learning task, study the task, take a test, receive
feedback from the computer including a prescription or recommendation
for the next task.

LIBRARY ROUTINE
A special purpose program which may be maintained in storage for use
when needed.

LIGHT PEN
A pen–like device which can be pressed against the screen to provide
INPUT without using the KEYBOARD. The computer can detect what the
pen is pointed at so the user can choose an option from a list or
enter a shape (eg a map).

LINE–PRINTER
See PRINTER.

LOAD
To place data into main storage

LOGIC
The system in which on/off conditions at the inputs of digital circuits provide related on/off signals at the outputs.

LOGO
A powerful and easily learned PROGRAMMING LANGUAGE which has been developed by Seymour Papert at the Massachusetts Institute of Technology and used to develop learning through programming and debugging. It has recently been implemented on MICROCOMPUTERS.

LOOP
A group of instructions in a program which may be executed more than once before the program continues. The loop includes one instruction which increments some kind of counter and another which checks the counter to see if it has reached a specific exit number.

LOW LEVEL LANGUAGE
See PROGRAMMING LANGUAGE.

LOW RESOLUTION GRAPHICS
GRAPHICS, which any computer can produce, resolved to individual picture cells of about 40 across by 20 down, suitable for blocks, bar charts and crude diagrams.

LSI (Large scale integration)
This term is generally applied to integrated circuits containing from 100 to 5,000 logic gates or from 1,000 to 16,000 memory bits.

MACHINE CODE
The sequence of BINARY numbers which the computer can understand. All PROGRAMS written in computer languages have to be converted into machine code at some stage.

MAINFRAME
A large multi-purpose computer, usually serving the needs of a large community of both local and remote users. Each user communicates with the computer either through a TIME-SHARING TERMINAL or through a BATCH PROCESSING system.

MEDIA
A collective term used to describe those facilities which are used to store/transmit information and data.

MEDIUM RESOLUTION GRAPHICS
GRAPHICS, which are resolved to individual picture cells of about 200 down by 300 across, suitable for fairly fine lines and recognisable circles.

MEGA
Prefix meaning million. Megabit (one million bits) MEGABYTE (one million bytes).

MEGABYTE
Measure used for the MEMORY capacity of a computer. One megabyte represents approximately one million stored alphabetic characters. This is much more than current MICROCOMPUTERS, or even large computers, can hold in internal memory. But external memory capacities of several megabytes are now becoming available for microcomputers and can be provided on WINCHESTER disc drives. The cost of these is now low enough for them to be purchased for educational use.

MEMORY
Computers store some PROGRAMS and DATA inside their memory for immediate use while they are switched on. This is internal memory which is limited but quickly accessed. Computers can also store programs and data permanently in external memory, which can be much more extensive though it takes longer to retrieve from DISCS and much longer from cassettes. (See RAM and ROM.)

MEMORY MAP
A memory map is a diagram of memory showing which particular routines take up which memory locations.

MENU
A set of instructions for running a program which are built into the program so that they appear on the screen, allowing the user to merely select options rather than remember them. They are a great convenience and often eliminate the need for additional written instructions on paper. Menus are one of the features which are referred to when people speak of a microcomputer as 'friendly'.

MESSAGE
Group or sequence of words which must be transferred as a whole for its meaning to be understood. Typically a message consists of an identity label, which may include the address, the text of the message and an EOM (end of message) symbol.

MICROCOMPUTER
A compact portable computer based on MICROPROCESSORS and silicon chips. It can be operated wherever there is electric power, or even by battery, and is often used by just one person or for a single purpose. Microcomputers have become fairly cheap – from $50 to $500 – though the PERIPHERALS needed to use them (eg DISC DRIVES, PRINTERS) may cost more.

MICROELECTRONICS
The branch of electronics which deals with very small voltages and currents. Usually in connection with silicon chip technology. (See MICROPROCESSOR, RAM AND ROM.)

MICROFICHE
A photographic representation of text or graphic data in microscopic form, needing a special machine to examine it. It is now both possible and convenient for computers to produce their results directly in this form and the advantages of reduced storage needs are thought to outweigh the need for special microfiche readers. They are widely used in connection with the production of reports from major information retrieval systems.

MICROPROCESSOR
A silicon chip containing the components needed to perform the operations determined by a PROGRAM. Microprocessors are now used in all computers and in control applications in industry and in the house (eg robot welding machines, washing machines and cameras).

MICROSECOND
One millionth of a second.

MILLISECOND
One thousandth of a second.

MINICOMPUTER
A computer which is smaller than a MAINFRAME, but which has similar facilities, such as TIME–SHARING. A minicomputer may be part of a larger system.

MNEMONIC
A memory aid. Mnemonic code is an ASSEMBLER LANGUAGE code in which the instruction names are easy to remember, like ADD for add, MPY for multiply and STO for store.

MODEM
Performs the same functions as an ACOUSTIC COUPLER, but is directly wired to the telephone system instead of using the handset.

MSI (Medium scale integration)
A term generally applied to integrated circuits containing from 20 to 100 logic gates or less than 1000 memory bits.

MULTI–USER SYSTEMS
Enable many users from different TERMINALS to use the same computer. Common on MAINFRAMES, but much less on MICROCOMPUTERS which do not have enough power to handle more than one user at a time.

NANOSECOND
One thousand–millionth of a second.

NETWORK
A system that lets computers (and their PERIPHERALS) communicate with each other using wires, optical fibres or terrestial/satellite broadcasting.

NETWORK INTERFACE
A device which allows computers and PERIPHERALS to link into a NETWORK.

OBJECT CODE
'Source code' or 'source programs' are what the programmer writes. The 'source language' will usually be one of the well known languages like BASIC or COBOL or it may be a low level ASSEMBLER LANGUAGE. Before it is acted upon by the computer it has to be translated into a form the computer can understand, and the results of the translation are called object code.

ON–LINE
Now a rather dated concept but once used to distinguish active connection to a computer through a TERMINAL as opposed to the then conventional way of preparing PUNCHED CARDS off–line and then feeding them directly into the computer.

OPERAND
That part of a computer instruction which contains the ADDRESS of the data.

OPERATING SYSTEM
The PROGRAM used by a computer to enable it to load a HIGH LEVEL LANGUAGE and to control its communication with the user and with PERIPHERALS like DISC DRIVES and PRINTERS.

OPTICAL READER
A device used for machine recognition of characters by recognition of their shapes.

OUTPUT
A general term for any result produced by the computer. Output can be in the form of voice, printed paper (print–out), magnetic tape, etc.

PAPER TAPE
A continuous narrow strip of paper with punched holes used as a means of storing information and PROGRAMS. This can be 'read' by the computer. It used to be a widespread method for sending programs from one computer to another.

PASSWORD
A string of characters which allows certain computer users to run restricted programs or to read restricted files. Handling passwords is a function of the operating system and not all microcomputers have it. Usually a computer, or rather its operating system, will request the user to type in his/her password; this is checked and access is either granted or denied.

PEEK
Most versions of the BASIC language have a statement which allows you to read the contents of a specified memory address. For example X = PEEK 18370 assigns the numeric value stored in memory address 18370 to the variable X. A companion statement is POKE, to put a value into a specific memory address.

PERIPHERALS
The 'plug-in' components which enable a computer to receive, store and transmit information. The more common peripherals are a VISUAL DISPLAY UNIT, PRINTER and DISC DRIVE.

PERSONAL COMPUTER
See MICROCOMPUTER.

PLASMA DISPLAY
Sometimes called a gas-discharge display. Originally developed for the PLATO system (qv). This is an alternative to the TV type cathode ray tube as a way of displaying human-machine communication. Currently they are more expensive per character than the conventional CRT display.

PLATO
A CAI system developed at the University of Illinois (Urbana-Champaign) and by Control Data Corporation. It is very powerful but has so far only been available on expensive hardware.

POKE
An instruction, available in most versions of BASIC, which stores integer values in a specified memory location. For example POKE 65, 15360 places the ASCII number 65 – which is the letter 'A' – in memory address 15360.

PORT
A socket on the computer into which a user can plug a terminal or some other input/output device.

PORTABILITY
The extent to which a PROGRAM can be run on different computer systems. This term essentially refers to the program itself, and not to the means of storage (eg DISC) in which it is contained. A highly portable program will run successfully on many computer systems. Unfortunately a disc can only be 'read' by the type of computer on which it was 'written'.

PRINTED CIRCUIT BOARD
A rigid plastic plate into which individual electronic components can be plugged or soldered to make contact with circuits printed on the board. At the other end of the circuit is the edge of the board which is equipped with EDGE CONNECTORS. These engage with further circuitry in the BACKPLANE.

PRINTER
A piece of equipment which, when connected to a computer, enables its OUTPUT to be printed on paper. Some printers are capable of printing characters only, while others are also capable of printing GRAPHICS.

PRINT-OUT
The results produced by the computer on paper.

PROGRAM
A set of instructions, written in a computer language, eg BASIC, FORTRAN. It is these instructions which instruct the computer to perform the specified tasks. A computer without a program is like a gramophone without a record. (See SOFTWARE.)

PROGRAMMED INSTRUCTION
Any instructional materials which use the principles of programmed instruction, namely (1) small steps; (2) active responding; (3) prompt feedback.

PROGRAMMING LANGUAGE
The language in which a computer PROGRAM is written. There are many such languages, of which BASIC is the most common in domestic and educational use. Others include FORTRAN, COBOL, ALGOL and Pascal. High level languages resemble natural language or mathematical notation whereas low level languages are closer to MACHINE CODE.

PROM (Programmable read only memory)
A memory into which information can be written after the device is manufactured, but thereafter cannot be altered.

PSYCHOMOTOR DOMAIN
The area of human learning that involves mind-muscle coordination. An example might be learning to work a computer based video game.

PUNCHED CARD
Thin cards, on which combinations of small holes have been punched as a means of storing and entering information and PROGRAMS. Standard punched cards can hold up to 80 characters. Now only found on a few MAINFRAME installations.

QUERY
Mode of using a data base system in order to retrieve information.

QWERTY
Refers to the standard, traditional typewriter keyboard layout which starts with these letters.

RAM (Random access memory)
That part of the computer's memory which stores PROGRAMS and DATA temporarily. The information is erased when the power is switched off.

RANDOM ACCESS
A technique for storing and retrieving data which does not require a strict sequential storage of the data nor a sequential search of an entire file to find a specific record. A record can be addressed and accessed directly at its location in the file.

REAL-TIME
The technique of computing while a process takes place so that the results can be used to control the progress of the process.

REGISTER
A high speed device used in a CENTRAL PROCESSING UNIT for temporary storage of small amounts of data or intermittent results generated during processing.

REINFORCEMENT
Any device, technique or action which serves to increase the likelihood that a given response will be made again, given functionally similar circumstances. Most instructional programmers regard the feedback given to confirm a correct response as reinforcement for that response.

RESIDENT
A PROGRAM which is always present in the computer, usually stored in ROM.

RESOLUTION
A measure of the fineness with which lines can be drawn on the screen. A colour transparency is high resolution, a TV picture is medium resolution and a newspaper photograph is lower resolution still. By computer standards, however, all are high. (See LOW, MEDIUM AND HIGH RESOLUTION GRAPHICS.)

ROM (Read only memory)
Memory which can only be 'read' not 'written on' (see RAM). It is used
to store PROGRAMS which are used frequently, or which are needed
before other programs can be implemented. ROM can be plugged into a
computer and is sometimes used as a way of distributing programs
(especially games).

ROUTINE
A sequence of machine instructions which carry out a specific
processing function.

ROUTING
The process of steering an individual student on a unique course
through a modularised curriculum.

SCREEN DIGITISING
A technique for turning a shape placed over the VDU screen into
DIGITAL form suitable for processing by the computer. This can be done
by directing the CURSOR around a transparency of the shape either with
GAMES PADDLES or with the KEYBOARD.

SCROLL
The manner in which text is sometimes moved on a CRT screen.
Specifically the text on the screen moves either up or down the screen
continuously, usually with each new line of text occurring at one end
of the screen simultaneously with the disappearance from the screen of
the oldest line of text.

SECOND PROCESSOR
An additional processor which can handle the computation while the
first handles the transfer of information from the KEYBOARD and to
the PERIPHERALS. It enables the computer to work much faster.

SELF-PACED LEARNING
Any instructional presentation technique in which the pace of the
lesson is adjusted to fit the requirements of the individual learner.
Technically, it should refer only to those lessons in which the
student is in complete control of the rate at which the lesson is
accomplished.

SEMICONDUCTOR MEMORY
Memory made from semiconducting devices, usually silicon transistors
and resistors which provide microminiature storage for data and
instructions.

SEQUENTIAL ACCESS
Information which must be reached in a simple predetermined sequence,
rather than according to more sophisticated criteria as in RANDOM
ACCESS

SIMULATION
The process of representing the real world in some easily manageable form. Educational simulations simplify the real world, to some extent, to assist learning. Simulated experiments allow students to interpret the results of an experiment that would be too difficult, dangerous, expensive or time–consuming to carry out 'for real'. Computer simulations may produce graphic or mathematical models, and for research purposes are often quite complex.

16–BIT PROCESSOR
This processes 16 BITS at once. Most MICROPROCESSORS in use handle only eight bits simultaneously and are slower and can directly access much less internal MEMORY than a 16–bit processor.

SOFTWARE
Computer PROGRAMS and DATA.

SOLID STATE COMPONENT
A component whose operation depends on electrical activity in solids, eg performance of a transistor or crystal diode. All silicon semiconductors are solid state devices.

SOURCE CODE
This is a program written by a human programmer. It compares with OBJECT CODE, which is the MACHINE CODE into which the program is translated. (See COMPILER.)

SOURCE LANGUAGE
A language nearest to the user's usual business or professional language, which enables him/her to instruct a computer more easily. FORTRAN, COBOL, ALGOL, BASIC PL/1 are a few examples.

SSI (Small scale integration)
A term applied to integrated circuits containing from one to twenty logic gates.

STORAGE DEVICES
Covers both internal RAM and ROM and external DISC and cassette MEMORY.

STORYBOARD
A paper and pencil rendition of each FRAME of a CAL sequence. It can be used to test an idea before extensive program writing takes place.

STRING
A sequence of records, words or characters, usually arranged in some specific order.

STRUCTURED PROGRAMMING
A method of programming whereby the computer **PROGRAM** consists of clearly labelled and defined sections, each of which performs a specific task. A standard structure enables quite complex programs to be read and understood.

STUDENT PROFILE
The computer–stored record of information about each individual student registered on a CML system.

SUBROUTINE
Within a computer program some operations will be repeated frequently, eg passing the results of a calculation to a printer. One way of programming this activity would be to duplicate the printer code at each point within the program where a print operation is required. An alternative approach (using a subroutine) is to embed the sequence of instructions within a routine that the program can 'call up' each time it needs to. A subroutine is thus a sequence of instructions which performs an often required function and which can be called from anywhere within the body of the main program. Getting into a subroutine is generally described as **BRANCHING**.

SUM CHECK
A procedure to check that the total number of digits transmitted in each block is correct. When using a telephone link it allows the automatic retransmission of a block if an error is detected.

TACTILE
A surface or instrument which is reactive to touch. A tactile terminal is one which can sense the fact that a student is touching a specific portion of the screen.

TASK ANALYSIS
The process of examining or studying the smallest unit of work in a job role, or the smallest transaction in a learning situation.

TELEPRINTER
Similar to a TELETYPE, but only able to receive information.

TELEPROCESSING
The use of telecommunications equipment to transmit data between two computers in different locations, or between input/output devices and a centralised computer where I/O is at a location remote from the computer.

TELESOFTWARE
A new development which allows SOFTWARE to be transmitted directly into a computer's MEMORY over a distance, by telephone (using VIEWDATA) or television (using TELETEXT). The computer receiving the PROGRAM needs a suitable DECODER.

TELETEXT
An information system which is broadcast as part of a television transmission. A suitable DECODER enables the information to be displayed on a domestic television screen. Unlike VIEWDATA services, telesoftware is basically a one way transmission of information.

TELETYPE
A rather crude electric typewriter that can be connected to a computer and used for INTERACTIVE computing. Both the user's entries and the responses made by the computer are typed on a continuous roll of paper.

TERMINAL
A piece of equipment containing a KEYBOARD with a PRINTER and/or a VDU, which enables the user to communicate with a computer (usually a MAINFRAME or MINICOMPUTER). The terminal may be distant from the computer. (See TIME-SHARING.)

TERMINAL BEHAVIOUR
The new skills, knowledge and abilities that students have at the completion of a lesson that they did not have at the beginning of the lesson constitute terminal behaviour.

TIME-SHARING
A system which lets a number of people have INTERACTIVE use of a single computer at the same time. Each user should have the illusion of sole use of the computer, though if the system is overloaded or inefficient there may be delays in response.

TOUCH-(SENSITIVE)-SCREEN
A VDU screen which is able to detect the position of the user's finger. This can be used to enable users who are not familiar with the use of the KEYBOARD to pick selections from a menu of choices.

TRANSDUCER
A device which converts energy from one form to another, as a hi-fi pick-up cartridge converts mechanical to electrical energy.

TRANSFERABILITY
The extent to which a PROGRAM will be run on another computer. This implies PORTABILITY, but it also involves the ease of use by a novice and depends on good DOCUMENTATION.

TRAP
Part of a computer PROGRAM which prevents the user from entering
information which is irrelevant or wrong, and which prevents the
computer from giving one of its own ERROR MESSAGES, which are not
usually easy for the user to understand. A trap will usually inform
the user of his/her mistake and then allows another attempt at typing
in the information to be made.

TTL
Transistor–transister logic. A standard design approach to
semiconductor integrated circuits.

TURING'S TEST
Research in ARTIFICIAL INTELLIGENCE (AI) is concerned with building
machines that can perform tasks which people would ordinarily claim
requires the intellectual abilities of a human–being. Turing's test is
an experiment proposed by AI researchers to determine whether or not a
machine possesses intelligence on a human level.

USER–FRIENDLY
Describes an interactive PROGRAM which gives helpful and informative
messages to guide the user. More generally used to describe any
computer SOFTWARE, system or environment which is friendly
and accessible to the user.

VALIDATION INSTRUCTION
Any instructional system which has undergone a aconscientious
validation process of testing and revision.

VDU
See VISUAL DISPLAY UNIT.

VIDEO DISC
A device which stores digital information on a DISC about the size of
a gramophone record. The initial application is for replaying
television quality material through a domestic television set. The
fact that enough information for one hour of video can be stored on a
disc indicates the enormous storage potential if used for text, DATA
or PROGRAMS. Access to sections of the disc can be under the control
of a computer program also contained on the disc so it has great
potential for the development of educational materials.

VIDEOTEX
A method of receiving electronic digital information at a distance and
displaying it on a screen. Videotex can be transmitted by telephone
lines (VIEWDATA) or broadcasting (TELETEXT).

VIEWDATA
The transmission of digital information by the use of a telephone system
that links DATA BASES on large MAINFRAME systems to local users.
VIEWDATA systems may be public (like Prestel and Antiope) or private
(like the Open University's Optel). Unlike the TELETEXT services,
Viewdata is INTERACTIVE, and the user can make choices, answer
questions and order information or goods using a KEYPAD.

VISUAL DISPLAY UNIT (VDU)
A television–like screen (black and white or colour), which displays
the output of the computer.

VOLATILE MEMORY
Digital MEMORY system which loses the information when the power
supply is switched off; that is the information evaporates and is
lost. Also devices from which such a memory is made. A typical example
is the SEMICONDUCTOR memory of which most types are volatile.

WAFER (or slice)
A thin disc of semiconductor material, usually silicon, in which many
semiconductor devices are fabricated at one time. The devices are
subsequently separated and assembled in individual packages.

WEIGHTING
The multiplication of a test score by some factor before it is added
to an item, subtotal or total score.

WINCHESTER
A type of HARD DISC which packs DATA very tightly and has to be
sealed against the entry of dust.

WORD
A set of characters which have one addressable location and are
treated as one unit.

WORD PROCESSING
A powerful technique for EDITING, storing and rearranging text. The
text is stored magnetically (on a DISC or in MEMORY) until it is ready
for the final PRINT–OUT. Word processing can be performed either by a
dedicated word processor (purpose built) or by general–purpose
computers. Although MICROCOMPUTERS can be used for word processing,
a disc–based system is almost essential.

INDEX

Numbers in parentheses indicate glossary entries.